DATA ENTRY
Skillbuilding and Applications

Doris D. Humphrey, Ph.D.
Career Solutions Training Group

Australia • Brazil • Japan • Korea • Mexico • Singapore • Spain • United Kingdom • United States

SOUTH-WESTERN
CENGAGE Learning™

Data Entry: Skillbuilding and Applications
Doris D. Humprhrey, Ph.D.
Career Solutions Training Group

Vice President/Editor-in-Chief: Dave Shaut

Senior Publisher: Karen Schmohe

Acquisition Editor: Jane Phelan

Media Developmental Editor: Matthew McKinney

Contributing Writer: Amy Stuart

Production Manager: Tricia Matthews Boies

Production Editor: Alan Biondi

Marketing Manager: Lori Pegg

Marketing Coordinator: Georgianna Wright

Manufacturing Coordinator: Charlene Taylor

Cover and Internal Design: Tippy McIntosh

Cover Images: ©Photodisc

Cover Photo Collage: Tippy McIntosh

Compositor: Cover to Cover Publishing, Inc.

Printer: Von Hoffmann Graphics, Eldridge, Iowa

For product information and technology assistance, contact us at **Cengage Learning, Customer & Sales Support**, **1-800-354-9706**

For permission to use material from this text or product, submit all requests online at **www.cengage.com/permissions**
Further permissions questions can be emailed to **permissionrequest@cengage.com**

ISBN-13: 978-0-538-43477-5
ISBN-10: 0-538-43477-5
Book + CD:
ISBN-13: 978-0-538-43476-8
ISBN-10: 0-538-43476-7

South-Western Cengage Learning
5191 Natorp Boulevard
Masan, Ohio 45040
USA

Printed in the United States of America
5 6 7 12 11 10

Table of Contents

Data Entry: The Intersection of Real-World Experience and Skill Building

Destination: Workplace Ready

Having the confidence to step into the job market requires real-world experiences plus strong skills. *Data Entry Skillbuilding and Applications* provides the kind of experiences a data entry specialist encounters every day on the job. Career profiles focus on real-world careers and workplace expectations.

Career Profiles

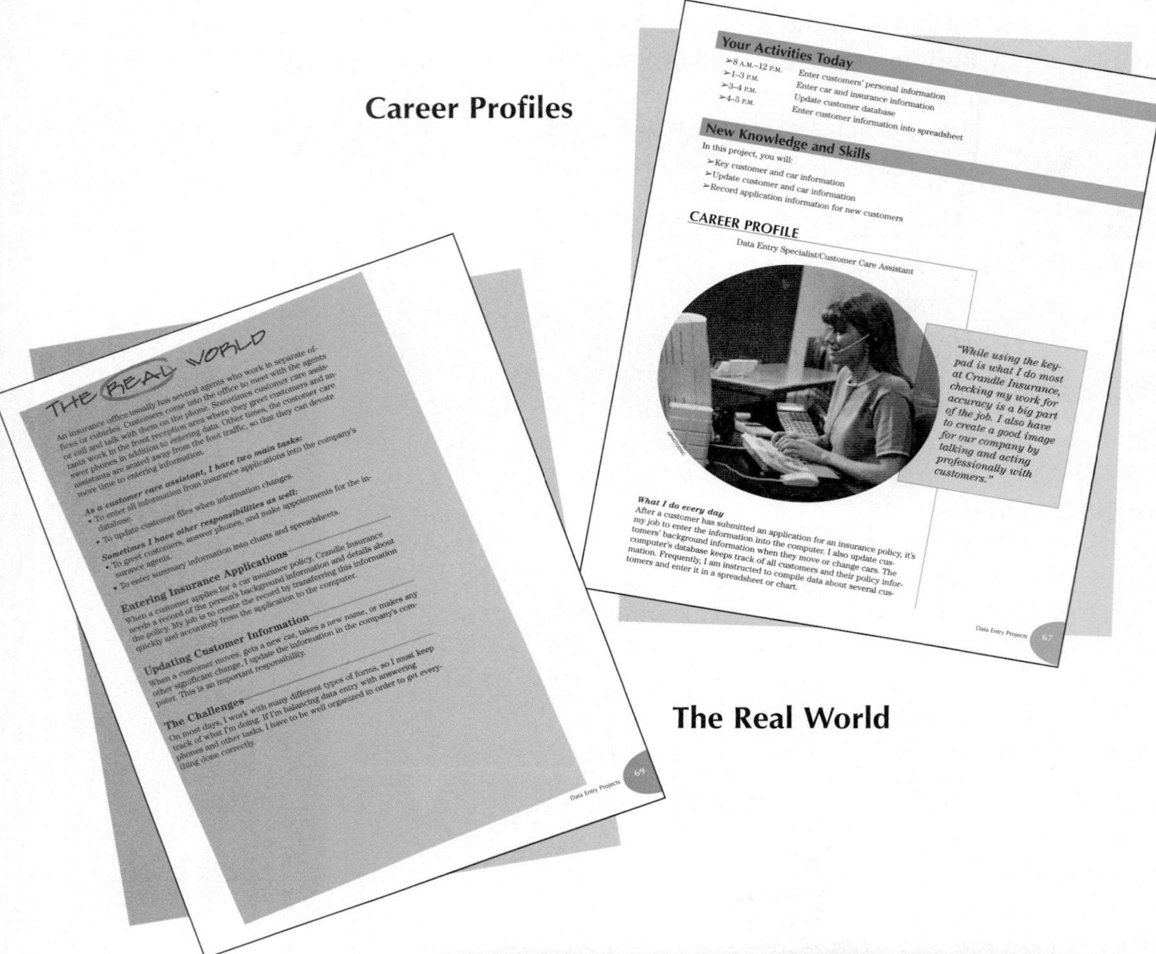

Your Activities Today

- 8 A.M.–12 P.M. Enter customers' personal information
- 1–3 P.M. Enter car and insurance information
- 3–4 P.M. Update customer database
- 4–5 P.M. Enter customer information into spreadsheet

New Knowledge and Skills

In this project, you will:

- Key customer and car information
- Update customer and car information
- Record application information for new customers

CAREER PROFILE

Data Entry Specialist/Customer Care Assistant

"While using the keypad is what I do most at Crandle Insurance, checking my work for accuracy is a big part of the job. I also have to create a good image for our company by talking and acting professionally with customers."

What I do every day
After a customer has submitted an application for an insurance policy, it's my job to enter the information into the computer. I also update customers' background information when they move or change cars. The computer's database keeps track of all customers and their policy information. Frequently, I am instructed to compile data about several customers and enter it in a spreadsheet or chart.

Data Entry Projects 67

THE REAL WORLD

An insurance office usually has several agents who work in separate offices or cubicles. Customers come into the office to meet with the agents or call and talk with them on the phone. Sometimes customer care assistants work in the front reception area where they greet customers and answer phones in addition to entering data. Other times, the customer care assistants are seated away from the foot traffic, so that they can devote more time to entering information.

As a customer care assistant, I have two main tasks:

- To enter all information from insurance applications into the company's database.
- To update customer files when information changes.

Sometimes I have other responsibilities as well:

- To greet customers, answer phones, and make appointments for the insurance agents.
- To enter summary information into charts and spreadsheets.

Entering Insurance Applications

When a customer applies for a car insurance policy, Crandle Insurance needs a record of the person's background information and details about the policy. My job is to create the record by transferring this information quickly and accurately from the application to the computer.

Updating Customer Information

When a customer moves, gets a new car, takes a new name, or makes any other significant change, I update the information in the company's computer. This is an important responsibility.

The Challenges

On most days, I work with many different types of forms, so I must keep track of what I'm doing. If I'm balancing data entry with answering phones and other tasks, I have to be well organized in order to get everything done correctly.

Data Entry Projects 69

The Real World

Main Menu

Fundamentals First

You'll begin in the **Training Center** and build your skills. And your practice will be fun! *Data Entry Skillbuilding and Applications* software uses graphics, audio, technique reminders, and a variety of speed and accuracy drills to help you improve.

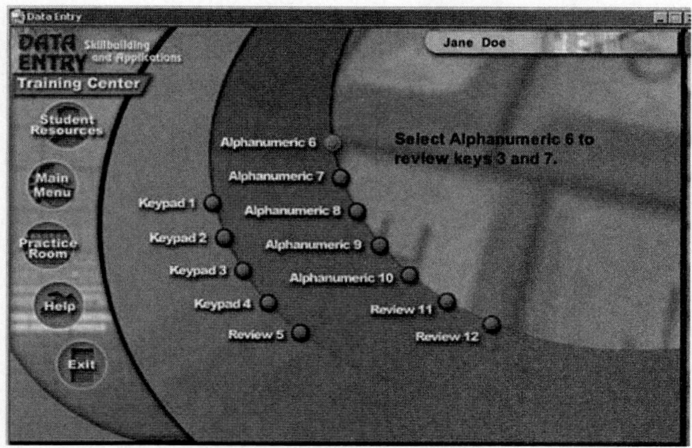

Training Center Main Menu

Lessons review reaches and build basic skills.

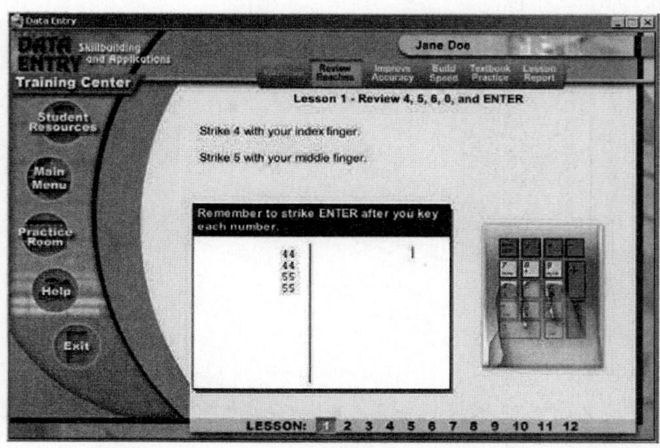

Lesson 1
Review Reaches

Lessons include both onscreen and textbook drills.

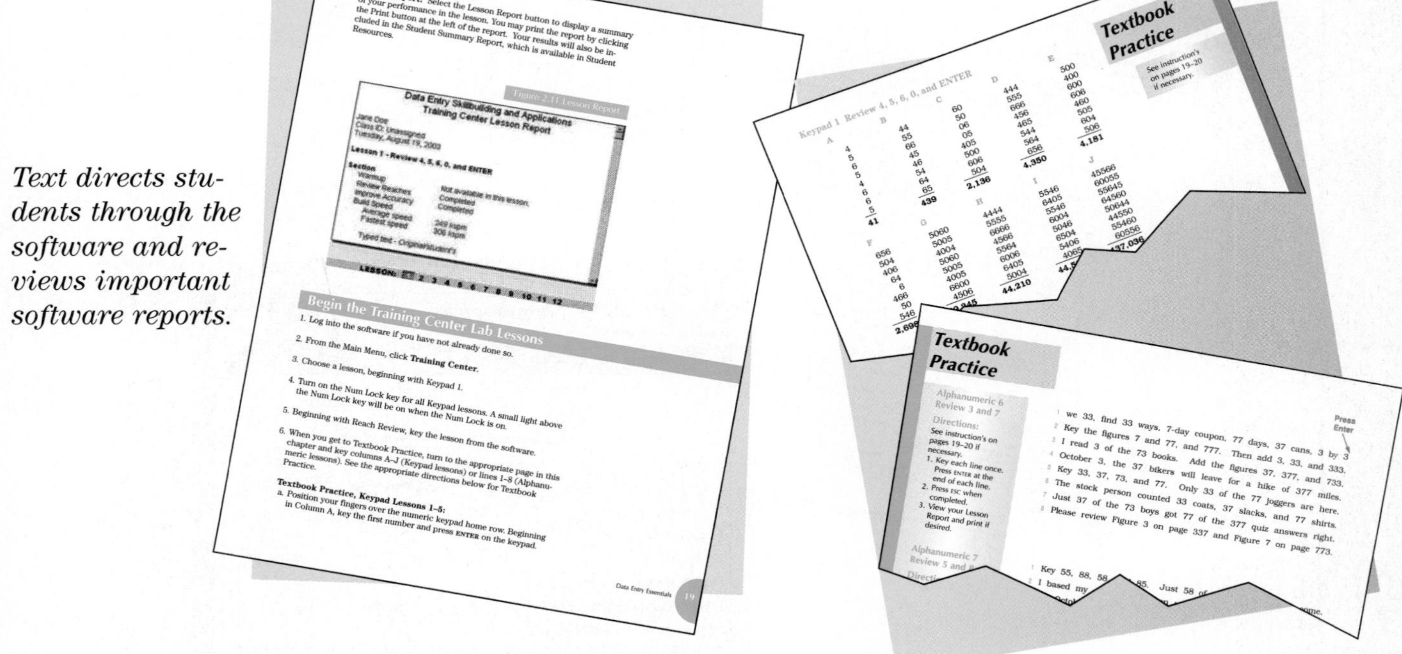

Lesson Report: Select the Lesson Report button to display a summary of your performance in the lesson. You may print the report by clicking the Print button at the left of the report. Your results will also be included in the Student Summary Report, which is available in Student Resources.

Figure 2.11 Lesson Report

Data Entry Skillbuilding and Applications
Training Center Lesson Report
Jane Doe
Class ID: Unassigned
Tuesday, August 19, 2003
Lesson 1 - Review 4, 5, 6, 0, and ENTER
Section
Warmup
Review Reaches — Not available in this lesson.
Improve Accuracy — Completed
Build Speed — Completed
Average speed — 249 kspm
Fastest speed — 306 kspm
Typed text - Original/Student's
LESSON: 1 2 3 4 5 6 7 8 9 10 11 12

Begin the Training Center Lab Lessons

1. Log into the software if you have not already done so.
2. From the Main Menu, click **Training Center**.
3. Choose a lesson, beginning with Keypad 1.
4. Turn on the Num Lock key for all Keypad lessons. A small light above the Num Lock key will be on when the Num Lock is on.
5. Beginning with Reach Review, key the lesson from the software.
6. When you get to Textbook Practice, turn to the appropriate page in this chapter and key columns A–J (Keypad lessons) or lines 1–8 (Alphanumeric lessons). See the appropriate directions below for Textbook Practice.

Textbook Practice, Keypad Lessons 1–5:
a. Position your fingers over the numeric keypad home row. Beginning in Column A, key the first number and press ENTER on the keypad.

Data Entry Essentials 19

Textbook Practice

See instruction's on pages 19–20 if necessary.

Keypad 1 Review 4, 5, 6, 0, and ENTER

Textbook Practice

Alphanumeric 6
Review 3 and 7

Directions:
See instruction's on pages 19–20 if necessary.
1. Key each line once. Press ENTER at the end of each line.
2. Press ESC when completed.
3. View your Lesson Report and print if desired.

Press Enter

1 we 33, find 33 ways, 7-day coupon, 77 days, 37 cans, 3 by 3
2 Key the figures 7 and 77, and 777. Then add 3, 33, and 333.
3 I read 3 of the 73 books. Add the figures 37, 377, and 733.
4 October 3, the 37 bikers will leave for a hike of 377 miles.
5 Key 33, 37, 73, and 77. Only 33 of the 77 joggers are here.
6 The stock person counted 33 coats, 37 slacks, and 77 shirts.
7 Just 37 of the 73 boys got 77 of the 377 quiz answers right.
8 Please review Figure 3 on page 337 and Figure 7 on page 773.

Alphanumeric 7
Review 5 and 8

1 Key 55, 88, 58 … 85. Just 58 of …
2 I based my …

Text directs students through the software and reviews important software reports.

The Project Lab is the heart of *Data Entry Skillbuilding Applications*. Four real-life projects capture the work performed on the job. Warmup and Stretch drills in each project help students to continue to build their skills. Real-world business forms provide the data for keying.

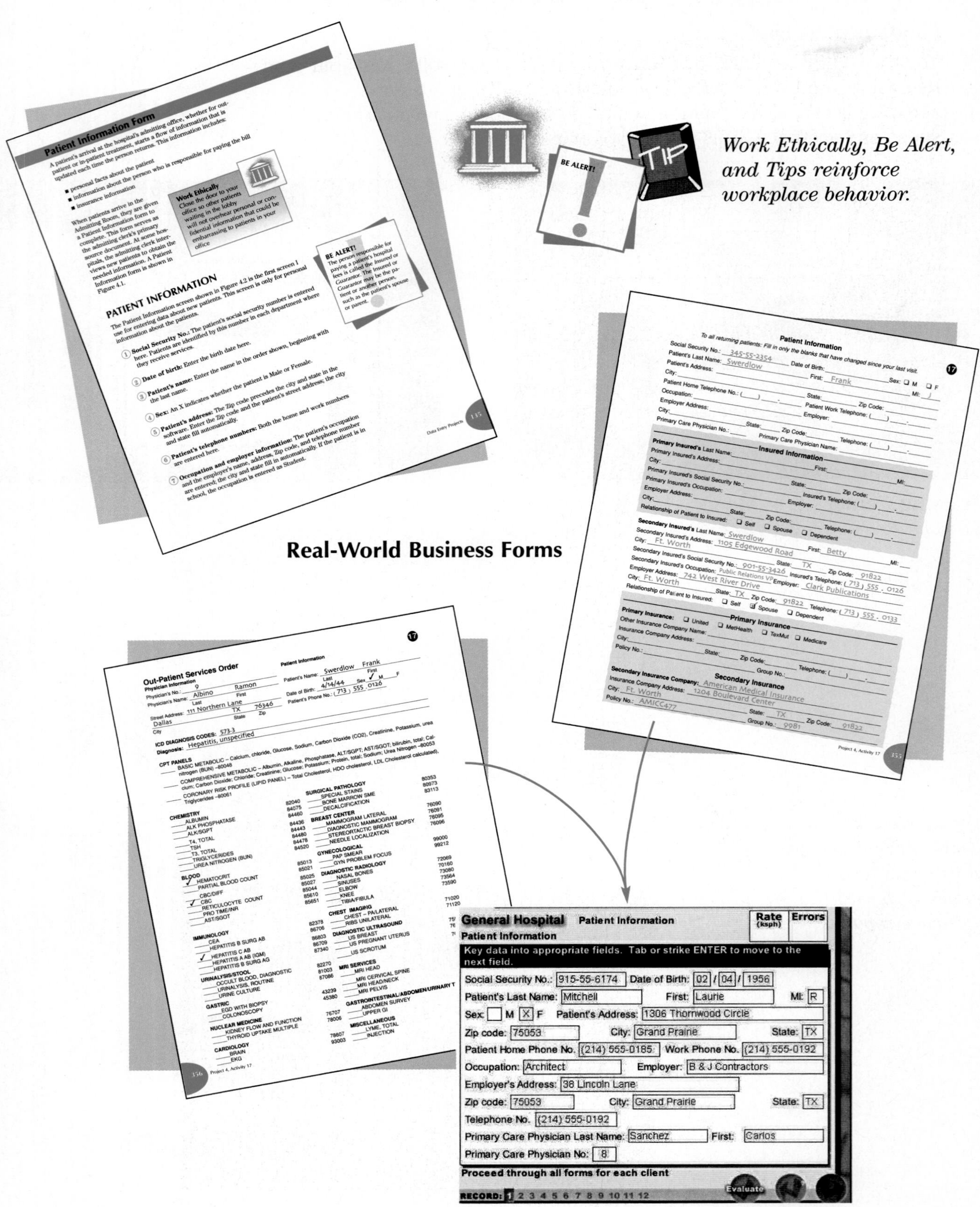

Work Ethically, Be Alert, and Tips reinforce workplace behavior.
Real-World Business Forms

The Practice Room provides timed writings, drills, and an Open Screen to practice on your own. Timings and some drills are keyed from the textbook. A variety of progress reports are available. These can be viewed on screen, printed, or e-mailed (distance education).

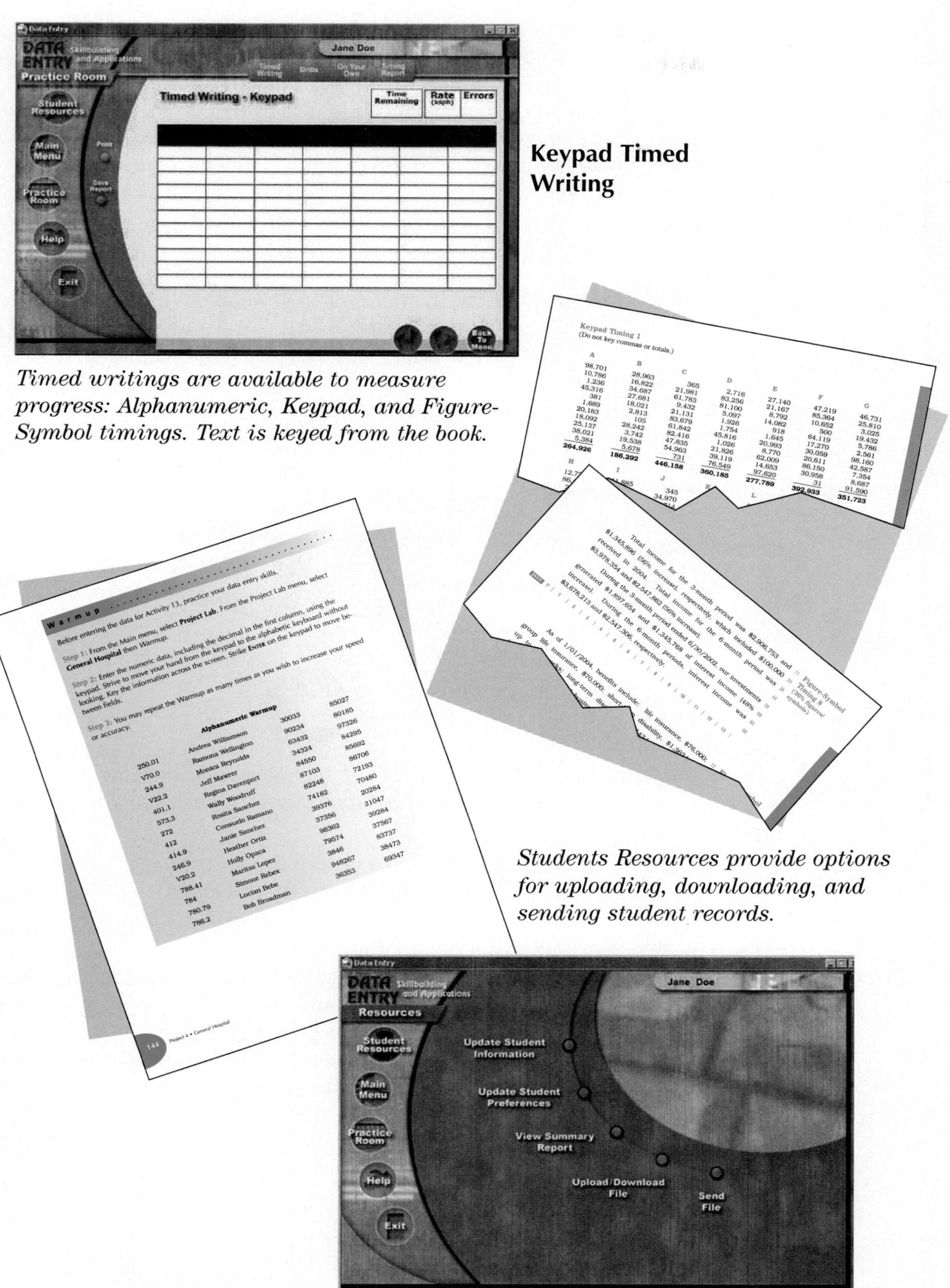

Keypad Timed Writing

Timed writings are available to measure progress: Alphanumeric, Keypad, and Figure-Symbol timings. Text is keyed from the book.

Students Resources provide options for uploading, downloading, and sending student records.

Preface

The best way to prepare for a career as a data entry specialist is to gain experience in real-life activities that data entry specialists encounter every day. *Data Entry Skillbuilding and Applications*, a combined textbook and program software solution, provides this type of experience. You'll begin by learning about the role of data entry in today's workplace; then you'll become familiar with the equipment, software, and terminology that are essential to the job. Since excellent customer service skills and strong ethical behaviors are essential to success, these important elements are presented in the first few pages and stressed throughout the textbook.

Four real-life projects, each slightly more complex than the previous project, capture the actual work performed by a data entry specialist. The projects are interesting and motivating, and they will help you build your data entry skill while also broadening your decision-making and problem solving abilities. Using source documents similar to those used in business, you will enter data for:

Funwear, a mail-order clothing catalog

Crandle Insuance,
an automobile insurance company

Western Suites, a hotel

General Hospital, a big-city hospital

Special Features

Each of the four projects in the Project Lab includes several elements that will help you become a successful data entry specialist. Look for these items in each project:

- Profile of a data entry specialist and a description of the organization
- The Real World—the challenges of the data entry position
- Projects-with at least four activities in each project
- Step-by-step instructions for completing each activity
- Real-world source documents, including handwritten documents, filled-in forms, audio interviews, e-mails, and Web sites

A variety of tips in each project will contribute to your overall success as a data entry specialist. Work Ethically comments describe behaviors that are expected of all data entry specialists. On the Alert and Tips suggest ways to deal with customers and provide reminders when working in the software.

About the Software

Data Entry Skillbuilding and Applications software works hand-in-hand with the book. Knowing how to manipulate data entry software in different settings will make you more employable. Therefore, the software that accompanies this book is specially tailored for each project and is similar to what you would use today if you were employed in a catalog company, an insurance company, a hotel, or a hospital. The software includes many features to make your data entry experience both fun and motivational:

Training Center: Twelve lessons that review the reaches to the top-row numbers and the keypad. Each lesson includes routines to review keyreaches, improve accuracy, build speed, and practice on your own. You'll key from data both onscreen and from the textbook.

Project Lab: Seventeen data entry activities that are based around four companies or projects. Each project also includes Warmup and Stretch activities to build skill and a Project Report.

Practice Room: Keypad and alphanumeric timed writings (15 seconds to 5 minutes), drills from the projects, an Open Screen for keying text, and a calculator for data. You will use the Practice Room throughout your study of data entry.

Student Resources: This area of the software allows you to create various reports and manage your student data. Special features include:

- Upload/Download File for transporting student data between the class room and home.
- Send File for sending your student record to your instructor.
- View Summary Report for viewing the final results of all activities. Click the hyperlink of each completed activity and you can view the data in the forms. If errors exist, they'll be shown in red.
- Update Student Preferences to change software options.
- Update Student Information to change your password.

Instructor Approved

A special thanks to the instructors who have reviewed these projects and provided valuable input. Thank you also to the many instructors who shared, through a questionnaire, their insights on teaching data entry, grading scales, and concerns.

Helen Gratton
Des Moines Area Community College

Kathy Locke
Spartanburg Technical College, South Carolina

Diane Kelly
Morgan Memorial Goodwill Industries

http://dataentry.swlearning.com

INSTRUCTOR WEB SITE

Installation Procedures

System Requirements

The following minimum system requirements are necessary to run the ***Data Entry Skillbuilding and Applications*** software.

- PC (or 100%-compatible) with 233 MHz Pentium II or higher processor
- 32 Megabytes of RAM (64MB recommended, 64MB required for Windows 2000 and XP)
- Hard disk with 40 MB free (plus 100 MB to run movies from hard drive instead of the CD-ROM)
- Windows 95, 98, Me, 2000 or XP
- CD-ROM drive
- SoundBlaster compatible sound card and speakers
- 800 x 600 monitor capable of displaying 24bit color
- Keyboard and Mouse

Installation Procedures

Follow the steps provided below to install the Data Entry Skillbuilding and Applications software at your computer.

1. Insert the Data Entry Skillbuilding and Applications disc into the CD-ROM drive.
2. If your Windows CD Autoplay is on, the installation will automatically begin. If it begins, proceed to Step 5.
3. Click the Start button, and choose Run.
4. Key x:\setup, where "x" is the letter of your CD-ROM drive, and strike ENTER.
5. Follow the instructions that appear on the screen to complete the installation process.

   After installing the software, store the disc in a secure location.

GETTING STARTED WITH *DATA ENTRY SKILLBUILDING and APPLICATIONS*

This section includes the start-up instructions for the Data Entry Skillbuilding and Applications software and explains how to create a new student record. Remember you can access the on-line help to learn more about the software.

1. Turn on the computer. Start Windows.
2. Click on the **Start** button and select Programs. Select the South-Western Keyboarding program group and click Data Entry.
3. Select the appropriate student name from the list that appears in the Log In dialog box. Then, enter the correct password to continue.
4. If you are using the program for the first time, you must click the **New** button and complete the New Student dialog box.
5. After you log in, the program will display the Main menu.

When the Main menu appears, you should choose the appropriate keyboarding module to display the lesson menu.

New Student

When you first use the *Data Entry Skillbuilding and Applications* program, you must enter the following information: name, Class ID, and password. Follow the appropriate instructions to register as a new user.

1. To register, click the **New** button shown in the Log In dialog box. The New Student dialog box appears.
2. Enter user name (first name, last name).
3. Choose a Class ID.
4. Enter a password. Be sure to write the password on a piece of paper and store it in a safe place.
5. Click the OK button to complete the registration process

Part 1

DATA ENTRY ESSENTIALS

F1
Esc
Tab

Chapter 1

Data Entry in an Information World

CHAPTER OBJECTIVES

- ❒ Understand the data entry process
- ❒ Apply appropriate data entry terminology
- ❒ Identify data entry software applications for different careers
- ❒ Relate customer service to data entry
- ❒ Use ethical standards when entering data

Each day tens of thousands of data entry specialists—called by a variety of titles—input numbers and words into computer systems. This data keeps information flowing around the world. Whether you apply for a driver's license, request admittance to an educational institution, purchase concert or movie tickets, order a meal at a restaurant, pay bills, list a home for sale with a realtor, or book an airline ticket, a person with data entry skills will be involved somewhere along the way. Every industry, government agency, educational system, and other type of organization relies on accurate, fast entry of information to accomplish its goals.

Getting Started with Data Entry

Information comes to data entry specialists in a variety of ways. You can expect to work from:

- ➢handwritten documents
- ➢filled-in forms
- ➢computer printouts
- ➢voice communications
- ➢e-mail
- ➢Web sites
- ➢other

➠ Process
➠ Equipment
➠ Software

Process

A data entry specialist becomes involved at the beginning of the information handling process. You can better understand the data entry specialist's role by thinking of this process in three steps:

Step 1: A data entry specialist enters numbers and words into a computer system.

Step 2: The computer organizes and manipulates the information, develops a report, calculates results, or reaches some other outcome.

Step 3: Managers and supervisors make decisions and solve problems based on the organized data.

Equipment

On a data entry specialist's desk, you'll find a (1) computer monitor, (2) a keyboard, and sometimes (3) a printer. The specialist must be able to use this equipment with ease. With frequent skill building practice on the keyboard, you will increase your data entry speed and accuracy and position yourself for a well-paying job.

Software

Data entry specialists generally use two types of application software. *Spreadsheet software* provides its users the tools to manage, present, and analyze numeric information. *Database software* stores both alphabetic and numeric information about related topics and provides an easy way to sort and select information. For example, information might be sorted by ZIP code, state, last name, age, gender, or other ways.

Database software uses on-screen forms to enter and edit the information. Reports organize information in a printed format. All information about a particular customer is referred to as a *record.* A specific piece of information is referred to as a *field.* Examples of fields are Last Name, First Name, and Middle Initial.

The application software used by data entry specialists differs depending on the type of information and the outcome or document that is required.

- An airline reservation specialist uses software that allows the traveler's name, flight numbers, and the cost of the ticket to be entered.
- A data entry specialist for a charitable agency uses software that allows the names of volunteers, the cities and countries where they serve, and other details to be entered.
- A data entry assistant in a law enforcement unit uses software that allows the names of criminals, the crimes they committed, and the time they will serve to be entered.
- Research assistants use software that allows statistics gathered during a long-term study to be entered and manipulated.
- Accounting assistants use software that allows income, expenses, and investments to be entered and totals and ratios to be calculated.

While the final use of the information determines the data entry features of software, your basic data entry skills will transfer easily from job to job. By combining (1) basic knowledge of how software works and (2) the ability to move about a keyboard quickly and accurately, you will be in high demand, no matter what career field you choose.

Speaking the Language

Every occupation has a special language that employees must understand if they are to communicate effectively with co-workers. Learning a few key terms now will help you become a more effective data entry specialist.

- data
- data entry
- database software
- decision making
- electronic database
- fields
- problem solving
- raw information
- source documents
- spreadsheet software

General Terms

The term *data entry* refers to the process of entering *raw information* such as alphabetic characters, numeric characters, and special symbols into a computer. The word *data* is used to describe information that will be processed into reports, forms, and records.

Raw information may be handwritten or keyed and is contained in forms, charts, and other materials called *source documents*. Source documents usually are filed as backup material in case they're needed again.

Employability Terms

As a data entry specialist, you may find discrepancies or mistakes in the material you enter. This will require you to engage in *decision making* about what should be entered and what should be set aside to discuss with your supervisor.

Other times, you may encounter problems with the format of the material you receive, or you may have questions about the priority for completing your work. In this case, you will do some *problem solving* to reach the right answer.

Building a Career

To reach your career goal, you should start thinking now about the first data entry job you will pursue and how you will use it to reach continuing levels of success. By developing a plan, you will be more likely to reach your career goal.

Career Pathways

- Career pathway
- Customer service
- Working ethically

As a data entry specialist, you will have the option of assisting others who work in many different career pathways. The career pathway you choose will depend on your interests and the opportunities available at the time you are looking for a job. The following career chart lists the six basic career pathways and a few careers in each pathway. Examples of the type of information a data entry specialist in each pathway would enter are also shown. By spending a little time with the list, you'll gain a better understanding of how your services can be utilized in the future.

Career Path	Career	Data to be Input
Communication and the arts	Artist	Sales reports
	Reporter	Charts of statistics
	Interior designer	Cost estimates
	Stage performer	Ticket purchases
Health and Medicine	Medical assistant	Patient information
	Billing clerk	Medical codes
	Laboratory technician	Test results
	Doctor	Patient appointment schedule
Human, Public, and Personal Service	Teacher	Grades
	Hair salon owner	Income and expenses
	Government employee	Tax data
	Fitness trainer	Client exercise regimen
Business	Accountant	Numbers for reports
	Bank teller	Deposit slips
	Architect	Estimates to build a house
	Small business owner	Sales and receipts
Science and Technology	Computer programmer	Programming code
	Scientist	Research data
	Engineer	Mathematical equations
	Animal researcher	Feeding data
Environment and Natural Resources	Forestry agent	Tree repopulation data
	Weatherperson	Weather tracking information
	Water researcher	Research data
	Owner of large farm	Seed and production data

Giving Excellent Customer Service

Successful companies and institutions know that the best way to beat the competition is to offer the best possible customer service. These employers want to hire individuals who truly believe in providing excellent customer service. As a data entry specialist, you'll improve your prospects for job success if you combine your data entry skills with behaviors that keep the customer coming back.

Here are some ways for a data entry specialist to inspire customers' trust and confidence.

Exhibit a good attitude. Attitude—like Jello™—is a little hard to describe. It's your outlook on life, the general feeling you communicate to others, the vibes you give off. To exhibit a good attitude, project a positive outlook as you work with customers, even when you may not feel positive.

Keep your customers' best interests at heart. Customers are smart. If you're thinking of yourself instead of them, they'll pick up on it.

Do what you say you'll do. Gaining a customer's trust is essential, and the best way to gain trust is to follow through when you make a promise. Don't promise more than you can do.

Always tell the truth. The hardest thing about telling a lie is that you often have to tell another to cover it up. Customers and your supervisor usually find out when you haven't told the truth.

Ask customers for feedback about the way you're handling a problem. You can't improve unless you know what you're doing wrong. Always act on customers' suggestions if possible, or they won't believe you are sincere.

Demonstrate self-confidence when you talk with customers. Lack of confidence is easily detectable. Even if you're a little unsure, act confident.

To a customer, each employee is the company. Every encounter with an employee—positive or negative—influences whether a customer continues to do business with the company. Many, though not all, data entry specialists work directly with customers. If you take a job working with customers, remember that your effort and attitude are important.

Work Ethically
Ethical characteristics that will increase your chances of success in a data entry career are:

Sincerity	Accountability
Honesty	Cooperation
Cooperation	Trustworthiness
Integrity	

Working Ethically

Companies are judged by how responsibly and ethically they perform their services or sell their products. The data entry specialist has a responsibility to work ethically also—by entering all data exactly as it appears, without changing it in any way. Changing data can be illegal; for example, a data entry specialist in a payroll department who improperly records employee hours could be charged for an illegal action.

Chapter 2

Getting Started with Data Entry: The Training Center

CHAPTER OBJECTIVES

- ❒ Understand keyboarding terminology
- ❒ Become familiar with the Data Entry software
- ❒ Learn to use the Training Center

You will complete the activities within this book using *Data Entry Skillbuilding and Applications* software. In addition to completing four projects, you will also review and develop basic data entry skills. In this chapter, you will review basic keyboarding and data entry concepts, learn to log into the software, and begin your work in the Training Center module of the software. The drills at the end of this chapter are used in the Training Center.

Understanding Keyboarding Concepts

The keyboard includes these groups of keys:

- *Alphanumeric keys:* Top row of numbers and three rows of alphabetic letters.
- *Numeric keypad:* Identical to a ten-key calculator in design, the numeric keypad consists of the numbers 0–9 plus the arithmetic functions +, –, ×, ÷, and directional arrows ← ↑ ↓ →. The numeric keypad is located on the right side of the keyboard and may be used in place of the top row number keys.

  When you key a large amount of numeric data, you will find that using the numeric keypad is more efficient than using the numbers above the alphabetic keys. Most data entry specialists spend the majority of their time entering numbers from the keypad, though personal names, street names, and similar information requires the use of the alphabetic keys.

  When using the keypad, press the Num Lock key at the top left of the keypad. The Num Lock key activates or turns on the keypad. The Keypad includes an ENTER key, a decimal key, and common operational keys (/, *, and –). The keypad is not a calculator; it does not divide, multiply, or add/subtract numbers unless software is specifically written to make the keypad operate in this manner.
- *Function keys:* Keys identified as F1 through F12 that are located at the top of the keyboard. Each function key serves a special purpose, for example, saving a document or moving to the next record. Functions can also be performed without using the function keys, as you will learn in later sections of this book.
- *Arrow keys:* The arrow keys allow you to navigate on the screen in the direction of the arrow.

Figure 2.1 Keyboard Arrangement

- *Backspace* and *Delete:* These keys allow you to erase text. Pressing the Backspace key erases text to the left of the insertion point. Pressing the Delete key erases text to the right of the insertion key.

Keyboarding Technique

Developing good technique while keying is perhaps the single most important event in the data entry operator's instructional life. You are training your muscles to respond in a specific way. Your goal is to continually key in the correct manner. Position at the keyboard is the constant point of reference; the mind and body should learn to key from a certain position. Position the keyboard directly in front of you at the edge of the desk. Sit directly in front of the keyboard about one-hand span away from the edge of the table.

Body: Sit upright before the keyboard. Ideally, feet are flat on the floor, one foot slightly ahead of the other. Center your body with the "B" key.

Arms and Wrists: Keep your arms close to your body. Keep your wrists low, but not resting on the keyboard.

Fingers: Drop your arms to the side and notice the natural curve of your fingers. Bring your fingers to the keyboard, keeping this natural, relaxed curve of the fingers.

Eyes: Keep your eyes on the source copy or the document from which you are keying.

Getting Started with the Software

To get started in the software you must first log in and create a student record. Follow the steps below to begin. Once you have logged into the software, you will be taken directly to the Main menu, which is explained a little later in the chapter.

Log In

1. Turn on the computer; Windows will load.

2. Click the **Start** button and select Programs.

3. Choose South-Western Keyboarding and click **Data Entry**. (If the program does not appear on the Start menu, click Programs to locate it.)

The first time you use the software, you must create a student record from the Log in dialog box. *You will only do this once.* Your student record will contain the results of what you do in the software.

To create a student record, click the **New** button from the Log In dialog box. In the New Student dialog box, key your first name, press Tab, key your middle initial, press Tab, and key your last name. If your instructor has set up a class, add yourself to the appropriate class. Enter a password. Remember your password because you will need it each time you enter the program. Click OK to continue.

Figure 2.2 New Student Dialog Box

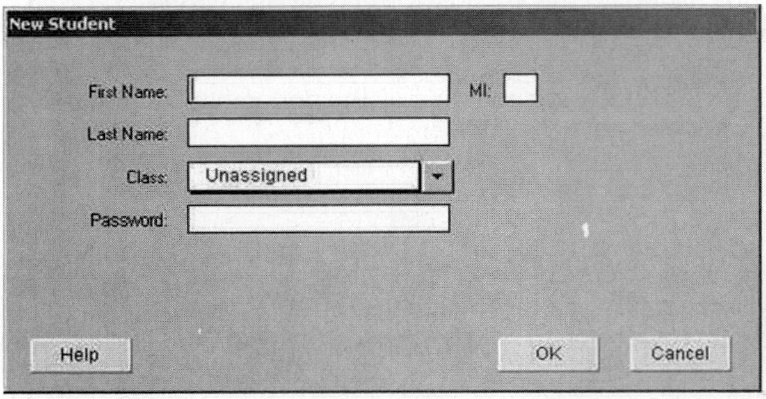

The next time you enter the program, select your name from the Log In menu and enter your password. Once you have logged into the software, a bookmark will remember where you left off.

Using the Main Menu

You will see the Main Menu after you have logged into the software. You can navigate anywhere in the software from the Main Menu. Note these features of the Main Menu:

- Navigation and resource buttons along the left edge of the screen.
- Practice Room: Timed writings, drills, and an open screen for keying information from other sources.
- Training Center: Skillbuilding lessons to build speed and accuracy.

- Project Lab: Four data entry projects where you will work as a data entry specialist for various companies. The Project Lab is the heart of the Data Entry software.

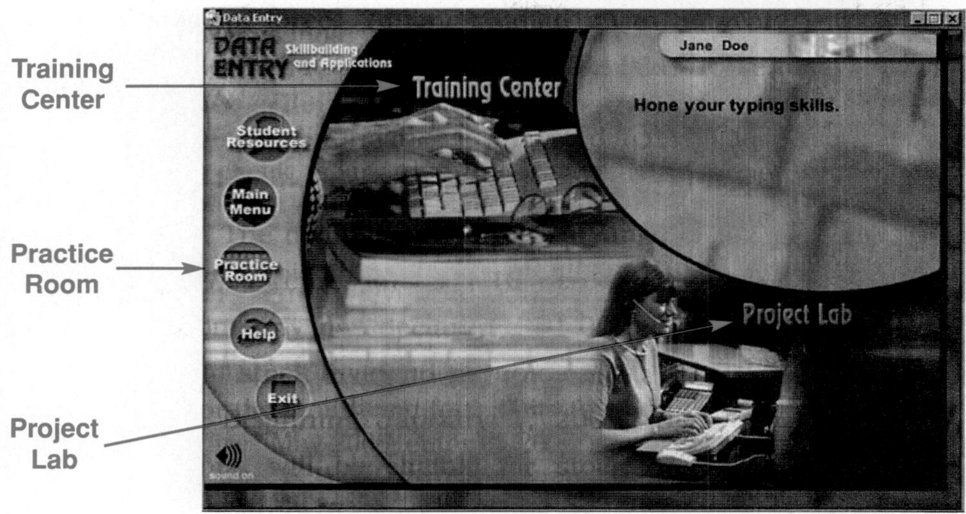

Figure 2.3 Main Menu

Navigating the Main Menu

The Main Menu includes buttons along the left edge of the screen that allow you to navigate within the software and provide access to special features. These features are discussed in the order in which they appear on the screen.

Student Resources: The Student Resources option allows you to change some of the preferences of the software and manage your student record. The Student Resources Menu is shown in Figure 2.4 and an explanation of each option follows.

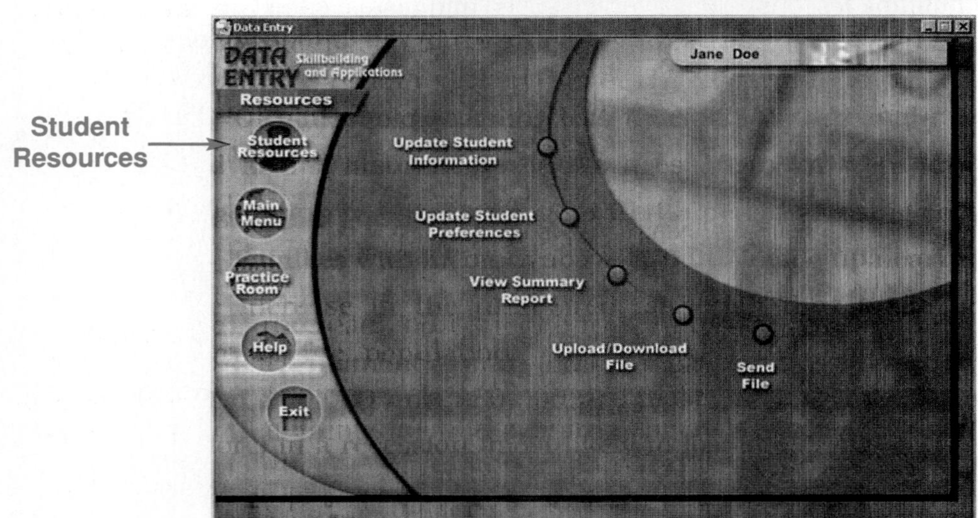

Figure 2.4 Student Resources Menu

Update Student Information: Select this option to change your password.

Update Student Preferences: Select this option to change the default settings for such elements as audio, number of spaces after a period, backspace option in the Training Center and Practice Room, and your choice of Spanish or English for directional copy and voice. Select the tab for each part of the software to view the options. To change options that are dimmed, click the Use Class Default box to remove the checkmark. If your instructor chooses to lock some of these options, you will not be able to change them.

Figure 2.5 Update Student Preferences

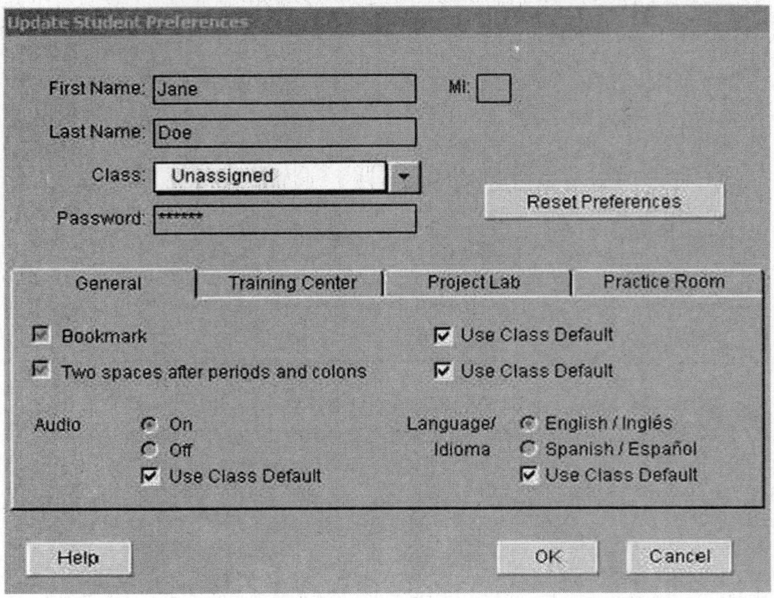

View Summary Report: Two reports summarize the work you have done within the Training Center and the Project Lab: the Training Center Summary Report and the Project Lab Summary Report. The Training Center Summary Report (Figure 2.6) indicates your progress on the skill-building lessons. Your average speed and fastest speed are reported for the Build Speed activity. Select the Print button to print the report. To display the Lesson Report for a lesson that has been completed, click the date of the lesson. The Project Lab Summary Report is discussed in Chapter 3.

Figure 2.6 Training Center Summary Report

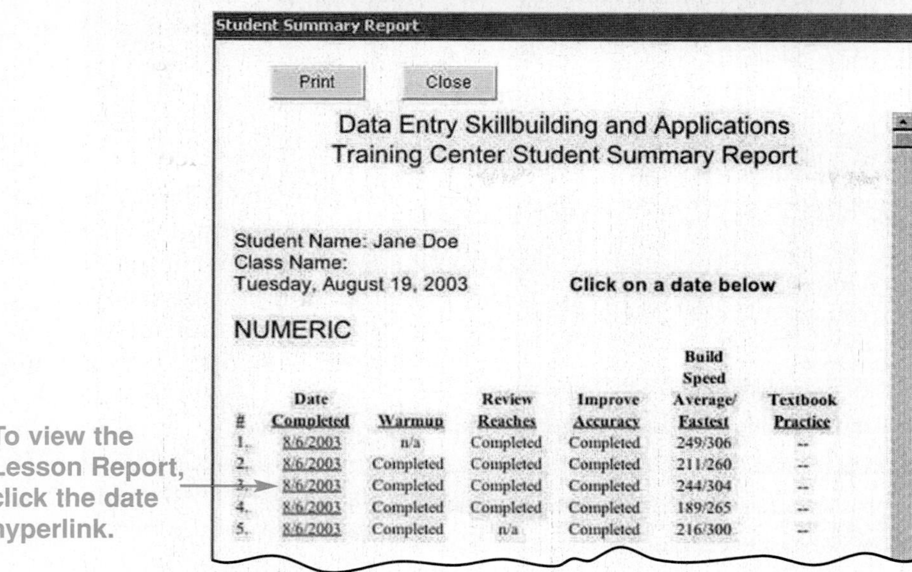

#	Date Completed	Warmup	Review Reaches	Improve Accuracy	Build Speed Average/ Fastest	Textbook Practice
1.	8/6/2003	n/a	Completed	Completed	249/306	--
2.	8/6/2003	Completed	Completed	Completed	211/260	--
3.	8/6/2003	Completed	Completed	Completed	244/304	--
4.	8/6/2003	Completed	Completed	Completed	189/265	--
5.	8/6/2003	Completed	n/a	Completed	216/300	--

Upload/Download File: The Upload/Download feature transfers your student record from one location to another. For example, use the *Import Data* option to transfer your student record from drive A to the program. When the Locate data file dialog box displays, browse to locate the folder in which your data file is saved.

Use the *Export Data* option to transfer your student record from the program to drive A. When the dialog box displays (Figure 2.7b), change the folder or drive in the Save In box. Use the down arrow to locate the desired drive.

Figure 2.7a Upload/Download Files

Figure 2.7b Locate the Drive

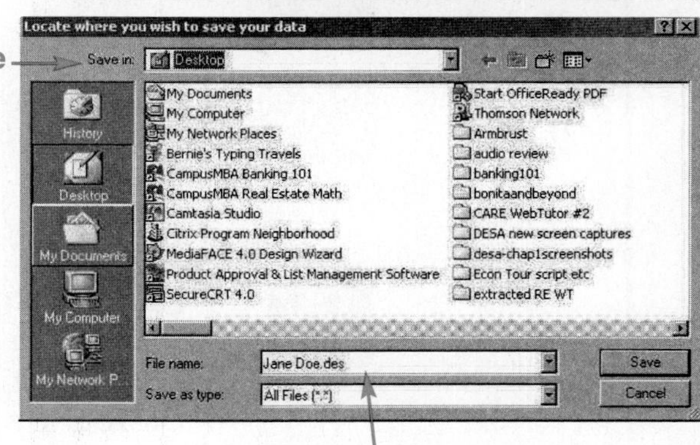

Send File: Select Send File to send your student record to your instructor. When you click this option, your student record file is automatically attached to an e-mail. Fill in your instructor's e-mail address and send the message.

Figure 2.8 Send File Option

Note: The Send file feature is dependent on your having a MAPI compliant e-mail program. If you are using an e-mail program such as Hotmail, Yahoo, or AOL, you must use the Upload/Download feature to export your student record. Select the *Export Data* option to transfer your student record from the program to drive A (see previous page). Once you have exported your student record, attach the file to an e-mail and send it to your instructor. Your student record consists of *FirstName LastName.des.*

Main Menu: The Main Menu button returns you to the Main Menu from any screen in the software.

Help: Help provides information about the features of the software.

Exit: The Exit button allows you to quit the software.

Sound: Select the Sound button to turn sound on or off. Sound on is the default setting.

Practice Room

Practice Room: The Practice Room is designed to build your speed and accuracy in data entry. It includes timed writings (alphanumeric and keypad), the drills from the projects, and an open screen or work area called On Your Own for keying text or data from other sources. Chapter 4 describes the Practice Room in detail.

Project Lab

The Project Lab is the heart of *Data Entry, Skillbuilding and Applications*. Here you will work as a data entry operator in four different companies using four different projects. Each project contains several activities that simulate data entry in the real world. Chapter 3 provides detailed information on the Project Lab.

Training Center

Before beginning the data entry projects, you will want to spend several hours in the Training Center. The Training Center includes 12 lessons that review the alphanumeric keys and keypad. You will have an opportunity to learn, review, and improve your keyboarding skills before moving onto the data entry projects.

Working in the Training Center

To enter the Training Center, click anywhere within the words **Training Center** on the Main Menu. The Training Center Menu displays. Lessons 1–5 review the keypad. Lessons 6–12 review and build skill on the alphabetic and top-row reaches. To select a lesson, click the lesson number. Complete these lessons in sequence. To do the Keypad lessons, press the **Num Lock** button before you begin to turn it on.

Figure 2.9 Training Center Menu

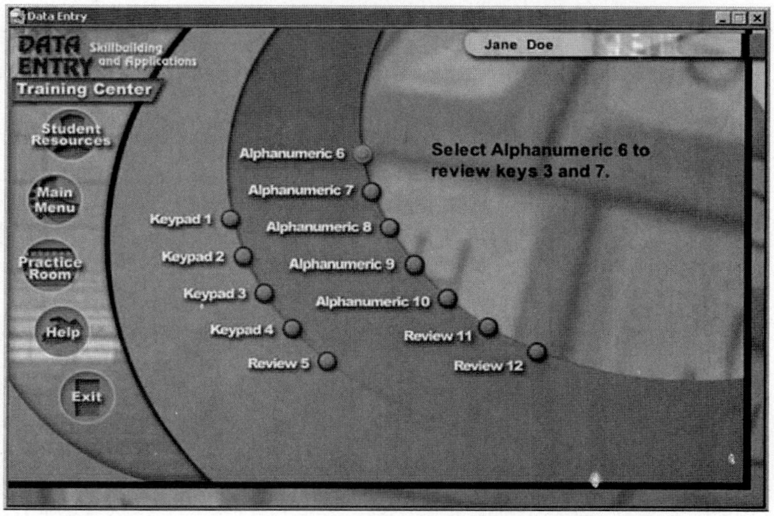

Lesson Design

The tabs at the top of the lesson screen display the exercises within each lesson. Lesson exercises should be completed in sequence. Begin with the first exercise, and the software will move automatically through the lesson. You can move to a new lesson by clicking a lesson tab at the bottom of the screen. You must complete all the drills in each lesson in order to receive credit for doing the lesson

Beginning with Lesson 2, each lesson includes the parts below. The Warmup exercise is not included in Lesson 1.

Warmup: You will key each column of numbers or lines twice; your speed is reported at the end of the second attempt.

Figure 2.10 Lesson Screen in the Training Center

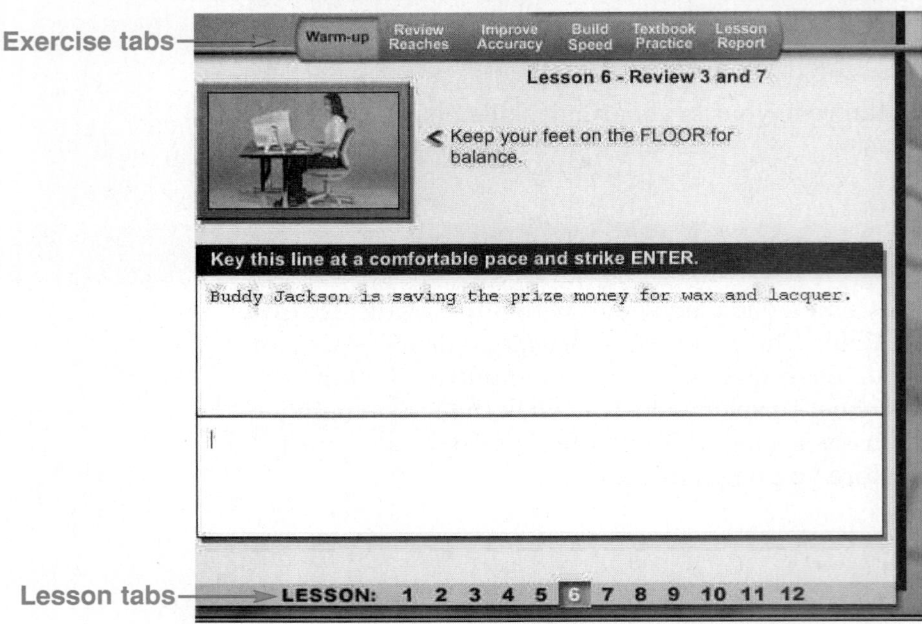

Review Reaches: Each lesson reviews two or more numbers. In Keypad, you will begin with the home row—numbers 4, 5, and 6. You must key each number correctly; if you make a mistake, the software will prompt you with the correct keystroke by flashing it on the screen.

Improve Accuracy: You will key four columns of numbers or four lines of text. Your goal is to key as accurately as possible. You will have three opportunities to enter each number correctly.

Build Speed: You will key each column of numbers or each line of text twice. Your *kpm* (keystrokes per minute) will be reported after you enter a column of numbers or *gwam* (gross words a minute) after entering a line of text. You will be challenged to increase your speed by 10 keystrokes.

Textbook Practice: The Textbook Practice exercise allows you to key directly from the textbook. The exercises are located at the end of this chapter. The directions for Textbook Practice in the software direct you to the page in the book. Each drill in the textbook is identified with a lesson number. Your goal is to keep your eyes on the textbook copy and enter the data. Speed and errors are reported. Textbook Practice lines in Alphanumeric will print in your Lesson Report.

The Textbook Practice for the Keypad lessons include a total below each column; you will not key the total. Instead, strike ENTER twice to obtain the total. Repeat the column until you obtain the correct answer. Strike **Y** to enter a new set of numbers or **N** to go to the Lesson Report. The remainder of this chapter includes the Textbook Practice for these 12 lessons.

Note: The Textbook Practice drills can also be used in On Your Own in the Practice Room.

Lesson Report: Select the Lesson Report button to display a summary of your performance in the lesson. You may print the report by clicking the Print button at the left of the report. Your results will also be included in the Student Summary Report, which is available in Student Resources.

Figure 2.11 Lesson Report

Data Entry Skillbuilding and Applications
Training Center Lesson Report

Jane Doe
Class ID: Unassigned
Tuesday, August 19, 2003

Lesson 1 - Review 4, 5, 6, 0, and ENTER

Section	
Warmup	Not available in this lesson.
Review Reaches	Completed
Improve Accuracy	Completed
Build Speed	
Average speed	249 kspm
Fastest speed	306 kspm

Typed text - *Original/student's*

LESSON: 1 2 3 4 5 6 7 8 9 10 11 12

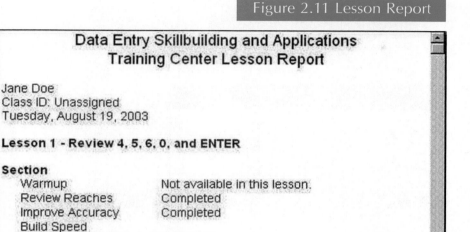

Begin the Training Center Lab Lessons

1. Log into the software if you have not already done so.

2. From the Main Menu, click **Training Center**.

3. Choose a lesson, beginning with Keypad 1.

4. Turn on the Num Lock key for all Keypad lessons. A small light above the Num Lock key will be on when the Num Lock is on.

5. Beginning with Review Reaches, key the lesson from the software.

6. When you get to Textbook Practice, turn to the appropriate page in this chapter and key columns A–J (Keypad lessons) or lines 1–8 (Alphanumeric lessons). See the appropriate directions below for Textbook Practice.

Textbook Practice, Keypad Lessons 1–5:

a. Position your fingers over the numeric keypad home row. Beginning in Column A, key the first number and press ENTER on the keypad.

b. After you have entered the last figure within a column, strike the ENTER key twice to get a total. If your total differs from the one shown in the book, rekey the group.

c. Key **Y** to the question Begin new practice? Follow this procedure as you key the numbers in Column B, C, etc. through column J.

Figure 2.12 Textbook Practice

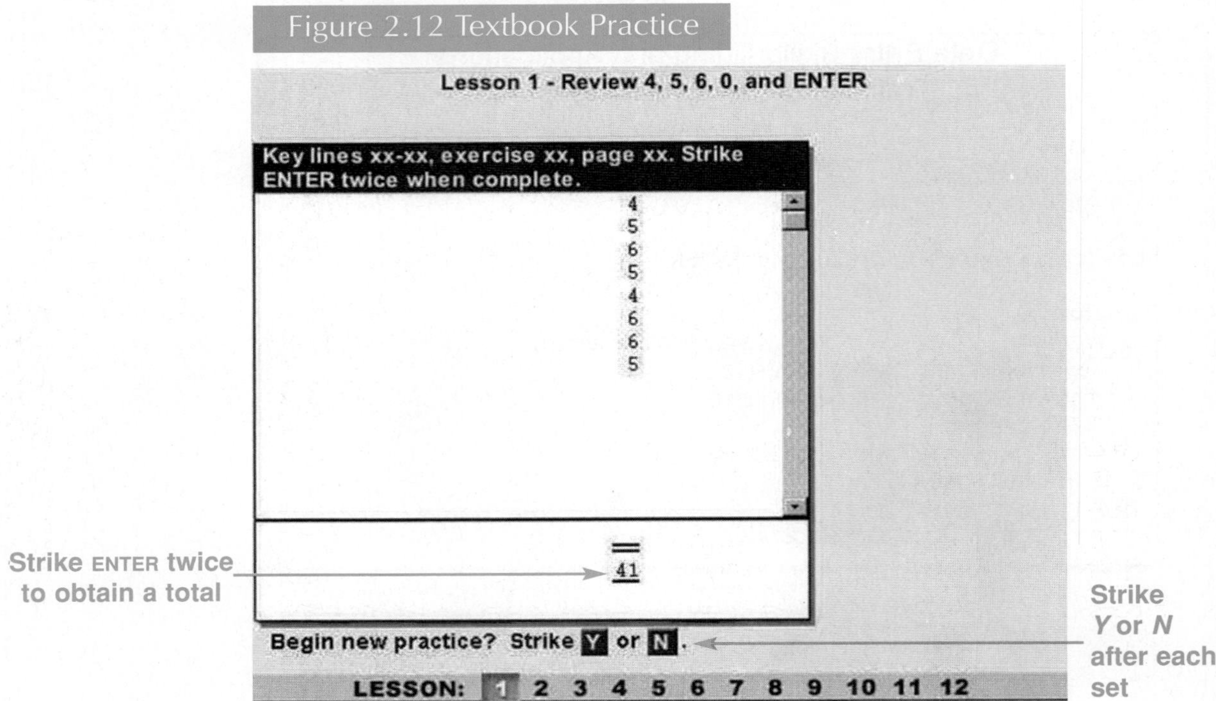

7. After keying the last column in Textbook Practice (column J), key **N** or press ESC to display your Lesson Report.

8. To print the report, select the Print button to the left of the report.

Textbook Practice, Alphanumeric Lessons 6–12: Key the lines from the textbook working for good control. Repeat the exercise if desired.

9. After keying the last sentence, press ESC. Press **Y** to repeat the exercise or **N** to display your Lesson Report.

10. To print the report, select the Print button to the left of the report. The Textbook Practice lines will print with the Lesson Report.

Keypad 1 Review 4, 5, 6, 0, and ENTER

A	B	C	D	E
4	44	60	444	500
5	55	50	555	400
6	66	06	666	600
5	45	05	456	606
4	46	405	465	460
6	54	500	544	505
6	64	606	564	604
5	65	504	656	506
41	**439**	**2,136**	**4,350**	**4,181**

F	G	H	I	J
656	5060	4444	5546	45566
504	5005	5555	6405	60055
406	4004	6666	5546	55645
64	5060	4566	6004	64560
6	5005	5564	5046	50644
466	4005	6006	6504	44550
50	6600	6405	5406	55460
546	4506	5004	4065	60556
2,698	**39,245**	**44,210**	**44,522**	**437,036**

Keypad 2 Review 7, 8, and 9

A	B	C	D	E
7	88	987	474	90
8	99	789	585	70
9	77	877	969	80
8	99	788	678	90
5	88	997	498	67
8	77	879	857	58
7	99	977	796	69
4	77	799	986	86
56	**704**	**7,093**	**5,843**	**610**

F	G	H	I	J
707	807	7080	4074	40700
798	945	8040	5085	47845
607	607	5009	6096	58459
498	854	9408	9446	94765
576	967	7506	8557	40706
890	907	6458	7884	56087
997	867	9846	4975	45905
856	705	5479	8575	79800
5,929	**6,659**	**58,826**	**54,692**	**464,267**

Textbook Practice

See instruction's on pages 19–20 if necessary.

Turn on Num Lock key before you begin.

Keypad 3 Review 1, 2, 3

A	B	C	D	E
1	22	321	414	40
2	33	123	525	10
3	11	211	636	20
2	33	133	634	30
1	44	332	431	62
3	55	213	521	62
2	66	311	416	36
3	33	122	324	36
17	**297**	**1,766**	**3,901**	**296**

F	G	H	I	J
56	321	365	504	3663
34	123	324	30	2552
46	211	416	200	1441
21	332	521	10	1321
34	213	431	5340	5314
45	311	634	2546	6423
23	122	110	2104	3005
33	532	210	1006	5043
292	**2,165**	**3,011**	**11,740**	**28,762**

Keypad 4 Review Decimal and Symbols

A	B	C	D	E
3.3	1.23	.45	3.34	.33
3.5	3.44	4.06	4.34	.36
3.6	4.66	7.88	.33	6.33
3.7	.55	.56	.34	3.98
6.3	.89	3.44	.93	3.70
6.3	.23	7.88	.36	.35
.33	3.44	.66	3.38	.79
.36	8.99	.09	5.39	2.31
27.39	**23.43**	**25.02**	**18.41**	**18.15**

F	G	H	I	J
3.55	.305	709.1	5.77	5.23
.13	.508	50.08	.13	311.25
.34	.803	400.57	7.00	423.59
.78	.203	89.04	8.05	587.34
1.59	.098	10.50	.67	768.74
7.88	.213	11.75	.56	824.74
4.07	.359	9.24	6.77	965.97
2.13	.872	.018	455.88	112.85
20.47	**3.361**	**1280.298**	**484.83**	**3,999.71**

Keypad 5 Review

A	B	C	D	E
10	111	3.21	9.30	34.41
20	222	2.34	4.10	67.84
30	333	1.23	5.50	45.52
40	444	9.98	8.07	45.61
50	555	7.75	1.10	56.63
60	666	3.21	1.04	67.83
34	777	4.32	1.24	23.41
25	888	5.43	2.25	23.31
14	999	7.65	9.87	56.61
47	000	8.76	4.33	67.88
58	122	9.87	6.60	12.22
69	233	1.21	9.76	13.33
93	344	2.32	5.08	16.59
82	566	4.54	2.53	94.44
71	677	7.76	1.00	98.77
17	788	2.21	5.06	33.88
28	899	6.65	5.66	77.55
39	633	9.98	8.30	88.22
45	899	3.63	2.01	26.26
65	766	5.50	8.29	79.35
897	**10,922**	**107.55**	**101.09**	**1029.66**

F	G	H	I	J
32638	6039.08	9.98	3559.51	3000.50
92563	4175.92	1.92	6324.10	2500.00
47739	9178.21	1.92	8575.34	800.00
13922	1204.51	9.10	734.67	5.60
94181	7833.23	8.29	3524.12	2300.78
77929	423.31	3.26	2167.27	6770.00
61893	8737.10	5.28	9483.52	88.99
94835	8315.94	2.21	6795.25	.66
35514	9144.89	8.04	4284.50	6.77
99487	8538.13	5.85	3.30	455.06
85109	671.28	5.89	8585.40	5660.56
10951	2.45	8.32	679.25	233.05
23305	8005.21	1.10	5706.37	650.00
50672	167.62	1.23	1.76	3.05
42940	1373.48	3.02	8.88	2038.99
55031	4795.61	2.00	19.57	1000.00
918,709	**78,605.97**	**77.41**	**60,452.81**	**25,514.01**

Textbook Practice

Press Enter

Alphanumeric 6 Review 3 and 7

Directions:

See instruction's on pages 19–20 if necessary.

1. Key each line once. Press ENTER at the end of each line.
2. Press ESC when completed.
3. View your Lesson Report and print if desired.

1 we 33, find 33 ways, 7-day coupon, 77 days, 37 cans, 3 by 3

2 Key the figures 7 and 77, and 777. Then add 3, 33, and 333.

3 I read 3 of the 73 books. Add the figures 37, 377, and 733.

4 October 3, the 37 bikers will leave for a hike of 377 miles.

5 Key 33, 37, 73, and 77. Only 33 of the 77 joggers are here.

6 The stock person counted 33 coats, 37 slacks, and 77 shirts.

7 Just 37 of the 73 boys got 77 of the 377 quiz answers right.

8 Please review Figure 3 on page 337 and Figure 7 on page 773.

Alphanumeric 7 Review 5 and 8

Directions:

Follow the directions as in Lesson 6.

Technique Reminders:

- Fingers curved and upright.
- Extend fingers and reach to the top row.

1 Key 55, 88, 58, and 85. Just 58 of the 88 skiers have come.

2 I based my April 5 report on pages 558 to 585 of Chapter 55.

3 On October 8, the 35 hikers left on a long hike of 58 miles.

4 Add the figures 5, 55, and 555. Have just 8 of 88 finished?

5 He keyed all 538 pages for Invoice 758, or 83 more than Joy.

6 Jack said Motor 73 is idling at 8 mph and Motor 85 at 5 mph.

7 Key 38, 58, and 738. Key the figures as units: 37, 57, 87.

8 My goal is to sell 55 tacos, 58 pizzas, and 37 cases of pop.

Alphanumeric 8 Review 0 and 4

1 Do you want 0, 00, or 000 paper? Snap the finger off the 0.

2 Of 44 members, 4 were 40 minutes late for the 4 meetings.

3 Did they key at the rate of 40, or was it 84 words a minute?

4 Enter the figures 0, 4, and 40; then try 400, 404, and 4440.

5 Reach up to 4, 45, and 454. Key 40 and 400. Study Item 40.

6 Car 477 had its trial run. Speeds of 380 mph. were reached.

7 Key 3 and 4 and 5 and 7 and 8 and 0 and 437 and 734 and 504.

8 Kris will be 47 on Tuesday, October 8; he weighs 300 pounds.

Alphanumeric 9 Review 1 and 9

My staff of 9 worked 49 hours each week from May 9 to May 9.

Do you want a size 9 or 11? I have 19 of each one in stock.

Please review Figure 11 on page 19 and Figure 19 on page 99.

My goal is to sell 99 tacos, 59 pizzas, and 5 cases of cola.

Sara used Volume 9, pages 419 to 490 for my April 19 report.

Key quickly pairs of figures: 10, 37, 48, 59, 919, and 733.

Two-digit numbers such as 19, 37, 74, and 85 are fun to key.

Our team planted 38 cedar, 375 walnut, and 1,590 pine trees.

Alphanumeric 10 Review 2 and 6

At 6 p.m., Channel 6 reported the August 6 score was 6 to 2.

Add the figures 6, 66, and 666. Have only 2 of 22 finished?

or 94 if 85 am 17 do 39; tug 575 lap 910 fork 4948 kept 8305

The stock person counted 28 coats, 16 slacks, and 49 shirts.

Do you need size 2 or 6; I have 8 of size 40 or 42 in stock.

Of the 16 numbers, only 3 were selected: 113, 519, and 578.

Key the figures as units: 27, 59, 17, 30, 48, 762, and 268.

Our group sold 850 chili dogs, 497 sandwiches, and 301 pies.

Alphanumeric 11 Review

or 94 is 83 me 73 so 29 the 563 and 166 apt 105 cow 392 form

my 76 I'm 87 via 481 wet 235 you 697 spa 201 fad 413 sir 284

Joe scored 26, 37, 48, and 50; Tim scored 28, 31, 46, and 59.

I'm 87 to 59 and 183 was 212 hop 690 fog 495 wet 235 pin 087

Please review Rules 1 to 12 in Chapter 5, pages 193 and 130.

She will need 12 copies of Z6417 and Z9843 by June 14, 2004.

On May 10, Rick drove 500 miles to New Mexico in car No. 84.

Tract 27 cites the date as 1850; Tract 170 says it was 1852.

Alphanumeric 12 Review

4 $4 $f f$ half $4; off $4; of $4; she saved $9; price is $5

2 @2 @2 @s jan@ubi-sw.com; matt@ubi-sw.com; doris@ubi-sw.com

5 5% %f %f 7& tariff; 9% increase; 15% less; 28% base; up 5% 24@

.26; 22 @ .35; sold 2 @ 87; were 12 @ .95; ellie@ubi.com

It was built for $96.90, not $102—about 5% less than planned.

Evlyn had $8; Sean, $9; and Cal, $7. The cash total was $7.

June 17, 2006; September 30, 1998; July 4, 1776, December 16

1598 West 218 Street; Apartment 35c; Suite 2058; 45230-1987

Chapter 3

Completing the Projects: The Project Lab

CHAPTER OBJECTIVES

- ❒ Learn to enter data correctly and efficiently
- ❒ Understand the common practices for entering data
- ❒ Learn to proofread and evaluate your work

In the Project Lab, you will gain experience completing four data entry projects that are similar to those performed by data entry specialists every day. Each project is slightly more complex than the previous one. You will apply standard data entry procedures and your knowledge and skill to complete each project. You will use a variety of forms to complete the projects for four organizations:

- ❒ Crandle Insurance, an automobile insurance company
- ❒ Funwear, a mail-order clothing catalog
- ❒ Western Suites, a hotel
- ❒ General Hospital, a big-city hospital

Overview of the Project Lab

To enter the Project Lab, select Project Lab from the Main Menu. The Project Lab menu displays and lists the four organizations: Crandle Insurance, Funwear, Western Suites, and General Hospital. The navigation bar to the left of the Project Lab menu provides the navigation to the Practice Room, Student Resources, Help, or Exit. To begin a project, simply select the project name. To return to the Main Menu, select the Main Menu button.

Figure 3.1 Project Lab Menu

Project Welcome Screen

The project welcome screen in Figure 3.2 is a brief introduction to the organization. The activities that you will be handling are listed on the Activity bar. Click the right arrow button to continue or click Warm-up. When you select an activity, the button will change to black lettering.

Figure 3.2 Project Welcome Screen

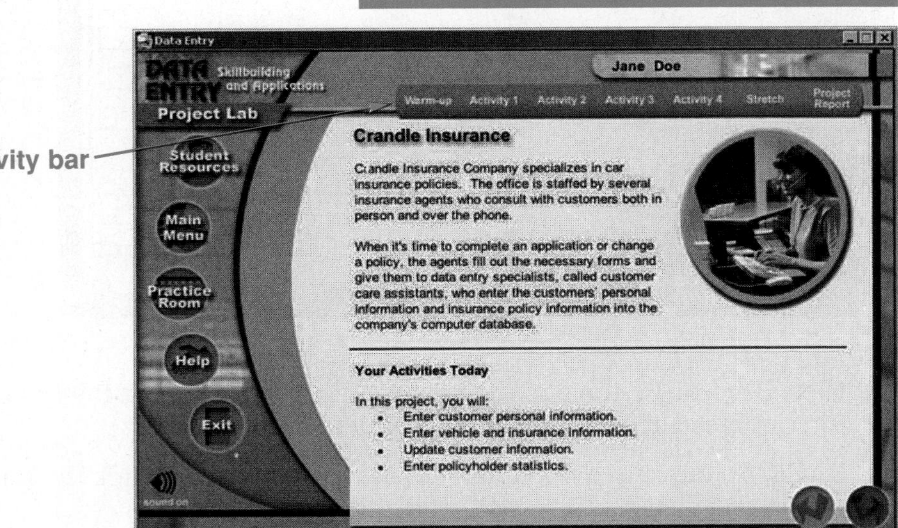

Each project begins with a **Warmup** exercise and ends with a **Stretch** exercise that are designed to increase your data entry skills. Enter the data as directed in the textbook. When exercises consist primarily of numbers, use the ENTER key on the keypad to move between fields. When exercises combine both numeric and alphabetic data, use the Tab key to move between fields. Your gross words a minute (*gwam*) for Alphanumeric exercises or keystrokes per hour (*ksph*) for Keypad exercises will display when you complete the exercise. You may choose to repeat the exercise to increase your speed and accuracy rate. (Note: The Warmup and Stretch exercises are also available from the Practice Room by selecting the Drills option.)

Activity Form Screen

Data for each activity is entered in an activity form that displays when you select an activity (see Figure 3.3). Note these points:

- The navigation bar at the left of the screen provides access to other parts of the program. Click the Main Menu button to return to the Main Menu.
- Data fields on the screen may be in a different order than the information on the printed form.
- The **record number** for each customer or client appears below the activity form. You can move between records by selecting the record number. You can move to the next record by pressing Tab or ENTER after completing the last field of a record. Enter all data for a customer before moving to the next customer.

Figure 3.3 Activity Form Screen

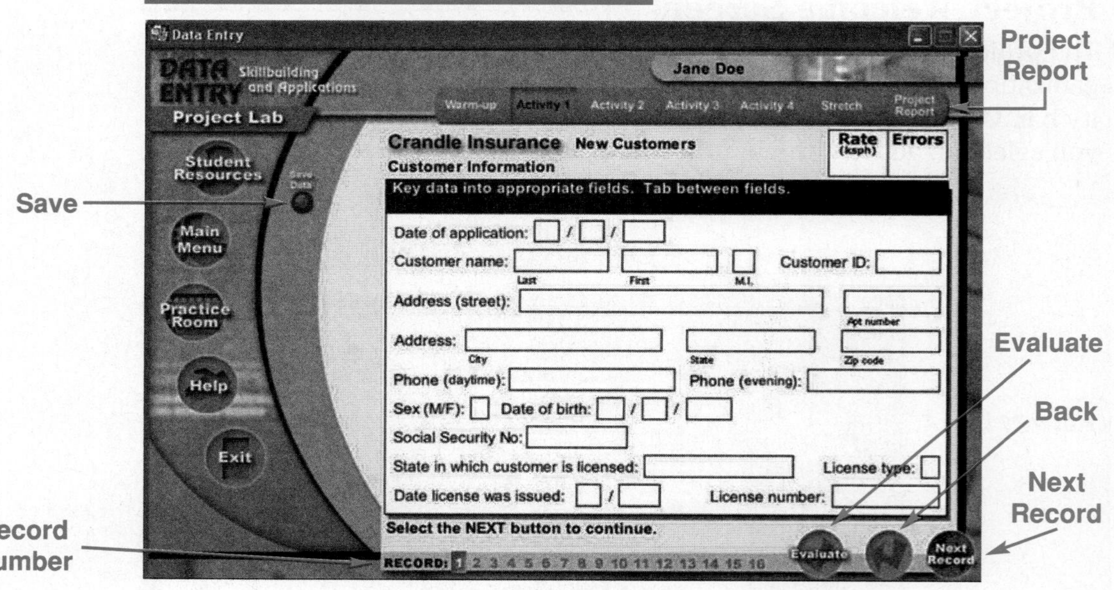

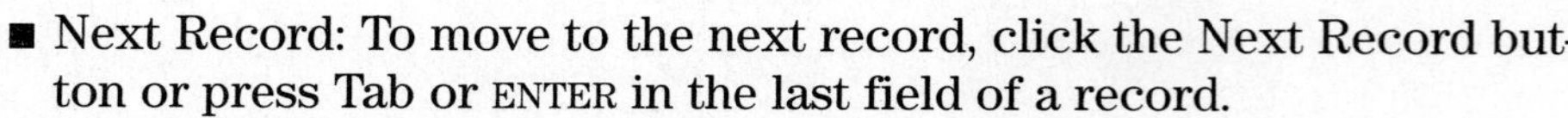

- Next Record: To move to the next record, click the Next Record button or press Tab or ENTER in the last field of a record.

- BACK: To move to a previous screen within a record, click the Back button.

- Save: After each record (customer) is completed within an activity, the data keyed to that point saves automatically. If you complete only a portion of a record before leaving an activity, however, you must click Save in order to return to it at a later time. **Note:** The Save feature saves only one partially completed activity within each project at a given time. Thus if you were to start Activity 2 (Project 1) before completing Activity 1 (Project 1), you would lose the data you had keyed in Activity 1. If you choose to begin another activity before completing a previous activity, two dialog boxes will appear warning you that you will lose the data keyed if you continue with the next activity. *Work with Caution.* Once you have saved an activity, you can work in the Practice Room or the Training Lab, however, without losing your data in the activity.

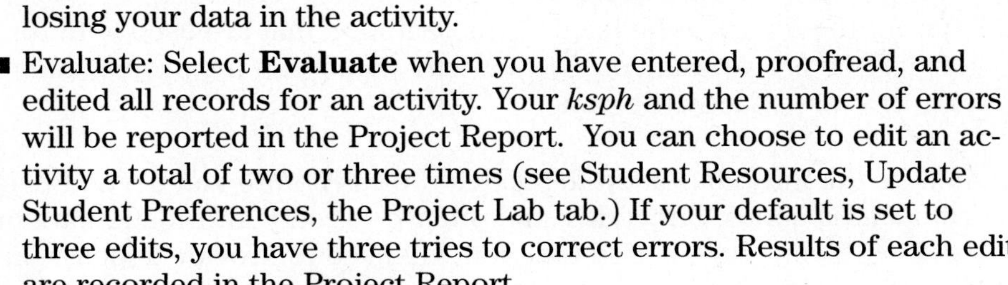

- Evaluate: Select **Evaluate** when you have entered, proofread, and edited all records for an activity. Your *ksph* and the number of errors will be reported in the Project Report. You can choose to edit an activity a total of two or three times (see Student Resources, Update Student Preferences, the Project Lab tab.) If your default is set to three edits, you have three tries to correct errors. Results of each edit are recorded in the Project Report.

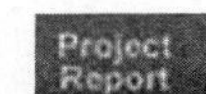

- Project Report: After an activity is proofread and checked (evaluated), select the Project Report button to view your results. If you choose to redo an activity from the beginning, results are saved as Pass 2. You can view the data you keyed in the most recent pass of an activity by selecting Student Resources, View Summary Report, Project Lab Summary, and then choosing the activity. **Note:** Only data from the most recent pass is saved.

Navigating within an Activity Form

Button Name	**Movement**
Tab	Next field or to the second or subsequent screen within a record
Next Record	Last field within a form to the next record
ENTER	Next or subsequent screen within a record
Back	Previous screen
Save	Stores current record if uncompleted when you must exit the software
Evaluate	Check your work after last record
Record tab/numbers	Move between records when proofreading or correcting errors
Next Activity	Move to the next activity
Shift + Tab	Previous field

Entering, Proofreading, and Evaluating Activities

Entering data effectively means keying data in an efficient manner, proofreading the data carefully so that it is 100 percent correct, and evaluating your work. Be effective by following these suggestions:

Entering and Proofreading Data

1. Read through a project carefully before you begin. Study the forms and the examples given so that you understand what needs to be keyed.

2. Tear out the forms in the back of the textbook that are used with the activity you are working on. The activity number in the project and on the forms are exactly the same.

3. Analyze the information on the activity forms before you begin. Check that all area codes, ZIP codes, and other necessary information are on the form. Some information that you will need to provide appears on the inside back cover. Fill in any missing information.

4. Organize the forms in a neat stack. Assuming that space is available, stack the forms on the side of your desk. Have a pen available for checking forms before you begin.

5. Toggle the Num Lock key on before entering data using the keypad (the light will be green when Num Lock is on).

6. Enter the data for the first record (customer). Correct mistakes as you key. Use the backspace key and mouse as you normally would in Windows software.

7. Proofread, that is, compare the data you keyed with the data on the source document (printed form). Correct mistakes that you may have made. When you are satisfied that the data for the first record is correct, turn the source document face down on your desk and continue with the second record. Correct mistakes using backspace or delete or selecting the data with the mouse and rekeying it.

When entering the data, follow these practices:

Proper names: Enter first and last names exactly as they appear on the form. Compound names such as Van Meter that should be keyed as one word. If a name includes an apostrophe, key the name without a space before or after the apostrophe.

Activity Form	Key Name
Van Meter	VanMeter
VanMeter	VanMeter
O'Henry	O'Henry (no spaces before or after apostrophe)

Dates: Enter two digits for the month and day and four digits for the year. Each part of the date is entered as a separate field. Tab between each field.

Activity Form	Key Date
November 15, 2004	11 **Tab** 15 **Tab** 2004
May 1, 1954	05 **Tab** 01 **Tab** 1954

Social Security Numbers: Enter the number as a single field. Do not key the hyphens. The software will automatically add the hyphen.

Activity Form	Key
326-78-0900	326780900

Street Names: Enter street names as shown on the form. Words such as Street, Avenue, and Boulevard may either be spelled out or abbreviated. Key them as they appear. Do not key ordinals such as 8th or 3d. Key periods as they appear on the form.

Activity Form	Key
121 W. Main St.	121 W. Main St.
68th Street	68 Street

ZIP Codes: Customers may use either a 5-digit ZIP code or a 9-digit ZIP code. Enter whatever number is given. If a ZIP code is not provided, check the inside back cover for the correct number. The entire ZIP code is considered to be one field. If a 9-digit ZIP code appears on the form, enter all 9 digits. It is not necessary to key the hyphen; it will be added automatically.

Activity Form	Key Data
45230-9876	452309876
45230	45230

Telephone Numbers: Enter phone numbers as one field without keying any parentheses or hyphens; they will be formatted automatically.

Activity Form	Key Data
(513) 555-0175	5135550175

Evaluating Your Work

After entering the data for an activity, evaluate or check your document. Follow these steps:

1. Select **Save** if you are interrupted before entering all of the source documents for an activity.

2. Select **Evaluate** to check your speed and accuracy. Your results will be recorded in your Project Report as *Pass 1, Edit 1.* If errors are present within records, the record number will be highlighted at the bottom of

the screen. Locate the source document for the first record that is highlighted. Proofread the screen against the source document and correct the error(s). Edit each highlighted tab. *Note:* If a record includes more than one screen, you will need to check each screen within the record. Use the Previous and Next arrows at the bottom of your screen to navigate to multiple screens within a record.

3. Select **Evaluate** again when you are ready to check your work the second time. Your *ksph* and errors will be displayed. The results will be recorded on your Project Report as *Pass 1, Edit 2*.

4. If errors still exist after the second evaluation, continue to proofread and edit the records with errors. The record numbers containing errors will be highlighted. Select **Evaluate** when you are ready to check your results. If mistakes are present within the activity, the errors will be highlighted in red on each form. The results will be saved in your Project Report as *Pass 1, Edit 3*.

You may repeat an activity after the third edit by starting all over. Results will be scored in the same manner but results will be listed as *Pass 2, Edit 1*, etc. in your Project Report.

Project Report

The results of your keying speed and accuracy are reported in the Project Report within an activity. The Project Report shows the date it was completed, your *ksph* (keystrokes per hour), number of errors, and percentage of accuracy. Results are reported for each edit within a pass and for all passes. Your instructor may ask you to print this report and turn it in.

Project Lab Summary Report

The Project Lab Summary Report shows your progress for all activities within all four projects. The Project Lab Summary Report is available by clicking the Student Resources button on the Main menu and choosing this option from the dialog box (Figure 3.4). The Project Lab Summary Report includes only the results of your last edit in the most recent pass of each activity.

Figure 3.4 Project Lab Summary Report

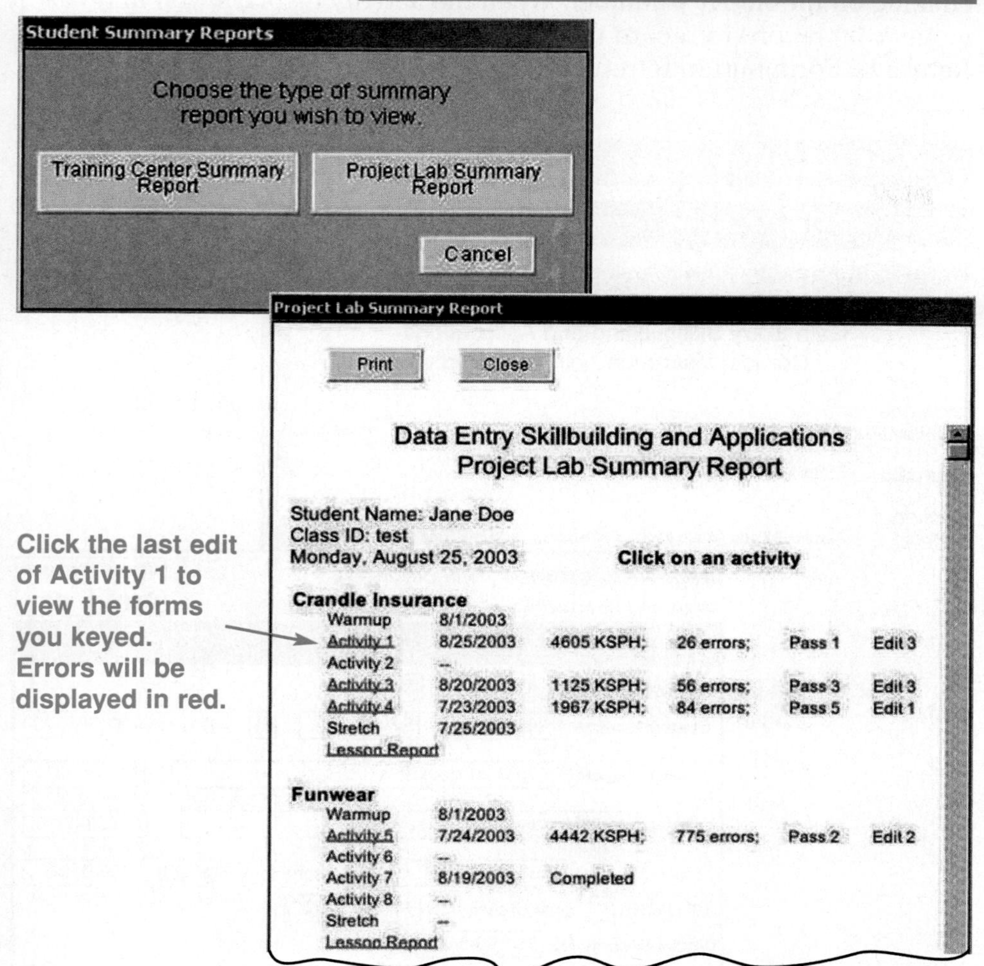

You can view the forms on screen as they appeared in your last edit by clicking on the Activity number. When the activity displays, you may move from record to record to view your forms (Figure 3.5). Click the Return to Form button to return to the Project Lab Summary Report.

Figure 3.5 View of Last Activity

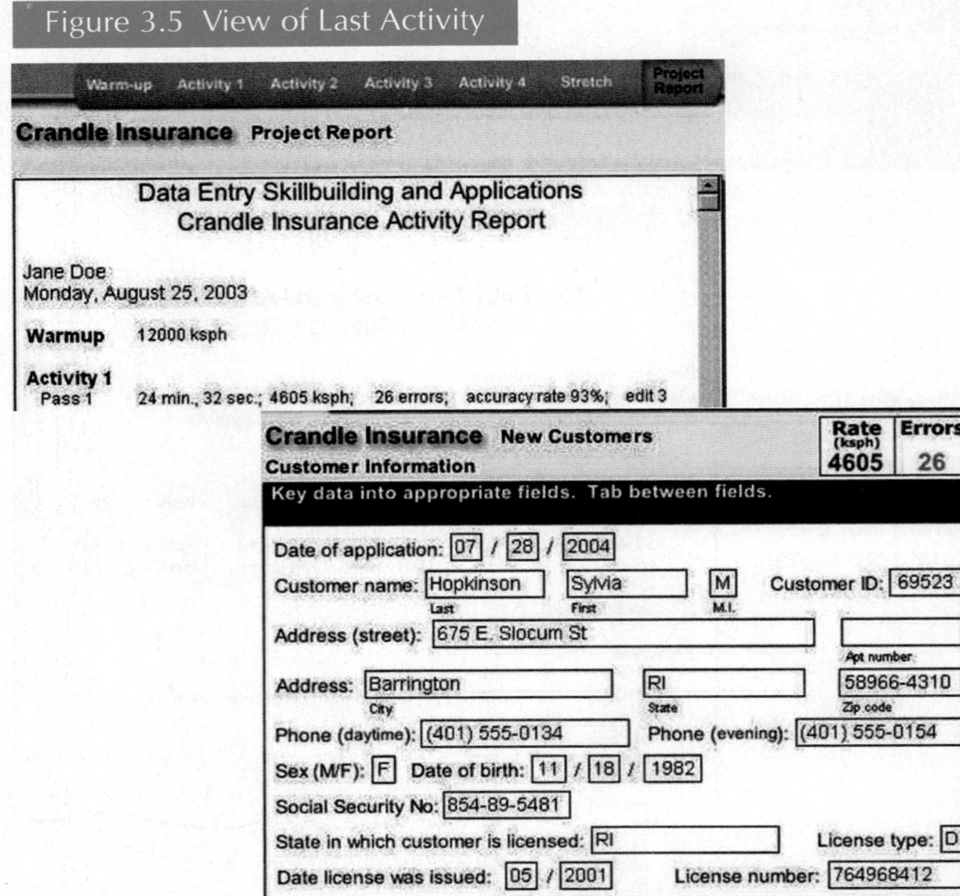

Chapter 4
Building Data Entry Skill: The Practice Room

CHAPTER OBJECTIVES

- ❒ Understand the purpose of the Practice Room
- ❒ Take a timed writing in the Practice Room

The Practice Room is designed to build your speed and accuracy when entering data or text. The more you practice your data entry skills, the better you will become at using the keyboard and navigating the software. In this chapter, you will learn about the Practice Room and take timed writings in the Practice Room.

Overview of the Practice Room

You can enter the Practice Room by clicking the Practice Room button on the Main Menu. As the menu shows, Timed Writings, Drills, and On Your Own (an open screen) are available in the Practice Room.

Figure 4.1 Practice Room Menu

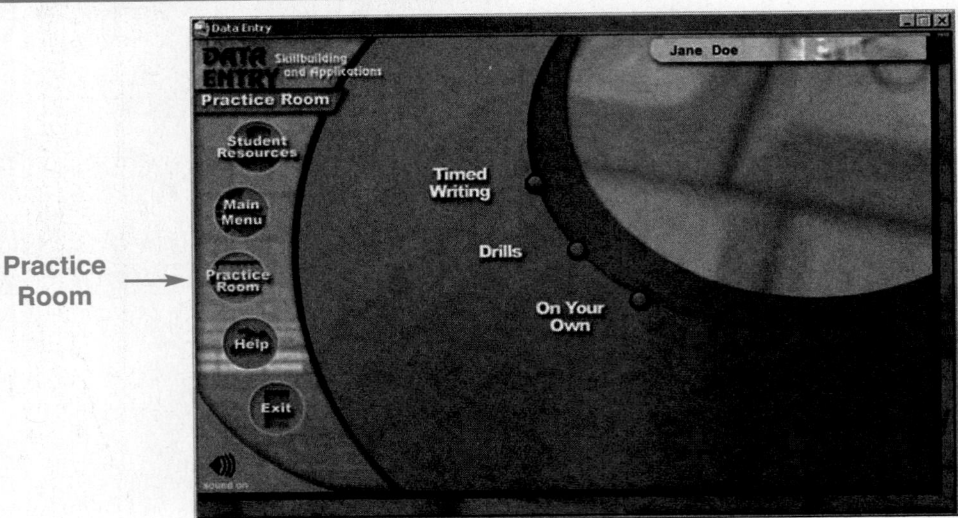

Timed Writings

You can measure your speed and accuracy using the timings located in this chapter. Three types of timings are available: Keypad timings, Alphanumeric timings, and Figure-Symbol timings. The timing numbers in the software correspond with those in this chapter (Figure 4.2). When you choose a particular timing, a dialog box will appear for you to select the length of the timing (15 seconds, 30 seconds, 1, 2, 3, or 5 minutes). The timing begins when you strike the first key. The results of the timings are saved automatically in your student record. When you have completed a timed writing, you will be able to review the errors you made while keying and print and save the timing.

After you complete the lessons in the Training Center, take at least one timed writing. Follow these directions for taking a timed writing. The Keypad timings are located on pages 41–52 and the Alphanumeric timings on pages 53–60. Figure-Symbol timings are located on pages 61–63.

To Take a Timed Writing
The Backspace mode is on by default. To change the Backspace mode to off, choose Student Resources from the Main Menu, then Update Preferences, Timed Writings.

1. From the Practice Room menu, click **Timed Writing**.

2. Select the timing you want to key. The timings listed on the menu are the same as the timings that appear later in this chapter. Notice there are 12 Keypad timings, 15 Alphanumeric timings, and 10 Figure-Symbol timings.

Figure 4.2 Timed Writings Menu

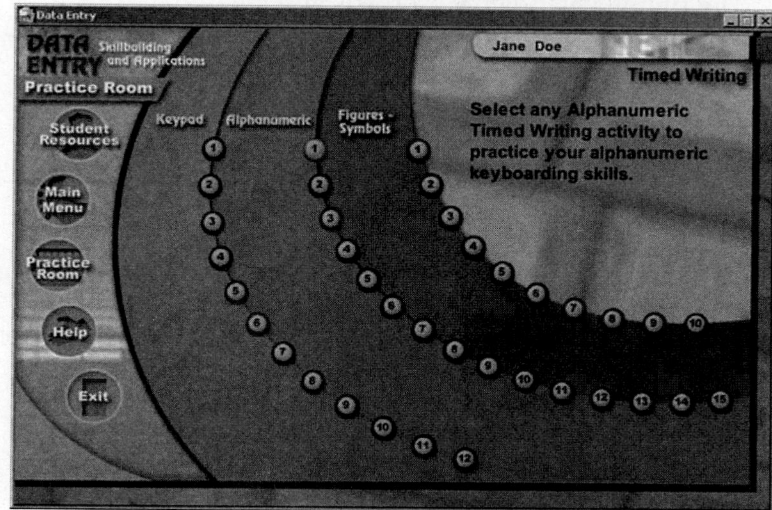

3. Enter the length of the timing and click OK.

4. Key the copy from the textbook. Tab to begin the first paragraph. Do not strike ENTER at the end of the line. The text will wrap automatically. If you finish the timing before time is called, continue keying from the beginning.

5. Print or save the timing if desired. Errors appear in bold on the print-out.

Figure 4.3 Timed Writing Dialog Box

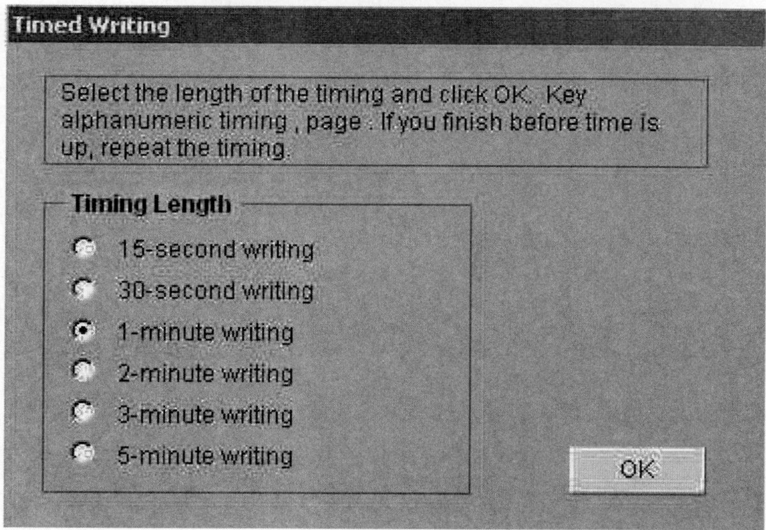

Keypad Timed Writing

1. The timing will begin as soon as you key the first digit. Beginning with Column A, key the data, moving down Column A and continue to Column B, etc.

2. Do not key the commas nor the totals.

3. Strike ENTER on the keypad to move to the next number.

4. Your keystrokes per hour (*ksph*) and number of errors will appear on screen. Errors will be highlighted.

5. You may repeat a Keypad timed writing or move to a new timed writing.

Saving a Timing

Timings can be saved as an image in a folder of your choice. Once saved, the timing can be attached to an e-mail for your instructor or opened and printed using Windows Explorer. The software will assign a file name to the timing. The file name includes your

- lastname and firstname separated by the underline key
- a two-letter abbreviation for the type of timing
- the timing number (such as 01)
- and T1 for Timing 1.

The abbreviations for the type of timing are AN for Alphanumeric, KP for Keypad, and FS for Figure Symbol. You may change the file name as desired. For example, if you repeat a timing, change the last part of the file name to T2 (second timing), T3 (third timing) etc. Examples of file names are

Alphanumeric Timing:	Lastname_Firstname_AN04T1.jpg
Keypad Timing:	Lastname_Firstname_KP04T1.jpg
Figure-Symbol	Lastname_Firstnamae_FS04T1.jpg

Tips for Taking Timed Writings

- Maintain good posture.
- Align body with the keyboard properly (body is centered with the I key).
- Concentrate on what you are keying—focus, focus, focus!
- Key quickly, but at a comfortable, controlled rate.
- Keep your eyes on the copy in the textbook.
- If you finish before time is up, start at the beginning and keep going until your time has elapsed.

Drills

Each of the four projects in the Project Lab include warmup and stretch drills to reinforce alphanumeric and keypad skills. The *Warmup* exercises located at the beginning of each project will help you get your fingers moving and your mind focused on keying data. *Stretch* exercises at the end of each project are designed to build speed and accuracy on alphanumeric data. Drills may be repeated more than once. The program stores the results of the most recent drill in the Project Summary Report. You can also access these drills from the Practice Room.

On Your Own

On Your Own is an open screen or practice area for keying text and data. The Open Screen for keying text displays by default. To switch to the Numeric Keypad screen, select the Keypad icon in the lower right corner.

In the Numeric Keypad open screen, strike ENTER after each number. Strike ENTER twice to obtain a total. The timed writing drills on pages 37–59 may be used to build skill in the Numeric Keypad screen. Compare your total on screen with the printed total (Figure 4.4).

Figure 4.4 On Your Own Numeric Keypad

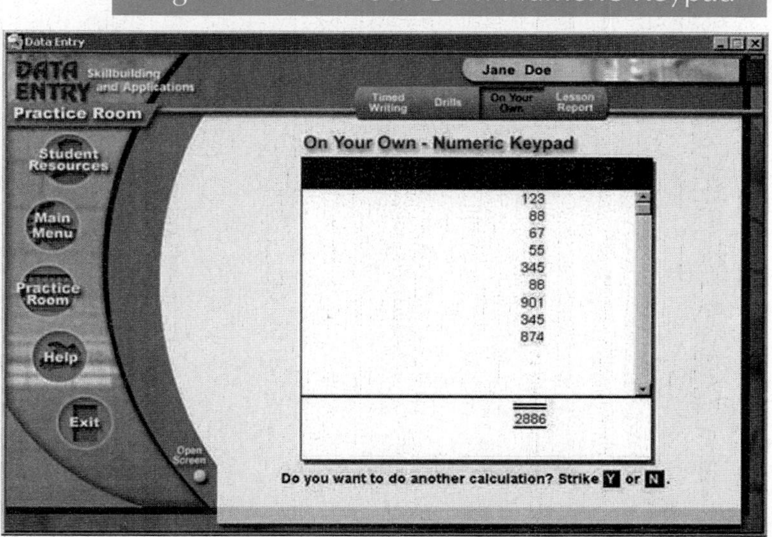

Drill Lines and Timed Writings

Keypad Timing 1

(Do not key commas or totals.)

A	B	C	D	E	F	G
98,701	28,963	365	2,716	27,140	47,219	46,731
10,786	16,822	21,981	83,256	21,167	85,364	25,810
1,236	34,687	61,783	81,100	8,792	10,652	3,025
45,316	27,681	9,432	5,097	14,082	500	19,432
381	18,021	21,131	1,926	918	64,119	5,786
1,689	2,813	83,679	1,754	1,645	17,270	2,561
20,183	105	61,842	45,816	20,993	30,059	98,160
18,092	28,242	82,416	1,026	8,770	20,611	42,587
25,137	3,742	47,835	21,826	62,009	86,150	7,354
38,021	19,538	54,963	39,119	14,653	30,958	8,687
5,384	5,678	731	76,549	97,620	31	91,590
264,926	**186,292**	**446,158**	**360,185**	**277,789**	**392,933**	**351,723**

H	I	J	K	L	M	N
12,720	41,885	345	19,043	80,123	87,291	64,597
86,414	17,251	34,970	17,408	41,878	36,648	46,312
2,588	61,665	96,714	42,034	3,341	10,217	4,591
6,135	17,880	4,206	4,597	719	38,238	10,200
7,600	4,300	10,714	654	84,128	3,574	371,964
94,409	2,330	8,322	20,345	2,274	273	574
2,330	64,110	34,126	60,567	37,753	31,910	3,416
14,500	444	41,367	56,320	85,139	42,712	6,879
1,435	8,168	52,476	3,587	84,118	44,823	16,487
13,207	21,382	1,305	2,281	23,707	95,858	32,746
51,403	11,007	90,909	34,689	3,314	151	5,492
292,741	**250,422**	**375,454**	**261,525**	**446,494**	**391,695**	**563,258**

O	P	Q	R	S	T	U
5,523	16,619	8,072	42,189	5,572	8,913	371,954
90,031	31,255	3,717	6,471	35,525	56,839	5,612
10,301	9,393	83,218	4,545	64,567	85,321	3,894
23,991	434	4,504	94,003	80,017	73,717	76,459
2,354	52,789	61,637	75,354	90,242	251	34,598
13,178	8,204	28,325	32,313	42,876	3,127	4,568
6,116	17,998	9,371	3,858	90,242	95,736	31,795
82,800	2,331	7,448	891	9,917	3,857	9,700
8,918	51,560	20,191	74,124	218	41,176	10,506
4,329	12,715	22,853	82,761	60,312	31,806	5,284
75,812	83,213	80,872	94,343	6,187	49,255	5,984
323,353	**286,511**	**330,208**	**510,852**	**485,675**	**449,998**	**560,354**

Keypad Timing 2

(Do not key commas or totals.)

A	B	C	D	E	F	G
61,589	1,035	76,413	94,572	2,554	3,498	9,421
34,516	489,762	5,449	60,450	6,432	24,561	51,296
87,435	3,168	13,348	54,132	17,987	679,840	3,487
30,210	64,887	4,657	84,125	74,591	948	5,060
50,489	5,564	27,910	9,752	2,053	6,105	94,137
48,916	3,257	3,645	6,419	60,479	4,354	6,432
345	87,641	95,413	7,354	10,300	91,854	7,460
6,743	35,641	73,789	18,315	61,558	3,258	58,913
1,215	89,045	66,498	5,690	76,441	64,951	29,746
1,394	4,152	8,216	37,461	2,156	11,547	23,248
57,941	2,671	8,731	3,489	5,467	78,641	42,654
380,793	**786,823**	**384,069**	**381,759**	**320,018**	**969,557**	**331,854**

H	I	J	K	L	M	N
12,720	41,885	345	19,043	80,123	87,291	64,597
86,414	17,251	34,970	17,408	41,878	36,648	46,312
2,588	61,665	96,714	42,034	3,341	10,217	4,591
6,135	17,880	4,206	4,597	719	38,238	10,200
7,600	4,300	10,714	654	84,128	3,574	371,964
94,409	2,330	8,322	20,345	2,274	273	574
2,330	64,110	34,126	60,567	37,753	31,910	3,416
14,500	444	41,367	56,320	85,139	42,712	6,879
1,435	8,168	52,476	3,587	84,118	44,823	16,487
13,207	21,382	1,305	2,281	23,707	95,858	32,746
51,403	11,007	90,909	34,689	3,314	151	5,492
292,741	**250,422**	**375,454**	**261,525**	**446,494**	**391,695**	**563,258**

O	P	Q	R	S	T	U
1,357	73,549	10,201	73,549	7,310	87,351	25,000
6,194	64,985	28,947	58,746	61,845	4,987	6,457
5,078	52,014	3,584	3,549	34,689	95,642	87,412
12,578	37,820	6,102	59,463	26,795	4,315	3,021
64,587	1,546	59,874	42,148	35,449	93,025	32,845
97,410	37,894	15,946	3,024	65,487	76,800	6,189
30,024	787	35,784	25,167	1,349	9,512	25,412
51,346	16,049	64,971	6,458	23,761	5,249	67,851
3,487	3,456	31,258	3,214	9,158	83,467	46,134
6,741	22,587	9,461	68,974	34,852	5,090	5,027
90,570	4,697	357	3,559	593	17,901	4,389
369,372	**315,384**	**266,485**	**347,851**	**301,288**	**483,339**	**309,737**

Keypad Timing 3

(Do not key commas or totals.)

A	B	C	D	E	F	G
14,220	1,506	57,459	3,024	2,627	5,964	25,879
6,540	2,970	6,981	6,509	4,985	75,364	64,875
23,587	5,461	3,548	480	24,560	1,258	1,015
4,986	48,970	4,569	48,795	32,587	6,851	39,478
321,476	54,897	21,036	3,489	116,489	2,579	25,566
61,278	32,148	19,435	65,410	592	3,521	64,902
315	46,997	35,746	948,756	4,060	65,487	4,870
6,489	31,569	95,431	312,574	85,467	98,741	1,589
27,354	15,794	1,679	5,009	6,987	32,105	6,487
94,587	358	3,654	91,500	13,469	64,820	19,487
5,347	61,890	15,975	4,896	53,491	19,850	2,003
566,179	**302,560**	**265,513**	**1,490,442**	**345,314**	**376,540**	**256,151**

H	I	J	K	L	M	N
8,241	159	65,789	6,675	3,579	6,479	5,466
1,184	43,489	4,265	25,498	68,951	6,497	8,977
3,574	5,678	9,154	5,587	1,476	6,479	8,965
10,230	649,875	8,561	1,159	25,496	34,796	12,567
30,258	12,587	3,247	16,497	60,548	10,254	95,120
60,456	756,314	6,510	93,164	1,358	60,289	64,905
50,487	98,420	29,587	9,158	27,649	34,871	3,197
79,850	1,360	12,304	74,862	3,574	27,964	67,319
15,946	4,596	67,845	2,014	1,584	18,960	34,897
3,479	159	50,620	42,587	13,645	1,478	11,504
5,784	13,574	46,798	49,521	92,817	3,465	3,498
269,489	**1,586,211**	**304,680**	**326,722**	**300,677**	**211,532**	**316,415**

O	P	Q	R	S	T	U
4,613	9,788	974	85,210	2,300	348,450	21,346
2,829	4,896	2,651	34,520	5,412	11,597	9,487
13,947	3,546	6,587	5,459	5,487	6,587	6,548
4,697	6,784	3,245	5,059	64,895	7,654	69,321
31,587	30,164	648,971	16,498	12,648	25,874	50,606
50,064	5,621	32,154	6,098	46,158	6,984	3,548
4,975	48,965	20,145	4,879	49,752	13,695	91,582
21,489	23,645	64,052	31,025	50,364	45,963	24,610
3,257	36,487	35,743	64,987	69,710	4,654	3,024
649,852	69,784	3,215	12,203	5,007	357	1,560
3,041	32,015	15,946	5,201	6,943	21,594	36,498
790,351	**271,695**	**833,683**	**271,139**	**318,676**	**493,409**	**318,130**

Keypad Timing 4

(Do not key commas or totals.)

A	B	C	D	E	F	G
43,456	2,158	3,491	4,175	32,741	1,253	8,934
9,876	4,316	6,752	14,259	3,458	35,786	6,159
443,215	58,794	2,894	62,458	6,874	26,498	8,745
2,369	24,580	8,459	3,541	5,982	50,500	2,548
64,879	25,910	57,820	90,274	3,024	94,210	12,036
32,456	30,148	15,948	5,048	61,549	1,678	65,847
90,508	64,973	73,534	3,540	35,789	31,865	30,210
6,423	59,432	9,154	90,548	3,654	5,948	1,594
5,846	2,587	64,875	2,680	98,452	4,896	16,458
9,746	3,648	25,846	23,739	10,250	3,243	96,548
3,256	5,827	69,325	56,128	46,951	76,210	35,749
712,030	**282,373**	**338,098**	**356,390**	**308,724**	**332,087**	**284,828**

H	I	J	K	L	M	N
29,450	7,861	40,560	12,841	16,489	8,189	654
4,561	4,879	89,889	2,589	431	4,132	35,948
3,247	5,896	3,658	32,105	509	35,749	3,154
25,987	4,985	89,632	69,548	35,987	6,159	30,265
45,698	50,140	2,563	5,215	31,548	36,841	25,813
6,541	60,258	32,465	3,210	65,498	91,548	3,549
2,587	30,254	50,184	71,265	78,215	35,789	36,945
15,946	6,944	20,306	954	3,154	36,541	358,740
63,578	33,458	3,005	325,410	94,521	32,158	12,500
3,694	15,879	9,450	1,052	20,654	60,159	9,487
52,549	64,922	4,987	36,548	23,014	649	3,254
253,838	**285,476**	**346,699**	**560,737**	**370,020**	**347,914**	**520,309**

O	P	Q	R	S	T	U
12,510	1,594	1,917	76,541	83,064	6,549	74,858
645	3,576	3,719	162	9,019	3,214	645
53,547	5,821	7,492	3,245	30,548	9,872	59,921
68,745	3,691	1,260	6,489	51,461	30,241	487
15,946	1,598	42,813	83,540	3,645	15,978	7,321
35,746	648,791	5,879	5,930	2,654	1,025	129,653
95,894	97,346	61,325	13,462	321	35,489	69,541
164	51,973	85,731	29,461	82,314	6,549	15,024
20,150	67,495	28,130	36,450	64,987	35,874	10,364
5,361	1,584	37,091	25,987	32,015	15,963	5,015
69,420	35,768	61,903	16,025	18,950	36,952	24,342
378,128	**919,237**	**337,260**	**297,292**	**378,978**	**197,706**	**397,171**

Keypad Timing 5

(Do not key commas or totals.)

A	B	C	D	E	F	G
16,497	321	34,697	7,789	3,021	2,438	278
2,589	42,580	21,560	6,549	63,124	6,450	3,548
48,961	6,540	40,560	53,099	98,510	9,452	654,987
14,657	59,410	60,587	51,469	67,489	2,587	3,554
32,010	1,498	4,890	35,480	54,780	4,569	32,456
610,580	31,632	6,120	148,997	654	5,874	25,694
206,034	7,895	69,750	3,456	99,456	1,023	501,405
259	3,256	1,587	578	3,579	3,259	608,970
678	123,654	48,905	45,021	1,564	32,648	267,951
591	985,159	34,915	5,649	3,894	369,547	25,648
36,548	3,576	178	36,498	1,560	325	3,257
969,404	**1,265,521**	**323,749**	**394,585**	**397,631**	**438,172**	**2,127,748**

H	I	J	K	L	M	N
3,054	4,985	2,015	64,987	5,123	51,638	32,729
6,213	16,548	31,540	235	5,002	36,542	6,985
35,846	9,623	54,802	6,489	16,453	2,546	41,563
36,541	23,457	5,201	36,548	254	93,215	72,548
59,461	6,512	21,300	2,031	36,987	64,598	2,795
32,158	2,587	4,921	65,120	46,902	364,872	604,591
1,564	59,621	48,752	13,654	26,487	645	3,201
95,641	19,875	64,589	95,412	30,215	1,456	4,025
36,541	64,132	59,840	23,654	12,189	3,215	15,246
1,010	25,014	459	72,589	21,902	1,613	3,128
2,050	9,254	53,591	3,456	3,024	32,148	7,952
310,079	**241,608**	**347,010**	**384,175**	**204,538**	**652,488**	**794,763**

O	P	Q	R	S	T	U
3,456	9,850	32,015	45,699	8,247	34,589	7,413
3,217	6,579	2,548	825	9,365	10,236	6,947
59,874	62,103	20,148	6,410	1,470	236,540	58,974
1,254	24,891	46,789	30,012	19,613	21,003	12,034
67,891	1,325	32,111	2,189	3,532	2,450	1,560
3,279	6,512	46,972	41,597	32,145	974,613	1,264
60,189	32,189	60,548	25,997	61,059	576	30,548
49,521	3,254	2,158	12,047	15,023	7,514	59,410
32,597	1,589	3,214	456,980	32,478	2,581	11,589
20,134	820,156	9,485	2,645	55,356	3,691	31,569
6,740	24,668	4,567	6,789	1,894	6,153	4,879
308,152	**993,116**	**260,555**	**631,190**	**240,182**	**1,299,946**	**226,187**

Keypad Timing 6

(Do not key commas or totals.)

A	B	C	D	E	F	G
16,497	321	34,697	7,789	3,021	2,438	278
2,589	42,580	21,560	6,549	63,124	6,450	3,548
48,961	6,540	40,560	53,099	98,510	9,452	654,987
14,657	59,410	60,587	51,469	67,489	2,587	3,554
32,010	1,498	4,890	35,480	54,780	4,569	32,456
610,580	31,632	6,120	148,997	654	5,874	25,694
206,034	7,895	69,750	3,456	99,456	1,023	501,405
259	3,256	1,587	578	3,579	3,259	608,970
678	123,654	48,905	45,021	1,564	32,648	267,951
591	985,159	34,915	5,649	3,894	369,547	25,648
36,548	3,576	178	36,498	1,560	325	3,257
969,404	**1,265,521**	**323,749**	**394,585**	**397,631**	**438,172**	**2,127,748**

H	I	J	K	L	M	N
29,486	56,987	9,201	2,719	95,120	94,687	5,879
3,456	46,000	45,016	3,376	15,987	4,895	6,548
62,110	65,489	32,549	1,592	46,431	25,496	9,021
1,594	12,504	16,497	25,048	2,588	3,245	159,630
41,203	32,548	6,456	80,089	33,256	1,258	465,210
352	15,540	3,258	36,459	5,999	6,054	149,890
59,820	8,997	9,951	102,620	4,587	9,084	250
41,259	3,584	2,357	34,650	4,590	72,897	4,596
4,567	2,015	50,124	2,580	12,504	53,215	23,770
98,413	3,024	32,045	3,697	9,651	96,478	1,354
81,549	2,000	61,289	1,002	32,584	82,160	4,652
423,809	**248,688**	**268,743**	**293,832**	**263,297**	**449,469**	**830,800**

O	P	Q	R	S	T	U
98,701	28,963	365	2,716	27,140	47,219	46,731
10,786	16,822	21,981	83,256	21,167	85,364	25,810
1,236	34,687	61,783	81,100	8,792	10,652	3,025
45,316	27,681	9,432	5,097	14,082	500	19,432
381	18,021	21,131	1,926	918	64,119	5,786
1,689	2,813	83,679	1,754	1,645	17,270	2,561
20,183	105	61,842	45,816	20,993	30,059	98,160
18,092	28,242	82,416	1,026	8,770	20,611	42,587
25,137	3,742	47,835	21,826	62,009	86,150	7,354
38,021	19,538	54,963	39,119	14,653	30,958	8,687
5,384	5,678	731	76,549	97,620	31	91,590
264,926	**186,292**	**446,158**	**360,185**	**277,789**	**392,933**	**351,723**

Keypad Timing 7

(Do not key commas or totals.)

A	B	C	D	E	F	G
16,497	321	34,697	7,789	3,021	2,438	278
2,589	42,580	21,560	6,549	63,124	6,450	3,548
48,961	6,540	40,560	53,099	98,510	9,452	654,987
14,657	59,410	60,587	51,469	67,489	2,587	3,554
32,010	1,498	4,890	35,480	54,780	4,569	32,456
610,580	31,632	6,120	148,997	654	5,874	25,694
206,034	7,895	69,750	3,456	99,456	1,023	501,405
259	3,256	1,587	578	3,579	3,259	608,970
678	123,654	48,905	45,021	1,564	32,648	267,951
591	985,159	34,915	5,649	3,894	369,547	25,648
36,548	3,576	178	36,498	1,560	325	3,257
969,404	**1,265,521**	**323,749**	**394,585**	**397,631**	**438,172**	**2,127,748**

H	I	J	K	L	M	N
43,456	2,158	3,491	4,175	32,741	1,253	8,934
9,876	4,316	6,752	14,259	3,458	35,786	6,159
443,215	58,794	2,894	62,458	6,874	26,498	8,745
2,369	24,580	8,459	3,541	5,982	50,500	2,548
64,879	25,910	57,820	90,274	3,024	94,210	12,036
32,456	30,148	15,948	5,048	61,549	1,678	65,847
90,508	64,973	73,534	3,540	35,789	31,865	30,210
6,423	59,432	9,154	90,548	3,654	5,948	1,594
5,846	2,587	64,875	2,680	98,452	4,896	16,458
9,746	3,648	25,846	23,739	10,250	3,243	96,548
3,256	5,827	69,325	56,128	46,951	76,210	35,749
712,030	**282,373**	**338,098**	**356,390**	**308,724**	**332,087**	**284,828**

O	P	Q	R	S	T	U
12,720	41,885	345	19,043	80,123	87,291	64,597
86,414	17,251	34,970	17,408	41,878	36,648	46,312
2,588	61,665	96,714	42,034	3,341	10,217	4,591
6,135	17,880	4,206	4,597	719	38,238	10,200
7,600	4,300	10,714	654	84,128	3,574	371,964
94,409	2,330	8,322	20,345	2,274	273	574
2,330	64,110	34,126	60,567	37,753	31,910	3,416
14,500	444	41,367	56,320	85,139	42,712	6,879
1,435	8,168	52,476	3,587	84,118	44,823	16,487
13,207	21,382	1,305	2,281	23,707	95,858	32,746
51,403	11,007	90,909	34,689	3,314	151	5,492
292,741	**250,422**	**375,454**	**261,525**	**446,494**	**391,695**	**563,258**

Keypad Timing 8

(Do not key commas or totals.)

A	B	C	D	E	F	G
12,720	41,885	345	19,043	80,123	87,291	64,597
86,414	17,251	34,970	17,408	41,878	36,648	46,312
2,588	61,665	96,714	42,034	3,341	10,217	4,591
6,135	17,880	4,206	4,597	719	38,238	10,200
7,600	4,300	10,714	654	84,128	3,574	371,964
94,409	2,330	8,322	20,345	2,274	273	574
2,330	64,110	34,126	60,567	37,753	31,910	3,416
14,500	444	41,367	56,320	85,139	42,712	6,879
1,435	8,168	52,476	3,587	84,118	44,823	16,487
13,207	21,382	1,305	2,281	23,707	95,858	32,746
51,403	11,007	90,909	34,689	3,314	151	5,492
292,741	**250,422**	**375,454**	**261,525**	**446,494**	**391,695**	**563,258**

H	I	J	K	L	M	N
8,241	159	65,789	6,675	3,579	6,479	5,466
1,184	43,489	4,265	25,498	68,951	6,497	8,977
3,574	5,678	9,154	5,587	1,476	6,479	8,965
10,230	649,875	8,561	1,159	25,496	34,796	12,567
30,258	12,587	3,247	16,497	60,548	10,254	95,120
60,456	756,314	6,510	93,164	1,358	60,289	64,905
50,487	98,420	29,587	9,158	27,649	34,871	3,197
79,850	1,360	12,304	74,862	3,574	27,964	67,319
15,946	4,596	67,845	2,014	1,584	18,960	34,897
3,479	159	50,620	42,587	13,645	1,478	11,504
5,784	13,574	46,798	49,521	92,817	3,465	3,498
269,489	**1,586,211**	**304,680**	**326,722**	**300,677**	**211,532**	**316,415**

O	P	Q	R	S	T	U
35,749	64,895	36,874	2,369	6,498	4,319	6,329
45,620	1,597	61,206	4,590	21,025	3,719	10,287
5,460	3,548	50,095	1,590	65,021	3,918	4,260
49,870	5,498	36,450	25,807	1,564	1,793	45,820
1,567	320	15,945	3,460	32,015	36,458	2,236
81,230	902,500	4,697	59,011	15,665	3,459	31,169
4,980	35,014	3,259	32,589	1,256	401,230	43,464
32,589	64,952	458	45,600	4,896	2,580	49,521
1,547	1,230	6,549	20,202	31,025	701,590	103,020
15,974	13,654	12,036	34,601	15,648	13,570	3,576
35,540	48,920	20,300	1,052	3,546	1,657	1,630
310,126	**1,142,128**	**247,869**	**230,871**	**198,159**	**1,174,293**	**301,312**

Keypad Timing 9

(Do not key commas or totals.)

A	B	C	D	E	F	G
16,497	321	34,697	7,789	3,021	2,438	278
2,589	42,580	21,560	6,549	63,124	6,450	3,548
48,961	6,540	40,560	53,099	98,510	9,452	654,987
14,657	59,410	60,587	51,469	67,489	2,587	3,554
32,010	1,498	4,890	35,480	54,780	4,569	32,456
610,580	31,632	6,120	148,997	654	5,874	25,694
206,034	7,895	69,750	3,456	99,456	1,023	501,405
259	3,256	1,587	578	3,579	3,259	608,970
678	123,654	48,905	45,021	1,564	32,648	267,951
591	985,159	34,915	5,649	3,894	369,547	25,648
36,548	3,576	178	36,498	1,560	325	3,257
969,404	**1,265,521**	**323,749**	**394,585**	**397,631**	**438,172**	**2,127,748**

H	I	J	K	L	M	N
16,497	321	34,697	7,789	3,021	2,438	278
2,589	42,580	21,560	6,549	63,124	6,450	3,548
48,961	6,540	40,560	53,099	98,510	9,452	654,987
14,657	59,410	60,587	51,469	67,489	2,587	3,554
32,010	1,498	4,890	35,480	54,780	4,569	32,456
610,580	31,632	6,120	148,997	654	5,874	25,694
206,034	7,895	69,750	3,456	99,456	1,023	501,405
259	3,256	1,587	578	3,579	3,259	608,970
678	123,654	48,905	45,021	1,564	32,648	267,951
591	985,159	34,915	5,649	3,894	369,547	25,648
36,548	3,576	178	36,498	1,560	325	3,257
969,404	**1,265,521**	**323,749**	**394,585**	**397,631**	**438,172**	**2,127,748**

O	P	Q	R	S	T	U
9,456	45,990	123	3,697	9,159	15,870	8,790
41,264	1,591	3,654	85,821	5,894	6,702	9,364
4,597	56,700	2,589	30,407	6,501	79,015	4,963
30,201	50,508	10,478	97,410	20,587	646	1,594
36,410	64,550	56,480	62,580	4,500	35,940	3,574
65,498	5,945	52,548	2,589	35,400	354,987	6,548
3,250	659	64,970	43,654	69,840	3,216	69,784
4,159	348	20,489	1,259	5,054	459	105,023
34,510	64,891	60,154	30,145	24,890	66,789	30,271
3,597	500,522	3,258	25,489	15,946	10,590	1,590
73,236	64,987	73,489	257	6,782	36,480	349,610
306,178	**856,691**	**348,232**	**383,308**	**204,553**	**610,694**	**591,111**

Keypad Timing 10

(Do not key commas or totals.)

A	B	C	D	E	F	G
1,123	5,280	4,534	6,654	3,917	277,211	1,721
17,321	35,870	3,247	2,987	6,197	86,548	6,498
6,459	159	60,598	4,321	6,791	35,894	38,954
4,879	3,657	80,950	1,230	4,961	5,612	5,201
26,497	64,984	15,967	5,560	6,731	12,103	1,206
78,910	25,490	34,012	80,890	5,012	2,645	356,021
2,059	12,036	16,470	36,459	346,790	46,548	12,000
53,024	697	03,169	235,740	29,184	895	64,587
5,018	342,645	6,490	15,901	76,845	2,147	36,450
97,809	30,214	1,097	45,647	6,159	76,495	4,591
13,648	93,649	8,456	3,264	632,000	5,000	3,257
306,747	**614,681**	**234,990**	**438,653**	**1,124,587**	**551,098**	**530,486**

H	I	J	K	L	M	N
12,720	41,885	345	19,043	80,123	87,291	64,597
86,414	17,251	34,970	17,408	41,878	36,648	46,312
2,588	61,665	96,714	42,034	3,341	10,217	4,591
6,135	17,880	4,206	4,597	719	38,238	10,200
7,600	4,300	10,714	654	84,128	3,574	371,964
94,409	2,330	8,322	20,345	2,274	273	574
2,330	64,110	34,126	60,567	37,753	31,910	3,416
14,500	444	41,367	56,320	85,139	42,712	6,879
1,435	8,168	52,476	3,587	84,118	44,823	16,487
13,207	21,382	1,305	2,281	23,707	95,858	32,746
51,403	11,007	90,909	34,689	3,314	151	5,492
292,741	**250,422**	**375,454**	**261,525**	**446,494**	**391,695**	**563,258**

O	P	Q	R	S	T	U
1,347	548,977	48,661	3,012	3,491	64,875	5,897
96,314	64,500	1,536	6,054	18,965	45,687	24,598
26,458	1,258	63,105	90,156	1,250	48,961	2,561
4,598	5,648	10,594	3,459	32,110	25,849	301,260
47,852	6,487	6,842	561,058	64,890	65,310	3,210
2,410	7,452	2,590	6,540	46,102	23,006	1,542
25,401	3,214	1,597	34,897	15,897	34,982	20,564
34,658	30,021	36,215	64,689	45,697	12,004	02,890
9,058	64,501	84,210	3,254	6,589	35,048	34,571
86,450	3,210	35,222	86,312	6,497	16,430	3,598
6,480	59,015	3,219	4,599	2,657	2,305	1,230
341,026	**794,283**	**293,791**	**864,030**	**244,145**	**374,457**	**401,921**

Keypad Timing 11

(Do not key commas or totals.)

A	B	C	D	E	F	G
3,456	9,850	32,015	45,699	8,247	34,589	7,413
3,217	6,579	2,548	825	9,365	10,236	6,947
59,874	62,103	20,148	6,410	1,470	236,540	58,974
1,254	24,891	46,789	30,012	19,613	21,003	12,034
67,891	1,325	32,111	2,189	3,532	2,450	1,560
3,279	6,512	46,972	41,597	32,145	974,613	1,264
60,189	32,189	60,548	25,997	61,059	576	30,548
49,521	3,254	2,158	12,047	15,023	7514	59,410
32,597	1,589	3,214	456,980	32,478	2,581	11,589
20,134	820,156	9,485	2,645	55,356	3,691	31,569
6,740	24,668	4,567	6,789	1,894	6,153	4,879
308,152	**993,116**	**260,555**	**631,190**	**240,182**	**1,299,946**	**226,187**

H	I	J	K	L	M	N
8,241	159	65,789	6,675	3,579	6,479	5,466
1,184	43,489	4,265	25,498	68,951	6,497	8,977
3,574	5,678	9,154	5,587	1,476	6,479	8,965
10,230	649,875	8,561	1,159	25,496	34,796	12,567
30,258	12,587	3,247	16,497	60,548	10,254	95,120
60,456	756,314	6,510	93,164	1,358	60,289	64,905
50,487	98,420	29,587	9,158	27,649	34,871	3,197
79,850	1,360	12,304	74,862	3,574	27,964	67,319
15,946	4,596	67,845	2,014	1,584	18,960	34,897
3,479	159	50,620	42,587	13,645	1,478	11,504
5,784	13,574	46,798	49,521	92,817	3,465	3,498
269,489	**1,586,211**	**304,680**	**326,722**	**300,677**	**211,532**	**316,415**

O	P	Q	R	S	T	U
16,497	321	34,697	7,789	3,021	2,438	278
2,589	42,580	21,560	6,549	63,124	6,450	3,548
48,961	6,540	40,560	53,099	98,510	9,452	654,987
14,657	59,410	60,587	51,469	67,489	2,587	3,554
32,010	1,498	4,890	35,480	54,780	4,569	32,456
610,580	31,632	6,120	148,997	654	5,874	25,694
206,034	7,895	69,750	3,456	99,456	1,023	501,405
259	3,256	1,587	578	3,579	3,259	608,970
678	123,654	48,905	45,021	1,564	32,648	267,951
591	985,159	34,915	5,649	3,894	369,547	25,648
36,548	3,576	178	36,498	1,560	325	3,257
969,404	**1,265,521**	**323,749**	**394,585**	**397,631**	**438,172**	**2,127,748**

Keypad Timing 12

(Do not key commas or totals.)

A	B	C	D	E	F	G
12,720	41,885	345	19,043	80,123	87,291	64,597
86,414	17,251	34,970	17,408	41,878	36,648	46,312
2,588	61,665	96,714	42,034	3,341	10,217	4,591
6,135	17,880	4,206	4,597	719	38,238	10,200
7,600	4,300	10,714	654	84,128	3,574	371,964
94,409	2,330	8,322	20,345	2,274	273	574
2,330	64,110	34,126	60,567	37,753	31,910	3,416
14,500	444	41,367	56,320	85,139	42,712	6,879
1,435	8,168	52,476	3,587	84,118	44,823	16,487
13,207	21,382	1,305	2,281	23,707	95,858	32,746
51,403	11,007	90,909	34,689	3,314	151	5,492
292,741	**250,422**	**375,454**	**261,525**	**446,494**	**391,695**	**563,258**

H	I	J	K	L	M	N
43,456	2,158	3,491	4,175	32,741	1,253	8,934
9,876	4,316	6,752	14,259	3,458	35,786	6,159
443,215	58,794	2,894	62,458	6,874	26,498	8,745
2,369	24,580	8,459	3,541	5,982	50,500	2,548
64,879	25,910	57,820	90,274	3,024	94,210	12,036
32,456	30,148	15,948	5,048	61,549	1,678	65,847
90,508	64,973	73,534	3,540	35,789	31,865	30,210
6,423	59,432	9,154	90,548	3,654	5,948	1,594
5,846	2,587	64,875	2,680	98,452	4,896	16,458
9,746	3,648	25,846	23,739	10,250	3,243	96,548
3,256	5,827	69,325	56,128	46,951	76,210	35,749
712,030	**282,373**	**338,098**	**356,390**	**308,724**	**332,087**	**284,828**

O	P	Q	R	S	T	U
35,749	64,895	36,874	2,369	6,498	4,319	6,329
45,620	1,597	61,206	4,590	21,025	3,719	10,287
5,460	3,548	50,095	1,590	65,021	3,918	4,260
49,870	5,498	36,450	25,807	1,564	1,793	45,820
1,567	320	15,945	3,460	32,015	36,458	2,236
81,230	902,500	4,697	59,011	15,665	3,459	31,169
4,980	35,014	3,259	32,589	1,256	401,230	43,464
32,589	64,952	458	45,600	4,896	2,580	49,521
1,547	1,230	6,549	20,202	31,025	701,590	103,020
15,974	13,654	12,036	34,601	15,648	13,570	3,576
35,540	48,920	20,300	1,052	3,546	1,657	1,630
310,126	**1,142,128**	**247,869**	**230,871**	**198,159**	**1,174,293**	**301,312**

Alphanumeric Timing 1

In 1935, social security was formed to provide people with 12
some income when they retire. If you were born before 1938, your 25
full retirement age is 65. This law was changed in 1983 to 37
increase the full retirement age to 67 for people who were born 50
in 1960 or later. 54

To qualify for benefits you must earn up to 4 credits each 66
year through work. For example, in 2001, you earn one credit for 79
each $870 of wages. When you have earned $3,840, you have earned 92
4 credits for the year. Most people need 40 credits earned over 105
their working lifetime to receive retirement benefits. 116

About 1 in 6 Americans receives social security benefits, 128
and about 98 percent of all workers are in jobs covered by social 141
security. Benefits make up about 7 percent of the nation's total 155
economic output. From 1940, when slightly more than 222,000 167
people received monthly benefits, until today, when almost 45 179
million people receive such benefits, social security has grown 192
steadily. Nearly 1 in 3 beneficiaries are not retirees. 203

gwam 1' | 1 | 2 | 3 | 4 | 5 | 6 | 7 | 8 | 9 | 10 | 11 | 12 | 13 |

Alphanumeric Timing 2

An individual may contribute up to $2,000 a year to an 11
individual retirement account, or $2,500 if there is a nonworking 24
spouse. All contributions are deductible from current income and 37
are not taxed until the time the individual withdraws the money 50
at retirement age. The most that can be contributed to your 62
traditional IRA is $2,000 for 2001, $3,000 for 2002, or $3,500 76
for 2002 if you are 50 or older. 82

If a person's taxable income is $30,900 and $2,000 of 93
income is deferred, taxes are paid on $28,000, for a savings of 105
$638 on a joint return. If money is taken out before age 59.5, 119
there is a 10 percent penalty. 125

Only 32 percent of all couples and about 17 percent of all 137
singles over the age of 65 qualify for a private pension plan. 150
As of January 1, 1982, all Americans under the age of 70.5 and 163
who work are eligible to open a tax-deferred savings account. 175
Prior to 1982, a person who had belonged to an organized pension 188
plan could not have a tax-deferred account. 197

gwam 1' | 1 | 2 | 3 | 4 | 5 | 6 | 7 | 8 | 9 | 10 | 11 | 12 | 13 |

Alphanumeric Timing 3

Owning a home is one of the best ways to trim your tax 11
bill. Under the current tax code, mortgage interest on first and 24
second homes is generally deductible as long as these loans total 38
less than $1.1 million. 42

Let's assume the following. Your gross income is $35,600 54
and you buy a $117,000 house with $23,000 down. The principal is 67
$94,000 and you have a 30-year fixed rate mortgage at 10 percent 80
and property taxes of 1.27 percent of the home value or $1,485. 93
You file a joint tax return with 4 exemptions. 103

According to the tax code, your deductions for mortgage 114
interest and property taxes would be evaluated at a 16 percent 127
marginal tax rate. Non-housing itemized deductions—i.e., state 140
and local taxes, non-mortgage interest, and so on—is estimated 153
at $2,300 and the standard deduction is $5,450. Under the 165
current tax system, you would save $1,891 because of the mortgage 177
interest deduction. You can figure what your own costs and 189
savings will be by substituting your tax figures for those on the 202
income tax charts. 206

gwam 1' | 1 | 2 | 3 | 4 | 5 | 6 | 7 | 8 | 9 | 10 | 11 | 12 | 13 |

Alphanumeric Timing 4

Equal pay isn't just a women's issue. The 4 million men 12
who work in predominately female occupations lose an average of 24
$6,259 each year. The 25.6 million women in these jobs lose an 37
average of $3,487 a year. 42

Women represented 45 percent of all persons (men and 53
women) in the civilian 60 percent of the labor force entrants 66
between 1990 and 2005 and will comprise 47 percent of the labor 79
force by the year 2008. 93

In 2000, women were paid 73 cents for every dollar men 96
received. That's $27 less to spend on groceries, housing, child 107
care, and other expenses for every $100 worth of work. Labor 129
force participation for women continues to be highest among those 132
in the 35-44 age group; 78 percent of women in this age group 145
were in the labor force in 1992; 74 percent, for those 25-34 158
years old; 73 percent, for those 45-54 years old; and 47 percent, 170
for those between the ages of 55-64. The average 25-year-old 183
working woman will lose more than $523,000 to unequal pay during 196
her working life. 209

gwam 1' | 1 | 2 | 3 | 4 | 5 | 6 | 7 | 8 | 9 | 10 | 11 | 12 | 13 |

Alphanumeric Timing 5

A new registration was effective as of June 4, 2001. The 12
new registration offers for sale an additional 5,750,000 shares 25
of beneficial interest. Of that amount, 750,000 shares were 37
registered for our dividend plan. The portfolio had an unpaid 49
balance of $69,355,000, and was purchased for $68,522,999. The 62
blended interest rate was 12.46 percent, the current annual yield 75
was 12.61 percent, and the investment to value ratio was 71.69 88
percent. 90

Operating expenses were $183,000 and $113,000, a 62 percent 102
increase for the 3-month period. These were made up of fees paid 115
to our advisor of $100,000 and $59,000—a 72 percent increase— 128
and loan service fees of $51,000 and $46,000, an 11 percent 140
increase. 142

Operating expense as a percentage of income was 8.073 153
percent and 8.547 percent. Interest expense during the 164
comparable 3-month periods decreased by 98 percent, and during 177
the 6-month periods decreased by 94 percent. 186

gwam 1' | 1 | 2 | 3 | 4 | 5 | 6 | 7 | 8 | 9 | 10 | 11 | 12 | 13 |

Alphanumeric Timing 6

The American consumer is becoming more affluent. The 11
number of households with incomes of $100,000 or more will grow 24
38 percent by 2009. The number with incomes above $75,000 will 37
grow 26 percent. 40

Surveys of employment growth by occupation show that during 52
the 1990s, employment grew by 27 to 28 percent in job categories 65
where pay is the highest. In the lowest wage occupations, the 78
growth of employment was between 15 and 16 percent. 88

In 1994, 70 percent of households had incomes under $50,000 101
and 30 percent had $50,000 and above. By 2010 the households 113
with incomes under $50,000 will have dropped to 53 percent, while 126
those with incomes above $50,000 will approach 46 percent. By 139
2010 the U.S. consumer market will be almost split, with half of 152
all households having incomes below $50,000 and half above. 164

This year, less than 17 percent of market potential is in 176
the 55 to 68 age group; however, their share may reach 19 percent 189
by 2010. The 45 and above age groups will gain market share, 201
while the under 45 groups will lose ground. The under 25 group 214
will constitute only 3 percent of total market potential. 225

gwam 1' | 1 | 2 | 3 | 4 | 5 | 6 | 7 | 8 | 9 | 10 | 11 | 12 | 13 |

Alphanumeric Timing 11

Have you been to the beautiful Great Smoky Mountains 11
National Park? This park has about 273,550 acres in North 23
Carolina and about 241,206 acres in Tennessee, for a total of 35
over 500,000 acres. It was approved on May 22, 1926, and 47
established for full development in 1934. The diverse plant life 60
is lovely and is seen by over 11 million persons each year. 72

Another beautiful park is The Grand Canyon National Park, 84
which is located in Arizona. It was established on February 26, 97
1919. Additional land was acquired by the park in 1975, making 109
the total acreage just over 1.2 million. This unique exposure of 123
rock is 217 miles long and from 4 to 18 miles wide. In recent 135
years, it has been seen by about 2,843,000 people each year. 147

Yellowstone National Park was established in 1872. It is 159
older and larger than any of the other national parks, and is 172
fascinating in a different way. Its more than 2,319,000 acres 184
cover parts of three states. It has over 10,000 geysers, dozens 197
of majestic waterfalls, canyons, and quiet wildlife areas. About 210
2,487,500 people from all over the world visit each year. 222

gwam 1' | 1 | 2 | 3 | 4 | 5 | 6 | 7 | 8 | 9 | 10 | 11 | 12 | 13 |

Alphanumeric Timing 12

Our company recently announced a Stock Incentive Plan for 12
the next several years. Beginning January 1, 2004, stock options 25
may be awarded to employees. Under this plan, employees with 37
outstanding performances may receive stock equal to 35 percent of 51
their income, not to exceed $17,400. The total number of shares 64
shall not exceed 350. The average price of our stock ranges from 77
$29.68 to $48.65. The managers adopted the 2004 plan by a vote 90
of 732 to 148. 93

In addition to the incentive plan, employees may purchase 104
stocks at the daily value (currently $34.65) with a minimum 116
purchase of 10 shares. The purchase option will remain in effect 130
for a minimum of 3 years or until the outstanding shares from 142
2002 and 2003 (1,823,419 and 1,457,608 respectively) are owned by 155
our employees. The managers believe that more than 65 percent of 168
their employees will take advantage of this offer during the next 181
15 months, if not sooner. 187

gwam 1' | 1 | 2 | 3 | 4 | 5 | 6 | 7 | 8 | 9 | 10 | 11 | 12 | 13 |

Alphanumeric Timing 13

We currently have a huge deficit in our budget for state 12
highways. In the last fiscal year, the state expenditure for 24
capital outlay ranked 49th in the entire nation. Presently, our 37
9-cent per gallon gasoline tax is lower than all but 3 other 49
states. The current tax schedule, which began in 1995, has not 62
undergone a major change for a longer period of time than the 74
rates of all but 14 other states. Bill 80645, which will create 87
a 6-cent increase in the gasoline tax and a 17-percent increase 100
in various transportation fees, may pass. However, this is not 113
enough to provide the money to complete the widening of Route 71 126
to the junction of Interstate 287. 133

We must make the 9-cent gasoline tax mandatory if we are to 145
reduce the highway budget deficit. In the past, the voters have 158
rejected 4- and 6-cent tax increases, and it is doubtful that 171
they will accept this 9-cent tax. Moreover, the state has lost 183
$45,891,200 in transportation revenues, and petitions are 195
circulating for a 37 percent cut in property tax. 205

gwam 1' | 1 | 2 | 3 | 4 | 5 | 6 | 7 | 8 | 9 | 10 | 11 | 12 | 13 |

Alphanumeric Timing 14

Existing home sales fell 1.7 percent to 5.29 million units 12
from last month's reported 5.37 million units. In January, the 25
industry sold homes at a record rate of 6.05 million, and since 38
then the pace has slowed in 5 out of 7 months. The rate of home 51
sales averaged 5.58 million over the first 8 months this year. 63
Realtors forecast record sales of 5.44 million units for all of 76
2002. The supply of homes for sale rose to 5.0 months from 4.7. 89

Economists had expected home resales in August to rise 1.3 102
percent to an annual pace of 5.4 million units, up from July's 115
originally reported 5.33 million units. Existing home sales 127
account for 85 percent of all sales. 135

The median price of a home rose 0.7 percent to $163,800 146
last month, up from $162,400 in July. The price is 6.4 percent 159
higher than the same month last year. The supply of homes that 172
are available for sale rose to 5 months' worth in August, up from 185
4.7 months' worth the previous month. 192

gwam 1' | 1 | 2 | 3 | 4 | 5 | 6 | 7 | 8 | 9 | 10 | 11 | 12 | 13 |

Alphanumeric Timing 15

The more education a woman has, the greater the likelihood 12
she will seek employment. Among women 25 to 56 years of age with 25
less than 4 years of high school, only 53 percent were labor 37
force participants. For female high school graduates with no 50
college, 74 percent were in the labor force. Among women of the 63
same age group with 4 or more years of college, 84 percent were 76
in the labor force. 80

Women have earned at least half of all bachelor's and 91
master's degrees since the 1980-81 school year. In engineering, 104
women earned 14 percent of bachelor's, 13 percent of master's, 116
and 9 percent of doctorates. In mathematics, women earned 47 129
percent of bachelor's, 40 percent of master's, and 19 percent of 142
doctorates. Over an 8-year period, women's share of degrees rose 166
from 14 to 26 percent in dentistry, 25 to 33 percent in medicine, 168
and 32 to 41 percent in law. 174

Of the 54 million employed women in the United States, 40 186
million worked full time (35 or more hours per week); nearly 14 198
million, or 27 percent of all women workers, held part-time jobs 211
(less than 35 hours per week). 217

gwam 1' | 1 | 2 | 3 | 4 | 5 | 6 | 7 | 8 | 9 | 10 | 11 | 12 | 13 |

Figure-Symbol Timing 1
(10% figures/ symbols)

The more education a woman has, the greater the likelihood 12
she will be employed. Among women 25 to 54 years of age with less 25
than 4 years of high school in 1991, only 51% were in the labor 38
force. 40

For female high school graduates with no college, 74% were in 52
the labor force. Among women 25 to 54 years with 4 or more years 65
of college in 1991, 84% were in the labor force. 75

gwam 1' | 1 | 2 | 3 | 4 | 5 | 6 | 7 | 8 | 9 | 10 | 11 | 12 | 13 |

Figure-Symbol Timing 2
(10% figures/ symbols)

The company reported earnings of 9.2 percent. Net income of 13
$351,714 represents a 1.16 percent return on assets. As a result, 26
the company has declared a $1.00 per share cash dividend and a 10 39
percent stock dividend payable on January 12, 2004. 50

Beginning January 1, 2005, all 1,746 employees in our 12 61
locations will be eligible for stock bonuses. Each employee may 74
allocate from 7-14 percent of his/her pay, not to exceed $15,000, 87
to purchase stock. A minimum of 25 shares must be purchased. We 101
hope that more than 522 people or 60 percent will participate. 113

gwam 1' | 1 | 2 | 3 | 4 | 5 | 6 | 7 | 8 | 9 | 10 | 11 | 12 | 13 |

Figure-Symbol Timing 3
(10% figures/ symbols)

Households with an average annual income of $10,500 in 2000, 12
have seen almost no gains since 1975. These are in the lower 20 25
percent of the distribution. 31

By comparison, average annual incomes among the top 20 42
percent have soared 55 percent to $145,600, with a more than 25 55
percent increase since 1991. 61

gwam 1' | 1 | 2 | 3 | 4 | 5 | 6 | 7 | 8 | 9 | 10 | 11 | 12 | 13 |

Figure-Symbol Timing 4
(10% figures/ symbols)

Of households earning less than $25,000 annually, 23 percent 12
lacked health insurance. Adults ages 18 to 24 were least likely of 26
any age group to have coverage, with 28 percent lacking coverage. 39

Families with incomes above $75,000 made up nearly 58 percent 52
of the increase in the uninsured, although they make up only 30 65
percent of the population. Experts said that those with incomes 78
between $50,000 and $80,000 are most likely to have coverage and, 91
therefore, in a recession, most likely to lose it. 101

gwam 1' | 1 | 2 | 3 | 4 | 5 | 6 | 7 | 8 | 9 | 10 | 11 | 12 | 13 |

Figure-Symbol Timing 5
(20% figures/ symbols)

Save $100 with a mail-in rebate, plus get 0% interest for 12 12
months on Model 1980426 computers. The Model 1980426 is a 2.40 GHz 26
computer with a 17-inch monitor (16-inch viewable, .24 dot pitch). 40
It also has a 533 MHz side bus; 412 MB RAM memory, an 80 gigabyte 53
hard drive, and a 16X DVD-ROM drive. 60

Prefer a laptop? We have one (Model 6241071) with a 1.80 GHz 73
processor, 512 MB RAM, and a 30 gigabyte hard drive. It weighs 86
just 8.46 pounds and is 1.8 inches thick. The display is 16.1 98
inches. Save $50 on this model with a coupon and another $25 with 112
a mail-in rebate. 115

gwam 1' | 1 | 2 | 3 | 4 | 5 | 6 | 7 | 8 | 9 | 10 | 11 | 12 | 13 |

Figure-Symbol Timing 6
(20% figures/ symbols)

Did you know that nearly 60% or 58.2 million of U.S. 11
households own a cat or dog? There are more than 52 million dogs 24
and 60 million cats in the U.S. People in the U.S. spend $2.3 37
billion annually on their pets. More than 91% of pet owners take 50
their dogs and cats to a veterinarian for care. 60

To get a dog from an animal shelter, expect to pay between 72
$15 and $85. If you buy from a breeder, expect to pay from $250- 85
$1,500. A small dog will cost about $100-$300 a year to feed; a 98
medium dog, about $200-$400; and a large dog about $300-$500. In 111
addition, there are veterinary care costs for shots ($50-$200 a 124
year), annual checkups ($50-$200 a year), and spaying or neutering 137
($30-$150). 139

gwam 1' | 1 | 2 | 3 | 4 | 5 | 6 | 7 | 8 | 9 | 10 | 11 | 12 | 13 |

Figure-Symbol Timing 7
(20% figures/ symbols)

As a percent, operating expenses were 8.73 and 8.47 and 11
average invested assets were 0.27 and 0.24 during the 3–month 24
periods of 2002 and 2001, respectively. During the 6-month 36
periods, the figures were 9.21% and 8.58% of income, and 0.56% and 49
0.47% of invested assets. 54

Net income was $1,810,000 and $1,096,000 for the 3 months 66
ended June 30, 2002 and 2001, respectively, and $3,293,000 and 79
$2,013,000 for the 6-month periods, making earnings per share 91
during the comparable 3-month periods $0.47 and $0.45 (a 4% 103
increase) and $0.90 during both 6-month periods. 113

gwam 1' | 1 | 2 | 3 | 4 | 5 | 6 | 7 | 8 | 9 | 10 | 11 | 12 | 13 |

Figure-Symbol Timing 8 (30% figures/ symbols)

Total income for the 3-month period was $2,906,753 and 11
$1,345,896 (56% increase), respectively, which included $100,000 24
received in 2004. Total income for the 6-month period was 36
$3,978,354 and $2,547,862 (56% increase). 44

During the 3-month period ended 6/30/2002, our investments 56
generated $1,897,654 and $1,345,768 of interest income (48% 68
increase). During the 6-month periods, interest income was 80
$3,678,213 and $2,547,306, respectively. 88

gwam 1' | 1 | 2 | 3 | 4 | 5 | 6 | 7 | 8 | 9 | 10 | 11 | 12 | 13 |

Figure-Symbol Timing 9 (30% figures/ symbols)

As of 1/01/2004, benefits include: life insurance, $76,000; 12
group life insurance, $70,000; short-term disability, $1,362/week 26
up to 26 weeks; long-term disability, $3,543/month; accident 38
insurance, $60,000; and business travel insurance, $377,000. The 51
company contributes $1,967; you contribute $719. 61

As of 12/31/2004, the company contributed: $3,393, incentive 73
plan; $2,059, retirement account; $1,870, employee retirement; and 87
$5,335, social security (total $15,709). As of 12/31/2004, you 100
contributed: $4,523, $0, $0, and $5,335, respectively (total, 112
$9,858). Your total contributions are $11,401; the company total 125
contributions are $15,709. 131

gwam 1' | 1 | 2 | 3 | 4 | 5 | 6 | 7 | 8 | 9 | 10 | 11 | 12 | 13 |

Figure-Symbol Timing 10 (30% figures/ symbols)

Last year's budget was $1,248,376. This year's budget is 12
$1,598,307. We've allocated $191,796.84 (12%) for supplies and 25
$751,204.29 (47%) for wages for a total of $943,300.13 (59%). We 38
expect the remainder, $655,006.90, to be used for other expenses. 51
We expect over 5,000 people to participate on 5/19/2003, between 8 64
a.m. and 6 p.m. The address for tickets is R/E Events, 46281 Main 78
Street, Columbus, Ohio, 43234-3666. 85

This year, there will be more than 250 vendors (up 22%). 97
Booth fees range from $205-$1,360, depending on location. Booths 110
can be reserved by calling 614-555-1234. The fax number is 614- 123
555-1235. Registration numbers (from 601983 through 602258) can be 137
picked up on 5/17/2004 between 8 a.m. and 4 p.m. 146

gwam 1' | 1 | 2 | 3 | 4 | 5 | 6 | 7 | 8 | 9 | 10 | 11 | 12 | 13 |

Part 2 DATA ENTRY PROJECTS

Project 1
Crandle Insurance

Project 2
Funwear

Project 3
Western Suites

Project 4
General Hospital

Project 1

Crandle Insurance

Crandle Insurance

Crandle Insurance Company specializes in car insurance policies. The office is staffed by several insurance agents who consult with customers both in person and over the phone. When it's time to complete an application or change a policy, the agents fill out the necessary forms and give them to data entry specialists, called *customer care assistants,* who key the customers' personal information and insurance policy information into the company's computer database.

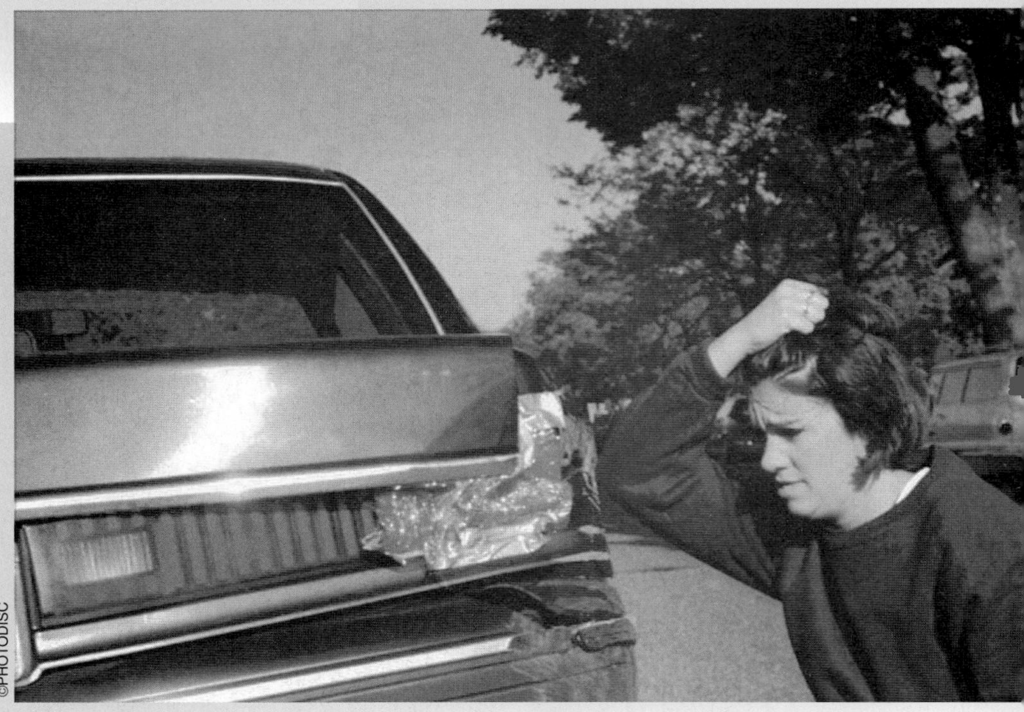

©PHOTODISC

Your Activities Today

- ➢8 A.M.–12 P.M. Enter customers' personal information
- ➢1–3 P.M. Enter car and insurance information
- ➢3–4 P.M. Update customer database
- ➢4–5 P.M. Enter customer information into spreadsheet

New Knowledge and Skills

In this project, you will:

- ➢Key customer and car information
- ➢Update customer and car information
- ➢Record application information for new customers

CAREER PROFILE

Data Entry Specialist/Customer Care Assistant

"While using the keypad is what I do most at Crandle Insurance, checking my work for accuracy is a big part of the job. I also have to create a good image for our company by talking and acting professionally with customers."

What I do every day

After a customer has submitted an application for an insurance policy, it's my job to enter the information into the computer. I also update customers' background information when they move or change cars. The computer's database keeps track of all customers and their policy information. Frequently, I am instructed to compile data about several customers and enter it in a spreadsheet or chart.

The best part of my job

I like being busy and working around people. Customers come in and out of Crandle Insurance all the time. The phones ring constantly, and I always have a stack of application forms to enter.

The worst part of my job

Most of my day is spent sitting and entering the same type of information. Sometimes this gets tedious.

What I need to know and be able to do

It's very important to have good keying skills, especially on the numeric keypad. The faster and more accurately I can enter numbers, the more efficiently I can get my tasks done. Because I work with a variety of forms, I have to recognize the differences among them. I also greet visitors since my desk is at the front of the office, so a positive attitude and good communication skills are important.

How I prepared to be a data entry specialist

I took keyboarding and other computer courses at a technical school. Then I had a three-month internship at a local insurance company. There, I learned how to deal with customers by observing the data entry specialists and agents. Later, Crandle offered me a higher paying job with an opportunity for promotion.

How I could have prepared better

Having a year or two of additional career training would have been helpful. I need more math experience and better people skills, so I plan to go back to school for advanced training.

Education needed: A customer care specialist in the insurance field needs a high school diploma plus data entry training or experience.

Salary range: $16,000 – $33,000

Job outlook: Data entry specialists are in high demand, especially those with good communication and computer skills. The insurance profession has many opportunities for data entry specialists, and the insurance career path can lead to higher-level jobs.

Related jobs: Word processor, file clerk, receptionist, customer service representative, order taker.

THE REAL WORLD

An insurance office usually has several agents who work in separate offices or cubicles. Customers come into the office to meet with the agents or call and talk with them on the phone. Sometimes customer care assistants work in the front reception area where they greet customers and answer phones in addition to entering data. Other times, the customer care assistants are seated away from the foot traffic, so that they can devote more time to entering information.

As a customer care assistant, I have two main tasks:

- To enter all information from insurance applications into the company's database.
- To update customer files when information changes.

Sometimes I have other responsibilities as well:

- To greet customers, answer phones, and make appointments for the insurance agents.
- To enter summary information into charts and spreadsheets.

Entering Insurance Applications

When a customer applies for a car insurance policy, Crandle Insurance needs a record of the person's background information and details about the policy. My job is to create the record by transferring this information quickly and accurately from the application to the computer.

Updating Customer Information

When a customer moves, gets a new car, takes a new name, or makes any other significant change, I update the information in the company's computer. This is an important responsibility.

The Challenges

On most days, I work with many different types of forms, so I must keep track of what I'm doing. If I'm balancing data entry with answering phones and other tasks, I have to be well organized in order to get everything done correctly.

Insurance Application Form

Each new customer fills out an application form that contains both personal and vehicle information. When this form is passed on to me, I enter these two types of data separately. I open one screen for the customer's personal information and a separate screen for information about the vehicle and insurance policy.

The complete application showing both parts is illustrated in Figure 1.1. It includes the following information:

- the date the application was submitted
- the customer's name, identification number, and address
- the customer's daytime and evening phone numbers
- the customer's sex, date of birth, and Social Security number
- the state where the customer is licensed to drive and the type of license
- the date the customer's driver's license was issued and the driver's license number
- the make, model, and year of the vehicle to be insured

Figure 1.1 Car Insurance Application Form

Crandle Insurance

Customer Information Update Form

Date of Application (MM/DD/YYYY):_____/_____/________

Customer name: ______________________________________ Customer ID:____________

Last First M.I.

Street: ______________________________________ Apt. Number:____________

City, State, Zip:______________________________________

Phone (daytime): (_____) _____-______ Phone (evening): (_____) _____-______

Sex (M/F):_______ Date of Birth (MM/DD/YYYY):_____/_____/_______

Social Security No.:_____-____-_______

State in which customer is licensed: __________________ License type:____________________

Date license was issued (MM//YYYY):_____/ ___________ License number: __________________

Vehicle Information

Customer name: ______________________________________ Customer ID:____________

Last First M.I.

Vehicle make:_____________________ Model:________________ Year: ________________

VIN: ______________________________________ Mileage:_______________

Date of purchase (MM//YYYY):_____/ _________ Usage code:_________ Miles per day: ____________

Coverage code: _____________________ Liability limit: ____________

- the vehicle's identification number (VIN) and the mileage on the odometer
- the date the vehicle was purchased, a code showing how the vehicle will be used, and the average number of miles driven each day
- a code showing the type of insurance coverage being purchased
- the maximum dollar amount of liability coverage the company will provide after an accident

Customer Information

When I receive an insurance application, I open the Customer Information screen in my software. If the customer is new, I start by entering all of the person's background information. A Customer Information screen is shown in Figure 1.2.

BE ALERT!
Double-check the spelling of each customer's name. Two-word names such as De Orio are keyed as one word without a space (DeOrio). Hyphenated names such as Atar-Brown, and other unusual forms are keyed as written, including all hyphens or other punctuation.

(1) **Date:** This is the date the application was submitted to Crandle Insurance. Enter two digits for the month, two digits for the day, and four digits for the year. If the application was submitted on January 3, 200x, the date is shown as 01/03/200x. Enter the current year for the letter x.

(2) **Customer name:** The customer's name may include a middle initial; keying the period is optional. When a customer has a double last name, both names are keyed without a space. For example, Van Buren is keyed as VanBuren. When a hyphen appears in a name, the hyphen is keyed, for example, Adams-Revell.

Figure 1.2 Customer Information Screen

Crandle Insurance New Customers
Customer Information
Rate (ksph) | Errors
Key data into appropriate fields. Tab between fields.
(1) Date of application: 07 / 28 / 2007
(2) Customer name: Hopkinson (Last) Sylvia (First) M (M.I.) (3) Customer ID: 695234
(4) Address (street): 675 E. Slocum St. Apt number:
(5) Address: Barrington (City) RI (State) 58966-4310 (Zip code)
(6) Phone (daytime): (401) 555-0134 Phone (evening): (401) 555-0154
(7) Sex (M/F): F Date of birth: 11 / 18 / 1982 (8)
(9) Social Security No: 854-89-5481
(10) State in which customer is licensed: RI (11) License type: D
(12) Date license was issued: 05 / 2001 (13) License number: 764968412
Select the NEXT button to continue.
RECORD: 1 2 3 4 5 6 7 8 9 10 11 12 13 14 15 16
Evaluate
Next Record

For use with Activities 1 and 3

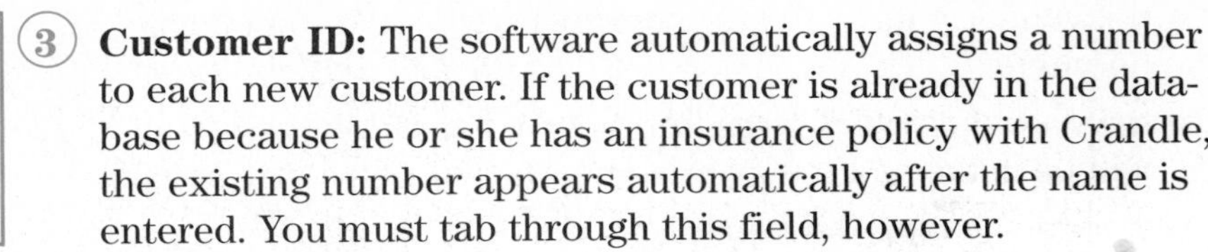

Work Ethically
Come to work on time and stay until the end of the day. Never take more than the allotted time for breaks.

3. **Customer ID:** The software automatically assigns a number to each new customer. If the customer is already in the database because he or she has an insurance policy with Crandle, the existing number appears automatically after the name is entered. You must tab through this field, however.

4. **Street:** The customer's street address may also include an apartment number.

5. **City, State, Zip:** This is the customer's city, two-letter state abbreviation, and Zip code. State abbreviations can be found on the Reference Sheet on the inside back cover of the text.

6. **Phone (daytime and evening):** Crandle Insurance needs numbers where the customer can be reached at any time.

7. **Sex:** M for male or F for female goes here.

8. **Date of birth:** This is the customer's birth date: Enter two digits for the month, two digits for the day, and four digits for the year.

BE ALERT!
If you own a car, you are required by the states to insure it.

9. **Social Security number:** Hyphens are not keyed in the customer's Social Security number.

10. **State in which customer is licensed:** This is the two-letter abbreviation for the state that issued the customer's driver's license.

11. **License class:** There are several different classes of driver's licenses. This license holder may drive different kinds of vehicles such as cars, buses, motorcycles, or others. The class will be A, B, C, or D.

12. **Date license was issued:** This is the date when the license was issued: enter two digits for the month, and four digits for the year.

13. **License number:** The customer's driver's license number is a number.

Vehicle Information

After I enter all the customer information data from an insurance application, the Vehicle Information screen appears and I enter information about the car. A Vehicle Information screen is shown in Figure 1.3.

1. **Customer ID:** Key the Customer ID and the customer's name will fill automatically.

2. **Vehicle Make:** This indicates the company that made the vehicle, for example, Toyota, Honda, or Ford.

3. **Model:** This is the specific type of vehicle, for example, Tercel (Toyota), Civic (Honda), or Taurus (Ford).

Figure 1.3 Vehicle Information Screen

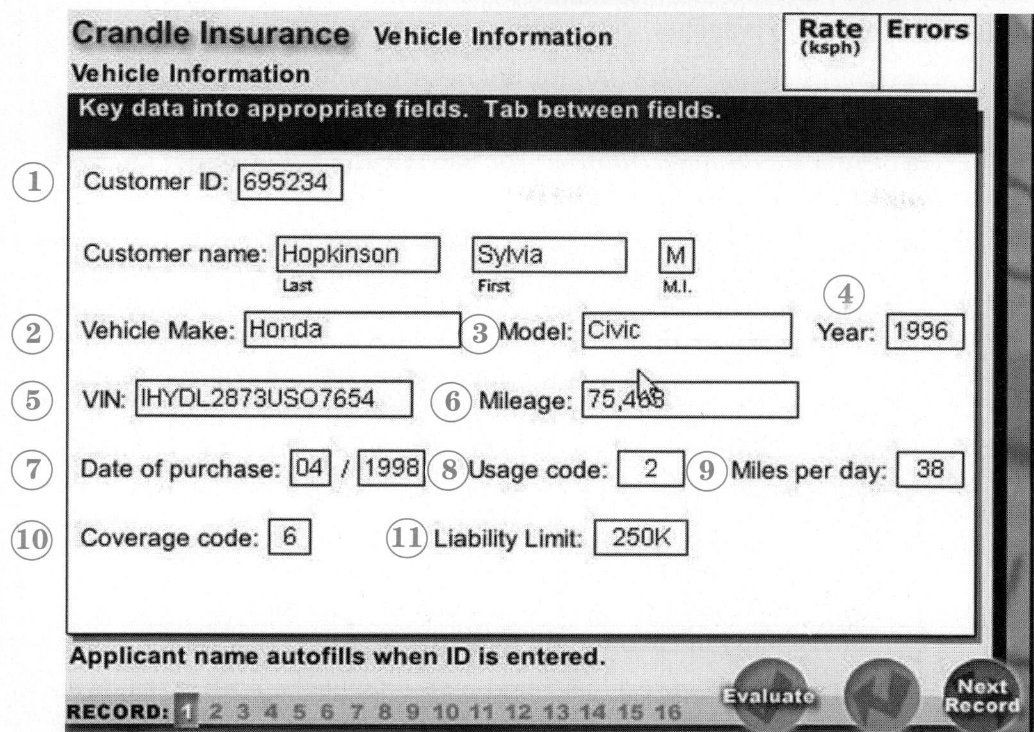

For use with Activities 2 and 3

(4) **Year:** This is the year the vehicle was manufactured.

(5) **VIN:** Each vehicle that is manufactured has a unique vehicle identification number (VIN), that identifies the vehicle in legal documents. Having the VIN number is very helpful in cases of theft or a traffic accident.

(6) **Mileage:** This is the mileage on the vehicle's odometer at the time the application was filed. An odometer is an instrument that indicates the distance traveled by a vehicle.

(7) **Date of purchase:** This is the date the vehicle was purchased: Enter two digits for the month and four digits for the year.

(8) **Usage code:** This code tells the company how the vehicle will be used. For example, cars are used for:

- commuting to work
- long-distance travel
- short-distance trips
- local errands and other

(9) **Miles per day:** This is the average number of miles the vehicle is driven each day.

When information to be entered is a mixture of alphabetic and numeric characters, use the top row to enter numbers. When information is all or mostly numeric, use the keypad to enter numbers.

(10) **Coverage code:** This number identifies the type of coverage the customer has chosen. Auto insurance is divided into several different types of coverage:

- *Bodily injury liability*, for injuries the policyholder causes to someone else.
- *Property damage liability*, for damage the policyholder causes to someone else's property.
- *Medical payments* insurance covers medical expenses for injuries. This "good faith" coverage guarantees immediate medical payments for the policyholder, his or her passengers, and other parties, regardless of who is at fault. It also covers the policyholder and members of the policyholder's household in any accident involving an automobile, whether the policyholder is on foot, on a bicycle, in a friend's car, or other.
- *Collision* covers damage to your own vehicle in an accident.
- *Comprehensive insurance* (fire, theft, and other non-collision damage) covers fire damage to the policyholder's vehicle, break-ins, vandalism or theft, as well as natural disasters such as earthquakes, hail, hurricanes, flood, and other.
- *Uninsured motorist* (UM) and *underinsured motorist* (UIM) coverage protects the policyholder if he or she is injured in an accident with others who carry insufficient or no liability insurance.
- Extra coverages are available for towing, labor, temporary replacement vehicles and similar expenses.

(11) **Liability Limit:** This is the highest dollar amount of coverage, which the customer can be reimbursed if he or she files a claim for damages incurred in an accident. The higher the limit, the more the policy costs the policyholder. K stands for thousands; for example, 100K means $100,000.

Policyholder Spreadsheet

Crandle keeps a spreadsheet of key information on policy holders. You will prepare a similar spreadsheet in Activity 4.

(1) **Last Name:** The customer's last name appears in the first column.

(2) **First Name:** The customer's first name appears in the second column.

(3) **Applicant ID:** This is the number that was automatically assigned to the customer when he or she submitted an application for insurance. It identifies the customer to the system.

(4) **License No:** This is the customer's driver's license number.

(5) **VIN:** This is the vehicle identification number.

(6) **Usage code:** This code identifies how the vehicle will be used.

Figure 1.4 Policyholder Spreadsheet

① ② ③ ④ ⑤ ⑥

Last Name	First Name	Customer ID	License No.	VIN	Usage code
Mitrano	John	652145	692354126	1HGCG165BWAO5285	4
Souder	Christine	584475	852647152	1TPER298WFEO8376	3
Forster	Glenn	625132	645278945	1IUGR234WGAO9382	4
Kingsley	Roderick	587496	236545826	1PUHT283YGIO2837	3
Romero	Angel	363251	789162531	1UYHT235IUKO2938	2
Jenkins	Dorothy	913764	421696233	1NBCK398KJHOØ683	4
McNaulty	Kevin	824691	652345621	1TFED987PKYO7463	5
Pottebaum	Susan	645281	951662351	1MJGF876YHSO9856	1
Atallah	Mustafa	789136	785463219	1KJSD466PLKO6322	2
Dematteo	Diane	526931	962321569	1HGDS756IWTO2756	4

For use with Activity 4

Warmup

Before entering the data for Activity 1, practice your data entry skills.

Step 1: Open the Data Entry Software.

Step 2: From the Main menu, select **Project Lab** then **Crandle Insurance**. Select the *WARMUP* button from the Activity bar located at the top of the screen.

Step 3: Enter the digits using the numeric keypad. Key the information across the screen. Strike ENTER on the keypad to move between fields or to the next row. Your speed and accuracy will be displayed at the end of the Warmup.

Step 4: You may repeat the Warmup as many times as you wish to increase your speed or accuracy.

Numeric Keypad Warmup

648275 Enter	794121567281 Enter	972864127 Enter	42157953 Enter	84216567 Enter
05728591	548724	5427928	764982130	021344275
9559849	451874	5144985	21546	7822403
301971	6144287	489967	45726	74516
1548932	652869354	55789	3216623	41726
942758	64572	978456	124567	5536244
6587524	4548	5442256	11424618	946125
578421	847965	87546842	2645	458263
45123	64245879	6320417	9874630	46127845
96635242	4516778	31207	12599	117458
6587723	495826	74547	1454258	031664
2597724	1238	24125	0058974876	45436

New Customers

In Activity 1, you will enter background information for 16 new insurance customers.

General Navigation

- Press *Tab* between fields as you enter the data.
- Press Tab, ENTER, or the *Next Record* button from the last field to move to the next screen.
- Select the *Back* arrow to move to the previous screen.
- Select the *Save* button to save the current record if you must exit the software before it is complete.
- When proofreading or correcting errors within records, select the highlighted tabs at the bottom of the screen to move between records.
- Select the *Evaluate* button to check your work
- Select the *Next Activity* button to move to the next activity. Move to the next activity only after you have completed and edited the activity you are working on.

Step 1: Remove all source documents for Crandle Insurance Activity 1 from the back of this book. They are marked with a large **1**.

Step 2: Analyze the applications by reviewing the source documents for each customer to be sure that all state abbreviations, Zip codes, and area codes are provided. Some of the information such as Zip codes or area codes may be missing. Refer to the Reference Sheet on the inside back cover for the missing information. Write the missing information on the source document. Do not add a period after the two-letter state abbreviation. Arrange the documents on your desktop so that you can turn completed documents face down as you complete them.

Step 3: From the Crandle Insurance Welcome screen, select **Activity 1**.

Step 4: A Customer Information screen similar to Figure 1.2 will appear. Instructions for entering records follow.

Date

Enter the application date as three fields. Press Tab between each field. Then press *Tab* to move to the Customer name field.

Name

Enter the customer's last name, first name, and middle initial. The name is entered as three fields; press *Tab* to move between fields. Periods are not required after initials.

BE ALERT!

Remember to enter two digits for the month, two digits for the day, and four digits for the year.

Customer ID

The computer will automatically assign an identification number to the customer. If the ID has not filled in by the time you have finished entering all data from the source document, you have likely made an error in entering the name. Press *Tab* to move to the next field.

Street

Enter the customer's street address and apartment number as separate fields; *Tab* between each field. Key only the apartment number. If no apartment is listed, you must tab through this field. Key periods after abbreviations as they appear on the form.

City, State, Zip

Enter the customer's city, state, and Zip code as separate fields; *Tab* between each field. If a Zip code is missing, remember to check the Reference Sheet on the inside back cover. Enter words such as *Road* or *Rd.* as they appear on the form. Enter nine-digit Zip codes without the hyphen.

Phone

Enter the customer' daytime and evening phone numbers as a ten-digit string; do not key the parentheses or the hyphen; they will appear automatically. *Tab* to the next field.

Sex

Enter M for male or F for female. *Tab* to the next field.

Date of Birth

Enter the customer's date of birth: two digits for the month, two digits for the day, and four digits for the year. Dates are considered three fields.

Social Security Number

Enter the customer's Social Security number as a single field (do not key the hyphens; they will appear automatically).

State where customer is licensed

Enter the two-letter abbreviation for the state where the driver's license was issued. If the abbreviation is missing, assume the driver is licensed in the state in which he/she lives and enter the state abbreviation.

License Type

Enter the letter that indicates the class of license held by the customer.

Date license was issued

Enter the month and year the license was issued: two digits for the month and four digits for the year.

Use the numeric keypad to enter a sequence of digits.

Step 5: Proofread the data entered for the first record against the source document. Correct errors that you find. To edit a field, select the field and rekey the correct information. Then turn the source document (application) over on its face to indicate that you are finished with it. Move to the next record.

Step 6: After entering and proofreading all orders, select **Evaluate** to check your work. The results will be recorded as Edit 1 in your student record.

If you are interrupted before entering all of the source documents for an activity, select the *SAVE* button.

Step 7: If errors occur in one or more records, the record numbers at the bottom of the screen will be highlighted in red. Locate the source document for the first record that is highlighted. Proofread the screen against the source document and correct errors. Select **Evaluate**. Your results will be recorded as Edit 2 in your student record.

Step 8: Edit the activity a third time if errors still exist. After the final Evaluate, the software will display errors by changing the text color within the fields from black to red.

Step 9: Store the source documents for Activity 1 in a folder or other safe place. You will use them again in Activity 4.

Step 10: Select the **Next Activity** button to move to Activity 2 or use the Activity menu located at the top of the screen.

Proofread all records for obvious errors before you Evaluate an activity.

- Check that phone numbers and area codes are formatted correctly. If they are not, they may be keyed incorrectly.
- Check that months are keyed with two digits (e.g. 01 for January)
- Check accuracy of all license numbers.

Activity 3

Customer Information

In Activity 3, you will update personal and vehicle information for nine customers whose records you prepared previously. An update is needed when a customer calls in to report a new address or telephone number, buys a different car, or makes some other change.

Step 1: Remove all source documents for Crandle Insurance Activity 3 from the back of this book. These forms are marked with a large 3.

Step 2: Analyze all source documents for completeness. Note that updates to the Customer or Vehicle information forms are shown in green on the source documents.

Step 3: Select **Activity 3** from the Activity menu located at the top of the screen. The screen will display a blank customer information form.

Step 4: Begin by entering the Customer ID from the first source document. The remainder of the screen will fill automatically with the information you entered previously for this customer. If the screen does not autofill, you have made an error entering the Customer ID. Update the form with the new customer information (shown in green on the form).

Data is recorded on two screens. Use the right arrow to move to the second screen.

Step 5: Proofread and edit each screen after data has been entered. To edit a field, select the field and rekey the correct information. After you have made all changes to the record, turn your source document over to indicate that you are finished with it.

Double-check VIN numbers for accuracy.

Step 6: Select **Evaluate** when you are ready to check your work.

Step 7: If errors are present in any record, the record number will be highlighted. Locate the source document for this record. Proofread the record against the source document and correct errors. Follow this procedure for each record containing errors. Evaluate your work.

Step 8: As before, you may edit the activity two more times.

Step 9: You will use these source documents for Activity 4; continue to Activity 4 or store them until you are ready to proceed.

Step 10: Select **Next Activity** to move to Activity 4 or use the Activity menu located at the top of the screen.

Activity 4

Policyholder Spreadsheet

In Activity 4, you will prepare a chart of customer information for the Crandle Insurance policyholders whose information you entered and updated.

Step 1: Retrieve the source documents for Activity 1 and Activity 2. Arrange them in alphabetic order by the customer's last name.

Step 2: Retrieve the source documents from Activity 3. For any record that has an Activity 3 form, replace the Activity 1 form with the Activity 3 form. Keep the documents in alphabetical order. Then, for all the Activity 1 forms that remain, put the Activity 2 form behind it. You now have a set of source documents for each customer. Write the Customer's ID which was supplied by the software earlier on each form. For example, Alvarez is 770526.

Step 3: Select **Activity 4** from the Activity menu located at the top of the screen.

Step 4: Double-check that forms are alphabetized by surname before you begin. Key the information requested on the form for the first **14 customers**. Use the updated data from Activity 3 when appropriate. For example, information for the first applicant will be as follows:

Alvarez	Ramon	770526	875921068	1UIHU288OUIO8276	4

Step 5: Follow the standard procedures for entering and proofreading each entry. Select **Evaluate** when you are ready to check your work.

Step 6: Edit and correct mistakes in the usual manner.

S T R E T C H . . . .

Now that you've learned to enter data for insurance policies, it's time to stretch your data entry speed and accuracy.

Step 1: From the Activity Menu, choose **Stretch**.

Step 2: Enter all information from Figure 1.4, page 75, as accurately and as quickly as possible. Do not stop to edit. Strike *Tab* to move to the next field.

Step 3: Select the **Evaluate** button to check your work. Your keystrokes per hour (*ksph*) and accuracy rate will be reported.

Step 4: Repeat the drill to increase your *ksph*.

Project 2

Funwear

Funwear Catalog is a popular mail-order company specializing in sportswear and casual clothing for men, women, and children. The customer service center is a busy office where data entry specialists called *customer service representatives* take and process orders from customers all over the country.

©PHOTODISC

Your Activities Today

- 8 A.M.–12 P.M. Enter mail-in orders on the computer
- 1–3 P.M. Answer phones and take call-in orders
- 3–4 P.M. Process returns and exchange requests
- 4–5 P.M. Record data for purchase orders

New Knowledge and Skills

In this project, you will:

- Enter, verify, and update customer information
- Process customer orders
- Enter shipping and billing information
- Record purchase order information

CAREER PROFILE

Data Entry Specialist/Customer Service Representative

"As a customer service representative and data entry specialist, I have many roles at Funwear. I speak with customers on the phone, help them find what they need, check for errors, and make sure that both phone orders and mail orders get filled on time."

What I do every day
I am the one who greets telephone customers and helps them order exactly what they need. I answer questions, clarify descriptions of merchandise, and sometimes make recommendations. I also enter orders that come by mail or fax and handle returns and exchanges. Finally, I record information about purchase orders. These are the forms that my company uses to order merchandise from the wholesalers so we can resell the merchandise to our customers.

The best part of my job
I talk to lots of different people throughout the day, and often I am able to help those who have questions or need recommendations. Most customers are friendly, and I enjoy interacting with them on the phone.

The worst part of my job
Sometimes people get angry because of mistakes in their shipments or because the company doesn't have what they want. I don't like it when people blame me for things I cannot control.

What I need to know and be able to do
Quick and accurate data entry skills are very important to my job. I also need good people skills since I spend a lot of time on the phone with customers. The customers often have questions, concerns, and problems that I must handle quickly and responsibly. When recording orders, I must recognize mistakes and make decisions about how to handle them. Even though the computers do the arithmetic for me, it helps to have good math skills so I can catch mistakes or problems.

How I prepared to be a customer service representative
In high school, I took keyboarding and other computer courses. When I enrolled in community college, I was able to take courses in data entry, which helped build my computer and customer relations skills. Finally, when I took this job, I was given special training in the programs and procedures that my company uses.

How I could have prepared better
Taking additional computer courses would have been helpful. The more I know about computers and the faster and more accurate my skills, the better opportunity I'll have for advancement.

Education needed: A customer service representative needs a high school diploma plus data entry training or experience.

Salary range: $16,000 — $33,000

Job outlook: Customer service representatives are in high demand. There is a particular need for people with good communication and computer skills.

Related jobs: Word processor, file clerk, receptionist, data entry specialist, order taker.

THE REAL WORLD

The inside of a mail-order company is an active, sometimes hectic scene. Several customer service representatives work together in a large room where phones ring constantly. Of course, there are times when the orders come in more slowly. That's when we take care of returns, problem orders, purchase orders, and other tasks. Part of the challenge of the job is balancing the slow times with the fast times and not getting either overwhelmed or bored.

As a customer service representative, I have three main tasks:

1. To greet telephone customers, answer their questions, and help them place their orders correctly.
2. To enter orders received through the mail or by fax.
3. To make sure that all customer information in the computer is correct and up to date.

When not working directly with customers, I have other responsibilities:

- To identify and correct mistakes in customer orders.
- To process returns and exchanges of mail-order merchandise.
- To prepare purchase orders.

Working with Customers

Some customers mail or fax their orders, and I enter the information directly from their order form. Other customers order by telephone. When a customer calls to place an order, I answer the phone with a cheerful greeting, then I enter the customer's identification code into the computer. If the customer has shopped with us previously, his or her name and address appear automatically on the screen. If the customer has not shopped with us before, I enter the new name and address. Then I use the chart on my screen to enter the code, description, price, and other information about each item the customer wants to order. Here are some sample codes and the products that go with them:

Code	Product
56831-674b	women's ribbed mock turtleneck t-shirt
78934-491g	men's khaki drawstring shorts
43068-934c	child's hooded windbreaker

Show respect during a conversation by using the customer's last name preceded by Mr. or Ms.

Verifying Shipping and Billing Information

When the customer's address and credit card information are already in the computer, I check to make sure all of the information is up to date. If not, I correct the shipping and billing addresses and the credit card number and expiration date.

THE CHALLENGES

As hard as the company tries, Funwear is not always able to fill the customer's order on the day it is requested. Some of the reasons include:

- The item a customer wants is out of stock, and the request has to be placed on **back order**. Orders that are back ordered are processed as soon as inventory is received.
- The customer provides the wrong item number. In this case, I contact the customer and determine which item is intended. For telephone customers, I get the correct information during the initial conversation.
- The customer's name, address, or credit card information are unreadable on a mail order. This requires a phone call to the customer for clarification of the confusing information.

©PHOTODISC

The Customer's Order Form

When customers want to order merchandise, they send their order forms to Funwear or call and read the information from the form over the phone. The form provides billing and shipping information and a list of all the items that are being ordered.

An order form is shown in Figure 2.1. Notice that it is divided into three sections: (1) billing and shipping, (2) payment method, and (3) merchandise. It contains the following information:

- the customer's identification number
- the date the customer filled out the form
- a stamped date added by Funwear showing when the order was received
- the customer's name and billing address.
- the name and address where merchandise should be shipped.
- the daytime and evening telephone numbers where the customer can be reached and the daytime and evening telephone numbers where the recipient of the merchandise can be reached.
- the customer's credit card or check/money order information.
- the item number, catalog page number where the item appears, description, size, color, second color, quantity, price of each item that is being purchased, subtotals, and total

Customer Mail Order

Customer ID: ______________________________ Date: ____________________
Last four digits of your Social Security number

Bill to:

Name: ______________________________

Street: ______________________ Apt: ______

City: ______________________________

State: __________ Zip: ______________

Phone: Day: (_____) _____-______

Evening: (_____) _____-______

Ship to (if different from billing address):

Name: ______________________________

Street: ______________________ Apt: ______

City: ______________________________

State: __________ Zip: ______________

Phone: Day: (_____) _____-______

Evening: (_____) _____-______

Payment Method:

Charge to:

- ❑ Visa
- ❑ Master Card
- ❑ Discover
- ❑ American Express
- ❑ Check/money order enclosed

Card number: ______-______-______-______

Expiration date: _____/_____
month/year

Signature: ______________________________

Item number	Page	Description	Size	Color	Color (2nd Choice)	Qty	Price per item	Subtotal
							Total:	

For use with Activities 5, 6, and 8

Billing and Shipping Information

The first time a customer places an order with Funwear, I create a new record by completing the Customer Order screen shown in Figure 2.2. Then I access this record each time the customer places an order. For repeat customers, I verify their information in the file and update it when needed.

TIP

If customers forget their ID, ask them to look at the address label of their catalog. The code usually is shown on the label.

(1) **Customer ID:** The Customer ID is the same as the last four digits of the customer's Social Security number. If a customer has ordered previously, the code is stored in the computer database. Each time the ID is entered for a repeat customer, the billing and shipping information fill automatically.

(2) **Date:** The date the order was completed by the customer is entered on this line. (Two digits for month, two digits for day, four digits for year.)

(3) **Bill To:** The Bill To section shows the name, address, and phone number (both day and evening) of the person who will be billed for the merchandise.

(4) **Ship To:** The Ship To information is the location where the order will be delivered. This section is completed only if the information is different than the Bill To information.

Figure 2.2 Bill To/Ship To Screen

Funwear New Customers
Customer Order
Rate (ksph) | Errors
Key data into appropriate fields. Tab between fields.

(1) Customer ID: 8954 (3) (2) Date: 07 / 11 / 2004

Bill To:
Last Name: Berkley First Name: William
Street: 1206 Pine Wood Lane Apt:
City: Tuskegee State: AL Zip code: 36083
Phone (daytime): (334) 555-0151 Phone (evening): (334) 555-0138

(4) Ship To:
Last Name: Berkley First Name: Suzanna
Street: 427 Oakdale Drive Apt:
City: Lebanon State: TN Zip code: 37087
Phone (daytime): (615) 555-0122 Phone (evening): (615) 555-0122

Proceed through all three forms for each client
RECORD: 1 2 3 4 5 6 7 8 9 10 11 12 13 14 15 16 Evaluate

For use with Activities 5 and 6

Payment Method Information

Funwear customers may pay by credit card, check, or money order. The Payment Method screen shown in Figure 2.3 appears after the customer information is entered.

⑤ **Charge To:** If a customer chooses to pay by credit card, the type of card to be used is indicated in this field.

⑥ **Check/money order:** If a customer chooses to pay by check or **money order**, the information is indicated in this field. A money order, like a check, is an order for the payment of money. It may be issued by the post office or a bank.

⑦ **Card number:** This field is for the credit card number. Hyphens are not keyed.

⑧ **Expiration date:** The credit card expiration date goes in this field, two digits for the month and four digits for the year. (For example, if the card expires May 2006, enter 05/2006.)

⑨ **Signature:** Customers must give permission for Funwear to place a charge against their credit card. Permission is indicated when the customer's signature is present. All mail and fax orders must be checked for this signature. The phrase "Signature Verified" will appear when a name is entered if the customer has ordered previously. For telephone orders, ask customers how the signature appears on the credit card.

Figure 2.3 Payment Method Screen

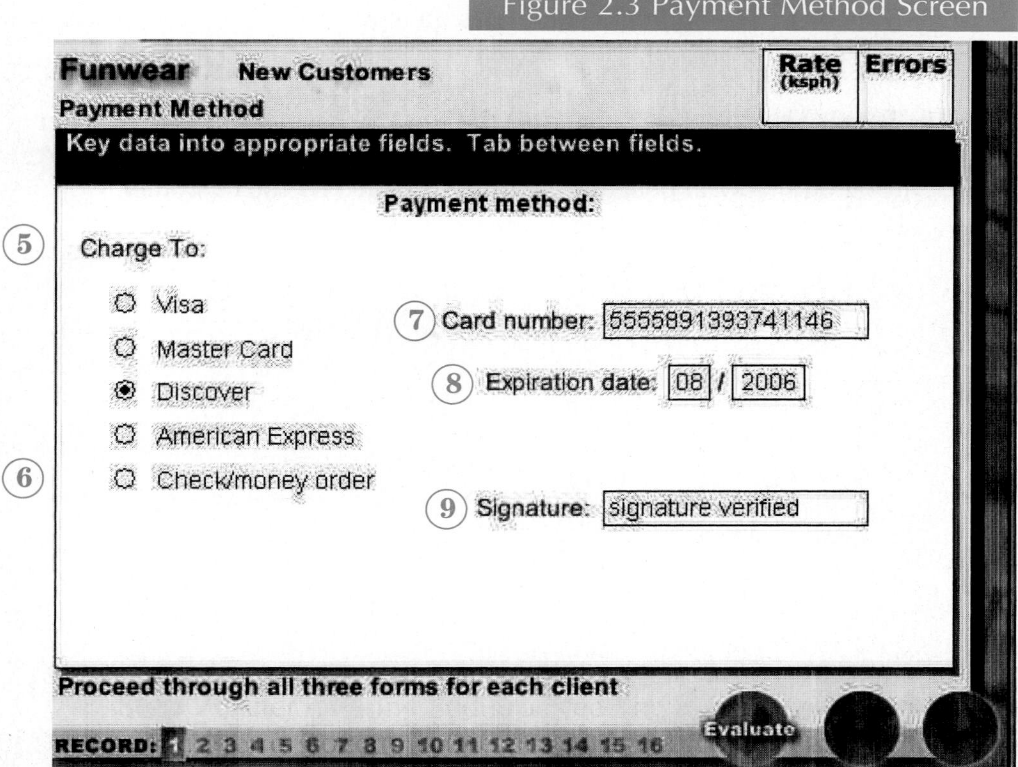

For use with Activities 5, 6, and 7

Merchandise Order Information

Once a customer's shipping and billing information have been entered and verified and the payment method has been designated, it's time to enter the order into the computer. The Merchandise Order screen is shown in Figure 2.4.

(10) **Item number:** Each item in the catalog has its own code number for identification.

(11) **Page:** This is the page number for the item in the catalog.

(12) **Description:** This is a description of the item being ordered (for example, "men's mesh t-shirt").

(13) **Size:** This is the size the customer wishes to order.

(14) **Color:** This is the color the customer wishes to order.

(15) **Color (second choice):** Customers are asked for a second choice in case the first choice is not available. If the customer writes "none" or leaves the space blank, enter "none" in this column.

(16) **Quantity:** This tells us how many of each item the customer wishes to order.

(17) **Price per item:** This refers to the price for one item, regardless of how many items are being ordered.

(18) **Subtotal:** The software calculates the subtotal automatically when the quantity and the unit price have been entered.

(19) **Total:** The software calculates the total automatically. It may differ from the customer's total. If the two totals differ, write the software total on the form beneath the total provided by the customer.

Work Ethically
Correct all entry mistakes so customers receive the merchandise they request.

Figure 2.4 Merchandise Order Screen

Funwear **New Customers**

Merchandise Order

Rate (ksph)	Errors

Key data into appropriate fields. Tab between fields.

Item Number	Page	Description	Size	Color	Color (2nd Choice)	Qty	Price per item	Sub total
43062-53g	14	Child's cotton t-shirt	6	Periwinkle	Raspberry	1	6.99	6.99
94045-183a	88	Men's flannel shirt	XL	Green/ blue plaid	Red/Blue plaid	1	21.99	21.99
(10)	(11)	(12)	(13)	(14)	(15)	(16)	(17)	(18)
					(19)	Total		$28.98

Proceed through all three forms for each client

RECORD: 1 2 3 4 5 6 7 8 9 10 11 12 13 14 15 16

Evaluate

Next Record

For use with Activities 5, 6, and 7

Funwear Purchases from Suppliers

Funwear Catalog purchases many clothing items from suppliers (vendors) each year to resell to catalog customers. I often enter the purchase order information for buyers. A Funwear purchase order to a clothing supplier is shown in Figure 2.5.

Figure 2.5 Purchase Order

Purchase Order

Vendor number: 87513

Vendor name and address:	**Ship to:**	**Bill to:**
Malcom and Malcom 9485 Collins Road Dryden, MI	Attn: Tom Jansen Funwear, Inc. 8990 Hamilton Boulevard Deer Creek, IA 67093	Accounts Payable Funwear, Inc. PO Box 6895 Deer Creek, IA 67093

Ship via: UPS 3-day

UPC Number	Qty	Description	Unit Price	Subtotal
95426	150	Men's cotton polo shirt	11.00	1,650.00
82415	300	Men's cotton crew-neck sweater	20.00	6,000.00
62187	250	Men's oxford dress shirt	14.00	3,500.00
24625	800	Ribbed cotton socks	3.00	2,400.00

Payment terms: Net 30 **Total:**

For use with Activity 8

Supplier Address Information

When Funwear places an order with a supplier for the first time, I enter the supplier's name and address into the system. For future orders, this information appears automatically when the supplier's identification number is entered.

1. **Supplier Number:** This is the identification number for the company from whom Funwear is purchasing merchandise. If we have ordered merchandise previously from this supplier, the company's name and address fill in automatically when the supplier number is entered.

2. **Date:** This is the date on which the order was placed with the supplier.

3. **Supplier name and address:** This is the name and street address of the company from which Funwear is ordering merchandise.

4. **Ship To:** This shows the name of Funwear's warehouse manager and the address of the warehouse. This information is preprinted on all purchase orders and autofills on the computer screen.

5. **Bill To:** This is the address of Funwear's billing office. It is also preprinted on the form.

Figure 2.6 Supplier Information Screen

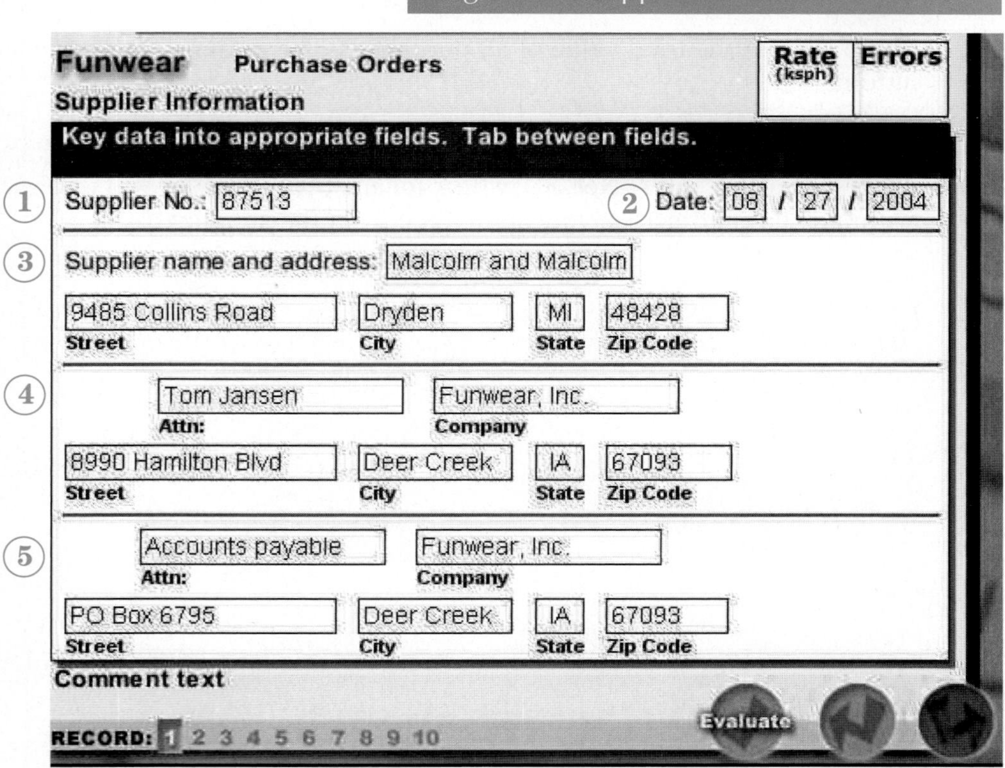

For use with Activity 8

Supplier Shipping and Merchandise Information

After the supplier's name and address have been entered and verified, the merchandise orders are entered into the system. The supplier merchandise screen is shown in Figure 2.7.

(6) **Ship Via:** The Ship Via box indicates the type of shipping that is requested. Funwear uses a variety of shipping methods, including United Parcel Service, FedEx, and the United States Postal Service. When orders are to be rushed, a special Overnight, One-day, or Two-Day service may be required.

(7) **UPC Number:** This abbreviation stands for Universal Product Code. It refers to the code number that identifies each item in the supplier's database.

(8) **Quantity:** This field shows the quantity of the each item Funwear is ordering.

(9) **Description:** This field contains a brief description of the item identified by the UPC number.

(10) **Unit Price:** This field shows the price of a single item.

(11) **Subtotal:** The computer automatically calculates the subtotal by multiplying the unit price times the number of items ordered.

(12) **Total:** This is the total value of all purchases. The total calculates automatically.

(13) **Payment Terms:** This lists the way that Funwear will pay for its order. Usually, I enter "Net 30," which means that Funwear will pay within 30 days after receiving an invoice from the supplier.

Figure 2.7 Supplier Merchandise Screen

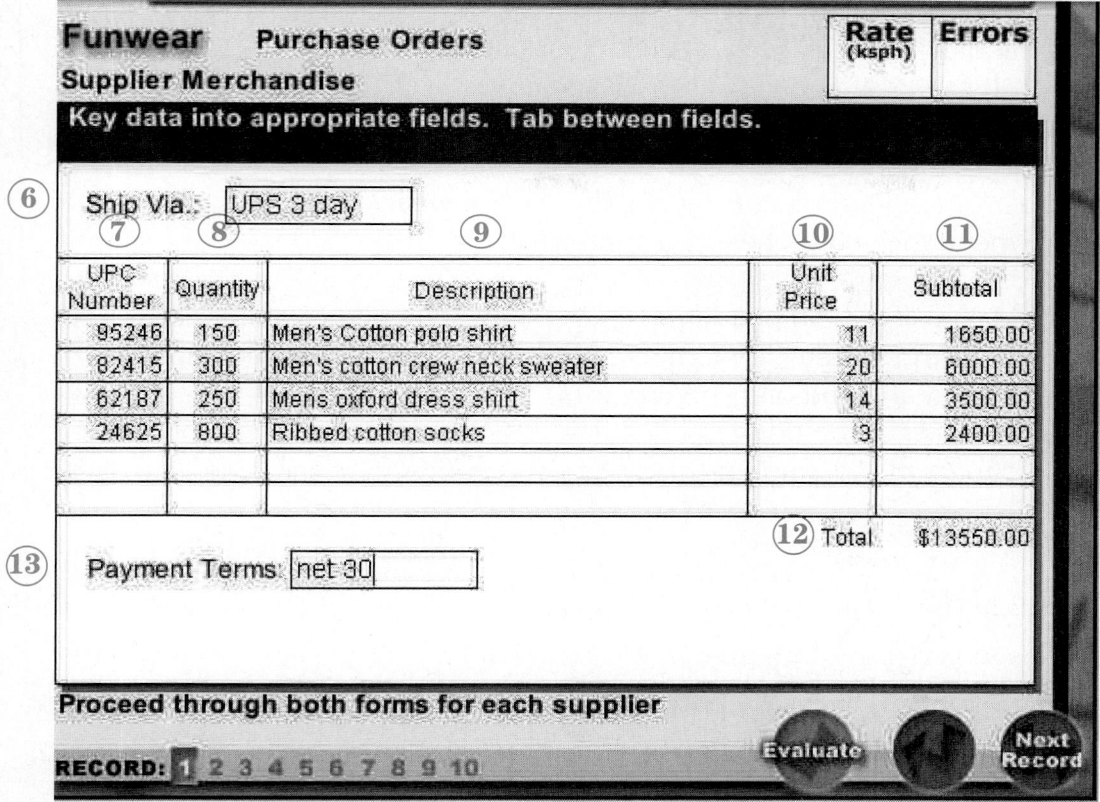

UPC Number	Quantity	Description	Unit Price	Subtotal
95246	150	Men's Cotton polo shirt	11	1650.00
82415	300	Men's cotton crew neck sweater	20	6000.00
62187	250	Mens oxford dress shirt	14	3500.00
24625	800	Ribbed cotton socks	3	2400.00

For use with Activity 8

Warmup

Before entering the data for Activity 5, practice your data entry skills.

Step 1: Open the Data Entry software.

Step 2: From the Main menu, select **Project Lab** then **Funwear**. Then select *Warmup* from the Activity menu located at the top of the screen.

Step 3: Enter the data using the alphanumeric keys. Key all hyphens and periods. Key the information across the screen. *Tab* to move between fields. Your speed and accuracy will be displayed at the end of the Warmup.

Step 4: You may repeat the Warmup as many times as you wish to increase your speed or accuracy.

56831-674b	Susan Hamilton	325.67	Red Oak Dr.	Auburn	334-555-9508
78934-491g	Justin Parker	122.95	Crestmont Dr.	San Diego	619-555-0176
59375-873g	Katrina Simpson	58.76	Walnut Ln.	Miami	305-555-0169
43068-934c	Christopher Delgado	528.66	Jessup Rd.	Dayton	937-555-0122
83659-835b	Sandra Wong	374.98	Tivoli Ln.	Flagstaff	928-555-0141
98472-845a	Enrique Gill	474.89	Sycamore Ave.	Raleigh	984-555-0121
83574-147g	Mara Estes	354.25	Marconi Ln.	Wausau	715-555-0113
28273-128b	Chris Sammons	787.54	Oakbrook Ct.	Laredo	956-555-0182

Activity 5

New Customers

In Activity 5, you will enter information from 16 mail order forms. Each order requires completing three screens. As you complete each screen for an order, proofread the data and correct errors before moving to the next screen.

Step 1: Remove all Customer Order forms for Funwear Activity 1 from the back of this book. These are marked with a large ❺.

Step 2: Analyze each order to make sure that it is complete. If area codes or Zip codes are missing, refer to the Reference Sheet on the inside back cover for the correct information. Write the missing information on the source document.

- Complete day and evening telephone numbers, including area codes.
- Complete billing and shipping addresses, including the Zip code.

Step 3: Select **Activity 5** from the Activity menu located at the top of the screen.

Step 4: The Customer Order screen shown in Figure 2.2 appears. Instructions for completing this section are given below. *Tab* between fields as you enter the data.

Customer ID

Enter the Customer ID number shown on the Customer Order form.

Date

Enter the date when the order form was filled out.

Bill To

Using the Bill To information from the Customer Order form, enter the name, address and telephone numbers. Key a phone number as a ten-digit string; do not key the parentheses or hyphen.

Ship To

If the Ship To box is blank on the order, the merchandise will automatically be sent to the billing address.

- If the merchandise will be sent to the billing address, click in the Ship To box and press **Ctrl + s**, and the data will fill automatically.
- If the Ship To box is different than the Bill To address, enter the new information.

BE ALERT!
The Ship to address often changes.

Step 5: Proofread the data on screen by comparing it to the source document. Correct errors. Select **Next**.

Step 6: The Payment Method screen, shown in Figure 2.3, appears.

Payment Method
If the customer is paying by credit card, *Tab* to the appropriate credit card box and enter an **X**. If the customer is paying by check or money order, *Tab* to *Check/Money Order* and enter an X. If the payment method is a check or money order, this screen is complete.

Credit Card or Check/Money Order
Enter the credit card number without hyphens and the credit card expiration date (two digits for the month and four digits for the year). Press **Ctrl + s** to indicate that the customer has signed the form.

Step 7: Proofread the data entered for the Payment Method screen and correct mistakes.

Step 8: Move to the Merchandise Order screen and enter the data for each item ordered. Totals will be entered automatically.

Step 9: Proofread the Merchandise Order screen against the source document. Correct errors. After you have made all corrections to a record, turn the source document over on its face to indicate that you are finished with it. Move to the next record and enter it.

Step 10: After entering and proofreading all orders, select **Evaluate** to check your work.

Step 11: If errors occur in one or more records, the tab will be highlighted in a different color. Locate the source document for the first incorrect record. Proofread the screen against the source document and correct errors. Follow this procedure for each record containing errors.

Step 12: You may repeat Step 11 twice more. After the final *Evaluate*, the software will display errors by changing the text color within the fields from black to red.

Step 13: If the screen totals do not match the source document totals, write the correct total below the total on the customer's order form. Cross through the customer's total. Store the source documents for Activity 5 in a folder.

Activity 6

Update Customer Information

Customer information often changes between orders. In Activity 6, you will update personal information for ten repeat customers and process their new orders. As you complete each screen for an order, proofread the data and correct errors that you have made before moving to the next screen.

Step 1: Remove all Customer Order forms for Funwear Activity 6 from the back of this book. These are marked with a large ❻.

Step 2: Review the orders to make sure that the customer has provided all necessary information. If area codes or Zip codes are missing, write the missing information on the source document.

Step 3: From the Funwear screen, click **Activity 6**. The *Shipping and Billing Information* screen shown in Figure 2.2 will appear. Instructions for completing this section are given below.

Customer ID Number

Enter the Customer ID and the Bill To and Ship To information from the customer's last order will appear automatically.

Date

Use the current year in the date.

Bill To Information

Compare the name, address, and phone numbers on the screen with those shown on the current order form. Edit as necessary.

Ship To Information

Ship To information changes often because customers order gifts or other items to be sent to family or friends. Compare the name, address, and phone numbers in the Ship To section with those shown on the current order. Edit as needed. Press **Ctrl** + **s** if the address is the same as the Bill to data.

If the customer's information changed in the Bill To: section, it will usually change in the Ship To: section also.

Step 4: Proofread your work against the source document and correct errors. Move to the Payment Method screen.

Step 5: Customers do not always use the same form of payment or the same credit card each time they order. Compare the information on the screen with the current order and edit as needed. Remember to press **Ctrl** + **s** to indicate that the customer has signed the credit card permission form.

Step 6: Process the customer's order in the usual manner. Proofread and correct errors.

Step 7: After entering all orders, select **Evaluate** to check your work.

Step 8: Follow the standard procedure to proofread each record that is highlighted at the bottom of the screen. Proofread the screen against the source document and correct errors. Edit and evaluate the activity as necessary.

Step 9: Compare the final Total for each customer order against the customer's order form. Write the correct total below the total on the customer's order form. Cross through the customer's total on the source document.

Step 10: Store the source documents for Activity 6 in a folder.

Step 11: Select **Next Activity** to move to Activity 7 or select the Activity menu located at the top of the screen.

Activity 7

Calculate Totals

In Activity 7, you will assume a new responsibility—calculating the total of the purchase orders to clothing suppliers.

Step 1: Turn to the Funwear purchase order forms for Activity 8 in the back of this book. These are marked with **8**.

Step 2: Add the subtotals for each of the Purchase Orders using the calculator. When you get the same total twice, write the total on the Purchase Order.

Activity 8

Purchase Orders

In Activity 8, you will enter ten purchase orders; data for each record will be entered on two screens. As you complete each screen for an order, proofread the data and correct errors before moving to the next screen. You will not be reminded to follow these standard procedures.

Step 1: Select **Activity 8**, from the Activity menu located at the top of the screen.

Step 2: Beginning with the first purchase order, enter the data required for the *Supplier Information* screen.

Supplier Number

Enter the supplier number from the purchase order. The supplier's name and address will be displayed automatically. If a name does not appear, this is the first time a purchase has been made from this supplier.

Ship To, Bill To

The shipping and billing addresses autofill.

BE ALERT!
If you are interruped before entering all of the source documents, select **Save**. This is the last time for this reminder.

Step 3: Enter the data from the purchase order in the *Supplier Merchandise* screen (Figure 2.7).

Ship Via

Enter the shipping method and the number of days that Funwear will allow for shipping.

Order Information

UPC and Quantity: For each item, enter the UPC code. The description and unit price for the item will display automatically. Fill in the quantity of each item. The subtotal will display automatically.

Payment Terms

Enter the payment terms.

Step 4: After entering all orders, select **Evaluate**. Proofread and correct the purchase orders, and re-evaluate your work in the standard manner.

STRETCH . . . .

Now that you've learned to enter data for customer orders and purchase orders, it's time to stretch your data entry speed and accuracy.

Step 1: From the Activity menu, choose **Stretch**.

Step 2. Enter all information below as accurately and as quickly as possible. Do not stop to edit.

Step 3: Review your performance by selecting **Evaluate** to check your work.

Step 4: Repeat this activity to increase your speed.

Customer Merchandise Order Screen

Item number	Page	Description	Size	Color	Color (2nd Choice)	Qty	Price per item	Subtotal
87365-941d	54	Women's terrycloth bathrobe	L	Green/ white	None	1	29.99	29.99
88361-524f	115	Women's suede sandals	9	Tan	None	1	19.49	19.49
97824-546c	90	Terrycloth hand towel	––	Forest green	Midnight mauve	2	7.99	15.98
54762-249a	8	Women's linen jacket	S	Moss	None	1	54.99	54.99
23971-625a	36	Men's V-neck cotton pullover	L	Lake blue	Coffee	1	34.99	34.99
24276-571b	64	Men's oxford shirt	16	Yellow	Ecru	1	21.49	21.49
77529-031d	27	Men's cotton twill shorts	32	Navy	Olive	1	29.99	29.99

Project 3
Western Suites

Western Suites is a hotel chain that prides itself on customer service. To keep guests happy—and returning—it surveys them with cards, telephone calls, e-mail, and a Web site. After guests respond, a *customer satisfaction specialist*, another name for data entry specialist, enters the responses into the hotel's computer database. The computer compiles all the information and generates a "report card" on the company's performance.

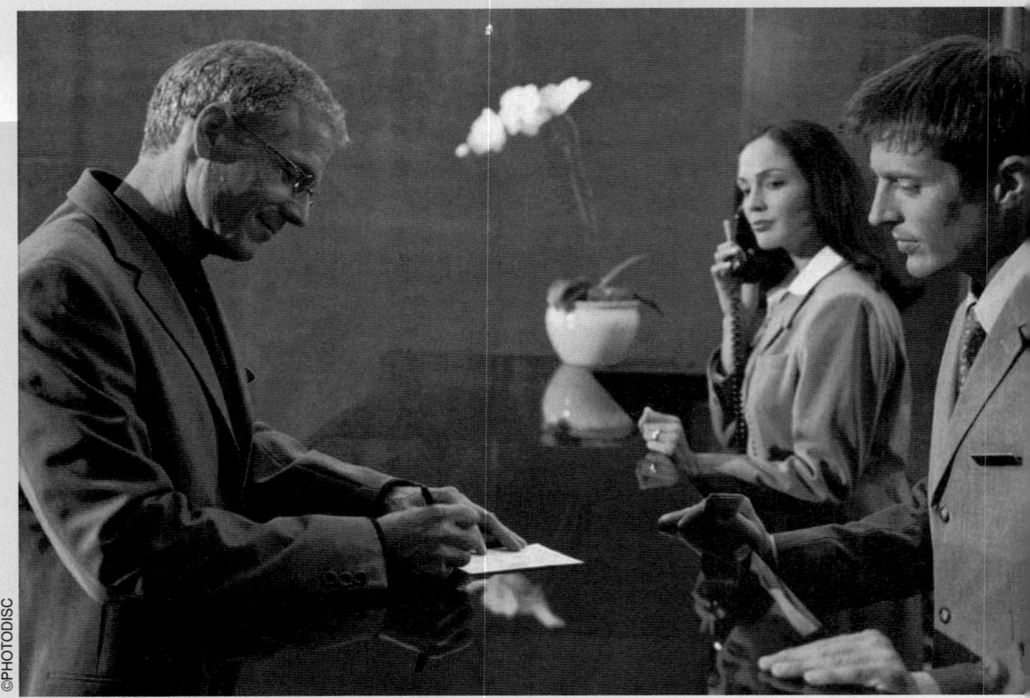

Your Activities Today

- ➢8–10:00 A.M. — Interpret, evaluate, and enter data from card and telephone surveys
- ➢10:00 A.M.–1:00 P.M. — Interpret, evaluate, and enter data from e-mail and Web site surveys

New Knowledge and Skills

In this project, you will:

- ➢Enter survey results for first-time guests
- ➢Enter survey results for repeat guests
- ➢Interpret guest comments and make decisions about which comment codes to use
- ➢Summarize guest comments

CAREER PROFILE

Data Entry Specialist/Customer Satisfaction Specialist

©PHOTODISC

"My job at Western Suites requires me to interpret comments from guest surveys. I translate the guests' comments into codes that can be easily organized by the computer and turned into a report for management."

What I do every day

Although my work at Western Suites is not visible to the guests, it is extremely important to the chain's success. I keep track of guest preferences—why they choose our hotel in the first place, which ones return and which ones don't, why they do or don't return, and how satisfied they are with their stay. After I enter information from surveys into the database, the computer sorts it for patterns about what guests like and dislike.

The best part of my job
I have good organizational skills, and I like sorting and interpreting data. I also enjoy learning what makes a business successful and the ways that a company can improve its service to customers.

The worst part of my job
Because my work is all behind the scenes, I miss interacting with guests. Faces and names are not attached to the information that I enter in the computer.

What I need to know and be able to do
My job involves a lot of interpretation, since I read or listen to guests' comments then sort the comments into specific categories for management's review. I have to pay close attention to what services the guests say they want and to the things they like and dislike. After I interpret the comments, I decide which comment codes to enter into the database. I need good decision-making skills and quick and accurate keying skills.

How I prepared to be a customer service representative
One summer I worked as a telemarketer. I learned to listen to customers and interpret their comments. Since I took many computer courses in high school and technical school, my data entry skills are excellent.

How I could have prepared better
Having better training in how to analyze data would be helpful. I may register for a data analysis course soon.

Education needed: A customer satisfaction specialist needs a high school diploma plus data entry training or experience.

Salary range: $16,000 – $33,000

Job outlook: Customer satisfaction specialists are in high demand. There is a particular need for people with good critical thinking and computer skills.

Related jobs: Word processor, file clerk, receptionist, data entry specialist, and order taker.

THE REAL WORLD

Guest is a hotel's term for customer.

Everything that goes on behind the scenes in a hotel is for one purpose—to keep guests happy and get them to return. One of the important ways that hotel managers assure that guests will return is to survey them to find out what they like and dislike, then to correct problems or make changes.

As a customer satisfaction clerk, I have three main tasks:

- To organize and categorize information from guest surveys.
- To enter guest survey information into the computer database.
- To make sure that all guest information in the hotel's computers is correct and up to date.

Reading and sorting guest satisfaction surveys

Most of Western Suites' information about guest satisfaction comes from survey cards completed by overnight guests. These cards consist of (1) items that guests rate according to how satisfied they were and (2) longer comments they write to describe their experiences at the hotel. My job is to read and interpret all the responses and then to enter the information into a form the hotel managers can read quickly and easily.

Give guests quality service by accurately recording their responses to the surveys.

Gathering information from e-mail and telephone surveys

Some of Western Suites' information comes from telephone and e-mail surveys and from guest feedback at our Web site. When I talk to a customer over the phone, I ask many questions and listen carefully in order to obtain the most helpful information. Responses that come by e-mail and the Web site provide less information than telephone conversations.

Entering guest information

For first-time guests, I create new files and enter background information. Since many of the hotel's customers are returning guests, I open the existing files and update their information.

The challenges

Some guests write long responses about their experiences at the hotel. My challenge is to organize the information into short comment codes so that it is useful to the managers. This means that I have to look for the main idea of the guest's response.

GUEST COMMENTS

Figure 3.3 shows the bottom of a survey card that has been filled in by a guest. Compare it to the screen that I use to enter this data in Figure 3.4. I interpret the guests' answers to the survey questions and enter comment codes that I believe best represent their answers. Guests sometimes give more than one answer, or more than one comment code applies. The screen allows me to enter up to three comment codes for each question. If the guest's answer is complex, I have to decide which three comment codes provide the best information.

Comment Codes

Friendliness of staff	100	Quality of room service	275
Ease of check-in/check-out	125	Convenience/location	300
Comfort of room	150	Message center capability	325
Spaciousness of room	175	Computer port accessibility	350
Décor of room	200	Business center	375
Cleanliness of room	225	Fitness center	400
Speed of room service	250	Overall	425

Figure 3.3 Guest Satisfaction Card (bottom)

Which were the most enjoyable aspects of your visit at Western Suites?

The room was very clean, comfortable and large. I was very comfortable.

What could Western Suites have done differently in order to serve you better?

All the business services were poor. I couldn't get a port for my computer. My messages got lost, and the business center was inadequate.

Would you return to Western Suites? __✓__Yes ______No ______Maybe

Yes, Overall, I was satisfied.

For use with Activity 9

THE REAL WORLD

Everything that goes on behind the scenes in a hotel is for one purpose—to keep guests happy and get them to return. One of the important ways that hotel managers assure that guests will return is to survey them to find out what they like and dislike, then to correct problems or make changes.

Guest is a hotel's term for customer.

As a customer satisfaction clerk, I have three main tasks:

- To organize and categorize information from guest surveys.
- To enter guest survey information into the computer database.
- To make sure that all guest information in the hotel's computers is correct and up to date.

Reading and sorting guest satisfaction surveys

Most of Western Suites' information about guest satisfaction comes from survey cards completed by overnight guests. These cards consist of (1) items that guests rate according to how satisfied they were and (2) longer comments they write to describe their experiences at the hotel. My job is to read and interpret all the responses and then to enter the information into a form the hotel managers can read quickly and easily.

Give guests quality service by accurately recording their responses to the surveys.

Gathering information from e-mail and telephone surveys

Some of Western Suites' information comes from telephone and e-mail surveys and from guest feedback at our Web site. When I talk to a customer over the phone, I ask many questions and listen carefully in order to obtain the most helpful information. Responses that come by e-mail and the Web site provide less information than telephone conversations.

Entering guest information

For first-time guests, I create new files and enter background information. Since many of the hotel's customers are returning guests, I open the existing files and update their information.

The challenges

Some guests write long responses about their experiences at the hotel. My challenge is to organize the information into short comment codes so that it is useful to the managers. This means that I have to look for the main idea of the guest's response.

A guest satisfaction card is left in each hotel room each day. The staff picks up the cards that have been filled out and sends them to me. I read each card, interpret the information, and enter it in the computer.

One part of the survey gives the guests several choices for rating their level of satisfaction with services and features the hotel provides. For this part, I key a number that matches the guest's rating. When a guest gives a longer, more complex comment, I read the response carefully and give it a comment code based on a standard list of codes provided by the hotel. That's harder to do. The top of the guest survey card is shown in Figure 3.1. The bottom is shown in Figure 3.3. This card is an example of one that has been filled out by a customer.

Figure 3.1 Guest Satisfaction Card (top)

Guest Satisfaction Survey

We hope you enjoyed your stay at Western Suites! In order to serve you better in the future, we would appreciate receiving your opinion about your stay. Please take a minute to fill out this card and leave it in your room at the end of your visit. Thank you!

Name: Norman Herndon Date of visit: 05/16/200x

Street Address: 415 E Lehigh Ave.

City, State, Zip Code: Duluth MN 55805-0753

Telephone: 218-555-0158

(Please circle your rating for each item listed below.)

Satisfaction Ratings:	Excellent	Very Good	Good	Satisfactory	Poor	Didn't Use
Friendliness of staff	5	(4)	3	2	1	0
Ease/speed of check-in/check-out	5	4	(3)	2	1	0
Comfort of room	(5)	4	3	2	1	0
Spaciousness of room	5	(4)	3	2	1	0
Décor	5	(4)	3	2	1	0
Cleanliness of room	(5)	4	3	2	1	0
Speed of room service	5	(4)	3	2	1	0
Quality of room service	5	4	(3)	2	1	0
Convenience/location	5	(4)	3	2	1	0
Message center capability	5	4	3	2	(1)	0
Computer port accessibility	5	4	3	2	(1)	0
Business center	5	4	3	2	(1)	0
Fitness center	5	4	(3)	2	1	0
Overall	5	(4)	3	2	1	0

For use with Activity 9

The first computer screen I use for entering information from the guest survey cards is shown in Figure 3.2. Though my screen is similar to the actual card, it is not identical. Compare my screen shown in Figure 3.2 to Figure 3.1. The guest circles the satisfaction ratings, but I key these choices.

Figure 3.2 Card Survey (Screen 1)

Western Suites **Card Surveys**
Guest Satisfaction

Rate (ksph)	Errors

Key data into appropriate fields. Tab between fields.

1 Last Name: Herndon First Name: Norman
2 Date of visit: 05 / 16 / 2007 3 ZIP code: 55805-0753
Street Address: 415 E. Lehigh Ave.
City: Duluth State: MN Phone: 218-555-0158

4 **Satisfaction Ratings:**

Friendliness of Staff:	4	Ease/speed of check-in/out:	3
Comfort of room:	5	Spaciousness of room:	4
Décor:	4	Cleanliness:	5
Speed of room service:	4	Quality of room service:	3
Convenience/location:	4	Message center capability:	1
Computer port accessibility:	1	Business center equipment:	1
Fitness center equipment:	3	Overall rating:	4

Proceed through all forms for each client

RECORD: 1 2 3 4 5 6 7 8 9 10 11 12 13 14 15 16 Evaluate

For use with Activity 9

1 **Name:** The guest's name is entered here as it appears on the survey card.

2 **Date of visit:** The date the guest registered at Western Suites is entered; the length of stay is not important.

3 **Zip Code:** Only the guest's Zip code is entered. The remainder of the address and the telephone number fill automatically from information that was obtained when the guest registered.

4 **Satisfaction Ratings:** The ratings circled by the guest are entered in the blank fields.

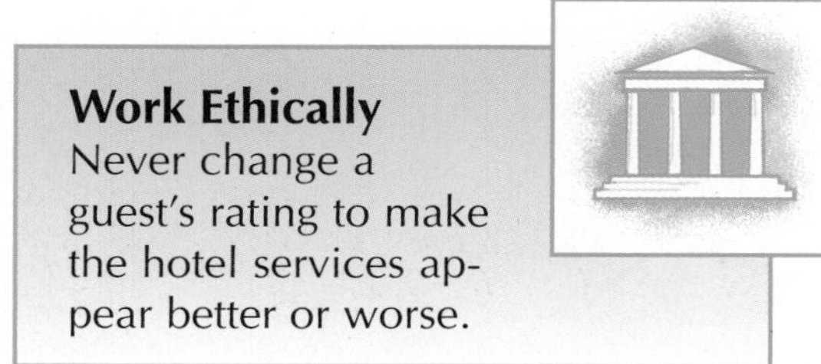

Work Ethically
Never change a guest's rating to make the hotel services appear better or worse.

GUEST COMMENTS

Figure 3.3 shows the bottom of a survey card that has been filled in by a guest. Compare it to the screen that I use to enter this data in Figure 3.4. I interpret the guests' answers to the survey questions and enter comment codes that I believe best represent their answers. Guests sometimes give more than one answer, or more than one comment code applies. The screen allows me to enter up to three comment codes for each question. If the guest's answer is complex, I have to decide which three comment codes provide the best information.

Comment Codes

Friendliness of staff	100	Quality of room service	275
Ease of check-in/check-out	125	Convenience/location	300
Comfort of room	150	Message center capability	325
Spaciousness of room	175	Computer port accessibility	350
Décor of room	200	Business center	375
Cleanliness of room	225	Fitness center	400
Speed of room service	250	Overall	425

Figure 3.3 Guest Satisfaction Card (bottom)

Which were the most enjoyable aspects of your visit at Western Suites?

The room was very clean, comfortable and large. I was very comfortable.

What could Western Suites have done differently in order to serve you better?

All the business services were poor. I couldn't get a port for my computer. My messages got lost, and the business center was inadequate.

Would you return to Western Suites? __✓__ Yes ______ No ______ Maybe

Yes, Overall, I was satisfied.

For use with Activity 9

Figure 3.4 Card Survey (Screen 2)

Western Suites Card Surveys
Guest Comments

Rate (ksph)	Errors

Key data into appropriate fields. Tab between fields.

Guest Comments:

(5) Which were the most enjoyable aspects of your visit at Western Suites?

[225] [175] [150]

(6) What could Western Suites have done differently to serve you better?

[375] [350] [325]

(7) Would you return to Western Suites? [X] Yes [ ] No [ ] Maybe

Proceed through all forms for each client

RECORD: 1 2 3 4 5 6 7 8 9 10 11 12 13 14 15 16 Evaluate Next Record

For use with Activity 9

(5) **Which were the most enjoyable aspects of your visit at Western Suites?** Analyze the customer's answer to this question and interpret the response. Enter up to three Comment Codes that most closely match what the customer has written. If the guest includes more than three comments, enter just the first three comments.

If a guest comments, "I liked the hotel because my room was comfortable," I enter 150 in one of the blanks. If the guest also says, "The room service food was great, and I really liked the fitness center," I enter 275 and 400 in the other blanks.

When a comment is complex, break it down into smaller parts.

(6) **What could Western Suites have done differently to serve you better?** Enter up to three Comment Codes that most closely match what the customer has written. If the guest includes more than three comments, enter only the first three comments.

If a guest comments, "There was a long line at check-in," I enter 125 in one of the blanks. A comment such as, "I couldn't find a computer port, and the business center wasn't up to date," leads me to enter 350 and 375.

(7) **Would you return to Western Suites?** Place an X in the box that applies.

Telephone Surveys

When guests stay at Western Suites on a regular basis, they are unlikely to fill out satisfaction cards each time. To stay in touch with these repeat guests, I contact them by telephone and ask about their experiences at our hotel. I ask a few questions that are not included on the in-room survey card and enter their responses as we talk. My telephone script is shown in Figure 3.5. The screens I filled in as I surveyed a guest over the phone are shown in Figure 3.6, 3.7, and 3.8.

1. **Guest information:** The guest's name, the current date, the address, telephone number, date of last visit, number of visits in past year, and average length of stay fill automatically for each client. In the real world the operator would confirm this information with the customer.

2. **Satisfaction ratings:** Convert the guest's oral response to the appropriate code

   Excellent 5; Very Good 4; Good 3; Satisfactory 2; Poor 1; Did not use service 0. The codes are the same as those used in Card Surveys.

3. **What guest likes best about staying at Western Suites:** Enter up to three comment codes.

4. **What Western Suites could do differently to serve the guest better:** Three spaces are provided for entering the codes that most closely match the guest's answers to this question.

5. **Guest stays at Western Suites primarily on business trips, personal trips, or both:** Enter an X in the box that applies.

6. **Other hotels or accommodations the guest uses regularly:** Many popular hotels are listed in the following chart. If the guest names one of these, enter the number that corresponds. If other hotels are named, enter the number 15. Include the first three choices the customer gives.

Belterra's	01	Hueston Inn	06	Shadway Inn	11
Chase Lodge	02	Manchester	07	Traveler's Delight	12
Chester's	03	McKinney's Inn	08	Washington Ritz	13
DeSimone Hotel	04	Millennium Suites	09	Winton	14
Four Corners`	05	Remington	10	Other	15

Guest Satisfaction Telephone Survey

Customer name: Arthur Eagan Date of conversation: Current Date

Customer address: 894 E. Haines St.

City, State, Zip Code: Wilmington DE 19894

Telephone: 302-555-0170

Date of last visit: 04/25/200x Number of visits in past year: 4

Average length of stay (days): 3

How would you rate the following: Please say Excellent, Very Good, Good, Satisfactory, Poor. If you didn't use a service, please let me know.

Friendliness of staff? Very good

Ease/speed of check-in/check-out? Good

Comfort of room? Excellent

Spaciousness of room? Very good

Décor? Very good

Cleanliness of room? Excellent

Speed of room service? Didn't use

Quality of room service? Didn't use

Convenience/location? Very good

Message center capability? Didn't use

Computer port accessibility? Didn't use

Business center equipment? Didn't use

Fitness center equipment? Didn't use

Overall satisfaction? Very good

What do you like most about Western Suites?

The rooms are big and the staff is always friendly. The main thing I like, though, is the convenience.

What could we do differently to serve you better?

Everything's fine.

Do you stay at Western Suites primarily on ☑ business trips, ☐ personal trips, or ☐ both?

What other hotels or accommodations do you use regularly?

Executive Suites, Comfort Inn

For use with Activity 10

Figure 3.6 Telephone Survey (Screen 1)

Western Suites Telephone Surveys

Guest Information

Rate (ksph)	Errors

Key data into appropriate fields. Tab or strike ENTER to move to the next field.

1 Last Name: Eagan First Name: Arthur

Date of conversation: 07 / 29 / 2003

Street Address: 894 E. Haines St.

City: Wilmington State: DE ZIP code: 19894

Phone: (302) 555-0170

Date of last visit: 04 / 25 / 2004

Number of visits in past year: 4

Average length of stay: 3

Proceed through all forms for each client

RECORD: 1 2 3 4 5 6 7 8 9 10 11 12 Evaluate

For use with Activity 10

Figure 3.7 Telephone Survey (Screen 2)

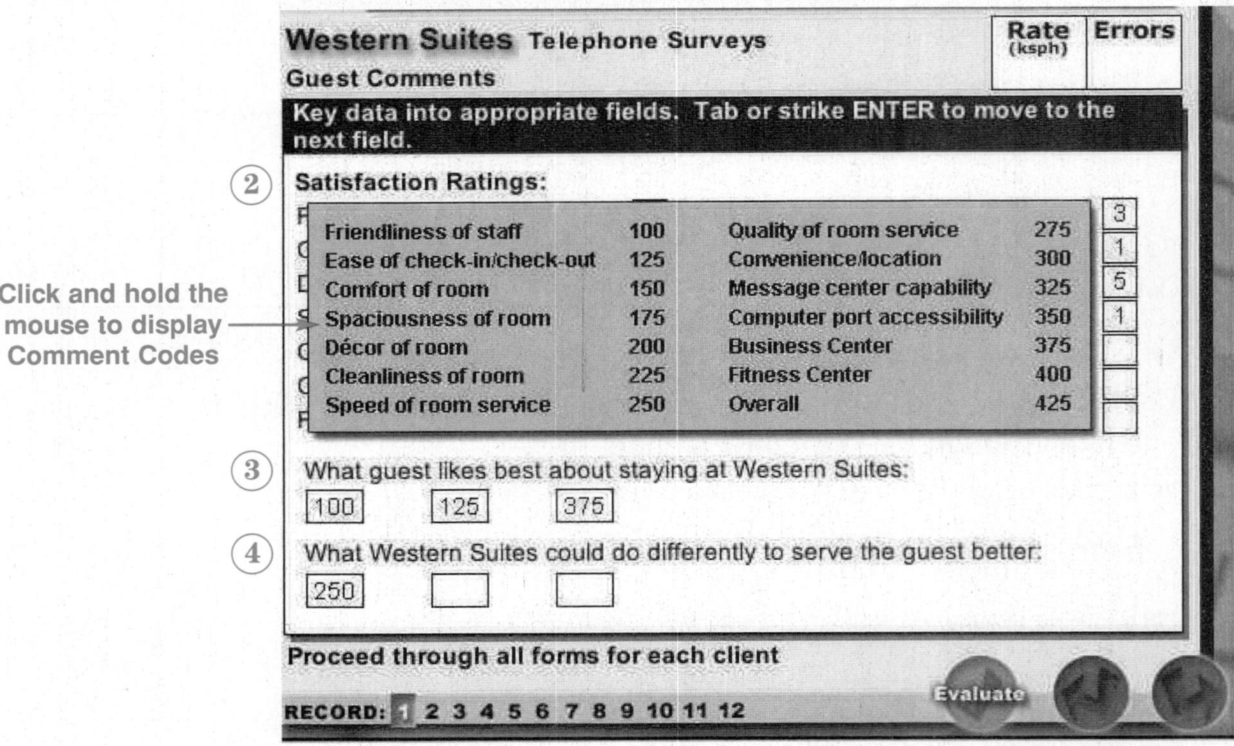

Western Suites Telephone Surveys

Guest Comments

Rate (ksph)	Errors

Key data into appropriate fields. Tab or strike ENTER to move to the next field.

2 **Satisfaction Ratings:**

Friendliness of staff	100	Quality of room service	275
Ease of check-in/check-out	125	Convenience/location	300
Comfort of room	150	Message center capability	325
Spaciousness of room	175	Computer port accessibility	350
Décor of room	200	Business Center	375
Cleanliness of room	225	Fitness Center	400
Speed of room service	250	Overall	425

3 1 5 1

Click and hold the mouse to display Comment Codes

3 What guest likes best about staying at Western Suites:

100 125 375

4 What Western Suites could do differently to serve the guest better:

250

Proceed through all forms for each client

RECORD: 1 2 3 4 5 6 7 8 9 10 11 12 Evaluate

For use with Activity 10

Figure 3.8 Telephone Survey (Screen 3)

Western Suites Telephone Surveys

Guest Comments

Rate (ksph)	Errors

Key data into appropriate fields. Tab or strike ENTER to move to the next field.

5 Guest stays at Western Suites primarily on business trips, personal trips, or both?

- [ ] Business
- [ ] Personal
- [X] Business and Personal

(Hit "x" to "check" a box.)

6 Other hotels or accommodations the guest uses regularly: 01 03 05

Hotel Key

Belterra's	01	Hueston Inn	06	Shadway Inn	11
Chase Lodge	02	Manchester	07	Traveler's Delight	12
Chester's	03	McKinney's Inn	08	Washington Ritz	13
DeSimone Hotel	04	Millennium Suites	09	Winton	14
Four Corners'	05	Remington	10	Other	15

Proceed through all forms for each client

RECORD: 1 2 3 4 5 6 7 8 9 10 11 12

Evaluate Next Record

For use with Activity 10

E-mail Surveys

Western Suites' management often surveys guests by e-mail in order to reduce the time needed for telephone interviews. An e-mail form is sent to the guest, who fills it out and sends a Reply e-mail. Figure 3.9 is an illustration of an e-mail survey that has been completed by a guest.

Figures 3.10 and 3.11 show the screens I use to enter the results of e-mail surveys. Since some guests write a lot of comments, the trickiest part of handling e-mail surveys is reducing the guests' comments to a few codes.

(1) **Guest name, e-mail address, and date of e-mail:** I key this information from the e-mail. The other fields containing the guest's address and personal history at the hotel fill automatically.

(2-5) **Satisfaction Ratings:** These responses are the same as the Telephone Survey.

(6) **Hotel code:** Enter the hotel codes for the first three choices the guest made.

1 **From:** Michael Vorion <mvorion@msb.com>
To: manager@westernsuites.com
Date: June 6, 200x
Subject: Western Suites Customer Satisfaction Survey

2-5 Please enter a number rating for each service or feature. The ratings are
5 Excellent **4** Very Good **3** Good **2** Satisfactory **1** Poor **0** Didn't Use

Satisfaction Ratings

Friendliness of Staff	5	Quality of room service	5
Ease/speed of check-in/out	4	Convenience/location	4
Comfort of room	4	Message center capability	5
Spaciousness of room	5	Computer port accessibility	2
Décor	0	Business center equipment	2
Cleanliness of room	5	Fitness center	0
Speed of room service	5	Overall	5

What do you like most about Western Suites?
The personal attention. The management keeps a record of my visits and the staff always greets me by name and knows my preferences and habits. The huge, clean rooms are a close second.

What could we do differently to serve you better?
Nothing; I am very happy with the service.

Do you stay at Western Suites primarily on business trips, personal trips, or both?
Both

6 **What other hotels or accommodations do you use regularly?**
Millennium Suites, Remington

For use with Activity 11

Figure 3.10 E-mail Questionnaires (Screen 1)

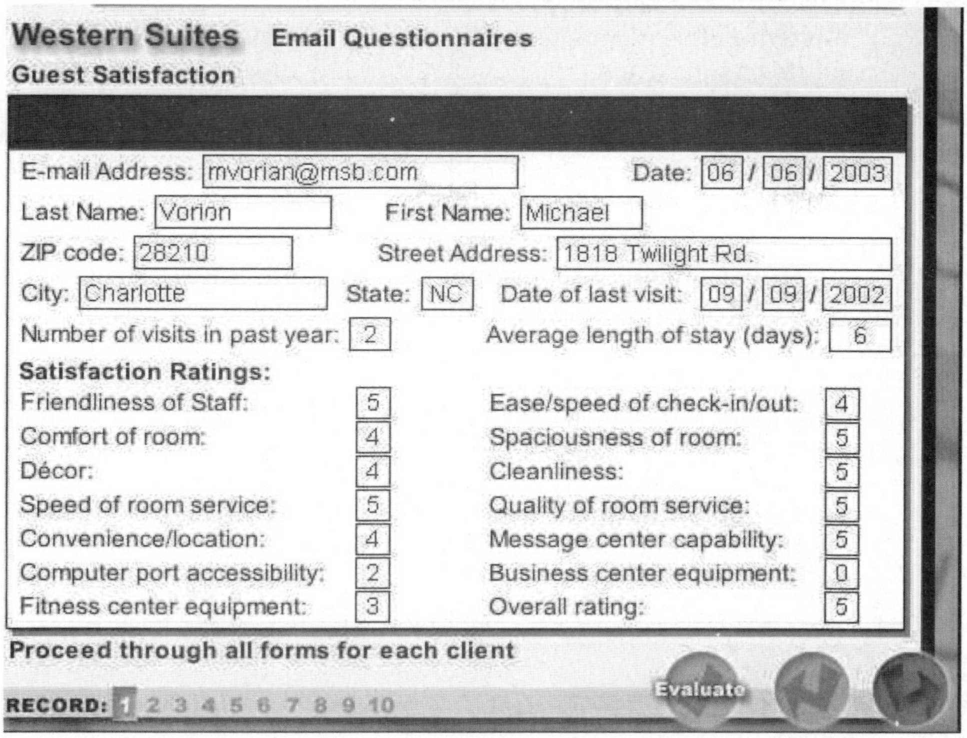

Western Suites **Email Questionnaires**

Guest Satisfaction

① E-mail Address: mvorian@msb.com Date: 06 / 06 / 2003
Last Name: Vorion First Name: Michael
ZIP code: 28210 Street Address: 1818 Twilight Rd.
City: Charlotte State: NC Date of last visit: 09 / 09 / 2002

Number of visits in past year: 2 Average length of stay (days): 6

② **Satisfaction Ratings:**

Friendliness of Staff:	5	Ease/speed of check-in/out:	4
Comfort of room:	4	Spaciousness of room:	5
Décor:	4	Cleanliness:	5
Speed of room service:	5	Quality of room service:	5
Convenience/location:	4	Message center capability:	5
Computer port accessibility:	2	Business center equipment:	0
Fitness center equipment:	3	Overall rating:	5

Proceed through all forms for each client

RECORD: 1 2 3 4 5 6 7 8 9 10 Evaluate

For use with Activity 11

Figure 3.11 E-mail Questionnaires (Screen 2)

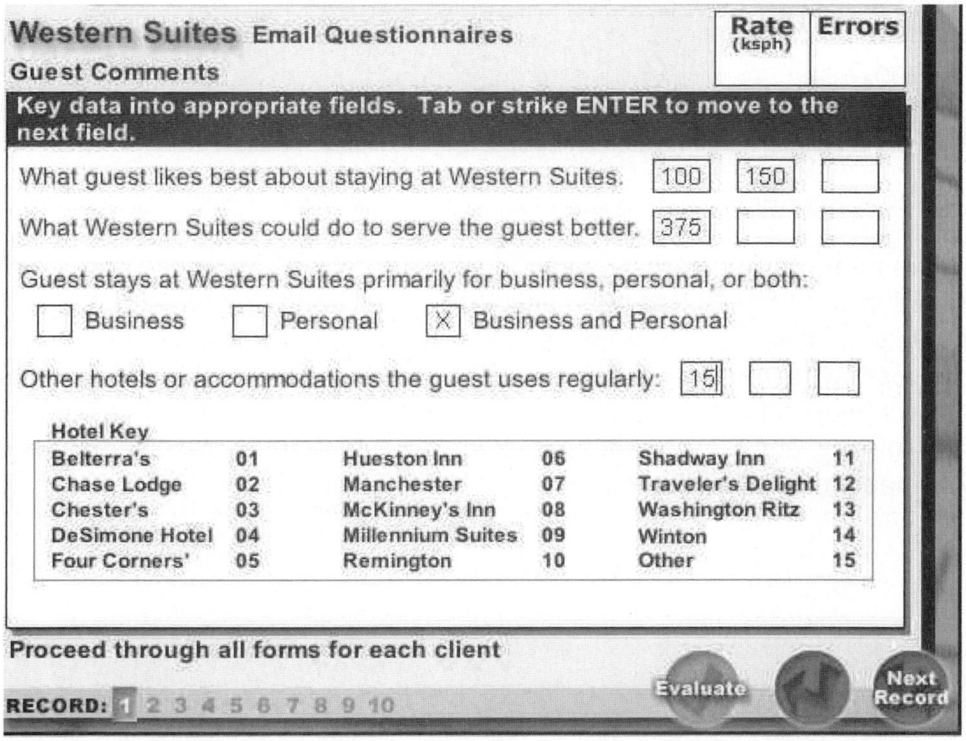

Western Suites **Email Questionnaires** Rate (ksph) Errors

Guest Comments

Key data into appropriate fields. Tab or strike ENTER to move to the next field.

③ What guest likes best about staying at Western Suites. 100 150

④ What Western Suites could do to serve the guest better. 375

⑤ Guest stays at Western Suites primarily for business, personal, or both:

☐ Business ☐ Personal ☒ Business and Personal

⑥ Other hotels or accommodations the guest uses regularly: 15

Hotel Key

Belterra's	01	Hueston Inn	06	Shadway Inn	11
Chase Lodge	02	Manchester	07	Traveler's Delight	12
Chester's	03	McKinney's Inn	08	Washington Ritz	13
DeSimone Hotel	04	Millennium Suites	09	Winton	14
Four Corners'	05	Remington	10	Other	15

Proceed through all forms for each client

RECORD: 1 2 3 4 5 6 7 8 9 10 Evaluate Next Record

For use with Activity 11

Web Site Feedback

Western Suites maintains a guest feedback page on its Web site where guests can make specific comments at any time. The feedback page does not ask all the detailed questions that appear on the survey forms. I read the guests' comments and enter the appropriate comment codes and summaries into my screen. Figure 3.12 shows the Web site feedback screen and Figure 3.13 shows my data entry screen.

1. **Guest name and personal information:** Enter the guest's name. The guest's address, date of last visit, number of visits in the past year, and the average length of stay fill automatically.

2. **Phone number and e-mail address:** Enter the guest's phone number and e-mail address.

3. **Comment codes:** Guests make both positive and negative comments. Enter the appropriate codes. See Comment Codes on page 114.

Figure 3.12 Web Site Feedback Form

Guest's Web Site Feedback

Name: Rosemary Thornton

Zip code: 99705

Today's date: 00/00/200x

Phone number: 907-555-0175

Email address: rthornton@rol.net

Comments: I just want to acknowledge the wonderful service I received from the manager on duty the night I arrived at your hotel. I had been delayed at the airport and had not had a chance to call to inform the hotel management that I would miss the arrival deadline. According to hotel policy, I should have lost my reservation, but the manager on duty, Mary Robbins, was extremely kind and went out of her way to have an extra room cleaned so that I would have a place to stay. She made my check-in easy, and I was made to feel very welcome and I greatly appreciate the extra effort that was made to accommodate me.

For use with Activity 12

Figure 3.13 Web Feedback Screen

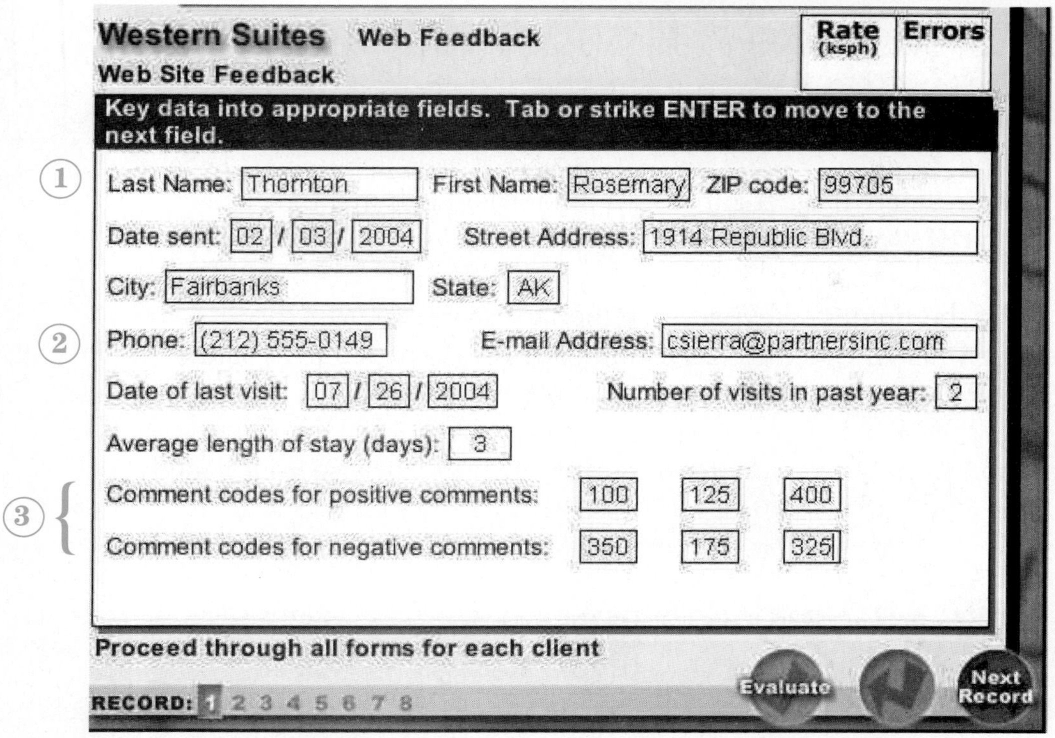

Western Suites Web Feedback

Web Site Feedback

Rate (ksph)	Errors

Key data into appropriate fields. Tab or strike ENTER to move to the next field.

① Last Name: Thornton First Name: Rosemary ZIP code: 99705

Date sent: 02 / 03 / 2004 Street Address: 1914 Republic Blvd.

City: Fairbanks State: AK

② Phone: (212) 555-0149 E-mail Address: csierra@partnersinc.com

Date of last visit: 07 / 26 / 2004 Number of visits in past year: 2

Average length of stay (days): 3

③ Comment codes for positive comments: 100 125 400

Comment codes for negative comments: 350 175 325

Proceed through all forms for each client

RECORD: 1 2 3 4 5 6 7 8 Evaluate Next Record

For use with Activity 12

Warmup

Before entering the data for Activity 9, practice your data entry skills.

Step 1: Open the Data Entry software.

Step 2: From the Main menu, select Project Lab. From the Project Lab menu, select Western Suites. Then select *WARMUP* from the Activity menu.

Step 3: Enter the data using the numeric keypad. Key the information across the screen. *Tab* to move between fields. Use the slash on the Numeric Keypad to separate parts of the date. Your speed and accuracy will be displayed at the end of the Warmup.

Step 4: You may repeat the Warmup as many times as you wish to increase your speed or accuracy.

642-555-6197	61524	326	05/02/2001	59283
965-555-3164	62301	876	01/31/2002	39826
674-555-1023	94782	420	11/30/1999	02983
602-555-7916	43161	216	02/05/2003	02946
963-555-7016	94782	210	11/26/1975	23986
156-555-4716	97450	647	07/15/1974	21039
247-555-9124	97485	826	08/24/1989	10846
876-555-7247	97448	510	11/19/2001	10484
890-555-2386	30415	419	07/05/2001	10937
129-555-9823	61027	982	09/10/2002	40598

Activity 9

Enter Card Surveys

In Activity 9, you will enter responses from 16 guest satisfaction survey cards. Each card requires completing two screens.

Step 1: Remove all Guest Satisfaction cards from the back of this book. These are marked with a large 9.

Step 2: From the Western Suites Welcome screen, select **Activity 9**.

Step 3: The *Guest Satisfaction* screen shown in Figure 3.2 appears. Instructions for completing the screen follow.

Guest information

Enter the guest's last name. The first name, address, and phone number will fill automatically. For the date of visit, enter the current year (for example, enter 04 02 2004).

Satisfaction ratings

Use the keypad to enter the rating the guest circled for each item on the survey. Use the keypad and press ENTER after each field.

Step 4: Proofread and correct errors. Move to the next screen.

Step 5:

Satisfaction rating

In the Guest Comments screen, enter the codes that best correspond to the guest's response. If fewer than three comment codes are needed, leave the additional spaces blank. If the guest did not respond to a question, enter no codes; you must Tab through each of the three columns, however, even if a code is not required. Note: Hold down the mouse to display the codes on your screen, or refer to page 114.

BE ALERT!
Sometimes the answer to "Would you return?" is not a simple yes, no, or maybe. A guest may write "probably" or "if I'm in the neighborhood" or something else. Use your judgment regarding the blank that applies.

Would guest return

Place an X in the blank that applies. Tab between fields.

Step 6: Proofread and correct errors. After you have made all corrections to a record, turn the source document over to indicate that you are finished with it. Move to the next record.

Step 7: After entering and proofreading all surveys, select the **Evaluate** button to check your work. If errors occur in one or more records, edit and evaluate as you have done in Projects 1 and 2.

Activity 10

Telephone Surveys

In Activity 10, you will enter responses from 12 telephone surveys. Check that the Audio Preference is on. The audio will play automatically as you tab to each field. The audio will simulate a phone conversation between the Western Suites representative (you) and the guest.

Option: You may also choose to complete this activity using the Guest Satisfaction Telephone Surveys from the back of the book. The forms are numbered 10-1, 10-2, 10-3. Enter the forms in sequential order.

Step 1: Select **Activity 10** from the Activity menu located at the top of the screen.

Step 2: **Screen 1** of *Telephone Surveys* displays with all guest information filled in automatically. Move to the next screen.

Satisfaction ratings

(Screen 2) As you tab to each item, the audio portion of the interview will play automatically. Listen carefully and then enter the proper rating that corresponds to the guest's response. If you need to replay the conversation for a particular field, press Ctrl + A in the field.

Excellent = 5 Very good = 4 Good = 3 Satisfactory = 2 Poor = 1

Questions and answers

Use your interpretation skills to translate the guests' comments into comment codes. If a guest says "nothing" or if fewer than three comments codes are needed, leave the additional spaces blank. You will need to Tab through each of the three fields, however, even if they are blank.

Business/personal

(Screen 3) Enter an X in the blank that applies.

Other hotels

Enter the hotel codes that correspond to the hotels that the guest uses as a two-digit number. If the guest names a hotel that is not listed, code it as 15 or "Other." List only the first three choices. See Figure 3.11 for an illustration.

Step 3: Proofread and correct errors. After you have made all corrections to a record, turn the source document over on its face to indicate that you are finished with it.

Step 4: After entering and proofreading all telephone surveys, select the **Evaluate** button to check your work. If errors occur in one or more records, follow the procedures for editing and evaluating records.

Activity 11

E-mail Questionnaires

In Activity 11, you will enter responses from 10 e-mail questionnaires to hotel guests. The source documents are Reply e-mails from the guests.

Step 1: Remove all e-mails from the back of the book. These are marked with a large **11**.

Step 2: Select **Activity 11** from the Activity menu located at the top of the screen.

Step 3: **Screen 1** of the *E-mail Questionnaire* screen displays. Instructions for completing the screen follow.

Guest information

Enter the guest's e-mail address. Enter only the information between arrow brackets. For example, enter the date the message was sent. Enter the current year. The guest's address, telephone number, date of last visit, number of visits in past year, and average length of stay will fill in automatically.

Satisfaction ratings

Enter the satisfaction ratings that the guest listed.

Questions and answers, reasons for staying at Western Suites, and other hotels

(Screen 2) Follow the same procedure used in Activities 9 and 10. See page 114 for comments or hold down the left mouse.

Step 3: Proofread, make corrections, and move to the next record.

Step 4: Select the **Evaluate** button to check your work. If errors occur in one or more records, follow the procedure from before.

Activity 12

Web Feedback

In Activity 12, you will interpret and enter feedback from eight guests who made comments at the Western Suites Web site. Analyze the comments carefully and choose the appropriate comment codes. In this activity, satisfaction ratings are not provided.

Step 1: Remove all Web Surveys from the back of the book. These are marked with a large **12**.

Step 2: Select **Activity 12** from the Activity menu located at the top of the screen.

Step 3: The *Web site Feedback* screen displays. Instructions for completing the screen follow.

Guest information

Enter the guest's last name. Other guest information autofills. Click the insertion point in the first Comment Code box.

Comment codes

Read and analyze the comments to determine those that are positive and those that are negative. If a comment is positive, match it to its code and enter the code in the appropriate space. Do the same for negative comments. A maximum of three negative and three positive codes may be entered.

Step 4: Proofread, make corrections, and move to the next record.

Step 5: Select the **Evaluate** button to check your work. If errors occur in one or more records, follow the standard procedures for correcting errors.

STRETCH . . . .

Now that you've learned to enter data for card and telephone surveys and for e-mail and Web sites, it's time to stretch your data entry speed and accuracy.

Step 1: From the Western Suites Activity menu, choose **Stretch**.

Step 2: Enter all information from the following chart as accurately and as quickly as possible. Do not stop to edit.

Step 3: Review your performance by selecting the **Evaluate** button to check your work.

Step 4: Repeat this activity to increase your speed by 10 *ksph*.

08/27/2005	Bruce Harkins	842-555-9624	462 Gratz St.	33671
03/18/2008	Amanda Oslick	682-555-3307	6394 Almond Dr.	61458
06/12/2008	Dr. Ward	314-555-3702	6229 Robins Ave.	96134
10/27/2007	Kevin Majus	926-555-2077	599 Devereux Rd.	61452
06/14/2006	Malachi O'Reilly	944-555-0681	234 S. Dungee Rd.	99478
09/12/2006	Josefa Martinez	346-555-9142	475 W. Poplar Ln.	41776
10/14/2008	Lien Phan	296-555-9421	6797 Palmetto Ave.	94126
02/14/2007	Claude Wildstein	246-555-9124	8735 Warsaw Ave.	62994
05/14/2006	Shawn Brozena	612-555-8863	1782 Lincoln Hwy.	87291

Project 4
General Hospital

General Hospital

Walk into General Hospital on the outskirts of Dallas, and you'll see a busy medical center that treats people who suffer from a variety of short-term or long-term illnesses. The hospital is well known for its excellent patient treatment and for the worldwide respect its physicians receive.

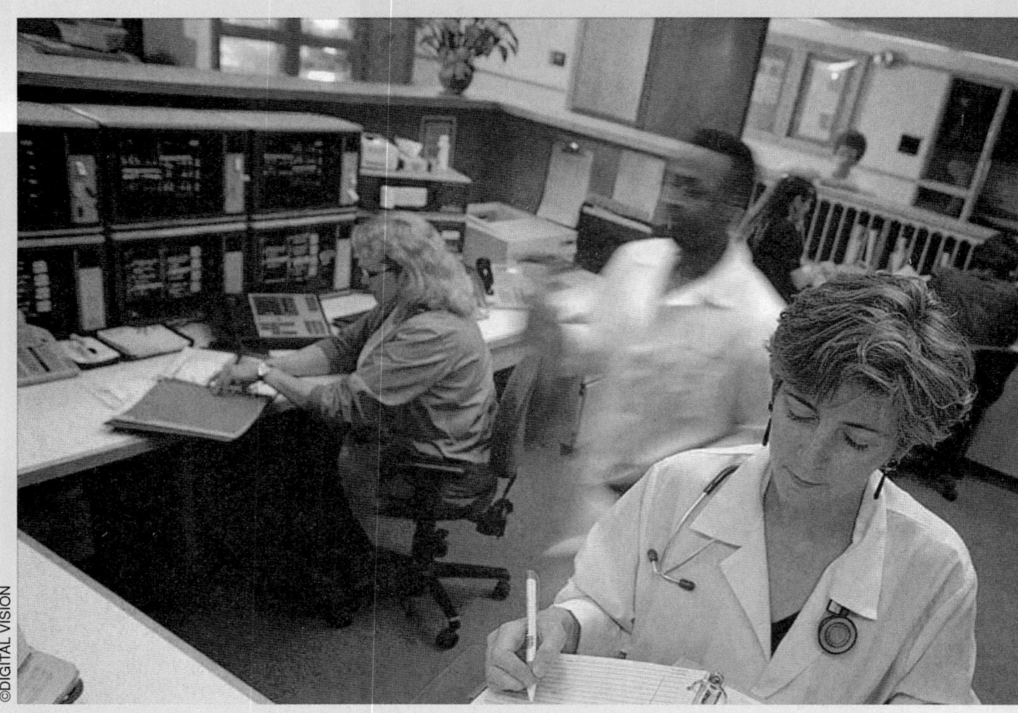

Your Activities Today

- ➢8–11:00 A.M. — Admit out-patients for service
- ➢12:00 noon to 3 P.M. — Update patient files
- ➢3–5 P.M. — Create coding charts

New Knowledge and Skills

In this project, you will:

- ➢Enter personal information about new patients
- ➢Update information about current or previous patients
- ➢Input diagnosis and procedure codes
- ➢Use a variety of source documents

CAREER PROFILE

Data Entry Specialist/Admitting Clerk

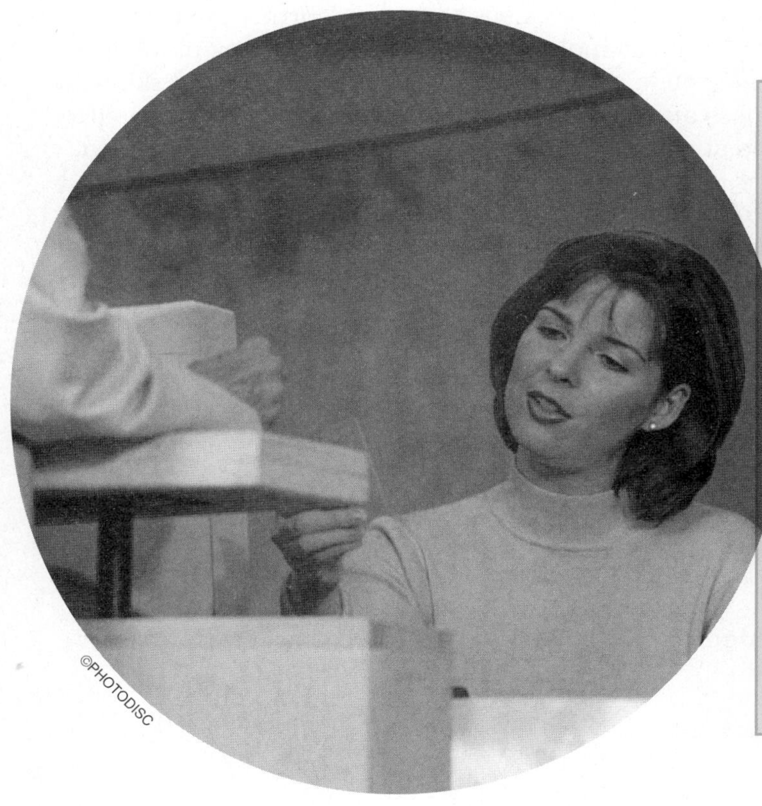

"Being a data entry specialist in the admitting office at General Hospital involves more than just keying numbers. In addition to communicating with patients and staff to obtain the correct information to enter, I must also understand medical terminology and medical coding procedures."

What I do every day

The admitting desk is the first stop patients make after arriving at the hospital for treatment or services. After I greet patients, I ask questions to obtain their personal and insurance information; then I enter the information into the hospital's database. In addition, I review the paperwork they bring from their referring physicians and enter the medical codes that identify the services or procedures to be performed.

Since patients receive services in different departments of the hospital, the information I enter can be recalled on each department's computers. Sometimes other departments add information. At the end of each patient's visit the Billing Department compiles all details about the treatments or services provided then bills the patient or the appropriate insurance company.

The best part of my job

Handling details and working with computers is what I like best about my job as a data entry specialist in the Admitting Department of General Hospital. I also like working directly with patients.

The worst part of my job

It's stressful to burden patients with questions when they are in pain or afraid of an upcoming procedure. I try to be sensitive in each situation.

What I need to know and be able to do

Entering complex or coded medical data into a computer quickly and accurately is the key to my success. It's also important for me to recognize when something is incorrect about the information I receive. When I see a mistake, I have to decide what steps to take to correct the problem. I need to know medical terminology, have an understanding of medical coding, be a good speller, and possess excellent proofreading skills. Exhibiting friendliness and understanding are important traits, too, since I must put patients at ease so I can probe for confidential information.

How I prepared to be a data entry clerk

During high school I took as many computer courses as I could, starting with keyboarding. Then I enrolled in a data entry program at a local career college. There I built my skills and took a variety of courses that provided a good background in working with customers. The hospital gave me additional training in medical terminology and medical coding.

How I could have prepared better

Accuracy on the 10-key pad has always been my biggest problem. If I had tried harder during school to increase my speed and accuracy, I would have scored better on the pre-employment test and been able to begin at a higher level. That would have meant a better starting salary.

Education needed: High school diploma plus data entry training or experience is required.

Salary range: $16,000 – $33,000

Job outlook: Job prospects will be favorable for individuals with the best technical skills, particularly those who show expertise with medical terminology, medical codes, and computer software applications.

Related jobs: Word processor, customer service representative, file clerk, receptionist, and order taker.

THE REAL WORLD

The admitting office of any hospital is a busy, sometimes chaotic, place. Many concerned patients and their worried relatives sit, stand, or wander around the office. Some may be crying. On a really challenging day, I enter information for 50 or more patients.

My work as an admitting room data entry specialist has two primary purposes:

- To enter personal information that starts the patient's billing record.
- To enter medical information that identifies (1) treatments, procedures, and services that will be performed for the patient and (2) the preliminary diagnosis of the patient's medical problem.

Identifying Treatments, Procedures, and Services

Patients arrive at the hospital with an Out-Patient Service Order completed by their primary care or referring physician. This form contains important information, including the physician's preliminary diagnosis of the patient's medical problem and the treatments, procedures, and services to be performed for the patient by the hospital.

After I enter personal information in the patient's record, I enter medical codes from the Out-Patient Service Order. I send the file electronically to each department where the patient will receive assistance or I print a copy for the patient to take along.

Here is a sample of the codes I enter and their matching information.

Code	Code No.	Diagnosis or Service
ICD	783.0	Anorexia (Diagnosis)
ICD	550.90	Inguinal hernia (Diagnosis)
ICD	788.41	Urinary frequency (Diagnosis)
CPT	81003	Urinalysis (Service)
CPT	85014	Hematocrit (Service)
CPT	71020	Chest X-ray, 2 views (Service)

BE ALERT!
ICD stands for International Statistical classification of Diseases and Related Health Problems. ICD codes identify a patient's diagnoses.

BE ALERT!
CPT Stands for Current Procedural Terminology. CPT codes identify treatments, procedures, and services that a patient receives.

Preparing to Bill

At every step of the treatment or service, the hospital staff accesses the patient's computer file and adds to the information. At the end of the hospital visit, the billing department retrieves the file, compiles a list of all services, and prints a bill that goes to the patient and to the patient's insurance company. The insurer may be a federal government program such as Medicare or Medicaid.

The Challenges

Compiling information from patients requires sensitivity and understanding. Sometimes patients forget their insurance information, so I help them call a family member to obtain what is needed, or I encourage them to return at another time with the information. Often, doctors fail to provide complete information on their Out-Patient Service Order. In this case, I have to call the doctor's office to obtain the information. Calling slows me down, which frustrates both the patients and me.

©Getty Images/PhotoDisc

Patient Information Form

A patient's arrival at the hospital's admitting office, whether for out-patient or in-patient treatment, starts a flow of information that is updated each time the person returns. This information includes:

- personal facts about the patient
- information about the person who is responsible for paying the bill
- insurance information

When patients arrive in the Admitting Room, they are given a Patient Information form to complete. This form serves as the admitting clerk's primary source document. At some hospitals, the admitting clerk interviews new patients to obtain the needed information. A Patient Information form is shown in Figure 4.1.

Work Ethically
Close the door to your office so other patients waiting in the lobby will not overhear personal or confidential information that could be embarrassing to patients in your office

PATIENT INFORMATION

The Patient Information screen shown in Figure 4.2 is the first screen I use for entering data about new patients. This screen is only for personal information about the patients.

BE ALERT!
The person responsible for paying a patient's hospital fees is called the *Insured* or *Guarantor*. The Insured or Guarantor may be the patient or another person, such as the patient's spouse or parent.

1. **Social Security No.:** The patient's social security number is entered here. Patients are identified by this number in each department where they receive services.

2. **Date of birth:** Enter the birth date here.

3. **Patient's name:** Enter the name in the order shown, beginning with the last name.

4. **Sex:** An X indicates whether the patient is Male or Female.

5. **Patient's address:** The Zip code precedes the city and state in the software. Enter the Zip code and the patient's street address; the city and state fill automatically.

6. **Patient's telephone numbers:** Both the home and work numbers are entered here.

7. **Occupation and employer information:** The patient's occupation and the employer's name, address, Zip code, and telephone number are entered; the city and state fill in automatically. If the patient is in school, the occupation is entered as Student.

Figure 4.1 patient Information Form

Patient Information

To all returning patients: Fill in only the blanks that have changed since your last visit.

Social Security No.: ____________________ Date of Birth: ____________________ Sex: ❑ M ❑ F

Patient's Last Name: ____________________ First: ____________________ MI: ______

Patient's Address: ____

City: ____________________ State: __________ Zip Code: __________

Patient Home Telephone No.: (_____) _____-_______ Patient Work Telephone: (_____) _____-_______

Occupation: ____________________ Employer: ____________________

Employer Address: ____

City: ____________________ State: ______ Zip Code: __________ Telephone: (_____) _____-_______

Primary Care Physician No.: _____ Primary Care Physician Name: ____________________

Insured Information

Primary Insured's Last Name: ____________________ First: ____________________ MI: ______

Primary Insured's Address: ____

City: ____________________ State: __________ Zip Code: __________

Primary Insured's Social Security No.: ____________________ Insured's Telephone: (_____) _____-_______

Primary Insured's Occupation: ____________________ Employer: ____________________

Employer Address: ____

City: ____________________ State: ______ Zip Code: __________ Telephone: (_____) _____-_______

Relationship of Patient to Insured: ❑ Self ❑ Spouse ❑ Dependent

Secondary Insured's Last Name: ____________________ First: ____________________ MI: ___

Secondary Insured's Address: ____

City: ____________________ State: __________ Zip Code: __________

Secondary Insured's Social Security No.: ____________________ Insured's Telephone: (_____) _____-_______

Secondary Insured's Occupation: ____________________ Employer: ____________________

Employer Address: ____

City: ____________________ State: ______ Zip Code: __________ Telephone: (_____) _____-_______

Relationship of Patient to Insured: ❑ Self ❑ Spouse ❑ Dependent

Primary Insurance

Primary Insurance: ❑ United ❑ MetHealth ❑ TexMut ❑ Medicare

Other Insurance Company Name: ____

Insurance Company Address: ____

City: ____________________ State: ______ Zip Code: __________ Telephone: (_____) _____-_______

Policy No.: ____________________ Group No.: ____________________

Secondary Insurance

Secondary Insurance Company: ____

Insurance Company Address: ____

City: ____________________ State: __________ Zip Code: __________

Policy No.: ____________________ Group No.: ____________________

For use with Activities 15, 16, 17

Figure 4.2 Patient Information (Screen 1)

General Hospital **Patient Information**

Patient Information

Rate (ksph)	Errors

Key data into appropriate fields. Tab or strike ENTER to move to the next field.

① Social Security No.: 915-55-6174 Date of Birth: 02 / 04 / 1956 ②

③ Patient's Last Name: Mitchell First: Laurie MI: R

④ Sex: [ ] M [X] F ⑤ Patient's Address: 1306 Thornwood Circle

Zip code: 75053 City: Grand Prairie State: TX

⑥ Patient Home Phone No. (214) 555-0185 Work Phone No. (214) 555-0192

⑦ Occupation: Architect Employer: B & J Contractors

Employer's Address: 38 Lincoln Lane

Zip code: 75053 City: Grand Prairie State: TX

Telephone No. (214) 555-0192

Primary Care Physician Last Name: Sanchez First: Carlos

⑧ Primary Care Physician No: 8

Proceed through all forms for each client

RECORD: 1 2 3 4 5 6 7 8 9 10 11 12 Evaluate

For use with Activities 15, 16, 17

⑧ **Primary care physician name and code:** After the physician's name is entered, the identifying code for the physician will fill in automatically.

INSURED INFORMATION

Work Ethically
Never share information about a patient, a client, or a customer

After I complete the Patient Information screen, two Insured Information screens display. All information about the persons carrying the insurance for the patient is entered on these screens. Some patients are insured by more than one company. For example, both the mother and father of a child may carry insurance through their work. One of the companies will be designated as the primary carrier and the other as the secondary. For some patients, Medicare or Medicaid serves as the primary carrier. The Insured Information screen matches the Insured Information part of the Patient Information form. Information about the primary insurance provider is shown in Figure 4.3.

⑨ **Primary insured's name, address, Social Security number, and telephone number:** The hospital needs complete information about the primary person who will pay the bill. This person is called the primary insured. This may be the patient or a parent, guardian or spouse.

⑩ **Primary insured's occupation:** Enter the appropriate information. The city and state names fill automatically when the Zip code is entered. If the insured is in school, the occupation is *Student*.

Figure 4.3 Primary Insured Information (Screen 2)

General Hospital Patient Information

Primary Insured Information

Rate (ksph)	Errors

Key data into appropriate fields. Tab or strike ENTER to move to the next field.

9 Primary Insured's Last Name: Mitchell First: Laurie MI: R
Primary Insured's Address: 1306 Thornwood Circle
Zip code: 75053 City: Grand Prairie State: TX
Primary Insured's Social Security No.: 915-55-6174
Primary Insured's Phone No. (214) 555-0185

10 Primary Insured's Occupation: Architect
Employer: B & J Contractors
Primary Insured's Employer's Address: 38 Lincoln Lane
Zip code: 75053 City: Grand Prairie State: TX
Telephone No. (214) 555-0192

11 Relationship of Patient to Insured: [X] Self [ ] Spouse [ ] Dependent

Proceed through all forms for each client

RECORD: 1 2 3 4 5 6 7 8 9 10 11 12 Evaluate

For use with Activities 15, 16, 17

11 **Relationship of patient to primary insured:** Insurance companies pay the hospital charges for the insured person and dependents of the insured person. Enter an X to identify the relationship.

Information about the secondary insured person is entered in the third screen, Figure 4.4.

12 **Secondary insured's name, address, Social Security number, and telephone number:** The hospital needs complete information about the person who is secondarily responsible for paying the patient's bill. The city and state autofill once the Zip code is entered.

13 **Secondary insured's occupation:** Enter the appropriate information about the secondary insured's occupation, employer, and employer's address.

14 **Relationship of patient to secondary insured:** Enter an X to identify the relationship of the patient to the secondary insured.

Figure 4.4 Secondary Insured Information (Screen 3)

General Hospital **Patient Information**

Secondary Insured Information

Rate (ksph)	Errors

Key data into appropriate fields. Tab or strike ENTER to move to the next field.

12 Secondary Insured's Last Name: Mitchell First: Simon MI: P
Secondary Insured's Address: 1306 Thornwood Circle
Zip code: 75053 City: Grand Prairie State: TX
Secondary Insured's Social Security No.: 234-55-9827
Secondary Insured's Phone No. (214) 555-0185

13 Secondary Insured's Occupation: Oil Rigger
Employer: TexMex Oil
Secondary Insured's Employer's Address: 30498 Olney Lane
Zip code: 75053 City: Grand Prairie State: TX
Telephone No. (214) 555-0144

14 Relationship of Patient to Insured: [ ] Self [X] Spouse [ ] Dependent

Proceed through all forms for each client

RECORD: 1 2 3 4 5 6 7 8 9 10 11 12 Evaluate

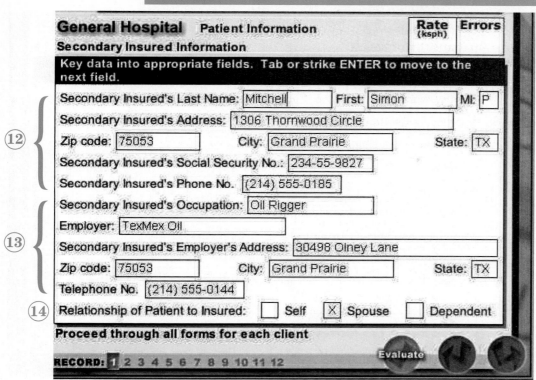

For use with Activities 15, 16, 17

INSURANCE INFORMATION

The Insurance Information screen contains information about all health insurance policies that cover the patient.

15 **Primary insurance:** United Medical Services, Metropolitan Health Insurance, Texas Mutual Medical Insurance, and Medicare are the primary insurance carriers for most General Hospital patients. Abbreviations for these carriers are shown on Line 15. If one of these carriers provides the primary insurance, enter an X in the appropriate box. The address and telephone number fill automatically.

16 **Other primary insurance company name:** If the name of the primary insurer is not listed on Line 15, the name of an "Other" insurance company is entered on Line 16.

17 **Primary insurance address:** Enter the address and Zip code; the city and state name fill automatically when the Zip code is entered.

18 **Policy and group numbers:** The insurance policy number and the group number are entered in this space. "Group" refers to people who are insured under one policy because they have something in common. Often, the group represents all the employees of one company.

BE ALERT!

Federal legislation will soon require all insurance claims to be submitted electronically. This will create a large number of new jobs for data entry specialists with excellent entry skills and knowledge of medical codes.

Figure 4.5 Insurance Information (Screen 4)

General Hospital **Patient Information**

Insurance Information

Rate (ksph)	Errors

Key data into appropriate fields. Tab or strike ENTER to move to the next field.

15 Primary Insurance: [ ] United [X] MetHealth [ ] TexMut [ ] Medicare

16 Other Insurance Company: [ ]

17 Primary Insurance Company Address: 1702 Broadway
Zip code: 66101 City: Kansas City State: KS
Telephone No. (913) 555-0125

18 Policy No: LM104-P Group No: TX-2938M

19 Secondary Insurance Company: Family Insurers of America
Secondary Insurance Address: 2203 Braxton Boulevard
Zip code: 73101 City: Oklahoma City State: OK

20 Policy No: 0044226-T Group No: TMO 2206

Proceed through all forms for each client

RECORD: 1 2 3 4 5 6 7 8 9 10 11 12 Evaluate

For use with Activities 15, 16, 17

(19) **Secondary insurance:** If the patient has secondary insurance, enter the company name, address, Zip code, and telephone number. When the Zip code is entered, the city and state fill automatically.

(20) **Policy and group numbers:** The numbers of the secondary insurer's policy and the group being insured are entered in this space.

Out-Patient Services Order

Physicians refer patients to the hospital for blood tests, X-rays, magnetic resonance imaging (MRI), mammograms, and other services, treatments, and procedures. The patient brings an Out-Patient Services Order prepared by the referring physician. It shows the patient's medical diagnosis and the treatments, procedures, and services to be performed. A typical Out-Patient Services Order is shown in Figure 4.6.

The first Out-Patient Services Order screen in Figure 4.7 provides fields for physician and patient information, diagnosis codes, and the physician's preliminary diagnosis of the patient's condition.

The Out-Patient Services Order screen requires information to be entered in a specific way. First, the information in the Physician Information column is entered, then the information for the Patient Information column is entered. Codes are entered in the ICD blocks last.

Out-Patient Services Order

Physician Information

Physician's No.: ____________________

Physician's Name: ____________________
Last First

Street Address: ____________________

____
City State Zip

Patient Information

Patient's Name: ____________________
Last First

Date of Birth: ____________ Sex_____M_____F

Patient's Phone No.: (_____) _____-_______

ICD DIAGNOSIS CODES: ____________________

Diagnosis: ____________________

CPT PANELS

_____ BASIC METABOLIC – Calcium, chloride, Glucose, Sodium, Carbon Dioxide (CO2), Creatinine, Potassium, urea nitrogen (BUN) –80048

_____ COMPREHENSIVE METABOLIC – Albumin, Alkaline, Phosphatase, ALT/SGPT; AST/SGOT; bilirubin, total; Calcium; Carbon Dioxide; Chloride; Creatinine; Glucose; Potassium; Protein, total; Sodium; Urea Nitrogen –80053

_____ CORONARY RISK PROFILE (LIPID PANEL) – Total Cholesterol, HDO cholesterol, LDL Cholesterol calculated), Triglycerides –80061

CHEMISTRY

_____ALBUMIN	82040
_____ALK PHOSPHATASE	84075
_____ALK/SGPT	84460
_____T4, TOTAL	84436
_____TSH	84443
_____T3, TOTAL	84480
_____TRIGLYCERIDES	84478
_____UREA NITROGEN (BUN)	84520

BLOOD

_____HEMATOCRIT	85013
_____PARTIAL BLOOD COUNT	85021
_____CBC/DIFF	85025
_____CBC	85027
_____RETICULOCYTE COUNT	85044
_____PRO TIME/INR	85610
_____AST/SGOT	85651

IMMUNOLOGY

_____CEA	82378
_____HEPATITIS B SURG AB	86706
_____HEPATITIS C AB	86803
_____HEPATITIS A AB (IGM)	86709
_____HEPATITIS B SURG AG	87340

URINALYSIS/STOOL

_____OCCULT BLOOD, DIAGNOSTIC	82270
_____URINALYSIS, ROUTINE	81003
_____URINE CULTURE	87086

GASTRIC

_____EGD WITH BIOPSY	43239
_____COLONOSCOPY	45380

NUCLEAR MEDICINE

_____KIDNEY FLOW AND FUNCTION	76707
_____THYROID UPTAKE MULTIPLE	78006

CARDIOLOGY

_____BRAIN	78607
_____EKG	93003

SURGICAL PATHOLOGY

_____SPECIAL STAINS	80353
_____BONE MARROW SME	80973
_____DECALCIFICATION	83113

BREAST CENTER

_____MAMMOGRAM LATERAL	76090
_____DIAGNOSTIC MAMMOGRAM	76091
_____STEREORTACTIC BREAST BIOPSY	76095
_____NEEDLE LOCALIZATION	76096

GYNECOLOGICAL

_____PAP SMEAR	99000
_____GYN PROBLEM FOCUS	99212

DIAGNOSTIC RADIOLOGY

_____NASAL BONES	72069
_____SINUSES	70160
_____ELBOW	73080
_____KNEE	73564
_____TIBIA/FIBULA	73590

CHEST IMAGING

_____CHEST – PA/LATERAL	71020
_____RIBS UNILATERAL	71120

DIAGNOSTIC ULTRASOUND

_____US BREAST	75545
_____US PREGNANT UTERUS	76805
_____US SCROTUM	76870

MRI SERVICES

_____MRI HEAD	70551
_____MRI CERVICAL SPINE	72141
_____MRI HEAD/NECK	70541
_____MRI PELVIS	72198

GASTROINTESTINAL/ABDOMEN/URINARY TRACT

_____ABDOMEN SURVEY	74000
_____UPPER GI	74240

MISCELLANEOUS

_____LYME, TOTAL	86618
_____INJECTION	90788

For use with Activities 15, 16, 17

Figure 4.7 Out-Patient Services Order (Screen 5)

General Hospital **Patient Information**
Out-Patient Services Order

Rate (ksph)	Errors

Key data into appropriate fields. Tab or strike ENTER to move to the next field.

21 Physician's Name: Sanchez (Last) Carlos (First)

22 Patient's Name: Mitchell (Last) Laurie (First)

Physician No: 8

Date of Birth: 02 / 04 / 1956

4802 Parkway Blvd.
Street Address

Sex: [ ] M [X] F

Dallas (**City**) TX (**State**) 75246 (**Zip Code**)

Patient's Phone: 214-555-0185

23 ICD DIAGNOSIS CODES: 466.0 — Diagnosis: BRONCHITIS, ACUTE

Proceed through all forms for each client

RECORD: 1 2 3 4 5 6 7 8 9 10 11 12 Evaluate

For use with Activities 15, 16, 17

21 **Physician's name, number, and address:** Enter the physician's name who is ordering the services, treatments, or procedures. The physician's number and address will fill in automatically when the name is entered.

22 **Patient's name, date of birth, sex, and telephone number:** Enter the patient's last name. All other patient information fills automatically since it was entered in a previous screen.

23 **ICD diagnosis codes:** The ICD codes identify the physician's preliminary diagnosis of the patient's condition. Tests and other procedures performed by the hospital will confirm the physician's diagnosis or identify a new diagnosis. If the diagnosis has previously been confirmed, the patient will receive services or procedures to treat the condition. After an ICD code is entered, the diagnosis displays automatically.

CPT CODES

The Service, Treatment, or Procedure screen (Figure 4.8) is for entering the CPT code for each service, treatment, or procedure the patient will receive at the hospital. These codes match the services, treatments, and procedures that the physician checked on the Out-Patient Services Order. Even though the form lists many codes, only the codes that apply to the patient are entered in the computer. Note that the columns shown on the screen are arranged differently from the CPT section of the Out-Patient Services order.

Work Ethically
Check CPT codes carefully. A patient could receive the improper medical service if you fail to check your entries. This could result in harm to the patient.

24 **CPT panels:** The Physician's Out-Patient Order, (Figure 4.6) lists three combinations of laboratory tests under the heading CPT Panels. When the CPT codes for these panels are entered on the screen, a brief description of the panel fills automatically. Enter the remaining CPT codes in a column. A short descriptive term that identifies the service, treatment, or procedure fills automatically.

Figure 4.8 Service, Treatment, or Procedures (Screen 6)

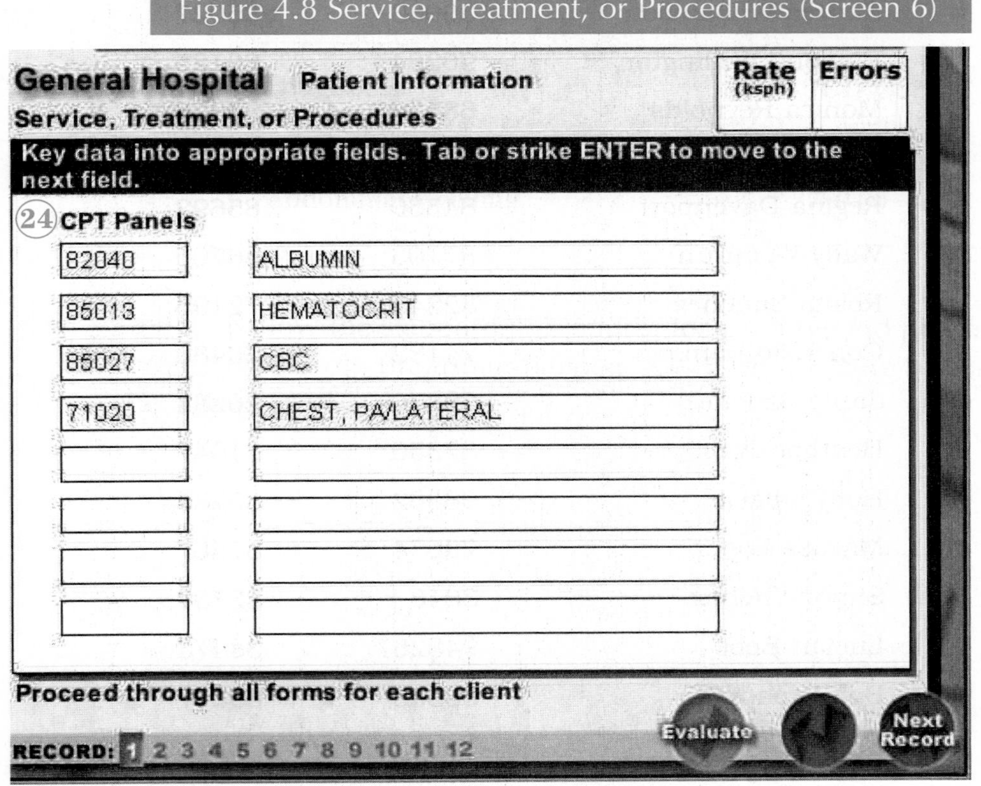

For use with Activities 15, 16, 17

Activity 14

CPT Coding Charts

In Activity 14, you will create a CPT coding chart to use as a reference when entering data in patient records. As an admittance clerk, you will refer to the chart when you have a question about a treatment, procedure, or service.

Step 1: Select **Activity 14** from the Activity menu located at the top of the screen. A blank screen with two headings will appear. Enter the first CPT code and the matching treatment, procedure, or service from the chart. Text will automatically format in uppercase.

CPT Code	Treatment, Procedure, Service
74000	Abdomen survey
73610	Albumin

Step 2: Follow the standard procedures for entering and proofreading each entry. Select the **Evaluate** button when you are ready to check your work.

CPT CODES

The Service, Treatment, or Procedure screen (Figure 4.8) is for entering the CPT code for each service, treatment, or procedure the patient will receive at the hospital. These codes match the services, treatments, and procedures that the physician checked on the Out-Patient Services Order. Even though the form lists many codes, only the codes that apply to the patient are entered in the computer. Note that the columns shown on the screen are arranged differently from the CPT section of the Out-Patient Services order.

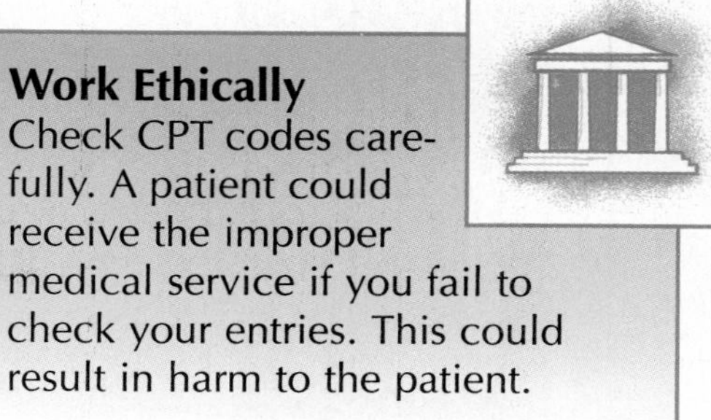

Work Ethically
Check CPT codes carefully. A patient could receive the improper medical service if you fail to check your entries. This could result in harm to the patient.

24 **CPT panels:** The Physician's Out-Patient Order, (Figure 4.6) lists three combinations of laboratory tests under the heading CPT Panels. When the CPT codes for these panels are entered on the screen, a brief description of the panel fills automatically. Enter the remaining CPT codes in a column. A short descriptive term that identifies the service, treatment, or procedure fills automatically.

Figure 4.8 Service, Treatment, or Procedures (Screen 6)

General Hospital Patient Information | Rate (ksph) | Errors

Service, Treatment, or Procedures

Key data into appropriate fields. Tab or strike ENTER to move to the next field.

24 CPT Panels

82040	ALBUMIN
85013	HEMATOCRIT
85027	CBC
71020	CHEST, PA/LATERAL

Proceed through all forms for each client

RECORD: 1 2 3 4 5 6 7 8 9 10 11 12 Evaluate Next Record

For use with Activities 15, 16, 17

Warmup

Before entering the data for Activity 13, practice your data entry skills.

Step 1: From the Main menu, select **Project Lab**. From the Project Lab menu, select **General Hospital** then *Warmup.*

Step 2: Enter the numeric data, including the decimal in the first column, using the keypad. Strive to move your hand from the keypad to the alphabetic keyboard without looking. Key the information across the screen. Strike **ENTER** on the keypad to move between fields.

Step 3: You may repeat the Warmup as many times as you wish to increase your speed or accuracy.

Alphanumeric Warmup

250.01	Andrea Williamson	30033	85027
V70.0	Ramona Wellington	90234	80185
244.9	Monica Reynolds	63432	97326
V22.2	Jeff Mawrer	34324	84295
401.1	Regina Davenport	84550	85692
573.3	Wally Woodruff	87103	86706
272	Rosita Sanchez	82248	72193
412	Consuelo Ramano	74182	70480
414.9	Janie Sanchez	39376	20284
246.9	Heather Ortiz	37356	21047
V20.2	Holly Opaca	98362	39284
788.41	Maritsa Lopez	79574	37567
784	Simone Rebex	3846	83737
780.79	Lucian Bebe	948267	38473
786.2	Bob Broadman	36353	69347

Activity 13

ICD Coding Charts

In Activity 13, you will create an ICD coding chart to use as a reference when entering data in patient records. As an admittance clerk, you will refer to the chart when you have a question about a diagnosis code.

ICD Codes

Step 1: From the General Hospital Welcome screen, select Activity 13.

Step 2: A blank screen with two headings will appear. Enter the first diagnosis and diagnosis code from the source document. Text will automatically format in uppercase. The zeros after the decimal are part of the code and must be keyed as shown.

Diagnosis	ICD Code
Abdominal pain, unspecified site	789.00
Abdominal swelling	789.30

Step 3: Follow the standard procedures for entering and proofreading each entry. Edit and correct mistakes in the usual manner. Select the **Evaluate** button when you are ready to check your work.

Activity 14

CPT Coding Charts

In Activity 14, you will create a CPT coding chart to use as a reference when entering data in patient records. As an admittance clerk, you will refer to the chart when you have a question about a treatment, procedure, or service.

Step 1: Select **Activity 14** from the Activity menu located at the top of the screen. A blank screen with two headings will appear. Enter the first CPT code and the matching treatment, procedure, or service from the chart. Text will automatically format in uppercase.

CPT Code	Treatment, Procedure, Service
74000	Abdomen survey
73610	Albumin

Step 2: Follow the standard procedures for entering and proofreading each entry. Select the **Evaluate** button when you are ready to check your work.

Activity 15

New Patients

In Activity 15, you will enter personal data for 10 new patients, using Patient Information Forms and Out-Patient Service Orders.

Step 1: Remove all source documents for Activity 15. Each patient will have a Patient Information Form and an Out-Patient Services Order, which is printed on the back side.

Step 2: Select **Activity 15** from the Activity menu. The Patient Information screen shown in Figure 4.2 will appear.

To complete the information for each patient, you will enter data on six different screens. After entering data for the first screen, proofread it by comparing it to the source document. Correct errors. Move to the second screen and so forth. You will enter all data for a single patient before moving to a new patient (record).

Patient information

Enter the patient's personal information. After keying the patient's street address and Zip code, the city and state names will fill in automatically. Enter the primary physician's name; the physician's code will fill in automatically.

When the patient is also the primary insured, data will autofill on the Primary Insured Information screen.

Insured Information

The second screen is for entering information about the person carrying the insurance. Enter all information about the Primary Insured. The city and state will fill automatically after the Zip code is entered. Move to the next screen. The third screen includes information about the secondary insured person.

Insurance Information

The fourth screen is for Insurance Information (Figure 4.4) If a patient does not have secondary insurance, leave this section blank. Move to the next screen.

Out-Patient Services Order

The fifth screen is for the Out-Patient Services Order (Figure 4.6). Enter the physician's name in the column on the left and other information about the physician will fill automatically.

Enter the patient's last name; the remaining patient information will fill automatically.

Enter all diagnosis codes listed. The name of the diagnosis will fill automatically below the codes. Move to the next screen.

Service, Treatment, or Procedure (ICD and CPT Codes)

The sixth screen is for the Service, Treatment, and Procedure (Figure 4.7). On the Out-Patient Services Order form, locate the first marked item under the heading CPT Panels. Enter the CPT code for the marked item. The service, treatment, or procedure information will display automatically.

Enter the CPT code for each remaining item the physician requested (marked). Note: the patient's form contains a list of all procedures; enter only those that are checked.

Step 3: Proofread and edit each record after data has been entered. Use the Back button to review a previous screen. When ready, move to the next patient.

Step 4: Select the **Evaluate** button when you are ready to check your work.

Activity 16

New Patients (Audio)

In Activity 16, you will enter personal data for 10 new patients using pre-recorded sound files. The sound files are similar to what an admitting clerk would experience in the real world. You will need to work from the printed copies of the Out-Patient Services Orders.

Option: You may also enter all records from the printed forms.

Step 1: Remove the Out-Patient Services Orders 16-1 through 16-10 from the back of the book.

Step 2: Select **Activity 16** from the Activity menu. Patients must be entered in the order they are interviewed in the audio files. When you Tab to the various fields, the audio will play automatically. Listen carefully, and pay attention to the spelling of names. All difficult words are spelled. Information on the first four screens will be entered from the audio files. If you need to replay the conversation for a particular field, press Ctrl + A within the field. Or simply click in a field after you have keyed the text. The later method is helpful when proofreading.

In addresses spell out words such as *Road* or *Street*.

After entering information about the patient and the insurance information, enter the data for the last two screens from the Out-Patient Services Order form.

Step 3: Select the **Evaluate** button when you are ready to check your work.

Activity 17

Patient Information

In Activity 17, 12 repeat patients visit the hospital for additional or continuing services. As a part of the admittance process, you will update their records if changes have occurred in their personal and insurance information.

Step 1: Remove the Patient Information sheets and Out-Patient Services Orders from the back of the book.

Step 2: Select Activity 17 from the Activity menu. The Patient Information screen will appear.

Step 3: Enter the first patient's Social Security number and wait for the screen to fill automatically with the remaining personal and insurance information.

Step 4: Edit the information on screen to include the changes shown on the form. To edit a field, select the field and key the correct information.

Step 5: Enter information from the Out-Patient's Services Order as you did in Activities 15 and 16. Continue by updating all patient records.

Step 6: Select the **Evaluate** button when you are ready to check your work.

S T R E T C H . . . .

Step 1: From the Activity menu, choose **Stretch**.

Step 2: Enter all figures using the keypad as accurately and as quickly as possible.

Step 3: Select the **Evaluate** button to check your work. Your keystrokes per hour (*ksph*) and accuracy rate will be reported.

Step 4: Repeat the drill to increase your *ksph*.

Numeric Stretch

250.01	90234	20532	228.2	37215	85027
244.2	84550	86706	414.9	97326	85692
272	82248	80185	20.2	30385	232
125.3	84295	78079	963.43	72193	293.5
412.8	29302	82927	786.2	30384	573.3
246.9	79803	70480	102.3	72196	784
576.8	74182	20345	401.1	20896	628.2
387.6	89323	39283	402.3	29382	694.9
836.7	27264	10482	204.5	08474	693.2
283.4	60483	13064	566.4	37364	19384
443.7	32948	10394	604.2	30493	4955
283.6	20485	70584	956.2	20383	12345
535.3	40545	89353	382.7	19373	29348
374.2	94722	63528	593.9	59532	50343
606.6	73635	25625	594.3	23918	83922

Forms

5

Customer Mail Order

Customer ID: 8954 Date: 07/11/200x

Last four digits of your Social Security number

Bill to:

Name: William Berkley

Street: 1206 Pine Wood Lane Apt:

City: Tuskegee

State: AL Zip: 36083

Phone: Day: (334) 555-0151

Evening: (334) 555-0138

Ship to (if different from billing address):

Name: Suzanna Berkley

Street: 427 Oakdale Drive Apt:

City: Lebanon

State: TN Zip: 37087

Phone: Day: (615) 555-0122

Evening: (615) 555-0122

Payment Method:

Charge to:

- ☐ Visa
- ☐ Master Card
- ☒ Discover
- ☐ American Express
- ☐ Check/money order enclosed

Card number: 5555-8913-9374-1146

Expiration date: 08 / 04
month/year

Signature: William Berkley

Item number	Page	Description	Size	Color	Color (2nd Choice)	Qty	Price per item	Subtotal
43062-539g	14	Child's cotton t-shirt	6	Periwinkle	Raspberry	1	6.99	6.99
94045-183a	88	Men's flannel shirt	XL	Green/blue plaid	Red/blue plaid	1	21.99	21.99
							Total:	$28.98

5

Customer Mail Order

Customer ID: 0943
Last four digits of your Social Security number

Date: 07/12/200X

Bill to:

Name: Andre Wilson
Street: 3108 McCarvey Street Apt: 3B
City: Madison
State: WI Zip: 53725
Phone: Day: (608) 555 - 0191
Evening: (608) 555 - 0122

Ship to (if different from billing address):

Name: Letitia Horowitz
Street: 501 W. Hanover Street Apt: 6
City: San Bernadino
State: CA Zip: 92408
Phone: Day: (909) 555 - 0116
Evening: (____) _____-______

Payment Method:

Charge to:

- ☐ Visa
- ☐ Master Card
- ☐ Discover
- ☒ American Express
- ☐ Check/money order enclosed

Card number: 5555 - 0663 8981 - 3247
Expiration date: 01 / 07
month/year
Signature: Andre Wilson

Item number	Page	Description	Size	Color	Color (2nd Choice)	Qty	Price per item	Subtotal
97243-849d	36	Women's cotton swimsuit cover	M	Blue floral	Red floral	1	24.99	24.99
64218-683c	84	Women's tank dress	10	Rose	Marine	1	32.99	32.99
							Total:	$59.98

5

Customer Mail Order

Customer ID: 5068
Last four digits of your Social Security number

Date: 07/12/200x

Bill to:

Name: Clarice Mohror

Street: 7041 West Wind Drive Apt: 82C

City: Newark

State: DE Zip: 19716

Phone: Day: (302) 555-0137

Evening: (302) 555-0125

Ship to (if different from billing address):

Name: ____

Street: ____ Apt: ____

City: ____

State: ____ Zip: ____

Phone: Day: (____) ____-____

Evening: (____) ____-____

Payment Method:

Charge to:

- ☐ Visa
- ☐ Master Card
- ☐ Discover
- ☐ American Express
- ☒ Check/money order enclosed

Card number: ____-____-____-____

Expiration date: ____/____
month/year

Signature: ____

Item number	Page	Description	Size	Color	Color (2nd Choice)	Qty	Price per item	Subtotal
68472-576a	18	Girl's tank swimsuit	8	Melon	None	1	17.99	17.99
48651-973b	41	Women's floral nightgown	12	Pistachio	Pink	1	24.99	24.99
97512-954d	89	Terrycloth bath towel	Long	Forest green	Midnight mauve	4	9.99	39.96
97824-546c	90	Terrycloth hand towel		Forest green	Midnight mauve	2	7.99	15.98
							Total:	$98.72

Customer Mail Order

Customer ID: 4264
Last four digits of your Social Security number

Date: 07/11/200x

Bill to:

Name: Christine Waterman

Street: 1634 Atkins Drive Apt: ______

City: El Dorado

State: AR Zip: 71730

Phone: Day: (907) 555-0158

Evening: (907) 555-0152

Ship to (if different from billing address):

Name: Susannah Waterman

Street: 816 Potter Street Apt: 7

City: Little Rock

State: AR Zip: 72211

Phone: Day: (907) 555-0135

Evening: (____) ____-____

Payment Method:

Charge to:

- ☐ Visa
- ☐ Master Card
- ☐ Discover
- ☐ American Express
- ☒ Check/money order enclosed

Card number: ______-______-______-______

Expiration date: ____/____
month/year

Signature: ______________________

Item number	Page	Description	Size	Color	Color (2nd Choice)	Qty	Price per item	Subtotal
54762-249a	8	Women's linen jacket	S	Moss	None	1	54.99	54.99
67129-542b	8	Women's linen skirt	8	Moss	None	1	42.99	42.99
							Total:	$97.98

Customer Mail Order

5

Customer ID: 8394 Date: 07/11/200x
Last four digits of your Social Security number

Bill to:

Name: Kimberly Cupovic
Street: 935 Arnold Street Apt: ______
City: Albany
State: NY Zip: 12202
Phone: Day: (518) 555 - 0102
Evening: (____) same

Ship to (if different from billing address):

Name: ______
Street: ______ Apt: ______
City: ______
State: ______ Zip: ______
Phone: Day: (____) ____-____
Evening: (____) ____-____

Payment Method:

Charge to:

- ☐ Visa
- ☐ Master Card
- ☒ Discover
- ☐ American Express
- ☐ Check/money order enclosed

Card number: 5555 - 3940 8212 - 9930
Expiration date: 08 / 06
month/year
Signature: Kimberly Cupovic

Item number	Page	Description	Size	Color	Color (2nd Choice)	Qty	Price per item	Subtotal
43062-539g	14	Child's cotton t-shirt	8	Teal	Navy	1	6.99	6.99
67928-412g	26	Men's windbreaker	Long	Gray	Black	1	22.99	22.99
27548-763b	99	Men's swim trunks	Long	Green	Royal	1	17.99	17.99
79682-642d	56	Cotton beach towel		Multi	Red	1	12.99	12.99
72459-174j	88	Women's lycra tank	M	Red	Mango	1	14.99	14.99
97243-849d	36	Women's cotton swimsuit cover	M	Blue floral	White	1	24.99	24.99
89145-265b	119	Women's lycra shorts	M	Tan	Cream	1	24.99	24.99
							Total:	$142.92

5

Customer Mail Order

Customer ID: 8892 Date: 07/15/200x
Last four digits of your Social Security number

Bill to:

Name: Grace Kushnir
Street: 357 Stenton Avenue Apt: 4
City: Northampton
State: MA Zip: 01060
Phone: Day: (413) 555-0143
Evening: (413) 555-0116

Ship to (if different from billing address):

Name: ____
Street: ____ Apt: ____
City: ____
State: ____ Zip: ____
Phone: Day: (____) ____-____
Evening: (____) ____-____

Payment Method:

Charge to:

- ☒ Visa
- ☐ Master Card
- ☐ Discover
- ☐ American Express
- ☐ Check/money order enclosed

Card number: 5555-0284-2943-9251
Expiration date: 08 / 05
month/year
Signature: Grace Kushnir

Item number	Page	Description	Size	Color	Color (2nd Choice)	Qty	Price per item	Subtotal
64218-683c	84	Women's tank dress	8	Marine	Melon	1	32.99	32.99
88361-524f	115	Women's suede sandals	7	Brown	Tan	1	19.49	19.49

Total: $52.48

5

Customer Mail Order

Customer ID: 9304
Last four digits of your Social Security number

Date: 07/05/200x

Bill to:

Name: David Saks
Street: 48 St vincent Place Apt:
City: Lexington
State: KY Zip: 40506
Phone: Day: (____) 555 - 0123
Evening: (____) 555 - 0179

Ship to (if different from billing address):

Name: Monica VonGroff
Street: 13 East Central Avenue Apt:
City: Paoli
State: PA Zip: 19301
Phone: Day: (610) 555 - 0122
Evening: (610) 555 - 0122

Payment Method:

Charge to:

- ☐ Visa
- ☒ Master Card
- ☐ Discover
- ☐ American Express
- ☐ Check/money order enclosed

Card number: 5555 - 9034 - 7323 - 9023
Expiration date: 05 / 08
month/year
Signature: David Saks

Item number	Page	Description	Size	Color	Color (2nd Choice)	Qty	Price per item	Subtotal
39827-274a	77	Men's cotton t-shirt	XL	Forest	Navy	1	14.99	14.99
38563-485c	86	Men's fleece vest	XL	Burgundy	Cafe	1	24.99	24.99
77529-031d	27	Men's cotton twill shorts	36	Navy	Black	1	29.99	29.99
							Total:	$66.77

5

Customer Mail Order

Customer ID: 9011
Last four digits of your Social Security number

Date: 07/06/200X

Bill to:

Name: Carmen Socorro

Street: 113 N. Mulberry Street Apt:

City: Denver

State: CO Zip: 80202

Phone: Day: (303) 555 - 0179

Evening: (303) 555 - 0119

Ship to (if different from billing address):

Name:

Street: Apt:

City:

State: Zip:

Phone: Day: (_____) _____-______

Evening: (_____) _____-______

Payment Method:

Charge to:

- ☒ Visa
- ☐ Master Card
- ☐ Discover
- ☐ American Express
- ☐ Check/money order enclosed

Card number: 5555 - 8212 - 9904 9369

Expiration date: 04 / 07
month/year

Signature: Carmen Socorro

Item number	Page	Description	Size	Color	Color (2nd Choice)	Qty	Price per item	Subtotal
32871-625c	65	Women's cotton roll-neck sweater	S	Peach	Lake	1	38.49	38.49
94045-183a	88	Men's flannel shirt	L	Red/blue plaid	None	1	21.99	21.99
							Total:	$60.48

5

Customer Mail Order

Customer ID: 4384 Date: 07/10/200x

Last four digits of your Social Security number

Bill to:

Name: Eli Dillon

Street: 844 Moore Street Apt:

City: Greenville

State: SC Zip: 29615

Phone: Day: (864) 555-0124

Evening: (864) 555-0199

Ship to (if different from billing address):

Name:

Street: Apt:

City:

State: Zip:

Phone: Day: (   )   -

Evening: (   )   -

Payment Method:

Charge to:

- ☒ Visa
- ☐ Master Card
- ☐ Discover
- ☐ American Express
- ☐ Check/money order enclosed

Card number: 5555-9022-6643-5342

Expiration date: 09 / 07
month/year

Signature: Eli Dillon

Item number	Page	Description	Size	Color	Color (2nd Choice)	Qty	Price per item	Subtotal
87246-246a	44	Child's overalls	6	Navy	Red	1	14.99	14.99
57249-145b	45	Child's canvas sneakers	8	White	None	1	12.99	12.99
87246-214h	64	Child's cotton socks	M	White	None	3	2.49	7.47
43809-065a	27	Women's cotton turtleneck shirt	M	Forest	Heather	1	11.99	11.99
45761-685c	56	Women's twill pants	12	Khaki	Brown	1	32.99	32.99
77529-031d	27	Men's cotton twill shorts	36	Black	Beige	1	29.99	29.99
24276-571b	64	Men's oxford shirt	18	Ecru	Sky blue	1	21.49	21.49
							Total:	$131.91

5

Customer Mail Order

Customer ID: 3920 Date: 07/14/200x
Last four digits of your Social Security number

Bill to:

Name: Alana Santorini
Street: 621 Powelton Road Apt: ____
City: Boulder
State: CO Zip: 80309
Phone: Day: (____) 555 - 0128
Evening: (____) 555 - 0136

Ship to (if different from billing address):

Name: ____
Street: ____ Apt: ____
City: ____
State: ____ Zip: ____
Phone: Day: (____) ____-____
Evening: (____) ____-____

Payment Method:

Charge to:

- ☒ Visa
- ☐ Master Card
- ☐ Discover
- ☐ American Express
- ☐ Check/money order enclosed

Card number: 5555 - 9056 - 8443 - 6201
Expiration date: 04 / 06
month/year
Signature: Alana Santorini

Item number	Page	Description	Size	Color	Color (2nd Choice)	Qty	Price per item	Subtotal
88361-524f	115	Women's suede sandals	9	Tan	None	1	19.49	19.49
89145-2656	119	Women's lycra shorts	L	Black	Brown	1	24.99	24.99
57196-254a	46	Women's cotton t-shirt	L	Mango	Peach	1	14.99	14.99
							Total:	$59.47

5

Customer Mail Order

Customer ID: 2486 Date: 07/14/200X
Last four digits of your Social Security number

Bill to:

Name: Timothy Yang

Street: 427 Langley Lane Apt:

City: Jackson

State: MI Zip: 39225

Phone: Day: (601) 555 - 0161

Evening: (601) 555 - 0166

Ship to (if different from billing address):

Name:

Street: Apt:

City:

State: Zip:

Phone: Day: (____) ____-____

Evening: (____) ____-____

Payment Method:

Charge to:

- ☐ Visa
- ☐ Master Card
- ☒ Discover
- ☐ American Express
- ☐ Check/money order enclosed

Card number: 5555 - 6952 - 5421 - 9362

Expiration date: 06 / 06
month/year

Signature: Timothy Yang

Item number	Page	Description	Size	Color	Color (2nd Choice)	Qty	Price per item	Subtotal
77529-031d	27	Men's cotton twill shorts	32	Navy	Olive	1	29.99	29.99
96022-654b	85	Men's fleece pullover	L	Eggplant	None	1	24.99	24.99
62590-554a	95	Men's nubuck sandals	11	Brown	Beige	1	44.99	44.99
							Total:	$109.97

5

Customer Mail Order

Customer ID: 7245 Date: 07/14/200x
Last four digits of your Social Security number

Bill to:

Name: Rakesh Mashru
Street: 914 Dewey Street Apt: 27A
City: Champaign
State: IL Zip: 61824
Phone: Day: (217) 555-0151
Evening: (____) same

Ship to (if different from billing address):

Name: Fay Brown
Street: 200 Cobbs Glenn Drive Apt: 14
City: Atlanta
State: GA Zip: 30033
Phone: Day: (404) 555-0142
Evening: (404) 555-0119

Payment Method:

Charge to:

- ☒ Visa
- ☐ Master Card
- ☐ Discover
- ☐ American Express
- ☐ Check/money order enclosed

Card number: 5555-0034-9408-7761
Expiration date: 11 / 07
month/year
Signature: Rakesh Mashru

Item number	Page	Description	Size	Color	Color (2nd Choice)	Qty	Price per item	Subtotal
68712-976g	54	Men's v-neck wool sweater	L	Charcoal	Heather gray	1	43.99	43.99
84627-981d	63	Men's khaki pants	34			1	37.99	37.99
24276-571b	64	Men's oxford shirt	16	Yellow	Ecru	1	21.49	21.49
54273-357a	68	Wool rib socks	M	Navy	Black	4	6.99	27.96
							Total:	$131.43

Customer Mail Order

5

Customer ID: 3239
Last four digits of your Social Security number

Date: 07/14/200x

Bill to:

Name: George Shentze
Street: 8406 Wooden Bridge Road Apt:
City: Bend
State: OR Zip: 97708
Phone: Day: (541) 555 - 0103
Evening: (541) 555 - 0148

Ship to (if different from billing address):

Name: Leila Hasan
Street: 675 Baltimore Avenue Apt:
City: Cleveland
State: OH Zip: 44138
Phone: Day: (216) 555 - 0155
Evening: (216) 555 - 0196

Payment Method:

Charge to:

- ☐ Visa
- ☒ Master Card
- ☐ Discover
- ☐ American Express
- ☐ Check/money order enclosed

Card number: 5555 - 7406 - 5503 - 3208
Expiration date: 10 / 05
month/year
Signature: George Shentze

Item number	Page	Description	Size	Color	Color (2nd Choice)	Qty	Price per item	Subtotal
62499-2416	74	Women's wool pea coat	S	Red	None	1	63.99	63.99
							Total:	$63.99

5

Customer Mail Order

Customer ID: 2284 Date: 07/14/200x
Last four digits of your Social Security number

Bill to:

Name: Irene Papandreou
Street: 438 McMaster Road Apt:
City: Milwaukee
State: WI Zip: 53237
Phone: Day: (414) 555 - 0125
Evening: (414) 555 - 0171

Ship to (if different from billing address):

Name:
Street: Apt:
City:
State: Zip:
Phone: Day: ( ) -
Evening: ( ) -

Payment Method:

Charge to:

- ☐ Visa
- ☐ Master Card
- ☐ Discover
- ☒ American Express
- ☐ Check/money order enclosed

Card number: 5555 - 9625 - 2514 - 0440
Expiration date: 08 / 05
month/year
Signature: Irene Papandreou

Item number	Page	Description	Size	Color	Color (2nd Choice)	Qty	Price per item	Subtotal
68275-223a	32	Men's striped rugby shirt	L	Eggplant	Navy	1	26.99	26.99
23971-625a	36	Men's v-neck cotton pullover	L	Lake blue	Coffee	1	34.99	34.99
32871-625c	65	Women's cotton roll-neck sweater	M	Black	Lupine	1	38.49	38.49

Total: $100.97

5

Customer Mail Order

Customer ID: 8181
Last four digits of your Social Security number

Date: 07/14/200x

Bill to:

Name: Alexander DiPaolo

Street: 729 Watkins Road Apt:

City: Rochester

State: MN Zip: 55903

Phone: Day: (507) 555-0189

Evening: (507) 555-0134

Ship to (if different from billing address):

Name: Marco DiPaolo

Street: 101 West End Avenue Apt:

City: New York

State: NY Zip: 10023

Phone: Day: (212) 555-0196

Evening: (212) 555-0148

Payment Method:

Charge to:

- ☐ Visa
- ☐ Master Card
- ☐ Discover
- ☒ American Express
- ☐ Check/money order enclosed

Card number: 5555-0987-3873-8253

Expiration date: 11 / 05
month/year

Signature: Alexander DiPaolo

Item number	Page	Description	Size	Color	Color (2nd Choice)	Qty	Price per item	Subtotal
84625-845f	58	Men's cotton hiking pants	L	Gray	Navy	1	34.99	34.99
23971-625a	36	Men's v-neck cotton pullover	L	Red wine	Coffee	1	34.99	34.99
							Total:	$59.98

6

Customer FAX Order

Customer ID: 8954 Date: 10/18/200x
Last four digits of your Social Security number

Bill to:

Name: William Berkley
Street: 1206 Pine Wood Lane Apt:
City: Tuskegee
State: AL Zip: 36083
Phone: Day: (480) 555-0151
Evening: (480) 555-0194

Ship to (if different from billing address):

Name: Harry Berkley
Street: 22 Southside Drive Apt: 7C
City: Mason
State: OH Zip: 45040
Phone: Day: (513) 555-0010
Evening: (513) 555-0010

Payment Method:

Charge to:

- ☐ Visa
- ☐ Master Card
- ☒ Discover
- ☐ American Express
- ☐ Check/money order enclosed

Card number: 5555-8913-9374-1146
Expiration date: 08 / 04
month/year
Signature: William Berkley

Item number	Page	Description	Size	Color	Color (2nd Choice)	Qty	Price per item	Subtotal
97512-954d	89	Terrycloth bath towel	Long	Cobalt blue	Fresh cream	2	9.99	19.98
97824-546c	90	Terrycloth hand towel	—	Cobalt blue	Fresh cream	2	7.99	15.98
							Total:	$35.96

6

Customer FAX Order

Customer ID: 2486 Date: 10/18/200x

Last four digits of your Social Security number

Bill to:

Name: Timothy Yang

Street: 427 Langley Lane Apt:

City: Jackson

State: MI Zip: 39225

Phone: Day: (601) 555 - 0161

Evening: (601) 555 - 0166

Ship to (if different from billing address):

Name:

Street: Apt:

City:

State: Zip:

Phone: Day: ( ) -

Evening: ( ) -

Payment Method:

Charge to:

- ☐ Visa
- ☐ Master Card
- ☐ Discover
- ☒ American Express
- ☐ Check/money order enclosed

Card number: 5555-4968-2210-3436

Expiration date: 09 / 07
month/year

Signature: Timothy Yang

Item number	Page	Description	Size	Color	Color (2nd Choice)	Qty	Price per item	Subtotal
97243-849d	36	Women's cotton swimsuit cover	M	Red floral	Green floral	1	24.99	24.99
							Total:	$24.99

6

Customer FAX Order

Customer ID: 2284 Date: 10/16/200x

Last four digits of your Social Security number

Bill to:

Name: Irene Papandreou

Street: 438 McMaster Road Apt:

City: Milwaukee

State: WI Zip: 53237

Phone: Day: (414) 555 - 0189

Evening: (414) 555 - 0171

Ship to (if different from billing address):

Name: Elana Sanchez

Street: 102 Wichita Street Apt:

City: Cincinnati

State: OH Zip: 45236

Phone: Day: (513) 555 - 0126

Evening: (513) 555 - 0134

Payment Method:

Charge to:

- ☐ Visa
- ☐ Master Card
- ☐ Discover
- ☒ American Express
- ☐ Check/money order enclosed

Card number: 5555-9625-2514-0440

Expiration date: 08 / 05
month/year

Signature: *Irene Papandreou*

Item number	Page	Description	Size	Color	Color (2nd Choice)	Qty	Price per item	Subtotal
96022-654b	85	Men's fleece pullover	L	Black	Navy	1	24.99	24.99
84627-981d	63	Men's khaki pants	34			1	37.99	37.99
							Total:	$62.98

6

Customer FAX Order

Customer ID: 5068
Last four digits of your Social Security number

Date: 10/14/200x

Bill to:

Name: Clarice Mohror
Street: 416 Campbell Avenue Apt: ______
City: Syracuse
State: NY Zip: 13225
Phone: Day: (315) 555-3506
Evening: (315) 555-3320

Ship to (if different from billing address):

Name: Same as bill to
Street: ______ Apt: ______
City: ______
State: ______ Zip: ______
Phone: Day: (____) ____-____
Evening: (____) ____-____

Payment Method:

Charge to:

- ☐ Visa
- ☐ Master Card
- ☐ Discover
- ☐ American Express
- ☒ Check/money order enclosed

Card number: ____-____-____-____

Expiration date: ____/____
month/year

Signature: ______________

Item number	Page	Description	Size	Color	Color (2nd Choice)	Qty	Price per item	Subtotal
62499-241b	74	Women's wool pea coat	S	Black	Red	1	63.99	63.99
32871-625c	65	Women's cotton roll-neck sweater	M	Mauve	Midnight	1	38.49	38.49
57196-254a	46	Women's cotton t-shirt	L	White	Cream	1	14.99	14.99
							Total:	$117.47

6

Customer FAX Order

Customer ID: 4264
Last four digits of your Social Security number

Date: 10/12/200x

Bill to:

Name: Christine Waterman
Street: 1429 West Carver Road Apt:
City: El Dorado
State: AR Zip: 71768
Phone: Day: (907) 555 - 0158
Evening: (907) 555 - 0190

Ship to (if different from billing address):

Name: Maritsa Sanchez
Street: 2402 West Carver Road Apt:
City: El Dorado
State: AR Zip: 71768
Phone: Day: (907) 555 - 0162
Evening: (907) 555 - 0168

Payment Method:

Charge to:

- ☐ Visa
- ☐ Master Card
- ☐ Discover
- ☐ American Express
- ☒ Check/money order enclosed

Card number: ____-____-____-____

Expiration date: ___/___ month/year

Signature: __________

Item number	Page	Description	Size	Color	Color (2nd Choice)	Qty	Price per item	Subtotal
89145-2656	119	Women's lycra shorts	L	Black	Brown	1	24.99	24.99
							Total:	$24.99

6

Customer FAX Order

Customer ID: 9304 Date: 10/20/200x
Last four digits of your Social Security number

Bill to:

Name: David Saks
Street: 674 Amsterdam Drive Apt:
City: Lexington
State: KY Zip: 40583
Phone: Day: (859) 555 - 0123
Evening: (859) 555 - 0179

Ship to (if different from billing address):

Name: Marthanna Saks
Street: 202 Hobson Lane Apt:
City: Nashville
State: TN Zip: 37201
Phone: Day: (615) 555 - 0124
Evening: (615) 555 - 0136

Payment Method:

Charge to:

- ☐ Visa
- ☒ Master Card
- ☐ Discover
- ☐ American Express
- ☐ Check/money order enclosed

Card number: 5555 - 3904 7323 - 9023
Expiration date: 05 / 08
month/year
Signature: David Saks

Item number	Page	Description	Size	Color	Color (2nd Choice)	Qty	Price per item	Subtotal
43062-539g	14	Child's cotton t-shirt	8	Mint	Raspberry	1	6.99	6.99
64218-683c	84	Women's tank dress	6	Fern	White	1	32.99	32.99
							Total:	$39.98

Customer FAX Order

Customer ID: 8394 Date: 10/19/200x

Last four digits of your Social Security number

Bill to:

Name: Kimberly Cupovic

Street: 935 Arnold Street Apt: ______

City: Albany

State: NY Zip: 12202

Phone: Day: (____) 555-0102

Evening: (____) same

Ship to (if different from billing address):

Name: ______

Street: ______ Apt: ______

City: ______

State: ______ Zip: ______

Phone: Day: (____) ____-____

Evening: (____) ____-____

Payment Method:

Charge to:

- ☒ Visa
- ☐ Master Card
- ☐ Discover
- ☐ American Express
- ☐ Check/money order enclosed

Card number: 5555-4573-9576-3944

Expiration date: 04 / 05
month/year

Signature: Kimberly Cupovic

Item number	Page	Description	Size	Color	Color (2nd Choice)	Qty	Price per item	Subtotal
43674-576g	66	Women's fleece vest	M	Lake	Navy	1	23.99	23.99
							Total:	$23.99

Customer FAX Order

Customer ID: 3239 Date: 10/11/200x

Last four digits of your Social Security number

Bill to:

Name: George Shentze

Street: 8406 Wooden Bridge Road Apt:

City: Bend

State: OR Zip: 97708

Phone: Day: (541) 555 - 0144

Evening: (541) 555 - 0148

Ship to (if different from billing address):

Name: SAME AS BILL TO

Street: ______ Apt: ______

City: ______

State: ______ Zip: ______

Phone: Day: (____) ____-____

Evening: (____) ____-____

Payment Method:

Charge to:

- ☐ Visa
- ☒ Master Card
- ☐ Discover
- ☐ American Express
- ☐ Check/money order enclosed

Card number: 5555-7406-5503-3208

Expiration date: 10 / 05
month/year

Signature: George Shentze

Item number	Page	Description	Size	Color	Color (2nd Choice)	Qty	Price per item	Subtotal
38466-904a	37	Men's flannel pajamas	L	Red	Pine	1	34.99	34.99
37564-947b	38	Men's felt slippers	11	Gray	None	1	19.99	19.99
							Total:	$54.98

6

Customer FAX Order

Customer ID: 4384 Date: 10/12/200x
Last four digits of your Social Security number

Bill to:

Name: Eli Dillon
Street: 844 Moore Street Apt: ______
City: Greenville
State: SC Zip: 29615
Phone: Day: (____) 555-0124
Evening: (____) 555-0199

Ship to (if different from billing address):

Name: Mary Ann Dillon
Street: 173 Sixth Street Apt: ______
City: Blue Ash
State: OH Zip: 45236
Phone: Day: (513) 555-0191
Evening: (513) 555-0124

Payment Method:

Charge to:

- ☐ Visa
- ☐ Master Card
- ☒ Discover
- ☐ American Express
- ☐ Check/money order enclosed

Card number: 5555-4755-3948-2736
Expiration date: 09 / 09
month/year
Signature: ______________________

Item number	Page	Description	Size	Color	Color (2nd Choice)	Qty	Price per item	Subtotal
84627-981d	63	Men's khaki pants	36			1	37.99	37.99
							Total:	$37.99

9

Guest Satisfaction Survey

We hope you enjoyed your stay at Western Suites! In order to serve you better in the future, we would appreciate receiving your opinion about your stay. Please take a minute to fill out this card and leave it in your room at the end of your visit. Thank you!

Name: Norman Herndon Date of visit: 05/16/200x

Street Address: 415 E Lehigh Ave.

City, State, Zip Code: Duluth MN 55805-0753

Telephone: 218-555-0158

Satisfaction Ratings:	**Excellent**	**Very Good**	**Good**	**Satisfactory**	**Poor**	**Didn't Use**
	(Please circle your rating for each item listed below.)					
Friendliness of staff	5	④	3	2	1	0
Ease/speed of check-in/check-out	5	4	③	2	1	0
Comfort of room	⑤	4	3	2	1	0
Spaciousness of room	5	④	3	2	1	0
Décor	5	④	3	2	1	0
Cleanliness of room	⑤	4	3	2	1	0
Speed of room service	5	④	3	2	1	0
Quality of room service	5	4	③	2	1	0
Convenience/location	5	④	3	2	1	0
Message center capability	5	4	3	2	①	0
Computer port accessibility	5	4	3	2	①	0
Business center	5	4	3	2	①	0
Fitness center	5	4	③	2	1	0
Overall	5	④	3	2	1	0

Which were the most enjoyable aspects of your visit at Western Suites?

The room was very clean, comfortable and large. I was very comfortable.

What could Western Suites have done differently in order to serve you better?

All the business services were poor. I couldn't get a port for my computer. My messages got lost, and the business center was inadequate.

Would you return to Western Suites? ✓ Yes ______ No ______ Maybe

Yes, Overall, I was satisfied.

9

Guest Satisfaction Survey

We hope you enjoyed your stay at Western Suites! In order to serve you better in the future, we would appreciate receiving your opinion about your stay. Please take a minute to fill out this card and leave it in your room at the end of your visit. Thank you!

Name: Janice Tancredi Date of visit: 05/16/200x

Street Address: 2448 Glendale Ave.

City, State, Zip Code: Wichita KS 67203-9856

Telephone: 316-555-0191

Satisfaction Ratings:	Excellent	Very Good	Good	Satisfactory	Poor	Didn't Use
	(Please circle your rating for each item listed below.)					
Friendliness of staff	(5)	4	3	2	1	0
Ease/speed of check-in/check-out	5	(4)	3	2	1	0
Comfort of room	(5)	4	3	2	1	0
Spaciousness of room	(5)	4	3	2	1	0
Décor	5	4	(3)	2	1	0
Cleanliness of room	(5)	4	3	2	1	0
Speed of room service	(5)	4	3	2	1	0
Quality of room service	(5)	4	3	2	1	0
Convenience/location	(5)	4	3	2	1	0
Message center capability	(5)	4	3	2	1	0
Computer port accessibility	(5)	4	3	2	1	0
Business center	(5)	4	3	2	1	0
Fitness center	5	4	3	2	1	(0)
Overall	(5)	4	3	2	1	0

Which were the most enjoyable aspects of your visit at Western Suites?

The staff was extremely friendly and helpful. Everyone went out of the way to help me. Check-in was fast.

What could Western Suites have done differently in order to serve you better?

Nothing--everything was fine.

Would you return to Western Suites? ✓ Yes ______ No ______ Maybe

9

Guest Satisfaction Survey

We hope you enjoyed your stay at Western Suites! In order to serve you better in the future, we would appreciate receiving your opinion about your stay. Please take a minute to fill out this card and leave it in your room at the end of your visit. Thank you!

Name: Frank Nakamura Date of visit: 05/14/200x

Street Address: 428 Westwind Dr.

City, State, Zip Code: Grand Junction CO 81501-4863

Telephone: 970-555-0166

Satisfaction Ratings:	Excellent	Very Good	Good	Satisfactory	Poor	Didn't Use
	(Please circle your rating for each item listed below.)					
Friendliness of staff	(5)	4	3	2	1	0
Ease/speed of check-in/check-out	5	4	(3)	2	1	0
Comfort of room	5	(4)	3	2	1	0
Spaciousness of room	5	(4)	3	2	1	0
Décor	(5)	4	3	2	1	0
Cleanliness of room	5	4	(3)	2	1	0
Speed of room service	(5)	4	3	2	1	0
Quality of room service	(5)	4	3	2	1	0
Convenience/location	5	(4)	3	2	1	0
Message center capability	5	4	3	2	1	(0)
Computer port accessibility	5	4	3	2	1	(0)
Business center	5	4	3	2	1	(0)
Fitness center	5	4	3	2	1	(0)
Overall	5	(4)	3	2	1	0

Which were the most enjoyable aspects of your visit at Western Suites?

Everyone was very friendly and the rooms were big. Room service was fast.

What could Western Suites have done differently in order to serve you better?

The bathroom could have been cleaner; we found some hair in the bathtub.

Would you return to Western Suites? __✓__Yes ______No ______Maybe

9

Guest Satisfaction Survey

We hope you enjoyed your stay at Western Suites! In order to serve you better in the future, we would appreciate receiving your opinion about your stay. Please take a minute to fill out this card and leave it in your room at the end of your visit. Thank you!

Name: Martha Edwards Date of visit: 05/16/200x

Street Address: 1548 Brant Dr.

City, State, Zip Code: Rapid City SD 55703

Telephone: 605-555-0187

(Please circle your rating for each item listed below.)

Satisfaction Ratings:	Excellent	Very Good	Good	Satisfactory	Poor	Didn't Use
Friendliness of staff	5	4	(3)	2	1	0
Ease/speed of check-in/check-out	5	(4)	3	2	1	0
Comfort of room	5	(4)	3	2	1	0
Spaciousness of room	(5)	4	3	2	1	0
Décor	5	4	(3)	2	1	0
Cleanliness of room	5	4	(3)	2	1	0
Speed of room service	5	4	3	2	(1)	0
Quality of room service	5	(4)	3	2	1	0
Convenience/location	5	4	(3)	2	1	0
Message center capability	5	4	(3)	2	1	0
Computer port accessibility	5	4	(3)	2	1	0
Business center	5	4	(3)	2	1	0
Fitness center	5	4	3	2	1	(0)
Overall	5	4	(3)	2	1	0

Which were the most enjoyable aspects of your visit at Western Suites?

Convenience, fitness center, fast check in.

What could Western Suites have done differently in order to serve you better?

Breakfast was not delivered at the time it was promised. I expected it to be there by 7 and it did not arrive until almost 7:30.

Would you return to Western Suites? ______Yes ______No ___✓___Maybe

Possibly. I was not terribly happy with the service but it was tolerable.

Guest Satisfaction Survey

We hope you enjoyed your stay at Western Suites! In order to serve you better in the future, we would appreciate receiving your opinion about your stay. Please take a minute to fill out this card and leave it in your room at the end of your visit. Thank you!

Name: Deborah Curran Date of visit: 05/10/200x

Street Address: 425 Snyder Ave.

City, State, Zip Code: Wakefield RI 02379

Telephone: 401-555-0198

Satisfaction Ratings:	Excellent	Very Good	Good	Satisfactory	Poor	Didn't Use
	(Please circle your rating for each item listed below.)					
Friendliness of staff	5	4	3	(2)	1	0
Ease/speed of check-in/check-out	5	4	(3)	2	1	0
Comfort of room	(5)	4	3	2	1	0
Spaciousness of room	5	(4)	3	2	1	0
Décor	(5)	4	3	2	1	0
Cleanliness of room	(5)	4	3	2	1	0
Speed of room service	5	4	(3)	2	1	0
Quality of room service	5	4	(3)	2	1	0
Convenience/location	5	(4)	3	2	1	0
Message center capability	5	(4)	3	2	1	0
Computer port accessibility	5	(4)	3	2	1	0
Business center	(5)	4	3	2	1	0
Fitness center	5	(4)	3	2	1	0
Overall	5	(4)	3	2	1	0

Which were the most enjoyable aspects of your visit at Western Suites?

The room was very pretty. It was comfortable and clean. The business center was good.

What could Western Suites have done differently in order to serve you better?

The staff could have been more helpful.

Would you return to Western Suites? ✓ Yes ______ No ______ Maybe

Yes, I would probably return. Overall, it was comfortable and satisfactory.

Guest Satisfaction Survey

[illegible]

Name: Jocelyn Carran [illegible] Date of stay: 12/11/2009 [illegible]

Street Address: 123 Parker Ave.

City, State, Zip Code: Wakefield, RI 02879

Telephone: 401-[illegible]

Satisfaction Rating: Excellent Very Good Good Satisfactory Poor Unacceptable

(Please circle your rating for each item listed below.)

Friendliness of staff	[illegible]	4	[illegible]	[illegible]	[illegible]	[illegible]
[illegible]	[illegible]	4	[illegible]	2	[illegible]	[illegible]
Comfort of room	[illegible]	[illegible]	[illegible]	[illegible]	[illegible]	[illegible]
Spaciousness of room	[illegible]	[illegible]	[illegible]	2	[illegible]	0
Decor	[illegible]	4	[illegible]	2	[illegible]	0
Cleanliness of room	[illegible]	4	[illegible]	2	[illegible]	[illegible]
[illegible]	[illegible]	[illegible]	[illegible]	2	[illegible]	[illegible]
[illegible]	[illegible]	[illegible]	[illegible]	2	[illegible]	[illegible]
[illegible]	[illegible]	[illegible]	[illegible]	[illegible]	[illegible]	[illegible]
[illegible]	[illegible]	4	[illegible]	2	[illegible]	[illegible]
[illegible]	[illegible]	[illegible]	[illegible]	[illegible]	[illegible]	[illegible]
[illegible]	[illegible]	[illegible]	[illegible]	[illegible]	[illegible]	[illegible]
[illegible]	[illegible]	4	[illegible]	[illegible]	[illegible]	[illegible]
Overall	[illegible]	4	[illegible]	[illegible]	[illegible]	[illegible]

[illegible]

The room was very pretty. It was comfortable and clean. The restaurant was good.

[illegible]

The staff could have been more helpful.

[illegible] Yes [illegible] No [illegible] Maybe

Yes, I would probably return. Overall, I was comfortable and satisfied.

Guest Satisfaction Survey

We hope you enjoyed your stay at Western Suites! In order to serve you better in the future, we would appreciate receiving your opinion about your stay. Please take a minute to fill out this card and leave it in your room at the end of your visit. Thank you!

Name: Jose Perez Date of visit: 05/16/200x

Street Address: 7109 Dobson St.

City, State, Zip Code: Escondido CA 92029

Telephone: 760-555-0127

Satisfaction Ratings:	**Excellent**	**Very Good**	**Good**	**Satisfactory**	**Poor**	**Didn't Use**
	(Please circle your rating for each item listed below.)					
Friendliness of staff	5	④	3	2	1	0
Ease/speed of check-in/check-out	5	④	3	2	1	0
Comfort of room	5	④	3	2	1	0
Spaciousness of room	⑤	4	3	2	1	0
Décor	5	4	③	2	1	0
Cleanliness of room	5	④	3	2	1	0
Speed of room service	5	④	3	2	1	0
Quality of room service	5	④	3	2	1	0
Convenience/location	5	④	3	2	1	0
Message center capability	5	④	3	2	1	0
Computer port accessibility	5	④	3	2	1	0
Business center	⑤	4	3	2	1	0
Fitness center	⑤	4	3	2	1	0
Overall	5	④	3	2	1	0

Which were the most enjoyable aspects of your visit at Western Suites?

The hotel was conveniently located and accessible to the downtown area. I liked the business center and the fitness center.

What could Western Suites have done differently in order to serve you better?

Nothing; I was quite satisfied.

Would you return to Western Suites? ✓ Yes ______ No ______ Maybe

Absolutely

9

Guest Satisfaction Survey

We hope you enjoyed your stay at Western Suites! In order to serve you better in the future, we would appreciate receiving your opinion about your stay. Please take a minute to fill out this card and leave it in your room at the end of your visit. Thank you!

Name: Janet Thongon Date of visit: 05/16/200x

Street Address: 2003 N. Felton Ave.

City, State, Zip Code: Gainesville FL 32611-8574

Telephone: 352-555-0195

Satisfaction Ratings:	Excellent	Very Good	Good	Satisfactory	Poor	Didn't Use
	(Please circle your rating for each item listed below.)					
Friendliness of staff	(5)	4	3	2	1	0
Ease/speed of check-in/check-out	5	4	(3)	2	1	0
Comfort of room	5	4	(3)	2	1	0
Spaciousness of room	5	4	(3)	2	1	0
Décor	5	4	(3)	2	1	0
Cleanliness of room	5	(4)	3	2	1	0
Speed of room service	5	4	(3)	2	1	0
Quality of room service	5	4	(3)	2	1	0
Convenience/location	5	4	(3)	2	1	0
Message center capability	5	(4)	3	2	1	0
Computer port accessibility	5	(4)	3	2	1	0
Business center	(5)	4	3	2	1	0
Fitness center	5	(4)	3	2	1	0
Overall	5	(4)	3	2	1	0

Which were the most enjoyable aspects of your visit at Western Suites?

The staff was very friendly, helpful and accessible.

What could Western Suites have done differently in order to serve you better?

I would have liked to be able to order late-night room service but the kitchen closed at 10 p.m.

Would you return to Western Suites? ✓ Yes ______No ______Maybe

Yes, probably

9

Guest Satisfaction Survey

We hope you enjoyed your stay at Western Suites! In order to serve you better in the future, we would appreciate receiving your opinion about your stay. Please take a minute to fill out this card and leave it in your room at the end of your visit. Thank you!

Name: Julia Bridges Date of visit: 05/16/200x

Street Address: 525 N. 23 St.

City, State, Zip Code: Chicago IL 60606-2987

Telephone: 312-555-0174

Satisfaction Ratings:	Excellent	Very Good	Good	Satisfactory	Poor	Didn't Use
	(Please circle your rating for each item listed below.)					
Friendliness of staff	5	4	(3)	2	1	0
Ease/speed of check-in/check-out	5	4	3	(2)	1	0
Comfort of room	5	(4)	3	2	1	0
Spaciousness of room	(5)	4	3	2	1	0
Décor	5	(4)	3	2	1	0
Cleanliness of room	5	4	(3)	2	1	0
Speed of room service	(5)	4	3	2	1	0
Quality of room service	(5)	4	3	2	1	0
Convenience/location	5	4	(3)	2	1	0
Message center capability	5	4	3	(2)	1	0
Computer port accessibility	5	4	3	(2)	1	0
Business center	5	4	3	(2)	1	0
Fitness center	5	4	(3)	2	1	0
Overall	5	4	(3)	2	1	0

Which were the most enjoyable aspects of your visit at Western Suites?

Very little was enjoyable.

What could Western Suites have done differently in order to serve you better?

Check-in definitely could have been a lot easier. The desk was understaffed, the staff was unfriendly, and the whole process took much too long.

Would you return to Western Suites? ______Yes ✓ No ______Maybe

Unlikely!

Guest Satisfaction Survey

We hope you enjoyed your stay at Western Suites! In order to serve you better in the future, we would appreciate receiving your opinion about your stay. Please take a minute to fill out this card and leave it in your room at the end of your visit. Thank you!

Name: Marcus Haggard Date of visit: 05/16/200X

Street Address: 525283 N. Hampton Rd.

City, State, Zip Code: Portland ME 04160

Telephone: 207-555-0126

Satisfaction Ratings:	Excellent	Very Good	Good	Satisfactory	Poor	Didn't Use
	(Please circle your rating for each item listed below.)					
Friendliness of staff	(5)	4	3	2	1	0
Ease/speed of check-in/check-out	5	(4)	3	2	1	0
Comfort of room	(5)	4	3	2	1	0
Spaciousness of room	(5)	4	3	2	1	0
Décor	5	(4)	3	2	1	0
Cleanliness of room	(5)	4	3	2	1	0
Speed of room service	(5)	4	3	2	1	0
Quality of room service	(5)	4	3	2	1	0
Convenience/location	(5)	4	3	2	1	0
Message center capability	(5)	4	3	2	1	0
Computer port accessibility	(5)	4	3	2	1	0
Business center	(5)	4	3	2	1	0
Fitness center	(5)	4	3	2	1	0
Overall	(5)	4	3	2	1	0

Which were the most enjoyable aspects of your visit at Western Suites?

Everything was great, especially the room – very bright, spacious and comfortable, and clean.

What could Western Suites have done differently in order to serve you better?

Nothing. I was very happy.

Would you return to Western Suites? ✓ Yes ____ No ____ Maybe

Definitely. I enjoyed my stay here very much.

9

Guest Satisfaction Survey

We hope you enjoyed your stay at Western Suites! In order to serve you better in the future, we would appreciate receiving your opinion about your stay. Please take a minute to fill out this card and leave it in your room at the end of your visit. Thank you!

Name: George Witherspoon Date of visit: 05/16/200x

Street Address: 428 Kensington Blvd.

City, State, Zip Code: Fort Wayne IN 46855-6342

Telephone: 260-555-0184

(Please circle your rating for each item listed below.)

Satisfaction Ratings:	Excellent	Very Good	Good	Satisfactory	Poor	Didn't Use
Friendliness of staff	(5)	4	3	2	1	0
Ease/speed of check-in/check-out	5	(4)	3	2	1	0
Comfort of room	(5)	4	3	2	1	0
Spaciousness of room	(5)	4	3	2	1	0
Décor	5	(4)	3	2	1	0
Cleanliness of room	(5)	4	3	2	1	0
Speed of room service	(5)	4	3	2	1	0
Quality of room service	(5)	4	3	2	1	0
Convenience/location	(5)	4	3	2	1	0
Message center capability	(5)	4	3	2	1	0
Computer port accessibility	(5)	4	3	2	1	0
Business center	(5)	4	3	2	1	0
Fitness center	(5)	4	3	2	1	0
Overall	(5)	4	3	2	1	0

Which were the most enjoyable aspects of your visit at Western Suites?

The staff was very pleasant and friendly. My room was big.

What could Western Suites have done differently in order to serve you better?

Some of the services could have been improved, like pool hours and speed of room service.

Would you return to Western Suites? ✓ Yes ______ No ______ Maybe

Yes, I would return.

9

Guest Satisfaction Survey

We hope you enjoyed your stay at Western Suites! In order to serve you better in the future, we would appreciate receiving your opinion about your stay. Please take a minute to fill out this card and leave it in your room at the end of your visit. Thank you!

Name: Ricardo Lopez Date of visit: 05/16/200x

Street Address: 913 Rodney Place

City, State, Zip Code: Harrisonburg VA 22807

Telephone: 540-555-0188

Satisfaction Ratings: (Please circle your rating for each item listed below.)

	Excellent	Very Good	Good	Satisfactory	Poor	Didn't Use
Friendliness of staff	5	4	3	(2)	1	0
Ease/speed of check-in/check-out	5	4	3	(2)	1	0
Comfort of room	5	4	(3)	2	1	0
Spaciousness of room	5	(4)	3	2	1	0
Décor	5	4	3	(2)	1	0
Cleanliness of room	5	(4)	3	2	1	0
Speed of room service	5	4	3	2	(1)	0
Quality of room service	5	4	3	2	(1)	0
Convenience/location	5	4	(3)	2	1	0
Message center capability	(5)	4	3	2	1	0
Computer port accessibility	5	4	3	2	(1)	0
Business center	5	4	3	2	(1)	0
Fitness center	5	4	3	2	(1)	0
Overall	5	4	3	(2)	1	0

Which were the most enjoyable aspects of your visit at Western Suites?

What could Western Suites have done differently in order to serve you better?

The staff could have been a lot more helpful and efficient. It took me a long time to check in, and it was difficult to get answers to my questions.

Would you return to Western Suites? ______Yes __✓__No ______Maybe

Guest Satisfaction Survey

We hope you enjoyed your stay at Western Suites! In order to serve you better in the future, we would appreciate receiving your opinion about your stay. Please take a minute to fill out this card and leave it in your room at the end of your visit. Thank you!

Name: Tariz Albez Date of visit: 05/16/200X

Street Address: 902 Dexter St.

City, State, Zip Code: Grand Junction CO 81501

Telephone: 970-555-0195

Satisfaction Ratings:	Excellent	Very Good	Good	Satisfactory	Poor	Didn't Use
	(Please circle your rating for each item listed below.)					
Friendliness of staff	5	(4)	3	2	1	0
Ease/speed of check-in/check-out	5	4	(3)	2	1	0
Comfort of room	(5)	4	3	2	1	0
Spaciousness of room	5	(4)	3	2	1	0
Décor	5	4	3	(2)	1	0
Cleanliness of room	(5)	4	3	2	1	0
Speed of room service	5	4	3	2	1	(0)
Quality of room service	5	4	3	2	1	(0)
Convenience/location	5	(4)	3	2	1	0
Message center capability	5	(4)	3	2	1	0
Computer port accessibility	5	4	3	2	1	(0)
Business center	5	4	3	2	1	(0)
Fitness center	(5)	4	3	2	1	0
Overall	5	(4)	3	2	1	0

Which were the most enjoyable aspects of your visit at Western Suites?

The pool and sauna in the fitness center were great.

What could Western Suites have done differently in order to serve you better?

Check-in could have been more efficient.

Would you return to Western Suites? ✓ Yes ______No ______Maybe

9

Guest Satisfaction Survey

We hope you enjoyed your stay at Western Suites! In order to serve you better in the future, we would appreciate receiving your opinion about your stay. Please take a minute to fill out this card and leave it in your room at the end of your visit. Thank you!

Name: Andrew Hrynko Date of visit: 05/12/200x

Street Address: 3148 Pearson Ave.

City, State, Zip Code: Seattle WA 98151

Telephone: 206-555-0186

Satisfaction Ratings:	Excellent	Very Good	Good	Satisfactory	Poor	Didn't Use
	(Please circle your rating for each item listed below.)					
Friendliness of staff	5	(4)	3	2	1	0
Ease/speed of check-in/check-out	5	(4)	3	2	1	0
Comfort of room	5	(4)	3	2	1	0
Spaciousness of room	5	(4)	3	2	1	0
Décor	5	4	(3)	2	1	0
Cleanliness of room	5	(4)	3	2	1	0
Speed of room service	(5)	4	3	2	1	0
Quality of room service	(5)	4	3	2	1	0
Convenience/location	5	(4)	3	2	1	0
Message center capability	5	(4)	3	2	1	0
Computer port accessibility	5	4	3	2	1	(0)
Business center	5	4	3	2	1	(0)
Fitness center	5	4	3	2	1	(0)
Overall	5	(4)	3	2	1	0

Which were the most enjoyable aspects of your visit at Western Suites?

We enjoyed the room service - delicious and very quick!

What could Western Suites have done differently in order to serve you better?

Nothing.

Would you return to Western Suites? ✓ Yes ______ No ______ Maybe

Yes. We were very pleased.

9

Guest Satisfaction Survey

We hope you enjoyed your stay at Western Suites! In order to serve you better in the future, we would appreciate receiving your opinion about your stay. Please take a minute to fill out this card and leave it in your room at the end of your visit. Thank you!

Name: Michael Quintana Date of visit: 05/06/200x

Street Address: 628 Vista Bonita

City, State, Zip Code: Las Cruces NM 88007

Telephone: 505-555-0155

Satisfaction Ratings:	Excellent	Very Good	Good	Satisfactory	Poor	Didn't Use
	(Please circle your rating for each item listed below.)					
Friendliness of staff	(5)	4	3	2	1	0
Ease/speed of check-in/check-out	5	(4)	3	2	1	0
Comfort of room	5	(4)	3	2	1	0
Spaciousness of room	(5)	4	3	2	1	0
Décor	5	4	(3)	2	1	0
Cleanliness of room	5	4	(3)	2	1	0
Speed of room service	5	4	(3)	2	1	0
Quality of room service	(5)	4	3	2	1	0
Convenience/location	(5)	4	3	2	1	0
Message center capability	5	4	(3)	2	1	0
Computer port accessibility	5	4	3	2	1	(0)
Business center	5	4	3	2	1	(0)
Fitness center	5	4	3	2	1	(0)
Overall	(5)	4	3	2	1	0

Which were the most enjoyable aspects of your visit at Western Suites?

The staff was very professional and polite. The room was relaxing.

What could Western Suites have done differently in order to serve you better?

I saw a bug in the bathroom and in the closet!

Would you return to Western Suites? ______Yes ______No __✓___Maybe

I haven't decided.

Guest Satisfaction Survey

We hope you enjoyed your stay at Western Suites! In order to serve you better in the future, we would appreciate receiving your opinion about your stay. Please take a minute to fill out this card and leave it in your room at the end of your visit. Thank you!

Name: Anthony D'Aio Date of visit: 05/16/200X

Street Address: 3614 /rutland Dr.

City, State, Zip Code: Youngstown OH 44555-3827

Telephone: 234-555-0134

Satisfaction Ratings: (Please circle your rating for each item listed below.)

	Excellent	**Very Good**	**Good**	**Satisfactory**	**Poor**	**Didn't Use**
Friendliness of staff	5	4	③	2	1	0
Ease/speed of check-in/check-out	5	④	3	2	1	0
Comfort of room	5	④	3	2	1	0
Spaciousness of room	⑤	4	3	2	1	0
Décor	5	④	3	2	1	0
Cleanliness of room	5	④	3	2	1	0
Speed of room service	5	④	3	2	1	0
Quality of room service	⑤	4	3	2	1	0
Convenience/location	5	④	3	2	1	0
Message center capability	5	4	3	②	1	0
Computer port accessibility	5	4	3	②	1	0
Business center	5	4	3	②	1	0
Fitness center	⑤	4	3	2	1	0
Overall	5	④	3	2	1	0

Which were the most enjoyable aspects of your visit at Western Suites?

The fitness equipment was good, and the room was nice and big—also clean and pretty.

What could Western Suites have done differently in order to serve you better?

The message center and business center were old technology.

Would you return to Western Suites? ______Yes ______No ✓ Maybe

I'll think about it.

Guest Satisfaction Survey

We hope you enjoyed your stay at Western Suites! In order to serve you better in the future, we would appreciate receiving your opinion about your stay. Please take a minute to fill out this card and leave it in your room at the end of your visit. Thank you!

Name: Benjamin Frebowitz Date of visit: 05/16/200x

Street Address: 2728 Griffith St.

City, State, Zip Code: Altoona PA 16603

Telephone: 814-555-0156

Satisfaction Ratings:

(Please circle your rating for each item listed below.)

	Excellent	**Very Good**	**Good**	**Satisfactory**	**Poor**	**Didn't Use**
Friendliness of staff	5	4	(3)	2	1	0
Ease/speed of check-in/check-out	5	(4)	3	2	1	0
Comfort of room	(5)	4	3	2	1	0
Spaciousness of room	(5)	4	3	2	1	0
Decor	5	4	(3)	2	1	0
Cleanliness of room	(5)	4	3	2	1	0
Speed of room service	5	4	(3)	2	1	0
Quality of room service	5	4	(3)	2	1	0
Convenience/location	5	(4)	3	2	1	0
Message center capability	5	4	(3)	2	1	0
Computer port accessibility	5	(4)	3	2	1	0
Business center	5	(4)	3	2	1	0
Fitness center	5	4	(3)	2	1	0
Overall	5	(4)	3	2	1	0

Which were the most enjoyable aspects of your visit at Western Suites?

Big room, nice and comfortable

What could Western Suites have done differently in order to serve you better?

The staff could have been friendlier.

Would you return to Western Suites? ✓ Yes ____ No ____ Maybe

9

Guest Satisfaction Survey

We hope you enjoyed your stay at Western Suites! In order to serve you better in the future, we would appreciate receiving your opinion about your stay. Please take a minute to fill out this card and leave it in your room at the end of your visit. Thank you!

Name: Anthony D'Aio Date of visit: 05/16/200x

Street Address: 3614 /rutland Dr.

City, State, Zip Code: Youngstown OH 44555-3827

Telephone: 234-555-0134

Satisfaction Ratings:	Excellent	Very Good	Good	Satisfactory	Poor	Didn't Use
	(Please circle your rating for each item listed below.)					
Friendliness of staff	5	4	③	2	1	0
Ease/speed of check-in/check-out	5	④	3	2	1	0
Comfort of room	5	④	3	2	1	0
Spaciousness of room	⑤	4	3	2	1	0
Décor	5	④	3	2	1	0
Cleanliness of room	5	④	3	2	1	0
Speed of room service	5	④	3	2	1	0
Quality of room service	⑤	4	3	2	1	0
Convenience/location	5	④	3	2	1	0
Message center capability	5	4	3	②	1	0
Computer port accessibility	5	4	3	②	1	0
Business center	5	4	3	②	1	0
Fitness center	⑤	4	3	2	1	0
Overall	5	④	3	2	1	0

Which were the most enjoyable aspects of your visit at Western Suites?

The fitness equipment was good, and the room was nice and big—also clean and pretty.

What could Western Suites have done differently in order to serve you better?

The message center and business center were old technology.

Would you return to Western Suites? ______Yes ______No ___✓___Maybe

I'll think about it.

9

Guest Satisfaction Survey

We hope you enjoyed your stay at Western Suites! In order to serve you better in the future, we would appreciate receiving your opinion about your stay. Please take a minute to fill out this card and leave it in your room at the end of your visit. Thank you!

Name: Benjamin Frebowitz Date of visit: 05/16/200x

Street Address: 2728 Griffith St.

City, State, Zip Code: Altoona PA 16603

Telephone: 814-555-0156

Satisfaction Ratings:	**Excellent**	**Very Good**	**Good**	**Satisfactory**	**Poor**	**Didn't Use**
	(Please circle your rating for each item listed below.)					
Friendliness of staff	5	4	(3)	2	1	0
Ease/speed of check-in/check-out	5	(4)	3	2	1	0
Comfort of room	(5)	4	3	2	1	0
Spaciousness of room	(5)	4	3	2	1	0
Décor	5	4	(3)	2	1	0
Cleanliness of room	(5)	4	3	2	1	0
Speed of room service	5	4	(3)	2	1	0
Quality of room service	5	4	(3)	2	1	0
Convenience/location	5	(4)	3	2	1	0
Message center capability	5	4	(3)	2	1	0
Computer port accessibility	5	(4)	3	2	1	0
Business center	5	(4)	3	2	1	0
Fitness center	5	4	(3)	2	1	0
Overall	5	(4)	3	2	1	0

Which were the most enjoyable aspects of your visit at Western Suites?

Big room, nice and comfortable

What could Western Suites have done differently in order to serve you better?

The staff could have been friendlier.

Would you return to Western Suites? ✓ Yes ______No ______Maybe

10–1

Guest Satisfaction Telephone Survey

Customer name: Arthur Eagan Date of conversation: ______

Customer address: 894 E. Haines St.

City, State, Zip Code: Wilmington DE 19894

Telephone: 302-555-0170

Date of last visit: 04/25/200x Number of visits in past year: 4

Average length of stay (days): 3

How would you rate the following: Please say Excellent, Very Good, Good, Satisfactory, Poor. If you didn't use a service, please let me know.

Friendliness of staff?	Very good
Ease/speed of check-in/check-out?	Good
Comfort of room?	Excellent
Spaciousness of room?	Very good
Décor?	Very good
Cleanliness of room?	Excellent
Speed of room service?	Didn't use
Quality of room service?	Didn't use
Convenience/location?	Very good
Message center capability?	Didn't use
Computer port accessibility?	Didn't use
Business center equipment?	Didn't use
Fitness center equipment?	Didn't use
Overall satisfaction?	Very good

What do you like most about Western Suites?

The rooms are big and the staff is always friendly. The main thing I like, though, is the convenience.

What could we do differently to serve you better?

Everything's fine.

Do you stay at Western Suites primarily on ☑ business trips, ☐ personal trips, or ☐ both?

What other hotels or accommodations do you use regularly?

Executive Suites, Comfort Inn

10–2

Guest Satisfaction Telephone Survey

Customer name: Victor Chesson Date of conversation: ____

Customer address: 7885 Pine St.

City, State, Zip Code: Reading PA 19601

Telephone: 610-555-0104

Date of last visit: 07/23/200x Number of visits in past year: 4

Average length of stay (days): 2

How would you rate the following: Please say Excellent, Very Good, Good, Satisfactory, Poor. If you didn't use a service, please let me know.

Friendliness of staff?	Good
Ease/speed of check-in/check-out?	Poor, actually
Comfort of room?	Very good; no complaints
Spaciousness of room?	Good
Décor?	Don't usually notice
Cleanliness of room?	Very good
Speed of room service?	Didn't use
Quality of room service?	Didn't use
Convenience/location?	Good
Message center capability?	Good
Computer port accessibility?	Didn't use
Business center equipment?	Satisfactory
Fitness center equipment?	Didn't use
Overall satisfaction?	Overall, I'd say it's satisfactory

What do you like most about Western Suites?

The hotel is conveniently located—easy to get to and from.

What could we do differently to serve you better?

Often the front desk is understaffed, which makes check-in and check-out times very slow.

Do you stay at Western Suites primarily on ☑ business trips, ☐ personal trips, or ☐ both?

What other hotels or accommodations do you use regularly?

Executive Suites, Comfort Inn

Guest Satisfaction Telephone Survey

Customer name: Katrina Gallagher Date of conversation: ________

Customer address: 459 W. Palace Ave.

City, State, Zip Code: Santa Fe NM 87502

Telephone: 505-555-0105

Date of last visit: 01/30/200x Number of visits in past year: 3

Average length of stay (days): 2.8

How would you rate the following: Please say Excellent, Very Good, Good, Satisfactory, Poor.
If you didn't use a service, please let me know.

Friendliness of staff?	Wonderful, excellent
Ease/speed of check-in/check-out?	Very good. I don't usually have a problem
Comfort of room?	Great, excellent
Spaciousness of room?	Very good, spacious
Décor?	Good
Cleanliness of room?	Great, excellent
Speed of room service?	Fair, satisfactory
Quality of room service?	Very good
Convenience/location?	Great, excellent
Message center capability?	Good
Computer port accessibility?	Satisfactory
Business center equipment?	Satisfactory
Fitness center equipment?	Poor
Overall satisfaction?	Good

What do you like most about Western Suites?

The staff is very friendly and the rooms are very comfortable.

What could we do differently to serve you better?

Speed up the room service.

Do you stay at Western Suites primarily on ☐ business trips, ☐ personal trips, or ☑ both?

What other hotels or accommodations do you use regularly?

Many others: I generally use whatever is convenient. I don't have a particular favorite.

Guest Satisfaction Telephone Survey

Customer name: Evelyn Mudrick Date of conversation: ______

Customer address: 904 St. Patrick Ave.

City, State, Zip Code: Des Moines IA 50318-7843

Telephone: 515-555-0168

Date of last visit: 02/07/200x Number of visits in past year: 1

Average length of stay (days): 3

How would you rate the following: Please say Excellent, Very Good, Good, Satisfactory, Poor.
If you didn't use a service, please let me know.

Friendliness of staff?	Very good
Ease/speed of check-in/check-out?	Excellent, no problems
Comfort of room?	Very good. The beds are especially comfortable.
Spaciousness of room?	Excellent
Décor?	Excellent
Cleanliness of room?	Excellent
Speed of room service?	Satisfactory
Quality of room service?	Excellent, delicious and good variety.
Convenience/location?	Very good
Message center capability?	Good
Computer port accessibility?	Good
Business center equipment?	Didn't use
Fitness center equipment?	Didn't use
Overall satisfaction?	It's very good

What do you like most about Western Suites?

The rooms are great, big and comfortable. I also enjoy the room service food—it's delicious.

What could we do differently to serve you better?

Speed up the room service.

Do you stay at Western Suites primarily on ☑ business trips, ☐ personal trips, or ☐ both?

What other hotels or accommodations do you use regularly?

Comfort Inn, Belterra's

Guest Satisfaction Telephone Survey

Customer name: Tim Van Der Vort Date of conversation: ____________

Customer address: 225 Fairhill Ln.

City, State, Zip Code: Marietta GA 30006

Telephone: 678-555-0178

Date of last visit: 03/08/200x Number of visits in past year: 2

Average length of stay (days): 3.5

How would you rate the following: Please say Excellent, Very Good, Good, Satisfactory, Poor. If you didn't use a service, please let me know.

Friendliness of staff? Excellent

Ease/speed of check-in/check-out? Very good

Comfort of room? Very good

Spaciousness of room? Excellent

Décor? Good

Cleanliness of room? Very good

Speed of room service? We haven't used room service

Quality of room service? We don't use room service

Convenience/location? Excellent

Message center capability? Good

Computer port accessibility? Didn't use

Business center equipment? Didn't use

Fitness center equipment? Poor

Overall satisfaction? Very good

What do you like most about Western Suites?

The hotel is conveniently located and the staff is very helpful.

What could we do differently to serve you better?

Nothing. We're very happy.

Do you stay at Western Suites primarily on ☐ business trips, ☑ personal trips, or ☐ both?

What other hotels or accommodations do you use regularly?

Millennium Suites, Belterra's

Guest Satisfaction Telephone Survey

Customer name: Fred Moccio Date of conversation: ______

Customer address: 9025 Catherine St.

City, State, Zip Code: Utica NY 13505

Telephone: 315-555-0137

Date of last visit: 06/16/200x Number of visits in past year: 3

Average length of stay (days): 2.6

How would you rate the following: Please say Excellent, Very Good, Good, Satisfactory, Poor. If you didn't use a service, please let me know.

Friendliness of staff? Good

Ease/speed of check-in/check-out? Satisfactory, but a little slow

Comfort of room? Excellent

Spaciousness of room? Excellent

Décor? Excellent

Cleanliness of room? Excellent

Speed of room service? Good

Quality of room service? Very good

Convenience/location? Very good

Message center capability? Satisfactory

Computer port accessibility? Satisfactory

Business center equipment? Didn't use

Fitness center equipment? Satisfactory

Overall satisfaction? Good

What do you like most about Western Suites?

I find the rooms very clean and comfortable.

What could we do differently to serve you better?

Sometimes check-out is a bit slow and room service is really slow.

Do you stay at Western Suites primarily on ☐ business trips, ☑ personal trips, or ☐ both?

What other hotels or accommodations do you use regularly?

McKinney's Inn, Manchester, Winton, Chase Lodge, a bunch of others.

Guest Satisfaction Telephone Survey

Customer name: Walter Hanton   Date of conversation: ____________

Customer address: 156 Summer St.

City, State, Zip Code: West Babylon   NY   11704-9867

Telephone: 631-555-0168

Date of last visit: 04/18/200x   Number of visits in past year: 5

Average length of stay (days): 4.2

How would you rate the following: Please say Excellent, Very Good, Good, Satisfactory, Poor. If you didn't use a service, please let me know.

Friendliness of staff?	Very good
Ease/speed of check-in/check-out?	Good
Comfort of room?	Very good
Spaciousness of room?	Excellent
Décor?	Good
Cleanliness of room?	Very good
Speed of room service?	Satisfactory
Quality of room service?	Excellent
Convenience/location?	Excellent
Message center capability?	Satisfactory
Computer port accessibility?	Didn't use
Business center equipment?	Didn't use
Fitness center equipment?	Good
Overall satisfaction?	Very good

What do you like most about Western Suites?

It's very comfortable and conveniently located.

What could we do differently to serve you better?

Can't think of anything.

Do you stay at Western Suites primarily on ☐ business trips, ☐ personal trips, or ☑ both?

What other hotels or accommodations do you use regularly?

Remington, Millennium, Chester's

Guest Satisfaction Telephone Survey

Customer name: Alex Orr Date of conversation: ______

Customer address: 538 W. York Dr.

City, State, Zip Code: Rockville MD 20857

Telephone: 301-555-0191

Date of last visit: 04/11/200x Number of visits in past year: 4

Average length of stay (days): 3.2

How would you rate the following: Please say Excellent, Very Good, Good, Satisfactory, Poor.
If you didn't use a service, please let me know.

Friendliness of staff?	Excellent
Ease/speed of check-in/check-out?	Good
Comfort of room?	Excellent
Spaciousness of room?	Very good
Décor?	Very good
Cleanliness of room?	Excellent
Speed of room service?	Good
Quality of room service?	Excellent
Convenience/location?	Very good
Message center capability?	Excellent
Computer port accessibility?	Excellent
Business center equipment?	Didn't use
Fitness center equipment?	Didn't use
Overall satisfaction?	Very good

What do you like most about Western Suites?

The rooms are excellent and the staff is very friendly.

What could we do differently to serve you better?

I wish room service quality were more consistent.

Do you stay at Western Suites primarily on ☑ business trips, ☐ personal trips, or ☐ both?

What other hotels or accommodations do you use regularly?

Any that are convenient.

Guest Satisfaction Telephone Survey

Customer name: Lonnie Ramsey Date of conversation: ______

Customer address: 629 Chester Springs Rd.

City, State, Zip Code: Escanaba MI 49829

Telephone: 906-555-0144

Date of last visit: 06/30/200x Number of visits in past year: 7

Average length of stay (days): 3.4

How would you rate the following: Please say Excellent, Very Good, Good, Satisfactory, Poor.
If you didn't use a service, please let me know.

Friendliness of staff? Excellent

Ease/speed of check-in/check-out? Good

Comfort of room? Excellent

Spaciousness of room? Very good

Décor? Very good

Cleanliness of room? Very good

Speed of room service? Didn't use

Quality of room service? Didn't use

Convenience/location? Excellent

Message center capability? Didn't use

Computer port accessibility? Didn't use

Business center equipment? Excellent

Fitness center equipment? Didn't use

Overall satisfaction? Very good

What do you like most about Western Suites?

It's very conveniently located and the staff is always very professional and helpful.

What could we do differently to serve you better?

Can't think of anything.

Do you stay at Western Suites primarily on ☐ business trips, ☐ personal trips, or ☑ both?

What other hotels or accommodations do you use regularly?

Millennium Suites, Comfort Inn, Belterra's

Guest Satisfaction Telephone Survey

Customer name: Shelly Abramson Date of conversation: ____________

Customer address: 735 West Lakes Dr.

City, State, Zip Code: Manchester NH 03103

Telephone: 603-555-0166

Date of last visit: 03/02/200x Number of visits in past year: 2

Average length of stay (days): 2

How would you rate the following: Please say Excellent, Very Good, Good, Satisfactory, Poor. If you didn't use a service, please let me know.

Friendliness of staff? Good

Ease/speed of check-in/check-out? Good

Comfort of room? Excellent

Spaciousness of room? Excellent

Décor? Excellent

Cleanliness of room? Very good, clean and neat

Speed of room service? Didn't use

Quality of room service? Didn't use

Convenience/location? Excellent

Message center capability? Good

Computer port accessibility? Didn't use

Business center equipment? Good

Fitness center equipment? Didn't use

Overall satisfaction? Very good

What do you like most about Western Suites?

It's convenient for both business and shopping, and we love the big well-decorated rooms.

What could we do differently to serve you better?

Keep more people on duty at the front desk during heavy check in times.

Do you stay at Western Suites primarily on ☐ business trips, ☐ personal trips, or ☑ both?

What other hotels or accommodations do you use regularly?

DeSimone Hotel, Four Corners, Remington, Shadway Inn, Traveler's Delight, Washington Ritz, a bunch of others.

Guest Satisfaction Telephone Survey

Customer name: Frank Cutillo Date of conversation: ____

Customer address: 534 Fox Chase Rd.

City, State, Zip Code: Poughkeepsie NY 12603-2763

Telephone: 845-555-0127

Date of last visit: 01/31/200x Number of visits in past year: 3

Average length of stay (days): 3.3

How would you rate the following: Please say Excellent, Very Good, Good, Satisfactory, Poor. If you didn't use a service, please let me know.

Friendliness of staff? Wonderful, excellent

Ease/speed of check-in/check-out? Great, excellent

Comfort of room? Excellent

Spaciousness of room? Very big, excellent

Décor? Great, excellent

Cleanliness of room? Excellent

Speed of room service? Good

Quality of room service? Very good

Convenience/location? Very good

Message center capability? Didn't use

Computer port accessibility? Didn't use

Business center equipment? Very good

Fitness center equipment? Didn't use

Overall satisfaction? Very good

What do you like most about Western Suites?

Everything—check-in service, location, comfort.

What could we do differently to serve you better?

Nothing.

Do you stay at Western Suites primarily on ☐ business trips, ☑ personal trips, or ☐ both?

What other hotels or accommodations do you use regularly?

none

Guest Satisfaction Telephone Survey

Customer name: Joseph Sigouin Date of conversation: ______

Customer address: 994 Robbins St.

City, State, Zip Code: Hoboken NJ 07030

Telephone: 551-555-0171

Date of last visit: 05/12/200x Number of visits in past year: 8

Average length of stay (days): 2.7

How would you rate the following: Please say Excellent, Very Good, Good, Satisfactory, Poor.
If you didn't use a service, please let me know.

Friendliness of staff?	Very good
Ease/speed of check-in/check-out?	Poor
Comfort of room?	Very good
Spaciousness of room?	Very good
Décor?	Very good
Cleanliness of room?	Excellent
Speed of room service?	Very good
Quality of room service?	Excellent
Convenience/location?	Very good
Message center capability?	Excellent
Computer port accessibility?	Very good
Business center equipment?	Excellent
Fitness center equipment?	Didn't use
Overall satisfaction?	Very good

What do you like most about Western Suites?

The people are very friendly and helpful, and the hotel is convenient to both the airport and the downtown area.

What could we do differently to serve you better?

Get high speed check in and check out

Do you stay at Western Suites primarily on ☐ business trips, ☐ personal trips, or ☑ both?

What other hotels or accommodations do you use regularly?

Executive Suites, Remington

From: Michael Vorion <mvorion@msb.com>

To: manager@westernsuites.com

Date: June 6, 200x

Subject: Western Suites Customer Satisfaction Survey

11

Please enter a number rating for each service or feature. The ratings are
5 Excellent **4** Very Good **3** Good **2** Satisfactory **1** Poor **0** Didn't Use

Satisfaction Ratings

Friendliness of Staff	5	Quality of room service	5
Ease/speed of check-in/out	4	Convenience/location	4
Comfort of room	4	Message center capability	5
Spaciousness of room	5	Computer port accessibility	2
Décor	0	Business center equipment	2
Cleanliness of room	5	Fitness center	0
Speed of room service	5	Overall	5

What do you like most about Western Suites?

The personal attention. The management keeps a record of my visits and the staff always greets me by name and knows my preferences and habits. The huge, clean rooms are a close second.

What could we do differently to serve you better?

Nothing; I am very happy with the service.

Do you stay at Western Suites primarily on business trips, personal trips, or both?

Both

What other hotels or accommodations do you use regularly?

Millennium Suites, Remington

From: John Anders <john1234@home.net>

To: manager@westernsuites.com

Date: April 28, 200x

Subject: Western Suites Customer Satisfaction Survey

Please enter a number rating for each service or feature. The ratings are
5 Excellent **4** Very Good **3** Good **2** Satisfactory **1** Poor **0** Didn't Use

Satisfaction Ratings

Service or feature	Rating	Service or feature	Rating
Friendliness of Staff	5	Quality of room service	5
Ease/speed of check-in/out	3	Convenience/location	4
Comfort of room	3	Message center capability	5
Spaciousness of room	5	Computer port accessibility	2
Décor	4	Business center equipment	2
Cleanliness of room	3	Fitness center	3
Speed of room service	3	Overall	5

What do you like most about Western Suites?

Convenience, convenience, convenience.

What could we do differently to serve you better?

I would appreciate 24-hour business center accessibility. I often work very late into the night.

Do you stay at Western Suites primarily on business trips, personal trips, or both?

Both

What other hotels or accommodations do you use regularly?

I like the Marriott and Hyatt.

From: Jessica Sierra <j.sierra@wilkerson.com>

To: manager@westernsuites.com

Date: June 8, 200x

Subject: Western Suites Customer Satisfaction Survey

11

Please enter a number rating for each service or feature. The ratings are
5 Excellent **4** Very Good **3** Good **2** Satisfactory **1** Poor **0** Didn't Use

Satisfaction Ratings

Friendliness of Staff	4	Quality of room service	5
Ease/speed of check-in/out	3	Convenience/location	5
Comfort of room	5	Message center capability	5
Spaciousness of room	5	Computer port accessibility	3
Décor	4	Business center equipment	2
Cleanliness of room	5	Fitness center	0
Speed of room service	3	Overall	5

What do you like most about Western Suites?
Convenience, comfortable room, good room service meals.

What could we do differently to serve you better?
Room service is sometimes slow.

Do you stay at Western Suites primarily on business trips, personal trips, or both?
Business

What other hotels or accommodations do you use regularly?
Chase Lodge, DeSimone Hotel, Fairfield Inn

From: Erin Samuelson <samuelson@neotech.com>

To: manager@westernsuites.com

Date: July 3, 200x

Subject: Western Suites Customer Satisfaction Survey

11

Please enter a number rating for each service or feature. The ratings are
5 Excellent **4** Very Good **3** Good **2** Satisfactory **1** Poor **0** Didn't Use

Satisfaction Ratings

Friendliness of Staff	5	Quality of room service	4
Ease/speed of check-in/out	4	Convenience/location	4
Comfort of room	4	Message center capability	4
Spaciousness of room	5	Computer port accessibility	4
Décor	4	Business center equipment	4
Cleanliness of room	5	Fitness center	3
Speed of room service	5	Overall	4

What do you like most about Western Suites?

Friendly people, comfortable rooms.

What could we do differently to serve you better?

Nothing.

Do you stay at Western Suites primarily on business trips, personal trips, or both?

Business

What other hotels or accommodations do you use regularly?

I like the Radisson.

From: Sarah Freeman <freeman@sampler.net>

To: manager@westernsuites.com

Date: March 14, 200x

Subject: Western Suites Customer Satisfaction Survey

11

Please enter a number rating for each service or feature. The ratings are
5 Excellent **4** Very Good **3** Good **2** Satisfactory **1** Poor **0** Didn't Use

Satisfaction Ratings

Friendliness of Staff	4	Quality of room service	0
Ease/speed of check-in/out	3	Convenience/location	4
Comfort of room	5	Message center capability	4
Spaciousness of room	4	Computer port accessibility	4
Décor	3	Business center equipment	4
Cleanliness of room	5	Fitness center	3
Speed of room service	0	Overall	4

What do you like most about Western Suites?

Comfortable and clean rooms, friendly staff, convenience, business center.

What could we do differently to serve you better?

Everything's fine.

Do you stay at Western Suites primarily on business trips, personal trips, or both?

Personal

What other hotels or accommodations do you use regularly?

I stay at a whole lot of different places—Chester's, Manchester, Winton.

From: Jon Stuart <jstuart@msb.com>

To: manager@westernsuites.com

Date: August 4, 200x

Subject: Western Suites Customer Satisfaction Survey

11

Please enter a number rating for each service or feature. The ratings are
5 Excellent **4** Very Good **3** Good **2** Satisfactory **1** Poor **0** Didn't Use

Satisfaction Ratings

Friendliness of Staff	3	Quality of room service	0
Ease/speed of check-in/out	4	Convenience/location	4
Comfort of room	3	Message center capability	0
Spaciousness of room	3	Computer port accessibility	0
Décor	0	Business center equipment	0
Cleanliness of room	5	Fitness center	0
Speed of room service	0	Overall	5

What do you like most about Western Suites?
Location.

What could we do differently to serve you better?
Nothing; I use very few of the services.

Do you stay at Western Suites primarily on business trips, personal trips, or both?
Business

What other hotels or accommodations do you use regularly?
McKinney's Inn, Winton, Shadway Inn

From: Sarah Shoence <sarahh@live.net>

To: manager@westernsuites.com

Date: April 21, 200x

Subject: Western Suites Customer Satisfaction Survey

11

Please enter a number rating for each service or feature. The ratings are
5 Excellent **4** Very Good **3** Good **2** Satisfactory **1** Poor **0** Didn't Use

Satisfaction Ratings

Friendliness of Staff	5	Quality of room service	3
Ease/speed of check-in/out	4	Convenience/location	4
Comfort of room	4	Message center capability	3
Spaciousness of room	4	Computer port accessibility	0
Décor	3	Business center equipment	0
Cleanliness of room	3	Fitness center	0
Speed of room service	3	Overall	3

What do you like most about Western Suites?
The staff.

What could we do differently to serve you better?
Speed up room service.

Do you stay at Western Suites primarily on business trips, personal trips, or both?
Both

What other hotels or accommodations do you use regularly?
Belterra's, Chase Lodge

From: Reka Manna <rmanna@wilkerson.com>

To: manager@westernsuites.com

Date: October 4, 200x

Subject: Western Suites Customer Satisfaction Survey

11

Please enter a number rating for each service or feature. The ratings are
5 Excellent **4** Very Good **3** Good **2** Satisfactory **1** Poor **0** Didn't Use

Satisfaction Ratings

Friendliness of Staff	5	Quality of room service	4
Ease/speed of check-in/out	2	Convenience/location	5
Comfort of room	5	Message center capability	5
Spaciousness of room	5	Computer port accessibility	5
Décor	5	Business center equipment	5
Cleanliness of room	5	Fitness center	5
Speed of room service	4	Overall	5

What do you like most about Western Suites?

Convenience and comfortable rooms.

What could we do differently to serve you better?

Better check-in, check-out procedure.

Do you stay at Western Suites primarily on business trips, personal trips, or both?

Business

What other hotels or accommodations do you use regularly?

Executive Suites

From: Ebert Tinner <tinner@tech.net>

To: manager@westernsuites.com

Date: July 3, 200x

Subject: Western Suites Customer Satisfaction Survey

11

Please enter a number rating for each service or feature. The ratings are
5 Excellent **4** Very Good **3** Good **2** Satisfactory **1** Poor **0** Didn't Use

Satisfaction Ratings

Friendliness of Staff	3	Quality of room service	0
Ease/speed of check-in/out	3	Convenience/location	5
Comfort of room	4	Message center capability	0
Spaciousness of room	4	Computer port accessibility	0
Décor	4	Business center equipment	4
Cleanliness of room	4	Fitness center	3
Speed of room service	0	Overall	4

What do you like most about Western Suites?

The convenience to the convention center, nice clean rooms.

What could we do differently to serve you better?

Limo service to the airport.

Do you stay at Western Suites primarily on business trips, personal trips, or both?

Both

What other hotels or accommodations do you use regularly?

Manchester, Traveler's Delight

Diagnosis	ICD Code
Abdominal pain	789.00
Abdominal swelling	789.30
Abnormal EKG	790
Abscess	682.9
Acne	706.1
Anemia	285.9
Anemia, iron deficiency	281.0
Aneurysm, aorta	441.9
Angina pectoris	411.1
Angina, heart pain	413.9
Angioplasty	443.9
Asthma, unspecified	493.90
Atrial fibrillation	427.31
Breast cyst	610.0
Bronchitis, acute	466.0
Camp physical	v70.3
Cardiac murmur	785.2
Cardiovascular disease	v17.4
Cataracts	366.9
Chemical inhalation (fumes, vapor)	506.4
Chest pain, unspecified	786.59
Cholesterol	272.0
Congestive heart failure	428
Contact viral disease	v01.7
Contusion	924.9
Convulsions, other	780.39
Coronary atherosclerosis	414.00
Coronary insufficiency	411.8
Cough	788.2
Cramps, lower extremities	729.82
Cyst, bone	733.20
Cystic breast	610.1
Cystitis (bladder infection)	595.9
Depressive disorder	311
Diarrhea	787.91
Dizziness and giddiness	780.4
Dyspnea and respiratory abnormalities	786.09
Edema	782.3
Elevated blood pressure	796.2
Endometriosis	617.9
Faint	780.2
Fatigue and malaise	780.79
Fibroids	218.9
Fibrocystic disease	610.1
Fluid retention	276.6

Foreign body, eye	360.60
Foreign body, swallowed	938
Fractures, ankle	824.8
Fractures, arm	813.90
Fractures, elbow	820.8
Fractures, pelvis	808.8
Frequent urination	788.42
Fungus infection	117.9
G.I. bleed	578.9
Gallstones	574.20
Gastric lymphoma	202.02
Gastritis	535.0
Gastroenteritis and colitis	558.9
General symptoms	780.9
Genital disease, female	629.9
Genital disease, male	608.9
Glucose abnormal, pregnancy	648.80
Goiter	204.9
Gout	274.9
Graves disease	240.9
Gynecological exam	v72.3
Headache	784.0
Heart disease, unspecified	429.9
Hepatitis, unspecified	573.3
Hypertension, essential, benign	401.1
Hypothyroidism, unspecified	244.9
Infant or child health check, routine	v20.2
Iron deficiency anemia	280.9
Long term current use of medications	v58.69
Malignant neoplasm, bronchus and lung	162.9
Multiple sclerosis	340
Osteoarthritis	715
Pain in foot	719.46
Pain in leg	719.47
Palpitations	785.1
Pneumonia	486
Rectal polyps	569.0
Sinusitis, acute	461.0
Tetanus/Diphtheria vaccination	v06.6
Thyroid disorder, unspecified	246.9
Tonsillitis, acute	463
Unspecified	285.9
Urinary frequency	788.41
Weight gain, abnormal	783.1
Weight loss, abnormal	783.2

CPT Code	Treatment, Procedure, Service
74000	ABDOMEN SURVEY
82040	ALBUMIN
84075	ALK PHOSPHATASE
84460	ALK/SGPT
86038	ANTINUCLEAR AB-ANA
85651	AST/SGOT
80048	BASIC METABOLIC
80973	BONE MARROW SME
78607	BRAIN
82310	CALCIUM
85027	CBC
85025	CBC/DIFF
82378	CEA
71010	CHEST, 1 VIEW
71020	CHEST PA/LATERAL
45380	COLONOSCOPY
80053	COMPREHENSIVE METABOLIC
80061	CORONARY RISK PROFILE (LIPID PANEL)
74150	CT ABDOMEN
83113	DECALCIFICATION
76075	DEXA BONE DENSITY
76091	DIAGNOSTIC MAMMOGRAM
43239	EGD WITH BIOPSY
93003	EKG
80051	ELECTROLYTES
73080	ELBOW
70150	FACIAL BONES
92230	FLUORESCEIN ANGIOSCOPY
73630	FOOT
73090	FOREARM
99384	GYN EXAM
99212	GYN PROBLEM FOCUS
73130	HAND
83718	HDL CHOLESTEROL
85013	HEMATOCRIT
86706	HEPATITIS B SURG AB
86709	HEPATITIS A AB (IGM)
87340	HEPATITIS B SURG AG
86803	HEPATITIS C AB
90788	INJECTION
83540	IRON, SERUM
76701	KIDNEY FLOW
76707	KIDNEY FLOW AND FUNCTION
73564	KNEE
73560	KNEE AP & LATERAL

79216	LIVER/SPLEEN
86618	LYME, TOTAL
76090	MAMMOGRAM LATERAL
74181	MRI ABDOMEN
70551	MRI HEAD
72141	MRI CERVICAL SPINE
70541	MRI HEAD/NECK
72198	MRI PELVIS
72069	NASAL BONES
76096	NEEDLE LOCALIZATION
82270	OCCULT BLOOD, DIAGNOSTIC
99000	PAP SMEAR
85021	PARTIAL BLOOD COUNT
72170	PELVIC AP VIEW
85610	PRO TIME/INR
80069	RENAL FUNCTION
85044	RETICULOCYTE COUNT
71120	RIBS UNILATERAL
72069	SCOLIOSIS STUDY
85651	SED RATE
70160	SINUSES
80353	SPECIAL STAINS
76095	STEREORTACTIC BREAST BIOPSY
87081	STREP CULTURE, THROAT
72072	THORACIC SPINE
78006	THYROID UPTAKE MULTIPLE
73590	TIBIA/FIBULA
84443	TSH
84480	T3, TOTAL
84439	T4, FREE (FT4)
84436	T4, TOTAL
84479	T-UPTAKE
84478	TRIGLYCERIDES
89993	UA W/REFLEX CULTURE
74240	UPPER GI
74245	UPPER GI W/AIR
84520	UREA NITROGEN (BUN)
84550	URIC ACID
81003	URINALYSIS, ROUTINE
87086	URINE CULTURE
76700	US ABDOMEN
75545	US BREAST
76805	US PREGNANT UTERUS
76870	US SCROTUM
73880	US CAROTID ARTERIES

Patient Information

15

To all returning patients: Fill in only the blanks that have changed since your last visit.

Social Security No.: 915-55-6174 Date of Birth: 02/04/1956 Sex: ☐ M ☑ F

Patient's Last Name: Mitchell First: Laurie MI: R

Patient's Address: 1306 Thornwood Circle

City: Grand Prairie State: TX Zip Code: 75053

Patient Home Telephone No.: (214) 555-0185 Patient Work Telephone: (214) 555-0192

Occupation: Architect Employer: B & J Contractors

Employer Address: 38 Lincoln Lane

City: Grand Prairie State: TX Zip Code: 75053 Telephone: (214) 555-0192

Primary Care Physician No.: _____ Primary Care Physician Name: Carlos Sanchez

Insured Information

Primary Insured's Last Name: Mitchell First: Laurie MI: R

Primary Insured's Address: 1306 Thornwood Circle

City: Grand Prairie State: TX Zip Code: 75053

Primary Insured's Social Security No.: 915-55-6174 Insured's Telephone: (214) 555-0185

Primary Insured's Occupation: Architect Employer: B & J Contractors

Employer Address: 38 Lincoln Lane

City: Grand Prairie State: TX Zip Code: 75053 Telephone: (214) 555-0192

Relationship of Patient to Insured: ☑ Self ☐ Spouse ☐ Dependent

Secondary Insured's Last Name: Mitchell First: Simon MI: P

Secondary Insured's Address: 1306 Thornwood Circle

City: Grand Prairie State: TX Zip Code: 75053

Secondary Insured's Social Security No.: 234-55-9827 Insured's Telephone: (214) 555-0185

Secondary Insured's Occupation: Oil Rigger Employer: TexMex Oil

Employer Address: 30498 Olney Lane

City: Grand Prairie State: TX Zip Code: 75053 Telephone: (214) 555-0144

Relationship of Patient to Insured: ☐ Self ☑ Spouse ☐ Dependent

Primary Insurance

Primary Insurance: ☐ United ☑ MetHealth ☐ TexMut ☐ Medicare

Other Insurance Company Name: ____________

Insurance Company Address: 1702 Broadway

City: Kansas City State: KS Zip Code: 66101 Telephone: (913) 555-0125

Policy No.: LM104-P Group No.: TX-2938M

Secondary Insurance

Secondary Insurance Company: Family Insurers of America

Insurance Company Address: 2203 Braxton Boulevard

City: Oklahoma City State: OK Zip Code: 73101

Policy No.: 0044226-T Group No.: TMO 2206

Out-Patient Services Order

15

Physician Information

Physician's No.: 8

Physician's Name: Sanchez Carlos
Last First

Street Address: 4802 Parkway Blvd.

Dallas TX 75246
City State Zip

Patient Information

Patient's Name: Mitchell Laurie
Last First

Date of Birth: 2/4/1956 Sex ____M ✓ F

Patient's Phone No.: (214) 555-0185

ICD DIAGNOSIS CODES: 569.0

Diagnosis: Rectal polyps

CPT PANELS

____ BASIC METABOLIC – Calcium, chloride, Glucose, Sodium, Carbon Dioxide (CO2), Creatinine, Potassium, urea nitrogen (BUN) –80048

____ COMPREHENSIVE METABOLIC – Albumin, Alkaline, Phosphatase, ALT/SGPT; AST/SGOT; bilirubin, total; Calcium; Carbon Dioxide; Chloride; Creatinine; Glucose; Potassium; Protein, total; Sodium; Urea Nitrogen –80053

____ CORONARY RISK PROFILE (LIPID PANEL) – Total Cholesterol, HDO cholesterol, LDL Cholesterol calculated), Triglycerides –80061

CHEMISTRY

____ ALBUMIN 82040
____ ALK PHOSPHATASE 84075
____ ALK/SGPT 84460
____ T4, TOTAL 84436
____ TSH 84443
____ T3, TOTAL 84480
____ TRIGLYCERIDES 84478
____ UREA NITROGEN (BUN) 84520

BLOOD

✓ HEMATOCRIT 85013
____ PARTIAL BLOOD COUNT 85021
____ CBC/DIFF 85025
____ CBC 85027
____ RETICULOCYTE COUNT 85044
____ PRO TIME/INR 85610
____ AST/SGOT 85651

IMMUNOLOGY

____ CEA 82378
____ HEPATITIS B SURG AB 86706
____ HEPATITIS C AB 86803
____ HEPATITIS A AB (IGM) 86709
____ HEPATITIS B SURG AG 87340

URINALYSIS/STOOL

✓ OCCULT BLOOD, DIAGNOSTIC 82270
____ URINALYSIS, ROUTINE 81003
____ URINE CULTURE 87086

GASTRIC

____ EGD WITH BIOPSY 43239
✓ COLONOSCOPY 45380

NUCLEAR MEDICINE

____ KIDNEY FLOW AND FUNCTION 76707
____ THYROID UPTAKE MULTIPLE 78006

CARDIOLOGY

____ BRAIN 78607
____ EKG 93003

SURGICAL PATHOLOGY

____ SPECIAL STAINS 80353
____ BONE MARROW SME 80973
____ DECALCIFICATION 83113

BREAST CENTER

____ MAMMOGRAM LATERAL 76090
____ DIAGNOSTIC MAMMOGRAM 76091
____ STEREORTACTIC BREAST BIOPSY 76095
____ NEEDLE LOCALIZATION 76096

GYNECOLOGICAL

____ PAP SMEAR 99000
____ GYN PROBLEM FOCUS 99212

DIAGNOSTIC RADIOLOGY

____ NASAL BONES 72069
____ SINUSES 70160
____ ELBOW 73080
____ KNEE 73564
____ TIBIA/FIBULA 73590

CHEST IMAGING

____ CHEST – PA/LATERAL 71020
____ RIBS UNILATERAL 71120

DIAGNOSTIC ULTRASOUND

____ US BREAST 75545
____ US PREGNANT UTERUS 76805
____ US SCROTUM 76870

MRI SERVICES

____ MRI HEAD 70551
____ MRI CERVICAL SPINE 72141
____ MRI HEAD/NECK 70541
____ MRI PELVIS 72198

GASTROINTESTINAL/ABDOMEN/URINARY TRACT

____ ABDOMEN SURVEY 74000
____ UPPER GI 74240

MISCELLANEOUS

____ LYME, TOTAL 86618
____ INJECTION 90788

Patient Information

To all returning patients: Fill in only the blanks that have changed since your last visit.

Social Security No.: 642-55-6407 Date of Birth: 07/15/1968 Sex: ☐ M ☑ F

Patient's Last Name: Leffler First: Anne MI: T

Patient's Address: 102 Fitzgerald St.

City: Dallas State: TX Zip Code: 75238-1459

Patient Home Telephone No.: (214) 555-0163 Patient Work Telephone: (____) ____-____

Occupation: Homemaker Employer: ________

Employer Address: ________

City: ________ State: ____ Zip Code: ______ Telephone: (____) ____-____

Primary Care Physician No.: ____ Primary Care Physician Name: Su Ling

Insured Information

Primary Insured's Last Name: Leffler First: Matthew MI: R

Primary Insured's Address: 102 Fitzgerald St.

City: Dallas State: TX Zip Code: 75238-1459

Primary Insured's Social Security No.: 523-23-8367 Insured's Telephone: (214) 555-0163

Primary Insured's Occupation: Business Owner Employer: Premier Check Printers

Employer Address: 8295 Canterbury Lane

City: Ft. Worth State: TX Zip Code: 76115 Telephone: (817) 555-0178

Relationship of Patient to Insured: ☐ Self ☑ Spouse ☐ Dependent

Secondary Insured's Last Name: ________ First: ________ MI: ___

Secondary Insured's Address: ________

City: ________ State: ____ Zip Code: ______

Secondary Insured's Social Security No.: ________ Insured's Telephone: (____) ____-____

Secondary Insured's Occupation: ________ Employer: ________

Employer Address: ________

City: ________ State: ____ Zip Code: ______ Telephone: (____) ____-____

Relationship of Patient to Insured: ☐ Self ☐ Spouse ☐ Dependent

Primary Insurance

Primary Insurance: ☑ United ☐ MetHealth ☐ TexMut ☐ Medicare

Other Insurance Company Name: ________

Insurance Company Address: 2329 Lexton Lane

City: Ft. Worth State: TX Zip Code: 91822 Telephone: (817) 555-0149

Policy No.: UMS38-432 Group No.: 485710-C

Secondary Insurance

Secondary Insurance Company: ________

Insurance Company Address: ________

City: ________ State: ____ Zip Code: ______

Policy No.: ________ Group No.: ________

Out-Patient Services Order

15

Physician Information

Physician's No.: 6

Physician's Name: Ling (Last) Su (First)

Street Address: 6208 Medical Center

Dallas (City) TX (State) 75246 (Zip)

Patient Information

Patient's Name: Leffler (Last) Anne (First)

Date of Birth: 7/15/68 Sex ___M ✓ F

Patient's Phone No.: (214) 555-0163

ICD DIAGNOSIS CODES: 202.02

Diagnosis: Gastric lymphoma

CPT PANELS

_____ BASIC METABOLIC – Calcium, chloride, Glucose, Sodium, Carbon Dioxide (CO2), Creatinine, Potassium, urea nitrogen (BUN) –80048

_____ COMPREHENSIVE METABOLIC – Albumin, Alkaline, Phosphatase, ALT/SGPT; AST/SGOT; bilirubin, total; Calcium; Carbon Dioxide; Chloride; Creatinine; Glucose; Potassium; Protein, total; Sodium; Urea Nitrogen –80053

_____ CORONARY RISK PROFILE (LIPID PANEL) – Total Cholesterol, HDO cholesterol, LDL Cholesterol calculated), Triglycerides –80061

CHEMISTRY

_____	ALBUMIN	82040
_____	ALK PHOSPHATASE	84075
_____	ALK/SGPT	84460
_____	T4, TOTAL	84436
_____	TSH	84443
_____	T3, TOTAL	84480
_____	TRIGLYCERIDES	84478
_____	UREA NITROGEN (BUN)	84520

BLOOD

✓	HEMATOCRIT	85013
_____	PARTIAL BLOOD COUNT	85021
✓	CBC/DIFF	85025
✓	CBC	85027
_____	RETICULOCYTE COUNT	85044
_____	PRO TIME/INR	85610
_____	AST/SGOT	85651

IMMUNOLOGY

_____	CEA	82378
_____	HEPATITIS B SURG AB	86706
_____	HEPATITIS C AB	86803
_____	HEPATITIS A AB (IGM)	86709
_____	HEPATITIS B SURG AG	87340

URINALYSIS/STOOL

_____	OCCULT BLOOD, DIAGNOSTIC	82270
✓	URINALYSIS, ROUTINE	81003
_____	URINE CULTURE	87086

GASTRIC

_____	EGD WITH BIOPSY	43239
_____	COLONOSCOPY	45380

NUCLEAR MEDICINE

_____	KIDNEY FLOW AND FUNCTION	76707
_____	THYROID UPTAKE MULTIPLE	78006

CARDIOLOGY

_____	BRAIN	78607
_____	EKG	93003

SURGICAL PATHOLOGY

✓	SPECIAL STAINS	80353
✓	BONE MARROW SME	80973
✓	DECALCIFICATION	83113

BREAST CENTER

_____	MAMMOGRAM LATERAL	76090
_____	DIAGNOSTIC MAMMOGRAM	76091
_____	STEREORTACTIC BREAST BIOPSY	76095
_____	NEEDLE LOCALIZATION	76096

GYNECOLOGICAL

_____	PAP SMEAR	99000
_____	GYN PROBLEM FOCUS	99212

DIAGNOSTIC RADIOLOGY

_____	NASAL BONES	72069
_____	SINUSES	70160
_____	ELBOW	73080
_____	KNEE	73564
_____	TIBIA/FIBULA	73590

CHEST IMAGING

_____	CHEST – PA/LATERAL	71020
_____	RIBS UNILATERAL	71120

DIAGNOSTIC ULTRASOUND

_____	US BREAST	75545
_____	US PREGNANT UTERUS	76805
_____	US SCROTUM	76870

MRI SERVICES

_____	MRI HEAD	70551
_____	MRI CERVICAL SPINE	72141
_____	MRI HEAD/NECK	70541
_____	MRI PELVIS	72198

GASTROINTESTINAL/ABDOMEN/URINARY TRACT

✓	ABDOMEN SURVEY	74000
_____	UPPER GI	74240

MISCELLANEOUS

_____	LYME, TOTAL	86618
_____	INJECTION	90788

Patient Information

15

To all returning patients: Fill in only the blanks that have changed since your last visit.

Social Security No.: 915-55-6120 Date of Birth: 11/16/1994 Sex: ☑ M ☐ F

Patient's Last Name: Swenson First: Joshua MI: R

Patient's Address: 1434 West Queen St.

City: Carrollton State: TX Zip Code: 75264

Patient Home Telephone No.: (972) 555-0127 Patient Work Telephone: (____) ____-____

Occupation: Student Employer: ________

Employer Address: ________

City: ________ State: ____ Zip Code: ______ Telephone: (____) ____-____

Primary Care Physician No.: ____ Primary Care Physician Name: Ad-Med Mair

Insured Information

Primary Insured's Last Name: Swenson First: Andrea MI: J

Primary Insured's Address: 1434 West Queen St.

City: Carrollton State: TX Zip Code: 75264

Primary Insured's Social Security No.: 416-55-3087 Insured's Telephone: (972) 555-0127

Primary Insured's Occupation: Office manager Employer: Bristol Technologies

Employer Address: 1286 Ashurst Rd, Suite 12

City: Dallas State: TX Zip Code: 75339 Telephone: (214) 555-0101

Relationship of Patient to Insured: ☐ Self ☐ Spouse ☑ Dependent

Secondary Insured's Last Name: Swenson First: Anthony MI: R

Secondary Insured's Address: 3653 Valley Forge Road

City: Wayne State: PA Zip Code: 19807

Secondary Insured's Social Security No.: 416-62-3087 Insured's Telephone: (610) 555-0139

Secondary Insured's Occupation: Banker Employer: First American Bank

Employer Address: 2204 Devon Drive

City: Wayne State: PA Zip Code: 19807 Telephone: (610) 555-0193

Relationship of Patient to Insured: ☐ Self ☐ Spouse ☑ Dependent

Primary Insurance

Primary Insurance: ☐ United ☑ MetHealth ☐ TexMut ☐ Medicare

Other Insurance Company Name: ________

Insurance Company Address: 1702 Broadway

City: Kansas City State: KS Zip Code: 66101 Telephone: (913) 555-0125

Policy No.: AS 194-W Group No.: TX-3937S

Secondary Insurance

Secondary Insurance Company: National Insurance

Insurance Company Address: 2302 Patriot Drive

City: Ft. Lauderdale State: FL Zip Code: 33329

Policy No.: NI247 Group No.: FAB023

Out-Patient Services Order

15

Physician Information

Physician's No.: 7

Physician's Name: Mair (Last) Ad-Med (First)

Street Address: 7109 Medical Center

Dallas (City) TX (State) 75246 (Zip)

Patient Information

Patient's Name: Swenson (Last) Joshua (First)

Date of Birth: 11/16/94 Sex ✓ M ___ F

Patient's Phone No.: (972) 555 - 0127

ICD DIAGNOSIS CODES: V7Ø.3, VØ6.6

Diagnosis: Camp physical, Tetanus/Diphtheria vaccination

CPT PANELS

____ BASIC METABOLIC – Calcium, chloride, Glucose, Sodium, Carbon Dioxide (CO2), Creatinine, Potassium, urea nitrogen (BUN) –80048

____ COMPREHENSIVE METABOLIC – Albumin, Alkaline, Phosphatase, ALT/SGPT; AST/SGOT; bilirubin, total; Calcium; Carbon Dioxide; Chloride; Creatinine; Glucose; Potassium; Protein, total; Sodium; Urea Nitrogen –80053

____ CORONARY RISK PROFILE (LIPID PANEL) – Total Cholesterol, HDO cholesterol, LDL Cholesterol calculated), Triglycerides –80061

CHEMISTRY

____	ALBUMIN	82040
____	ALK PHOSPHATASE	84075
____	ALK/SGPT	84460
____	T4, TOTAL	84436
____	TSH	84443
____	T3, TOTAL	84480
____	TRIGLYCERIDES	84478
____	UREA NITROGEN (BUN)	84520

BLOOD

✓	HEMATOCRIT	85013
____	PARTIAL BLOOD COUNT	85021
____	CBC/DIFF	85025
✓	CBC	85027
____	RETICULOCYTE COUNT	85044
____	PRO TIME/INR	85610
____	AST/SGOT	85651

IMMUNOLOGY

____	CEA	82378
____	HEPATITIS B SURG AB	86706
____	HEPATITIS C AB	86803
____	HEPATITIS A AB (IGM)	86709
____	HEPATITIS B SURG AG	87340

URINALYSIS/STOOL

____	OCCULT BLOOD, DIAGNOSTIC	82270
✓	URINALYSIS, ROUTINE	81003
____	URINE CULTURE	87086

GASTRIC

____	EGD WITH BIOPSY	43239
____	COLONOSCOPY	45380

NUCLEAR MEDICINE

____	KIDNEY FLOW AND FUNCTION	76707
____	THYROID UPTAKE MULTIPLE	78006

CARDIOLOGY

____	BRAIN	78607
____	EKG	93003

SURGICAL PATHOLOGY

____	SPECIAL STAINS	80353
____	BONE MARROW SME	80973
____	DECALCIFICATION	83113

BREAST CENTER

____	MAMMOGRAM LATERAL	76090
____	DIAGNOSTIC MAMMOGRAM	76091
____	STEREORTACTIC BREAST BIOPSY	76095
____	NEEDLE LOCALIZATION	76096

GYNECOLOGICAL

____	PAP SMEAR	99000
____	GYN PROBLEM FOCUS	99212

DIAGNOSTIC RADIOLOGY

____	NASAL BONES	72069
____	SINUSES	70160
____	ELBOW	73080
____	KNEE	73564
____	TIBIA/FIBULA	73590

CHEST IMAGING

____	CHEST – PA/LATERAL	71020
____	RIBS UNILATERAL	71120

DIAGNOSTIC ULTRASOUND

____	US BREAST	75545
____	US PREGNANT UTERUS	76805
____	US SCROTUM	76870

MRI SERVICES

____	MRI HEAD	70551
____	MRI CERVICAL SPINE	72141
____	MRI HEAD/NECK	70541
____	MRI PELVIS	72198

GASTROINTESTINAL/ABDOMEN/URINARY TRACT

____	ABDOMEN SURVEY	74000
____	UPPER GI	74240

MISCELLANEOUS

____	LYME, TOTAL	86618
✓	INJECTION	90788

Patient Information

15

To all returning patients: Fill in only the blanks that have changed since your last visit.

Social Security No.: 621-55-3021 Date of Birth: 06/12/1960 Sex: ☐ M ☑ F

Patient's Last Name: Lehman First: Susannah MI: T

Patient's Address: 894 Race St.

City: Mesquite State: TX Zip Code: 75185

Patient Home Telephone No.: (214) 555-0164 Patient Work Telephone: (214) 555-0187

Occupation: Photographer Employer: M & P Designs

Employer Address: 6120 Locust St.

City: Dallas State: TX Zip Code: 75336 Telephone: (214) 555-0187

Primary Care Physician No.: ____ Primary Care Physician Name: Mary Larusso

Insured Information

Primary Insured's Last Name: Lehman First: Susannah MI: T

Primary Insured's Address: 894 Race St.

City: Mesquite State: TX Zip Code: 75185

Primary Insured's Social Security No.: 621-55-3021 Insured's Telephone: (214) 555-0164

Primary Insured's Occupation: Photographer Employer: M & P Designs

Employer Address: 6120 Locust St.

City: Dallas State: TX Zip Code: 75336 Telephone: (214) 555-0187

Relationship of Patient to Insured: ☑ Self ☐ Spouse ☐ Dependent

Secondary Insured's Last Name: Lehman First: Daniel MI: C

Secondary Insured's Address: 894 Race St.

City: Mesquite State: TX Zip Code: 75185

Secondary Insured's Social Security No.: 465-55-2203 Insured's Telephone: (214) 555-0164

Secondary Insured's Occupation: Marketing Supervisor Employer: Hadley Corporation

Employer Address: 6120 Plantation Lane

City: Dallas State: TX Zip Code: 75336 Telephone: (214) 555-0137

Relationship of Patient to Insured: ☐ Self ☑ Spouse ☐ Dependent

Primary Insurance

Primary Insurance: ☐ United ☑ MetHealth ☐ TexMut ☐ Medicare

Other Insurance Company Name: ____

Insurance Company Address: 1702 Broadway

City: Kansas City State: KS Zip Code: 66101 Telephone: (913) 555-0125

Policy No.: SL493-KC Group No.: TX-2983-L

Secondary Insurance

Secondary Insurance Company: American Medical Insurance

Insurance Company Address: 1204 Boulevard Center

City: Ft. Worth State: TX Zip Code: 91822

Policy No.: AM493 Group No.: TX2983-L

Out-Patient Services Order

15

Physician Information

Physician's No.: 10

Physician's Name: Larusso (Last) Mary (First)

Street Address: 2302 Parkway Blvd.

Dallas (City) TX (State) 75336 (Zip)

Patient Information

Patient's Name: Lehman (Last) Susannah (First)

Date of Birth: 6/12/60 Sex ___M ✓ F

Patient's Phone No.: (214) 555-0164

ICD DIAGNOSIS CODES: 280.9. 285.9

Diagnosis: Iron deficiency anemia, Anemia

CPT PANELS

____ BASIC METABOLIC – Calcium, chloride, Glucose, Sodium, Carbon Dioxide (CO2), Creatinine, Potassium, urea nitrogen (BUN) –80048

✓ COMPREHENSIVE METABOLIC – Albumin, Alkaline, Phosphatase, ALT/SGPT; AST/SGOT; bilirubin, total; Calcium; Carbon Dioxide; Chloride; Creatinine; Glucose; Potassium; Protein, total; Sodium; Urea Nitrogen –80053

____ CORONARY RISK PROFILE (LIPID PANEL) – Total Cholesterol, HDO cholesterol, LDL Cholesterol calculated), Triglycerides –80061

CHEMISTRY

____	ALBUMIN	82040
____	ALK PHOSPHATASE	84075
____	ALK/SGPT	84460
____	T4, TOTAL	84436
____	TSH	84443
____	T3, TOTAL	84480
____	TRIGLYCERIDES	84478
____	UREA NITROGEN (BUN)	84520

BLOOD

✓	HEMATOCRIT	85013
____	PARTIAL BLOOD COUNT	85021
✓	CBC/DIFF	85025
✓	CBC	85027
____	RETICULOCYTE COUNT	85044
____	PRO TIME/INR	85610
____	AST/SGOT	85651

IMMUNOLOGY

____	CEA	82378
____	HEPATITIS B SURG AB	86706
____	HEPATITIS C AB	86803
____	HEPATITIS A AB (IGM)	86709
____	HEPATITIS B SURG AG	87340

URINALYSIS/STOOL

____	OCCULT BLOOD, DIAGNOSTIC	82270
✓	URINALYSIS, ROUTINE	81003
____	URINE CULTURE	87086

GASTRIC

____	EGD WITH BIOPSY	43239
____	COLONOSCOPY	45380

NUCLEAR MEDICINE

____	KIDNEY FLOW AND FUNCTION	76707
____	THYROID UPTAKE MULTIPLE	78006

CARDIOLOGY

____	BRAIN	78607
____	EKG	93003

SURGICAL PATHOLOGY

____	SPECIAL STAINS	80353
____	BONE MARROW SME	80973
____	DECALCIFICATION	83113

BREAST CENTER

____	MAMMOGRAM LATERAL	76090
____	DIAGNOSTIC MAMMOGRAM	76091
____	STEREORTACTIC BREAST BIOPSY	76095
____	NEEDLE LOCALIZATION	76096

GYNECOLOGICAL

____	PAP SMEAR	99000
____	GYN PROBLEM FOCUS	99212

DIAGNOSTIC RADIOLOGY

____	NASAL BONES	72069
____	SINUSES	70160
____	ELBOW	73080
____	KNEE	73564
____	TIBIA/FIBULA	73590

CHEST IMAGING

____	CHEST – PA/LATERAL	71020
____	RIBS UNILATERAL	71120

DIAGNOSTIC ULTRASOUND

____	US BREAST	75545
____	US PREGNANT UTERUS	76805
____	US SCROTUM	76870

MRI SERVICES

____	MRI HEAD	70551
____	MRI CERVICAL SPINE	72141
____	MRI HEAD/NECK	70541
____	MRI PELVIS	72198

GASTROINTESTINAL/ABDOMEN/URINARY TRACT

____	ABDOMEN SURVEY	74000
____	UPPER GI	74240

MISCELLANEOUS

____	LYME, TOTAL	86618
____	INJECTION	90788

Patient Information

15

To all returning patients: Fill in only the blanks that have changed since your last visit.

Social Security No.: 612-55-9421 Date of Birth: 05/12/1975 Sex: ☑ M ☐ F

Patient's Last Name: Tylo First: Charles MI: M

Patient's Address: 921 Algon Ave.

City: Duncanville State: TX Zip Code: 75116-9623

Patient Home Telephone No.: (972) 555-0156 Patient Work Telephone: (972) 555-0182

Occupation: Realtor Employer: Prudential

Employer Address: 7805 S. Campbell St.

City: Dallas State: TX Zip Code: 75287 Telephone: (972) 555-0128

Primary Care Physician No.: ____ Primary Care Physician Name: Robert Killey

Insured Information

Primary Insured's Last Name: Tylo First: Charles MI: M

Primary Insured's Address: 921 Algon Ave.

City: Duncanville State: TX Zip Code: 75116-9623

Primary Insured's Social Security No.: 612-55-9421 Insured's Telephone: (972) 555-0156

Primary Insured's Occupation: Realtor Employer: Prudential

Employer Address: 7805 S. Campbell St.

City: Dallas State: TX Zip Code: 75287 Telephone: (972) 555-0128

Relationship of Patient to Insured: ☑ Self ☐ Spouse ☐ Dependent

Secondary Insured's Last Name: ____ First: ____ MI: ____

Secondary Insured's Address: ____

City: ____ State: ____ Zip Code: ____

Secondary Insured's Social Security No.: ____ Insured's Telephone: (____) ____-____

Secondary Insured's Occupation: ____ Employer: ____

Employer Address: ____

City: ____ State: ____ Zip Code: ____ Telephone: (____) ____-____

Relationship of Patient to Insured: ☐ Self ☐ Spouse ☐ Dependent

Primary Insurance

Primary Insurance: ☑ United ☐ MetHealth ☐ TexMut ☐ Medicare

Other Insurance Company Name: ____

Insurance Company Address: 2329 Lexton Lane

City: Ft. Worth State: TX Zip Code: 91822 Telephone: (817) 555-0149

Policy No.: UMS21-323 Group No.: 485710-C

Secondary Insurance

Secondary Insurance Company: ____

Insurance Company Address: ____

City: ____ State: ____ Zip Code: ____

Policy No.: ____ Group No.: ____

Out-Patient Services Order

15

Physician Information

Physician's No.: 3

Physician's Name: Killey (Last) Robert (First)

Street Address: 23-R Rodes Dr

Dallas (City) TX (State) 75246 (Zip)

Patient Information

Patient's Name: Tylo (Last) Charles (First)

Date of Birth: 5/12/75 Sex ✓ M ____ F

Patient's Phone No.: (972) 555-0156

ICD DIAGNOSIS CODES: 789.00, 796.2

Diagnosis: Abdominal pain, Elevated blood pressure

CPT PANELS

____ BASIC METABOLIC – Calcium, chloride, Glucose, Sodium, Carbon Dioxide (CO2), Creatinine, Potassium, urea nitrogen (BUN) –80048

✓ COMPREHENSIVE METABOLIC – Albumin, Alkaline, Phosphatase, ALT/SGPT; AST/SGOT; bilirubin, total; Calcium; Carbon Dioxide; Chloride; Creatinine; Glucose; Potassium; Protein, total; Sodium; Urea Nitrogen –80053

____ CORONARY RISK PROFILE (LIPID PANEL) – Total Cholesterol, HDO cholesterol, LDL Cholesterol calculated), Triglycerides –80061

CHEMISTRY

____	ALBUMIN	82040
____	ALK PHOSPHATASE	84075
____	ALK/SGPT	84460
____	T4, TOTAL	84436
____	TSH	84443
____	T3, TOTAL	84480
____	TRIGLYCERIDES	84478
____	UREA NITROGEN (BUN)	84520

BLOOD

____	HEMATOCRIT	85013
____	PARTIAL BLOOD COUNT	85021
____	CBC/DIFF	85025
____	CBC	85027
____	RETICULOCYTE COUNT	85044
____	PRO TIME/INR	85610
____	AST/SGOT	85651

IMMUNOLOGY

____	CEA	82378
____	HEPATITIS B SURG AB	86706
____	HEPATITIS C AB	86803
____	HEPATITIS A AB (IGM)	86709
____	HEPATITIS B SURG AG	87340

URINALYSIS/STOOL

____	OCCULT BLOOD, DIAGNOSTIC	82270
____	URINALYSIS, ROUTINE	81003
____	URINE CULTURE	87086

GASTRIC

____	EGD WITH BIOPSY	43239
____	COLONOSCOPY	45380

NUCLEAR MEDICINE

____	KIDNEY FLOW AND FUNCTION	76707
____	THYROID UPTAKE MULTIPLE	78006

CARDIOLOGY

____	BRAIN	78607
____	EKG	93003

SURGICAL PATHOLOGY

____	SPECIAL STAINS	80353
____	BONE MARROW SME	80973
____	DECALCIFICATION	83113

BREAST CENTER

____	MAMMOGRAM LATERAL	76090
____	DIAGNOSTIC MAMMOGRAM	76091
____	STEREORTACTIC BREAST BIOPSY	76095
____	NEEDLE LOCALIZATION	76096

GYNECOLOGICAL

____	PAP SMEAR	99000
____	GYN PROBLEM FOCUS	99212

DIAGNOSTIC RADIOLOGY

____	NASAL BONES	72069
____	SINUSES	70160
____	ELBOW	73080
____	KNEE	73564
____	TIBIA/FIBULA	73590

CHEST IMAGING

____	CHEST – PA/LATERAL	71020
____	RIBS UNILATERAL	71120

DIAGNOSTIC ULTRASOUND

____	US BREAST	75545
____	US PREGNANT UTERUS	76805
____	US SCROTUM	76870

MRI SERVICES

____	MRI HEAD	70551
____	MRI CERVICAL SPINE	72141
____	MRI HEAD/NECK	70541
____	MRI PELVIS	72198

GASTROINTESTINAL/ABDOMEN/URINARY TRACT

✓	ABDOMEN SURVEY	74000
✓	UPPER GI	74240

MISCELLANEOUS

____	LYME, TOTAL	86618
____	INJECTION	90788

Patient Information

To all returning patients: Fill in only the blanks that have changed since your last visit.

Social Security No.: 415-55-9101 Date of Birth: 06/06/1922 Sex: ☑ M ☐ F

Patient's Last Name: Volpe First: Clyde MI: N

Patient's Address: 490 Lawrence Road

City: Arlington State: TX Zip Code: 76094

Patient Home Telephone No.: (214) 555-0188 Patient Work Telephone: (____) ____-____

Occupation: Retired Employer: ________

Employer Address: ________

City: ________ State: ____ Zip Code: ______ Telephone: (____) ____-____

Primary Care Physician No.: ____ Primary Care Physician Name: Steven Lincoln

Insured Information

Primary Insured's Last Name: Volpe First: Clyde MI: N

Primary Insured's Address: 490 Lawrence Road

City: Arlington State: TX Zip Code: 76094

Primary Insured's Social Security No.: 415-55-9101 Insured's Telephone: (214) 555-0188

Primary Insured's Occupation: Retired Employer: ________

Employer Address: ________

City: ________ State: ____ Zip Code: ______ Telephone: (____) ____-____

Relationship of Patient to Insured: ☑ Self ☐ Spouse ☐ Dependent

Secondary Insured's Last Name: ________ First: ________ MI: ___

Secondary Insured's Address: ________

City: ________ State: ____ Zip Code: ______

Secondary Insured's Social Security No.: ________ Insured's Telephone: (____) ____-____

Secondary Insured's Occupation: ________ Employer: ________

Employer Address: ________

City: ________ State: ____ Zip Code: ______ Telephone: (____) ____-____

Relationship of Patient to Insured: ☐ Self ☐ Spouse ☐ Dependent

Primary Insurance

Primary Insurance: ☐ United ☐ MetHealth ☐ TexMut ☑ Medicare

Other Insurance Company Name: ________

Insurance Company Address: 42 Bellvue

City: Dallas State: TX Zip Code: 75201 Telephone: (214) 555-0189

Policy No.: 415-55-9101 Group No.: A

Secondary Insurance

Secondary Insurance Company: ________

Insurance Company Address: ________

City: ________ State: ____ Zip Code: ______

Policy No.: ________ Group No.: ________

Out-Patient Services Order

15

Physician Information

Physician's No.: 7

Physician's Name: Mair (Last) Ad-Med (First)

Street Address: 7109 Medical Center

Dallas (City) TX (State) 75246 (Zip)

Patient Information

Patient's Name: Harlan (Last) Tabitha (First)

Date of Birth: 2/1/51 Sex ___ M ✓ F

Patient's Phone No.: (214) 555-0198

ICD DIAGNOSIS CODES: 240.9, 780.9

Diagnosis: Graves disease, General symptoms

CPT PANELS

___ BASIC METABOLIC – Calcium, chloride, Glucose, Sodium, Carbon Dioxide (CO2), Creatinine, Potassium, urea nitrogen (BUN) –80048

✓ COMPREHENSIVE METABOLIC – Albumin, Alkaline, Phosphatase, ALT/SGPT; AST/SGOT; bilirubin, total; Calcium; Carbon Dioxide; Chloride; Creatinine; Glucose; Potassium; Protein, total; Sodium; Urea Nitrogen –80053

✓ CORONARY RISK PROFILE (LIPID PANEL) – Total Cholesterol, HDO cholesterol, LDL Cholesterol calculated), Triglycerides –80061

CHEMISTRY

	Test	Code
	ALBUMIN	82040
	ALK PHOSPHATASE	84075
	ALK/SGPT	84460
✓	T4, TOTAL	84436
✓	TSH	84443
	T3, TOTAL	84480
	TRIGLYCERIDES	84478
	UREA NITROGEN (BUN)	84520

BLOOD

	Test	Code
	HEMATOCRIT	85013
	PARTIAL BLOOD COUNT	85021
✓	CBC/DIFF	85025
	CBC	85027
	RETICULOCYTE COUNT	85044
	PRO TIME/INR	85610
	AST/SGOT	85651

IMMUNOLOGY

	Test	Code
	CEA	82378
	HEPATITIS B SURG AB	86706
	HEPATITIS C AB	86803
	HEPATITIS A AB (IGM)	86709
	HEPATITIS B SURG AG	87340

URINALYSIS/STOOL

	Test	Code
	OCCULT BLOOD, DIAGNOSTIC	82270
✓	URINALYSIS, ROUTINE	81003
	URINE CULTURE	87086

GASTRIC

	Test	Code
	EGD WITH BIOPSY	43239
	COLONOSCOPY	45380

NUCLEAR MEDICINE

	Test	Code
	KIDNEY FLOW AND FUNCTION	76707
	THYROID UPTAKE MULTIPLE	78006

CARDIOLOGY

	Test	Code
	BRAIN	78607
	EKG	93003

SURGICAL PATHOLOGY

	Test	Code
	SPECIAL STAINS	80353
	BONE MARROW SME	80973
	DECALCIFICATION	83113

BREAST CENTER

	Test	Code
	MAMMOGRAM LATERAL	76090
	DIAGNOSTIC MAMMOGRAM	76091
	STEREORTACTIC BREAST BIOPSY	76095
	NEEDLE LOCALIZATION	76096

GYNECOLOGICAL

	Test	Code
	PAP SMEAR	99000
	GYN PROBLEM FOCUS	99212

DIAGNOSTIC RADIOLOGY

	Test	Code
	NASAL BONES	72069
	SINUSES	70160
	ELBOW	73080
	KNEE	73564
	TIBIA/FIBULA	73590

CHEST IMAGING

	Test	Code
	CHEST – PA/LATERAL	71020
	RIBS UNILATERAL	71120

DIAGNOSTIC ULTRASOUND

	Test	Code
	US BREAST	75545
	US PREGNANT UTERUS	76805
	US SCROTUM	76870

MRI SERVICES

	Test	Code
	MRI HEAD	70551
	MRI CERVICAL SPINE	72141
	MRI HEAD/NECK	70541
	MRI PELVIS	72198

GASTROINTESTINAL/ABDOMEN/URINARY TRACT

	Test	Code
	ABDOMEN SURVEY	74000
	UPPER GI	74240

MISCELLANEOUS

	Test	Code
	LYME, TOTAL	86618
	INJECTION	90788

Patient Information

To all returning patients: Fill in only the blanks that have changed since your last visit.

Social Security No.: 415-55-9101 Date of Birth: 06/06/1922 Sex: ☑ M ☐ F

Patient's Last Name: Volpe First: Clyde MI: N

Patient's Address: 490 Lawrence Road

City: Arlington State: TX Zip Code: 76094

Patient Home Telephone No.: (214) 555-0188 Patient Work Telephone: (____) ____-____

Occupation: Retired Employer: ________

Employer Address: ________

City: ________ State: ____ Zip Code: ____ Telephone: (____) ____-____

Primary Care Physician No.: ____ Primary Care Physician Name: Steven Lincoln

Insured Information

Primary Insured's Last Name: Volpe First: Clyde MI: N

Primary Insured's Address: 490 Lawrence Road

City: Arlington State: TX Zip Code: 76094

Primary Insured's Social Security No.: 415-55-9101 Insured's Telephone: (214) 555-0188

Primary Insured's Occupation: Retired Employer: ________

Employer Address: ________

City: ________ State: ____ Zip Code: ____ Telephone: (____) ____-____

Relationship of Patient to Insured: ☑ Self ☐ Spouse ☐ Dependent

Secondary Insured's Last Name: ________ First: ________ MI: ____

Secondary Insured's Address: ________

City: ________ State: ____ Zip Code: ____

Secondary Insured's Social Security No.: ________ Insured's Telephone: (____) ____-____

Secondary Insured's Occupation: ________ Employer: ________

Employer Address: ________

City: ________ State: ____ Zip Code: ____ Telephone: (____) ____-____

Relationship of Patient to Insured: ☐ Self ☐ Spouse ☐ Dependent

Primary Insurance

Primary Insurance: ☐ United ☐ MetHealth ☐ TexMut ☑ Medicare

Other Insurance Company Name: ________

Insurance Company Address: 42 Bellvue

City: Dallas State: TX Zip Code: 75201 Telephone: (214) 555-0189

Policy No.: 415-55-9101 Group No.: A

Secondary Insurance

Secondary Insurance Company: ________

Insurance Company Address: ________

City: ________ State: ____ Zip Code: ____

Policy No.: ________ Group No.: ________

Out-Patient Services Order

15

Physician Information

Physician's No.: 2

Physician's Name: Lincoln (Last) Steven (First)

Street Address: 2206 Bldg. B

Dallas (City) TX (State) 75204 (Zip)

Patient Information

Patient's Name: Volpe (Last) Clyde (First)

Date of Birth: 6/6/22 Sex ✓ M ___ F

Patient's Phone No.: (214) 555-0188

ICD DIAGNOSIS CODES: 79Ø, 411.1, 786.59

Diagnosis: Abnormal EKG, Angina pectoris, Chest pain, unspecified

CPT PANELS

___ BASIC METABOLIC – Calcium, chloride, Glucose, Sodium, Carbon Dioxide (CO2), Creatinine, Potassium, urea nitrogen (BUN) –80048

✓ COMPREHENSIVE METABOLIC – Albumin, Alkaline, Phosphatase, ALT/SGPT; AST/SGOT; bilirubin, total; Calcium; Carbon Dioxide; Chloride; Creatinine; Glucose; Potassium; Protein, total; Sodium; Urea Nitrogen –80053

✓ CORONARY RISK PROFILE (LIPID PANEL) – Total Cholesterol, HDO cholesterol, LDL Cholesterol calculated), Triglycerides –80061

CHEMISTRY

___	ALBUMIN	82040
___	ALK PHOSPHATASE	84075
___	ALK/SGPT	84460
___	T4, TOTAL	84436
___	TSH	84443
___	T3, TOTAL	84480
___	TRIGLYCERIDES	84478
___	UREA NITROGEN (BUN)	84520

BLOOD

✓	HEMATOCRIT	85013
___	PARTIAL BLOOD COUNT	85021
✓	CBC/DIFF	85025
___	CBC	85027
___	RETICULOCYTE COUNT	85044
___	PRO TIME/INR	85610
___	AST/SGOT	85651

IMMUNOLOGY

___	CEA	82378
___	HEPATITIS B SURG AB	86706
___	HEPATITIS C AB	86803
___	HEPATITIS A AB (IGM)	86709
___	HEPATITIS B SURG AG	87340

URINALYSIS/STOOL

___	OCCULT BLOOD, DIAGNOSTIC	82270
___	URINALYSIS, ROUTINE	81003
___	URINE CULTURE	87086

GASTRIC

___	EGD WITH BIOPSY	43239
___	COLONOSCOPY	45380

NUCLEAR MEDICINE

___	KIDNEY FLOW AND FUNCTION	76707
___	THYROID UPTAKE MULTIPLE	78006

CARDIOLOGY

___	BRAIN	78607
✓	EKG	93003

SURGICAL PATHOLOGY

___	SPECIAL STAINS	80353
___	BONE MARROW SME	80973
___	DECALCIFICATION	83113

BREAST CENTER

___	MAMMOGRAM LATERAL	76090
___	DIAGNOSTIC MAMMOGRAM	76091
___	STEREORTACTIC BREAST BIOPSY	76095
___	NEEDLE LOCALIZATION	76096

GYNECOLOGICAL

___	PAP SMEAR	99000
___	GYN PROBLEM FOCUS	99212

DIAGNOSTIC RADIOLOGY

___	NASAL BONES	72069
___	SINUSES	70160
___	ELBOW	73080
___	KNEE	73564
___	TIBIA/FIBULA	73590

CHEST IMAGING

___	CHEST – PA/LATERAL	71020
___	RIBS UNILATERAL	71120

DIAGNOSTIC ULTRASOUND

___	US BREAST	75545
___	US PREGNANT UTERUS	76805
___	US SCROTUM	76870

MRI SERVICES

___	MRI HEAD	70551
___	MRI CERVICAL SPINE	72141
___	MRI HEAD/NECK	70541
___	MRI PELVIS	72198

GASTROINTESTINAL/ABDOMEN/URINARY TRACT

___	ABDOMEN SURVEY	74000
___	UPPER GI	74240

MISCELLANEOUS

___	LYME, TOTAL	86618
___	INJECTION	90788

Patient Information

15

To all returning patients: Fill in only the blanks that have changed since your last visit.

Social Security No.: 876-55-4402 Date of Birth: 02/01/1951 Sex: ☐ M ☑ F

Patient's Last Name: Harlan First: Tabitha MI: S

Patient's Address: 22B University Lane

City: Dallas State: TX Zip Code: 75204-3217

Patient Home Telephone No.: (214) 555-0198 Patient Work Telephone: (_____) _____-_______

Occupation: Homemaker Employer: __________

Employer Address: __________

City: __________ State: _____ Zip Code: _______ Telephone: (_____) _____-_______

Primary Care Physician No.: _____ Primary Care Physician Name: Ad-Med Mair

Insured Information

Primary Insured's Last Name: Harlan First: Ronnie MI: _____

Primary Insured's Address: 22B University Lane

City: Dallas State: TX Zip Code: 75204-3217

Primary Insured's Social Security No.: 782-55-2203 Insured's Telephone: (214) 555-0198

Primary Insured's Occupation: Sales Employer: Casa de Ville

Employer Address: 9287 Twin Oaks Drive

City: Dallas State: TX Zip Code: 75204 Telephone: (214) 555-0163

Relationship of Patient to Insured: ☐ Self ☑ Spouse ☐ Dependent

Secondary Insured's Last Name: __________ First: __________ MI: ___

Secondary Insured's Address: __________

City: __________ State: _____ Zip Code: _______

Secondary Insured's Social Security No.: __________ Insured's Telephone: (_____) _____-_______

Secondary Insured's Occupation: __________ Employer: __________

Employer Address: __________

City: __________ State: _____ Zip Code: _______ Telephone: (_____) _____-_______

Relationship of Patient to Insured: ☐ Self ☐ Spouse ☐ Dependent

Primary Insurance

Primary Insurance: ☐ United ☐ MetHealth ☐ TexMut ☐ Medicare

Other Insurance Company Name: Merchant's Medical Insurance

Insurance Company Address: 1642 Parkway

City: Dallas State: TX Zip Code: 75204 Telephone: (214) 555-0104

Policy No.: 0203 Group No.: 1064B

Secondary Insurance

Secondary Insurance Company: __________

Insurance Company Address: __________

City: __________ State: _____ Zip Code: _______

Policy No.: __________ Group No.: __________

Out-Patient Services Order

15

Physician Information

Physician's No.: 7

Physician's Name: Mair (Last) Ad-Med (First)

Street Address: 7109 Medical Center

Dallas (City) TX (State) 75246 (Zip)

Patient Information

Patient's Name: Harlan (Last) Tabitha (First)

Date of Birth: 2/1/51 Sex ___ M ✓ F

Patient's Phone No.: (214) 555-0198

ICD DIAGNOSIS CODES: 240.9, 780.9

Diagnosis: Graves disease, General symptoms

CPT PANELS

_____ BASIC METABOLIC – Calcium, chloride, Glucose, Sodium, Carbon Dioxide (CO2), Creatinine, Potassium, urea nitrogen (BUN) –80048

✓ COMPREHENSIVE METABOLIC – Albumin, Alkaline, Phosphatase, ALT/SGPT; AST/SGOT; bilirubin, total; Calcium; Carbon Dioxide; Chloride; Creatinine; Glucose; Potassium; Protein, total; Sodium; Urea Nitrogen –80053

✓ CORONARY RISK PROFILE (LIPID PANEL) – Total Cholesterol, HDO cholesterol, LDL Cholesterol calculated), Triglycerides –80061

CHEMISTRY

_____	ALBUMIN	82040
_____	ALK PHOSPHATASE	84075
_____	ALK/SGPT	84460
✓	T4, TOTAL	84436
✓	TSH	84443
_____	T3, TOTAL	84480
_____	TRIGLYCERIDES	84478
_____	UREA NITROGEN (BUN)	84520

BLOOD

_____	HEMATOCRIT	85013
_____	PARTIAL BLOOD COUNT	85021
✓	CBC/DIFF	85025
_____	CBC	85027
_____	RETICULOCYTE COUNT	85044
_____	PRO TIME/INR	85610
_____	AST/SGOT	85651

IMMUNOLOGY

_____	CEA	82378
_____	HEPATITIS B SURG AB	86706
_____	HEPATITIS C AB	86803
_____	HEPATITIS A AB (IGM)	86709
_____	HEPATITIS B SURG AG	87340

URINALYSIS/STOOL

_____	OCCULT BLOOD, DIAGNOSTIC	82270
✓	URINALYSIS, ROUTINE	81003
_____	URINE CULTURE	87086

GASTRIC

_____	EGD WITH BIOPSY	43239
_____	COLONOSCOPY	45380

NUCLEAR MEDICINE

_____	KIDNEY FLOW AND FUNCTION	76707
_____	THYROID UPTAKE MULTIPLE	78006

CARDIOLOGY

_____	BRAIN	78607
_____	EKG	93003

SURGICAL PATHOLOGY

_____	SPECIAL STAINS	80353
_____	BONE MARROW SME	80973
_____	DECALCIFICATION	83113

BREAST CENTER

_____	MAMMOGRAM LATERAL	76090
_____	DIAGNOSTIC MAMMOGRAM	76091
_____	STEREORTACTIC BREAST BIOPSY	76095
_____	NEEDLE LOCALIZATION	76096

GYNECOLOGICAL

_____	PAP SMEAR	99000
_____	GYN PROBLEM FOCUS	99212

DIAGNOSTIC RADIOLOGY

_____	NASAL BONES	72069
_____	SINUSES	70160
_____	ELBOW	73080
_____	KNEE	73564
_____	TIBIA/FIBULA	73590

CHEST IMAGING

_____	CHEST – PA/LATERAL	71020
_____	RIBS UNILATERAL	71120

DIAGNOSTIC ULTRASOUND

_____	US BREAST	75545
_____	US PREGNANT UTERUS	76805
_____	US SCROTUM	76870

MRI SERVICES

_____	MRI HEAD	70551
_____	MRI CERVICAL SPINE	72141
_____	MRI HEAD/NECK	70541
_____	MRI PELVIS	72198

GASTROINTESTINAL/ABDOMEN/URINARY TRACT

_____	ABDOMEN SURVEY	74000
_____	UPPER GI	74240

MISCELLANEOUS

_____	LYME, TOTAL	86618
_____	INJECTION	90788

Patient Information

15

To all returning patients: Fill in only the blanks that have changed since your last visit.

Social Security No.: 650-55-8140 Date of Birth: 01/01/1948 Sex: ☑ M ☐ F

Patient's Last Name: Sierra First: Luis MI: S

Patient's Address: RFD #3

City: Abeline State: TX Zip Code: 78796

Patient Home Telephone No.: (817) 555-0158 Patient Work Telephone: (____) ____-____

Occupation: Farmer Employer: ____

Employer Address: ____

City: ____ State: ____ Zip Code: ____ Telephone: (____) ____-____

Primary Care Physician No.: ____ Primary Care Physician Name: Su Ling

Insured Information

Primary Insured's Last Name: Sierra First: Luis MI: S

Primary Insured's Address: RFD #3

City: Abeline State: TX Zip Code: 78796

Primary Insured's Social Security No.: 650-55-8140 Insured's Telephone: (817) 555-0158

Primary Insured's Occupation: Farmer Employer: ____

Employer Address: ____

City: ____ State: ____ Zip Code: ____ Telephone: (____) ____-____

Relationship of Patient to Insured: ☑ Self ☐ Spouse ☐ Dependent

Secondary Insured's Last Name: ____ First: ____ MI: ____

Secondary Insured's Address: ____

City: ____ State: ____ Zip Code: ____

Secondary Insured's Social Security No.: ____ Insured's Telephone: (____) ____-____

Secondary Insured's Occupation: ____ Employer: ____

Employer Address: ____

City: ____ State: ____ Zip Code: ____ Telephone: (____) ____-____

Relationship of Patient to Insured: ☐ Self ☐ Spouse ☐ Dependent

Primary Insurance

Primary Insurance: ☐ United ☐ MetHealth ☐ TexMut ☐ Medicare

Other Insurance Company Name: American Managed Care

Insurance Company Address: 1602 Plaza Center

City: Houston State: TX Zip Code: 77030 Telephone: (713) 555-0147

Policy No.: TXS2600010 Group No.: Farm

Secondary Insurance

Secondary Insurance Company: ____

Insurance Company Address: ____

City: ____ State: ____ Zip Code: ____

Policy No.: ____ Group No.: ____

Out-Patient Services Order

15

Physician Information

Physician's No.: 6

Physician's Name: Ling (Last) Su (First)

Street Address: 6208 Medical Center

Dallas (City) TX (State) 75246 (Zip)

Patient Information

Patient's Name: Sierra (Last) Luis (First)

Date of Birth: 1/1/48 Sex ✓ M ____ F

Patient's Phone No.: (817) 555-0158

ICD DIAGNOSIS CODES: 573.3

Diagnosis: Hepatitis, unspecified

CPT PANELS

_____ BASIC METABOLIC – Calcium, chloride, Glucose, Sodium, Carbon Dioxide (CO_2), Creatinine, Potassium, urea nitrogen (BUN) –80048

_____ COMPREHENSIVE METABOLIC – Albumin, Alkaline, Phosphatase, ALT/SGPT; AST/SGOT; bilirubin, total; Calcium; Carbon Dioxide; Chloride; Creatinine; Glucose; Potassium; Protein, total; Sodium; Urea Nitrogen –80053

_____ CORONARY RISK PROFILE (LIPID PANEL) – Total Cholesterol, HDO cholesterol, LDL Cholesterol calculated), Triglycerides –80061

CHEMISTRY

_____	ALBUMIN	82040
_____	ALK PHOSPHATASE	84075
_____	ALK/SGPT	84460
_____	T4, TOTAL	84436
_____	TSH	84443
_____	T3, TOTAL	84480
_____	TRIGLYCERIDES	84478
_____	UREA NITROGEN (BUN)	84520

BLOOD

_____	HEMATOCRIT	85013
_____	PARTIAL BLOOD COUNT	85021
✓	CBC/DIFF	85025
_____	CBC	85027
_____	RETICULOCYTE COUNT	85044
_____	PRO TIME/INR	85610
_____	AST/SGOT	85651

IMMUNOLOGY

_____	CEA	82378
_____	HEPATITIS B SURG AB	86706
	HEPATITIS C AB	86803
✓	HEPATITIS A AB (IGM)	86709
_____	HEPATITIS B SURG AG	87340

URINALYSIS/STOOL

_____	OCCULT BLOOD, DIAGNOSTIC	82270
_____	URINALYSIS, ROUTINE	81003
_____	URINE CULTURE	87086

GASTRIC

_____	EGD WITH BIOPSY	43239
_____	COLONOSCOPY	45380

NUCLEAR MEDICINE

_____	KIDNEY FLOW AND FUNCTION	76707
_____	THYROID UPTAKE MULTIPLE	78006

CARDIOLOGY

_____	BRAIN	78607
_____	EKG	93003

SURGICAL PATHOLOGY

_____	SPECIAL STAINS	80353
_____	BONE MARROW SME	80973
_____	DECALCIFICATION	83113

BREAST CENTER

_____	MAMMOGRAM LATERAL	76090
_____	DIAGNOSTIC MAMMOGRAM	76091
_____	STEREORTACTIC BREAST BIOPSY	76095
_____	NEEDLE LOCALIZATION	76096

GYNECOLOGICAL

_____	PAP SMEAR	99000
_____	GYN PROBLEM FOCUS	99212

DIAGNOSTIC RADIOLOGY

_____	NASAL BONES	72069
_____	SINUSES	70160
_____	ELBOW	73080
_____	KNEE	73564
_____	TIBIA/FIBULA	73590

CHEST IMAGING

_____	CHEST – PA/LATERAL	71020
_____	RIBS UNILATERAL	71120

DIAGNOSTIC ULTRASOUND

_____	US BREAST	75545
_____	US PREGNANT UTERUS	76805
_____	US SCROTUM	76870

MRI SERVICES

_____	MRI HEAD	70551
_____	MRI CERVICAL SPINE	72141
_____	MRI HEAD/NECK	70541
_____	MRI PELVIS	72198

GASTROINTESTINAL/ABDOMEN/URINARY TRACT

_____	ABDOMEN SURVEY	74000
_____	UPPER GI	74240

MISCELLANEOUS

✓	LYME, TOTAL	86618
_____	INJECTION	90788

Patient Information

15

To all returning patients: Fill in only the blanks that have changed since your last visit.

Social Security No.: 212-55-0620 Date of Birth: 02/03/1991 Sex: ☐ M ☑ F

Patient's Last Name: Lopez First: Alina MI: S

Patient's Address: 15 Denvyn Road

City: Dallas State: TX Zip Code: 75201-4632

Patient Home Telephone No.: (214) 555 - 0161 Patient Work Telephone: (____) ____-______

Occupation: Student Employer: ______

Employer Address: ______

City: ______ State: ______ Zip Code: ______ Telephone: (____) ____-______

Primary Care Physician No.: ______ Primary Care Physician Name: Suzanne Appleby

Insured Information

Primary Insured's Last Name: Lopez First: Margaritta MI: R

Primary Insured's Address: 15 Denvyn Road

City: Dallas State: TX Zip Code: 75201-4632

Primary Insured's Social Security No.: 810-55-0194 Insured's Telephone: (214) 555 - 0161

Primary Insured's Occupation: Accountant Employer: Maxim Acct. Ser.

Employer Address: 313 Highland Avenue

City: Dallas State: TX Zip Code: 75201 Telephone: (214) 555 - 0149

Relationship of Patient to Insured: ☐ Self ☐ Spouse ☑ Dependent

Secondary Insured's Last Name: ______ First: ______ MI: ___

Secondary Insured's Address: ______

City: ______ State: ______ Zip Code: ______

Secondary Insured's Social Security No.: ______ Insured's Telephone: (____) ____-______

Secondary Insured's Occupation: ______ Employer: ______

Employer Address: ______

City: ______ State: ______ Zip Code: ______ Telephone: (____) ____-______

Relationship of Patient to Insured: ☐ Self ☐ Spouse ☐ Dependent

Primary Insurance

Primary Insurance: ☐ United ☑ MetHealth ☐ TexMut ☐ Medicare

Other Insurance Company Name: ______

Insurance Company Address: 1702 Broadway

City: Kansas City State: KS Zip Code: 66101 Telephone: (913) 555 - 0125

Policy No.: ML714-KC Group No.: TX-4387-L

Secondary Insurance

Secondary Insurance Company: ______

Insurance Company Address: ______

City: ______ State: ______ Zip Code: ______

Policy No.: ______ Group No.: ______

Out-Patient Services Order

15

Physician Information

Physician's No.: 4

Physician's Name: Appleby Suzanne
Last First

Street Address: 16-B Hospital Tower

Dallas TX 75336
City State Zip

Patient Information

Patient's Name: Lopez Alina
Last First

Date of Birth: 2/3/91 Sex ___ M ✓ F

Patient's Phone No.: (214) 555 - 0161

ICD DIAGNOSIS CODES: 486, 788.2

Diagnosis: Pneumonia, Cough

CPT PANELS

____ BASIC METABOLIC – Calcium, chloride, Glucose, Sodium, Carbon Dioxide (CO2), Creatinine, Potassium, urea nitrogen (BUN) –80048

____ COMPREHENSIVE METABOLIC – Albumin, Alkaline, Phosphatase, ALT/SGPT; AST/SGOT; bilirubin, total; Calcium; Carbon Dioxide; Chloride; Creatinine; Glucose; Potassium; Protein, total; Sodium; Urea Nitrogen –80053

____ CORONARY RISK PROFILE (LIPID PANEL) – Total Cholesterol, HDO cholesterol, LDL Cholesterol calculated), Triglycerides –80061

CHEMISTRY

____ ALBUMIN 82040
____ ALK PHOSPHATASE 84075
____ ALK/SGPT 84460
____ T4, TOTAL 84436
____ TSH 84443
____ T3, TOTAL 84480
____ TRIGLYCERIDES 84478
____ UREA NITROGEN (BUN) 84520

BLOOD

✓ HEMATOCRIT 85013
____ PARTIAL BLOOD COUNT 85021
____ CBC/DIFF 85025
✓ CBC 85027
____ RETICULOCYTE COUNT 85044
____ PRO TIME/INR 85610
____ AST/SGOT 85651

IMMUNOLOGY

____ CEA 82378
____ HEPATITIS B SURG AB 86706
____ HEPATITIS C AB 86803
____ HEPATITIS A AB (IGM) 86709
____ HEPATITIS B SURG AG 87340

URINALYSIS/STOOL

____ OCCULT BLOOD, DIAGNOSTIC 82270
____ URINALYSIS, ROUTINE 81003
____ URINE CULTURE 87086

GASTRIC

____ EGD WITH BIOPSY 43239
____ COLONOSCOPY 45380

NUCLEAR MEDICINE

____ KIDNEY FLOW AND FUNCTION 76707
____ THYROID UPTAKE MULTIPLE 78006

CARDIOLOGY

____ BRAIN 78607
____ EKG 93003

SURGICAL PATHOLOGY

____ SPECIAL STAINS 80353
____ BONE MARROW SME 80973
____ DECALCIFICATION 83113

BREAST CENTER

____ MAMMOGRAM LATERAL 76090
____ DIAGNOSTIC MAMMOGRAM 76091
____ STEREORTACTIC BREAST BIOPSY 76095
____ NEEDLE LOCALIZATION 76096

GYNECOLOGICAL

____ PAP SMEAR 99000
____ GYN PROBLEM FOCUS 99212

DIAGNOSTIC RADIOLOGY

____ NASAL BONES 72069
____ SINUSES 70160
____ ELBOW 73080
____ KNEE 73564
____ TIBIA/FIBULA 73590

CHEST IMAGING

✓ CHEST – PA/LATERAL 71020
____ RIBS UNILATERAL 71120

DIAGNOSTIC ULTRASOUND

____ US BREAST 75545
____ US PREGNANT UTERUS 76805
____ US SCROTUM 76870

MRI SERVICES

____ MRI HEAD 70551
____ MRI CERVICAL SPINE 72141
____ MRI HEAD/NECK 70541
____ MRI PELVIS 72198

GASTROINTESTINAL/ABDOMEN/URINARY TRACT

____ ABDOMEN SURVEY 74000
____ UPPER GI 74240

MISCELLANEOUS

____ LYME, TOTAL 86618
____ INJECTION 90788

Patient Information

15

To all returning patients: Fill in only the blanks that have changed since your last visit.

Social Security No.: 659-55-9642 Date of Birth: 08/02/1951 Sex: ☑ M ☐ F

Patient's Last Name: McDonald First: Andrew MI: R

Patient's Address: 2165 Winfred Lane

City: Bedford State: TX Zip Code: 76021

Patient Home Telephone No.: (972) 555-0143 Patient Work Telephone: (972) 555-0196

Occupation: CPA Employer: DFK INTERNATIONAL

Employer Address: 1486 Belmont Parkway

City: Dallas State: TX Zip Code: 75228 Telephone: (214) 555-0123

Primary Care Physician No.: ____ Primary Care Physician Name: Anita Rambo

Insured Information

Primary Insured's Last Name: McDonald First: Andrew MI: R

Primary Insured's Address: 2165 Winfred Lane

City: Bedford State: TX Zip Code: 76021

Primary Insured's Social Security No.: 659-55-9642 Insured's Telephone: (972) 555-0143

Primary Insured's Occupation: CPA Employer: DFK INTERNATIONAL

Employer Address: 1486 Belmont Parkway

City: Dallas State: TX Zip Code: 75228 Telephone: (214) 555-0123

Relationship of Patient to Insured: ☑ Self ☐ Spouse ☐ Dependent

Secondary Insured's Last Name: McDonald First: Luanne MI: C

Secondary Insured's Address: 2165 Winfred Lane

City: Bedford State: TX Zip Code: 76021

Secondary Insured's Social Security No.: 354-55-8067 Insured's Telephone: (972) 555-0143

Secondary Insured's Occupation: Shipping Clerk Employer: URS Shipping

Employer Address: 2604 Transportation Drive

City: Dallas State: TX Zip Code: 75228 Telephone: (214) 555-0162

Relationship of Patient to Insured: ☐ Self ☑ Spouse ☐ Dependent

Primary Insurance

Primary Insurance: ☐ United ☑ MetHealth ☐ TexMut ☐ Medicare

Other Insurance Company Name: ____

Insurance Company Address: 1702 Broadway

City: Kansas City State: KS Zip Code: 66101 Telephone: (913) 555-0125

Policy No.: AM610 Group No.: TX-4392-M

Secondary Insurance

Secondary Insurance Company: Texas Mutual Medical Insurance

Insurance Company Address: 602 Insurance Center Drive

City: Houston State: TX Zip Code: 77030

Policy No.: TM834967-M Group No.: URS620-C

Out-Patient Services Order

15

Physician Information

Physician's No.: 1

Physician's Name: Rambo (Last) Anita (First)

Street Address: 6102 Medical Center

Dallas (City) TX (State) 75336 (Zip)

Patient Information

Patient's Name: McDonald (Last) Andrew (First)

Date of Birth: 8/2/51 Sex ✓ M ___ F

Patient's Phone No.: (972) 555-0143

ICD DIAGNOSIS CODES: 401.1

Diagnosis: Hypertension, essential, benign

CPT PANELS

___ BASIC METABOLIC – Calcium, chloride, Glucose, Sodium, Carbon Dioxide (CO2), Creatinine, Potassium, urea nitrogen (BUN) –80048

✓ COMPREHENSIVE METABOLIC – Albumin, Alkaline, Phosphatase, ALT/SGPT; AST/SGOT; bilirubin, total; Calcium; Carbon Dioxide; Chloride; Creatinine; Glucose; Potassium; Protein, total; Sodium; Urea Nitrogen –80053

✓ CORONARY RISK PROFILE (LIPID PANEL) – Total Cholesterol, HDO cholesterol, LDL Cholesterol calculated), Triglycerides –80061

CHEMISTRY

___	ALBUMIN	82040
___	ALK PHOSPHATASE	84075
___	ALK/SGPT	84460
___	T4, TOTAL	84436
___	TSH	84443
___	T3, TOTAL	84480
___	TRIGLYCERIDES	84478
___	UREA NITROGEN (BUN)	84520

BLOOD

___	HEMATOCRIT	85013
___	PARTIAL BLOOD COUNT	85021
✓	CBC/DIFF	85025
✓	CBC	85027
___	RETICULOCYTE COUNT	85044
___	PRO TIME/INR	85610
___	AST/SGOT	85651

IMMUNOLOGY

___	CEA	82378
___	HEPATITIS B SURG AB	86706
___	HEPATITIS C AB	86803
___	HEPATITIS A AB (IGM)	86709
___	HEPATITIS B SURG AG	87340

URINALYSIS/STOOL

___	OCCULT BLOOD, DIAGNOSTIC	82270
___	URINALYSIS, ROUTINE	81003
___	URINE CULTURE	87086

GASTRIC

___	EGD WITH BIOPSY	43239
___	COLONOSCOPY	45380

NUCLEAR MEDICINE

___	KIDNEY FLOW AND FUNCTION	76707
___	THYROID UPTAKE MULTIPLE	78006

CARDIOLOGY

___	BRAIN	78607
___	EKG	93003

SURGICAL PATHOLOGY

___	SPECIAL STAINS	80353
___	BONE MARROW SME	80973
___	DECALCIFICATION	83113

BREAST CENTER

___	MAMMOGRAM LATERAL	76090
___	DIAGNOSTIC MAMMOGRAM	76091
___	STEREORTACTIC BREAST BIOPSY	76095
___	NEEDLE LOCALIZATION	76096

GYNECOLOGICAL

___	PAP SMEAR	99000
___	GYN PROBLEM FOCUS	99212

DIAGNOSTIC RADIOLOGY

___	NASAL BONES	72069
___	SINUSES	70160
___	ELBOW	73080
___	KNEE	73564
___	TIBIA/FIBULA	73590

CHEST IMAGING

___	CHEST – PA/LATERAL	71020
___	RIBS UNILATERAL	71120

DIAGNOSTIC ULTRASOUND

___	US BREAST	75545
___	US PREGNANT UTERUS	76805
___	US SCROTUM	76870

MRI SERVICES

___	MRI HEAD	70551
___	MRI CERVICAL SPINE	72141
___	MRI HEAD/NECK	70541
___	MRI PELVIS	72198

GASTROINTESTINAL/ABDOMEN/URINARY TRACT

___	ABDOMEN SURVEY	74000
___	UPPER GI	74240

MISCELLANEOUS

___	LYME, TOTAL	86618
___	INJECTION	90788

Out-Patient Services Order

16–1

Physician Information

Physician's No.: 6

Physician's Name: Ling Su
Last First

Street Address: 6208 Medical Center

Dallas TX 75246
City State Zip

Patient Information

Patient's Name: Pilczarski Melissa
Last First

Date of Birth: 5/4/1949 Sex ___ M ✓ F

Patient's Phone No.: (817) 555-0122

ICD DIAGNOSIS CODES: 610.1

Diagnosis: Cystic breast

CPT PANELS

_____ BASIC METABOLIC – Calcium, chloride, Glucose, Sodium, Carbon Dioxide (CO2), Creatinine, Potassium, urea nitrogen (BUN) –80048

_____ COMPREHENSIVE METABOLIC – Albumin, Alkaline, Phosphatase, ALT/SGPT; AST/SGOT; bilirubin, total; Calcium; Carbon Dioxide; Chloride; Creatinine; Glucose; Potassium; Protein, total; Sodium; Urea Nitrogen –80053

_____ CORONARY RISK PROFILE (LIPID PANEL) – Total Cholesterol, HDO cholesterol, LDL Cholesterol calculated), Triglycerides –80061

CHEMISTRY

_____	ALBUMIN	82040
_____	ALK PHOSPHATASE	84075
_____	ALK/SGPT	84460
_____	T4, TOTAL	84436
_____	TSH	84443
_____	T3, TOTAL	84480
_____	TRIGLYCERIDES	84478
_____	UREA NITROGEN (BUN)	84520

BLOOD

_____	HEMATOCRIT	85013
_____	PARTIAL BLOOD COUNT	85021
_____	CBC/DIFF	85025
_____	CBC	85027
_____	RETICULOCYTE COUNT	85044
_____	PRO TIME/INR	85610
_____	AST/SGOT	85651

IMMUNOLOGY

_____	CEA	82378
_____	HEPATITIS B SURG AB	86706
_____	HEPATITIS C AB	86803
_____	HEPATITIS A AB (IGM)	86709
_____	HEPATITIS B SURG AG	87340

URINALYSIS/STOOL

_____	OCCULT BLOOD, DIAGNOSTIC	82270
_____	URINALYSIS, ROUTINE	81003
_____	URINE CULTURE	87086

GASTRIC

_____	EGD WITH BIOPSY	43239
_____	COLONOSCOPY	45380

NUCLEAR MEDICINE

_____	KIDNEY FLOW AND FUNCTION	76707
_____	THYROID UPTAKE MULTIPLE	78006

CARDIOLOGY

_____	BRAIN	78607
_____	EKG	93003

SURGICAL PATHOLOGY

_____	SPECIAL STAINS	80353
_____	BONE MARROW SME	80973
_____	DECALCIFICATION	83113

BREAST CENTER

_____	MAMMOGRAM LATERAL	76090
_____	DIAGNOSTIC MAMMOGRAM	76091
_____	STEREORTACTIC BREAST BIOPSY	76095
_____	NEEDLE LOCALIZATION	76096

GYNECOLOGICAL

_____	PAP SMEAR	99000
_____	GYN PROBLEM FOCUS	99212

DIAGNOSTIC RADIOLOGY

_____	NASAL BONES	72069
_____	SINUSES	70160
_____	ELBOW	73080
_____	KNEE	73564
_____	TIBIA/FIBULA	73590

CHEST IMAGING

_____	CHEST – PA/LATERAL	71020
_____	RIBS UNILATERAL	71120

DIAGNOSTIC ULTRASOUND

✓	US BREAST	75545
_____	US PREGNANT UTERUS	76805
_____	US SCROTUM	76870

MRI SERVICES

_____	MRI HEAD	70551
_____	MRI CERVICAL SPINE	72141
_____	MRI HEAD/NECK	70541
_____	MRI PELVIS	72198

GASTROINTESTINAL/ABDOMEN/URINARY TRACT

_____	ABDOMEN SURVEY	74000
_____	UPPER GI	74240

MISCELLANEOUS

_____	LYME, TOTAL	86618
_____	INJECTION	90788

Patient Information

16–1

To all returning patients: Fill in only the blanks that have changed since your last visit.

Social Security No.: 212-55-6201 Date of Birth: 05/04/1949 Sex: ☐ M ☑ F

Patient's Last Name: Pilczarski First: Melissa MI: A

Patient's Address: 59G Upton Lane

City: Ft. Worth State: TX Zip Code: 91822

Patient Home Telephone No.: (817) 555-0122 Patient Work Telephone: (817) 555-0145

Occupation: Dental Assistant Employer: Dr. Emilio Suarez

Employer Address: 22K Dental Building

City: Ft. Worth State: TX Zip Code: 91822-0349 Telephone: (817) 555-0145

Primary Care Physician No.: _____ Primary Care Physician Name: Su Ling

Insured Information

Primary Insured's Last Name: Pilczarski First: Melissa MI: A

Primary Insured's Address: 59G Upton Lane

City: Ft. Worth State: TX Zip Code: 91822

Primary Insured's Social Security No.: 212-55-6201 Insured's Telephone: (817) 555-0122

Primary Insured's Occupation: Dental Assistant Employer: Dr. Emilio Suarez

Employer Address: 22K Dental Building

City: Ft. Worth State: TX Zip Code: 91822-0349 Telephone: (817) 555-0145

Relationship of Patient to Insured: ☑ Self ☐ Spouse ☐ Dependent

Secondary Insured's Last Name: Pilczarski First: Frank MI: M

Secondary Insured's Address: 59G Upton Lane

City: Ft. Worth State: TX Zip Code: 91822

Secondary Insured's Social Security No.: 345-55-2201 Insured's Telephone: (817) 555-0122

Secondary Insured's Occupation: Reporter Employer: The Daily Mail

Employer Address: 556 Edgewood Drive

City: Ft. Worth State: TX Zip Code: 91822 Telephone: (817) 555-0198

Relationship of Patient to Insured: ☐ Self ☑ Spouse ☐ Dependent

Primary Insurance

Primary Insurance: ☐ United ☑ MetHealth ☐ TexMut ☐ Medicare

Other Insurance Company Name: _____

Insurance Company Address: 1702 Broadway

City: Kansas City State: KS Zip Code: 66101 Telephone: (913) 555-0125

Policy No.: MP435-KC Group No.: TX-2387-P

Secondary Insurance

Secondary Insurance Company: United Medical Services

Insurance Company Address: 2329 Lexton Lane

City: Ft. Worth State: TX Zip Code: 91822

Policy No.: UMS20-945 Group No.: 849029-P

Out-Patient Services Order

16–2

Physician Information

Physician's No.: 9

Physician's Name: Albino (Last) Ramon (First)

Street Address: 111 Northern Lane

Dallas (City) TX (State) 76346 (Zip)

Patient Information

Patient's Name: Daniels (Last) Louis (First)

Date of Birth: 1/1/59 Sex ✓ M ___ F

Patient's Phone No.: (214) 555-0119

ICD DIAGNOSIS CODES: 715, 719.46, 719.47

Diagnosis: Osteoarthritis, Pain in foot, Pain in leg

CPT PANELS

_____ BASIC METABOLIC – Calcium, chloride, Glucose, Sodium, Carbon Dioxide (CO2), Creatinine, Potassium, urea nitrogen (BUN) –80048

✓ COMPREHENSIVE METABOLIC – Albumin, Alkaline, Phosphatase, ALT/SGPT; AST/SGOT; bilirubin, total; Calcium; Carbon Dioxide; Chloride; Creatinine; Glucose; Potassium; Protein, total; Sodium; Urea Nitrogen –80053

✓ CORONARY RISK PROFILE (LIPID PANEL) – Total Cholesterol, HDO cholesterol, LDL Cholesterol calculated), Triglycerides –80061

CHEMISTRY

_____	ALBUMIN	82040
_____	ALK PHOSPHATASE	84075
_____	ALK/SGPT	84460
_____	T4, TOTAL	84436
_____	TSH	84443
_____	T3, TOTAL	84480
_____	TRIGLYCERIDES	84478
_____	UREA NITROGEN (BUN)	84520

BLOOD

_____	HEMATOCRIT	85013
_____	PARTIAL BLOOD COUNT	85021
_____	CBC/DIFF	85025
_____	CBC	85027
_____	RETICULOCYTE COUNT	85044
_____	PRO TIME/INR	85610
_____	AST/SGOT	85651

IMMUNOLOGY

_____	CEA	82378
_____	HEPATITIS B SURG AB	86706
_____	HEPATITIS C AB	86803
_____	HEPATITIS A AB (IGM)	86709
_____	HEPATITIS B SURG AG	87340

URINALYSIS/STOOL

_____	OCCULT BLOOD, DIAGNOSTIC	82270
_____	URINALYSIS, ROUTINE	81003
_____	URINE CULTURE	87086

GASTRIC

_____	EGD WITH BIOPSY	43239
_____	COLONOSCOPY	45380

NUCLEAR MEDICINE

_____	KIDNEY FLOW AND FUNCTION	76707
_____	THYROID UPTAKE MULTIPLE	78006

CARDIOLOGY

_____	BRAIN	78607
_____	EKG	93003

SURGICAL PATHOLOGY

_____	SPECIAL STAINS	80353
_____	BONE MARROW SME	80973
_____	DECALCIFICATION	83113

BREAST CENTER

_____	MAMMOGRAM LATERAL	76090
_____	DIAGNOSTIC MAMMOGRAM	76091
_____	STEREORTACTIC BREAST BIOPSY	76095
_____	NEEDLE LOCALIZATION	76096

GYNECOLOGICAL

_____	PAP SMEAR	99000
_____	GYN PROBLEM FOCUS	99212

DIAGNOSTIC RADIOLOGY

_____	NASAL BONES	72069
_____	SINUSES	70160
_____	ELBOW	73080
✓	KNEE	73564
✓	TIBIA/FIBULA	73590

CHEST IMAGING

_____	CHEST – PA/LATERAL	71020
_____	RIBS UNILATERAL	71120

DIAGNOSTIC ULTRASOUND

_____	US BREAST	75545
_____	US PREGNANT UTERUS	76805
_____	US SCROTUM	76870

MRI SERVICES

_____	MRI HEAD	70551
_____	MRI CERVICAL SPINE	72141
_____	MRI HEAD/NECK	70541
_____	MRI PELVIS	72198

GASTROINTESTINAL/ABDOMEN/URINARY TRACT

_____	ABDOMEN SURVEY	74000
_____	UPPER GI	74240

MISCELLANEOUS

_____	LYME, TOTAL	86618
_____	INJECTION	90788

Patient Information

16–2

To all returning patients: Fill in only the blanks that have changed since your last visit.

Social Security No.: 313-55-2203 Date of Birth: 01/01/1959 Sex: ☑ M ☐ F

Patient's Last Name: Daniels First: Louis MI: P

Patient's Address: 2323 Oak Avenue

City: Cooper State: TX Zip Code: 75432-0912

Patient Home Telephone No.: (214) 555-0119 Patient Work Telephone: (214) 555-0176

Occupation: Landscaper Employer: Prairie Landscaping

Employer Address: 9264 Laurel Lane

City: Cooper State: TX Zip Code: 75432 Telephone: (214) 555-0176

Primary Care Physician No.: ______ Primary Care Physician Name: Ramon Albino

Insured Information

Primary Insured's Last Name: Daniels First: Louis MI: P

Primary Insured's Address: 2323 Oak Avenue

City: Cooper State: TX Zip Code: 75432-0192

Primary Insured's Social Security No.: 313-55-2203 Insured's Telephone: (214) 555-0119

Primary Insured's Occupation: Landscaper Employer: Prairie Landscaping

Employer Address: 9264 Laurel Lane

City: Cooper State: TX Zip Code: 75432 Telephone: (214) 555-0176

Relationship of Patient to Insured: ☑ Self ☐ Spouse ☐ Dependent

Secondary Insured's Last Name: ______ First: ______ MI: ___

Secondary Insured's Address: ______

City: ______ State: ______ Zip Code: ______

Secondary Insured's Social Security No.: ______ Insured's Telephone: (____) ____-______

Secondary Insured's Occupation: ______ Employer: ______

Employer Address: ______

City: ______ State: ______ Zip Code: ______ Telephone: (____) ____-______

Relationship of Patient to Insured: ☐ Self ☐ Spouse ☐ Dependent

Primary Insurance

Primary Insurance: ☑ United ☐ MetHealth ☐ TexMut ☐ Medicare

Other Insurance Company Name: ______

Insurance Company Address: 2329 Lexton Lane

City: Ft. Worth State: TX Zip Code: 91822 Telephone: (817) 555-0149

Policy No.: UMS37-810 Group No.: 212102-C

Secondary Insurance

Secondary Insurance Company: ______

Insurance Company Address: ______

City: ______ State: ______ Zip Code: ______

Policy No.: ______ Group No.: ______

Out-Patient Services Order

16–3

Physician Information

Physician's No.: 8

Physician's Name: Sanchez (Last) Carlos (First)

Street Address: 4802 Parkway Blvd.

Dallas (City) TX (State) 75246 (Zip)

Patient Information

Patient's Name: Torres (Last) Serena (First)

Date of Birth: 5/14/77 Sex ____ M ✓ F

Patient's Phone No.: (817) 555 - 0142

ICD DIAGNOSIS CODES: 461.0

Diagnosis: Sinusitis acute

CPT PANELS

_____ BASIC METABOLIC – Calcium, chloride, Glucose, Sodium, Carbon Dioxide (CO2), Creatinine, Potassium, urea nitrogen (BUN) –80048

_____ COMPREHENSIVE METABOLIC – Albumin, Alkaline, Phosphatase, ALT/SGPT; AST/SGOT; bilirubin, total; Calcium; Carbon Dioxide; Chloride; Creatinine; Glucose; Potassium; Protein, total; Sodium; Urea Nitrogen –80053

_____ CORONARY RISK PROFILE (LIPID PANEL) – Total Cholesterol, HDO cholesterol, LDL Cholesterol calculated), Triglycerides –80061

CHEMISTRY

_____ALBUMIN 82040
_____ALK PHOSPHATASE 84075
_____ALK/SGPT 84460
_____T4, TOTAL 84436
_____TSH 84443
_____T3, TOTAL 84480
_____TRIGLYCERIDES 84478
_____UREA NITROGEN (BUN) 84520

BLOOD

_____HEMATOCRIT 85013
_____PARTIAL BLOOD COUNT 85021
_____CBC/DIFF 85025
_____CBC 85027
_____RETICULOCYTE COUNT 85044
_____PRO TIME/INR 85610
_____AST/SGOT 85651

IMMUNOLOGY

_____CEA 82378
_____HEPATITIS B SURG AB 86706
_____HEPATITIS C AB 86803
_____HEPATITIS A AB (IGM) 86709
_____HEPATITIS B SURG AG 87340

URINALYSIS/STOOL

_____OCCULT BLOOD, DIAGNOSTIC 82270
_____URINALYSIS, ROUTINE 81003
_____URINE CULTURE 87086

GASTRIC

_____EGD WITH BIOPSY 43239
_____COLONOSCOPY 45380

NUCLEAR MEDICINE

_____KIDNEY FLOW AND FUNCTION 76707
_____THYROID UPTAKE MULTIPLE 78006

CARDIOLOGY

_____BRAIN 78607
_____EKG 93003

SURGICAL PATHOLOGY

_____SPECIAL STAINS 80353
_____BONE MARROW SME 80973
_____DECALCIFICATION 83113

BREAST CENTER

_____MAMMOGRAM LATERAL 76090
_____DIAGNOSTIC MAMMOGRAM 76091
_____STEREORTACTIC BREAST BIOPSY 76095
_____NEEDLE LOCALIZATION 76096

GYNECOLOGICAL

_____PAP SMEAR 99000
_____GYN PROBLEM FOCUS 99212

DIAGNOSTIC RADIOLOGY

✓ NASAL BONES 72069
✓ SINUSES 70160
_____ELBOW 73080
_____KNEE 73564
_____TIBIA/FIBULA 73590

CHEST IMAGING

_____CHEST – PA/LATERAL 71020
_____RIBS UNILATERAL 71120

DIAGNOSTIC ULTRASOUND

_____US BREAST 75545
_____US PREGNANT UTERUS 76805
_____US SCROTUM 76870

MRI SERVICES

_____MRI HEAD 70551
_____MRI CERVICAL SPINE 72141
_____MRI HEAD/NECK 70541
_____MRI PELVIS 72198

GASTROINTESTINAL/ABDOMEN/URINARY TRACT

_____ABDOMEN SURVEY 74000
_____UPPER GI 74240

MISCELLANEOUS

_____LYME, TOTAL 86618
_____INJECTION 90788

Patient Information

16–3

To all returning patients: Fill in only the blanks that have changed since your last visit.

Social Security No.: 624-55-0319 Date of Birth: 05/14/1977 Sex: ☐ M ☑ F

Patient's Last Name: Torres First: Serena MI: I

Patient's Address: 8302 Ribber Road

City: Denton State: TX Zip Code: 76076

Patient Home Telephone No.: (817) 555 - 0142 Patient Work Telephone: (817) 555 - 0129

Occupation: Airline ticket agent Employer: West Airways

Employer Address: 2233 Prairie View

City: Houston State: TX Zip Code: 77030-6104 Telephone: (713) 555 - 0156

Primary Care Physician No.: ____ Primary Care Physician Name: Carlos Sanchez

Insured Information

Primary Insured's Last Name: Torres First: Serena MI: I

Primary Insured's Address: 8302 Ribber Road

City: Denton State: TX Zip Code: 76076

Primary Insured's Social Security No.: 624-55-0319 Insured's Telephone: (817) 555 - 0142

Primary Insured's Occupation: Airline ticket agent Employer: West Airways

Employer Address: 2233 Prairie View

City: Houston State: TX Zip Code: 77030-6104 Telephone: (713) 555 - 0156

Relationship of Patient to Insured: ☑ Self ☐ Spouse ☐ Dependent

Secondary Insured's Last Name: Torres First: Juan MI: S

Secondary Insured's Address: 8302 Ribber Road

City: Denton State: TX Zip Code: 76076

Secondary Insured's Social Security No.: 394-55-9382 Insured's Telephone: (817) 555 - 0142

Secondary Insured's Occupation: Florist Employer: Self

Employer Address: 6002 Carpenter Lane

City: Denton State: TX Zip Code: 76076 Telephone: (713) 555 - 0183

Relationship of Patient to Insured: ☐ Self ☑ Spouse ☐ Dependent

Primary Insurance

Primary Insurance: ☐ United ☐ MetHealth ☑ TexMut ☐ Medicare

Other Insurance Company Name: ____

Insurance Company Address: 602 Insurance Center Drive

City: Houston State: TX Zip Code: 77030 Telephone: (713) 555 - 0167

Policy No.: TM837729-T Group No.: WA392T

Secondary Insurance

Secondary Insurance Company: American Managed Care

Insurance Company Address: 1602 Plaza Center

City: Houston State: TX Zip Code: 77030

Policy No.: TXS2600010 Group No.: Floral

Out-Patient Services Order

16–4

Physician Information

Physician's No.: 9

Physician's Name: Albino (Last) Ramon (First)

Street Address: 111 Northern Lane

Dallas (City) TX (State) 76346 (Zip)

Patient Information

Patient's Name: Swerdlow (Last) Frank (First)

Date of Birth: 4/14/1944 Sex ✓ M ____ F

Patient's Phone No.: (713) 555-0126

ICD DIAGNOSIS CODES: 573.3

Diagnosis: Hepatitis, unspecified

CPT PANELS

_____ BASIC METABOLIC – Calcium, chloride, Glucose, Sodium, Carbon Dioxide (CO2), Creatinine, Potassium, urea nitrogen (BUN) –80048

_____ COMPREHENSIVE METABOLIC – Albumin, Alkaline, Phosphatase, ALT/SGPT; AST/SGOT; bilirubin, total; Calcium; Carbon Dioxide; Chloride; Creatinine; Glucose; Potassium; Protein, total; Sodium; Urea Nitrogen –80053

_____ CORONARY RISK PROFILE (LIPID PANEL) – Total Cholesterol, HDO cholesterol, LDL Cholesterol calculated), Triglycerides –80061

CHEMISTRY

_____ALBUMIN 82040
_____ALK PHOSPHATASE 84075
_____ALK/SGPT 84460
_____T4, TOTAL 84436
_____TSH 84443
_____T3, TOTAL 84480
_____TRIGLYCERIDES 84478
_____UREA NITROGEN (BUN) 84520

BLOOD

✓ HEMATOCRIT 85013
_____PARTIAL BLOOD COUNT 85021
✓ CBC/DIFF 85025
_____CBC 85027
_____RETICULOCYTE COUNT 85044
_____PRO TIME/INR 85610
_____AST/SGOT 85651

IMMUNOLOGY

_____CEA 82378
_____HEPATITIS B SURG AB 86706
✓ HEPATITIS C AB 86803
_____HEPATITIS A AB (IGM) 86709
_____HEPATITIS B SURG AG 87340

URINALYSIS/STOOL

_____OCCULT BLOOD, DIAGNOSTIC 82270
_____URINALYSIS, ROUTINE 81003
_____URINE CULTURE 87086

GASTRIC

_____EGD WITH BIOPSY 43239
_____COLONOSCOPY 45380

NUCLEAR MEDICINE

_____KIDNEY FLOW AND FUNCTION 76707
_____THYROID UPTAKE MULTIPLE 78006

CARDIOLOGY

_____BRAIN 78607
_____EKG 93003

SURGICAL PATHOLOGY

_____SPECIAL STAINS 80353
_____BONE MARROW SME 80973
_____DECALCIFICATION 83113

BREAST CENTER

_____MAMMOGRAM LATERAL 76090
_____DIAGNOSTIC MAMMOGRAM 76091
_____STEREORTACTIC BREAST BIOPSY 76095
_____NEEDLE LOCALIZATION 76096

GYNECOLOGICAL

_____PAP SMEAR 99000
_____GYN PROBLEM FOCUS 99212

DIAGNOSTIC RADIOLOGY

_____NASAL BONES 72069
_____SINUSES 70160
_____ELBOW 73080
_____KNEE 73564
_____TIBIA/FIBULA 73590

CHEST IMAGING

_____CHEST – PA/LATERAL 71020
_____RIBS UNILATERAL 71120

DIAGNOSTIC ULTRASOUND

_____US BREAST 75545
_____US PREGNANT UTERUS 76805
_____US SCROTUM 76870

MRI SERVICES

_____MRI HEAD 70551
_____MRI CERVICAL SPINE 72141
_____MRI HEAD/NECK 70541
_____MRI PELVIS 72198

GASTROINTESTINAL/ABDOMEN/URINARY TRACT

_____ABDOMEN SURVEY 74000
_____UPPER GI 74240

MISCELLANEOUS

_____LYME, TOTAL 86618
_____INJECTION 90788

Patient Information

16–4

To all returning patients: Fill in only the blanks that have changed since your last visit.

Social Security No.: 345-55-2354 Date of Birth: 04/14/1944 Sex: ☑ M ☐ F

Patient's Last Name: Swerdlow First: Frank MI: J

Patient's Address: 1105 Edgewood Road

City: Ft. Worth State: TX Zip Code: 91822

Patient Home Telephone No.: (713) 555-0126 Patient Work Telephone: (713) 555-0198

Occupation: Dry clean owner Employer: Self

Employer Address: 2204 Edgewood Road

City: Ft. Worth State: TX Zip Code: 91822 Telephone: (713) 555-0198

Primary Care Physician No.: _____ Primary Care Physician Name: Ramon Albino

Insured Information

Primary Insured's Last Name: Swerdlow First: Frank MI: J

Primary Insured's Address: 1105 Edgewood Road

City: Ft. Worth State: TX Zip Code: 91822

Primary Insured's Social Security No.: 345-55-2354 Insured's Telephone: (713) 555-0126

Primary Insured's Occupation: Dry clean owner Employer: Self

Employer Address: 2204 Edgewood Road

City: Ft. Worth State: TX Zip Code: 91822 Telephone: (713) 555-0198

Relationship of Patient to Insured: ☑ Self ☐ Spouse ☐ Dependent

Secondary Insured's Last Name: ______ First: ______ MI: ___

Secondary Insured's Address: ______

City: ______ State: ______ Zip Code: ______

Secondary Insured's Social Security No.: ______ Insured's Telephone: (_____) _____-______

Secondary Insured's Occupation: ______ Employer: ______

Employer Address: ______

City: ______ State: ______ Zip Code: ______ Telephone: (_____) _____-______

Relationship of Patient to Insured: ☐ Self ☐ Spouse ☐ Dependent

Primary Insurance

Primary Insurance: ☐ United ☐ MetHealth ☑ TexMut ☐ Medicare

Other Insurance Company Name: ______

Insurance Company Address: 602 Insurance Center Drive

City: Houston State: TX Zip Code: 77030 Telephone: (713) 555-0167

Policy No.: TM4659387-S Group No.: FS393T

Secondary Insurance

Secondary Insurance Company: ______

Insurance Company Address: ______

City: ______ State: ______ Zip Code: ______

Policy No.: ______ Group No.: ______

Out-Patient Services Order

16–5

Physician Information

Physician's No.: 1

Physician's Name: Rambo (Last) Anita (First)

Street Address: 6102 Medical Center

Dallas (City) TX (State) 75336 (Zip)

Patient Information

Patient's Name: Inella (Last) Mona (First)

Date of Birth: 2/10/22 Sex ___ M ✓ F

Patient's Phone No.: (713) 555-0122

ICD DIAGNOSIS CODES: V72.3, 617.9

Diagnosis: Gynecological exam, Endometriosis

CPT PANELS

_____ BASIC METABOLIC – Calcium, chloride, Glucose, Sodium, Carbon Dioxide (CO2), Creatinine, Potassium, urea nitrogen (BUN) –80048

_____ COMPREHENSIVE METABOLIC – Albumin, Alkaline, Phosphatase, ALT/SGPT; AST/SGOT; bilirubin, total; Calcium; Carbon Dioxide; Chloride; Creatinine; Glucose; Potassium; Protein, total; Sodium; Urea Nitrogen –80053

_____ CORONARY RISK PROFILE (LIPID PANEL) – Total Cholesterol, HDO cholesterol, LDL Cholesterol calculated), Triglycerides –80061

CHEMISTRY

_____ALBUMIN 82040
_____ALK PHOSPHATASE 84075
_____ALK/SGPT 84460
_____T4, TOTAL 84436
_____TSH 84443
_____T3, TOTAL 84480
_____TRIGLYCERIDES 84478
_____UREA NITROGEN (BUN) 84520

BLOOD

_____HEMATOCRIT 85013
_____PARTIAL BLOOD COUNT 85021
_____CBC/DIFF 85025
_____CBC 85027
_____RETICULOCYTE COUNT 85044
_____PRO TIME/INR 85610
_____AST/SGOT 85651

IMMUNOLOGY

_____CEA 82378
_____HEPATITIS B SURG AB 86706
_____HEPATITIS C AB 86803
_____HEPATITIS A AB (IGM) 86709
_____HEPATITIS B SURG AG 87340

URINALYSIS/STOOL

_____OCCULT BLOOD, DIAGNOSTIC 82270
_____URINALYSIS, ROUTINE 81003
_____URINE CULTURE 87086

GASTRIC

_____EGD WITH BIOPSY 43239
_____COLONOSCOPY 45380

NUCLEAR MEDICINE

_____KIDNEY FLOW AND FUNCTION 76707
_____THYROID UPTAKE MULTIPLE 78006

CARDIOLOGY

_____BRAIN 78607
_____EKG 93003

SURGICAL PATHOLOGY

_____SPECIAL STAINS 80353
_____BONE MARROW SME 80973
_____DECALCIFICATION 83113

BREAST CENTER

_____MAMMOGRAM LATERAL 76090
_____DIAGNOSTIC MAMMOGRAM 76091
_____STEREORTACTIC BREAST BIOPSY 76095
_____NEEDLE LOCALIZATION 76096

GYNECOLOGICAL

✓ PAP SMEAR 99000
✓ GYN PROBLEM FOCUS 99212

DIAGNOSTIC RADIOLOGY

_____NASAL BONES 72069
_____SINUSES 70160
_____ELBOW 73080
_____KNEE 73564
_____TIBIA/FIBULA 73590

CHEST IMAGING

_____CHEST – PA/LATERAL 71020
_____RIBS UNILATERAL 71120

DIAGNOSTIC ULTRASOUND

_____US BREAST 75545
_____US PREGNANT UTERUS 76805
_____US SCROTUM 76870

MRI SERVICES

_____MRI HEAD 70551
_____MRI CERVICAL SPINE 72141
_____MRI HEAD/NECK 70541
_____MRI PELVIS 72198

GASTROINTESTINAL/ABDOMEN/URINARY TRACT

_____ABDOMEN SURVEY 74000
_____UPPER GI 74240

MISCELLANEOUS

_____LYME, TOTAL 86618
_____INJECTION 90788

Patient Information

16–5

To all returning patients: Fill in only the blanks that have changed since your last visit.

Social Security No.: 216-55-2342 Date of Birth: 02/10/1922 Sex: ☐ M ☑ F

Patient's Last Name: Inella First: Mona MI: U

Patient's Address: 475 Hidden Lane

City: Houston State: TX Zip Code: 77030-2190

Patient Home Telephone No.: (713) 555-0122 Patient Work Telephone: (_____) _____-_______

Occupation: Retired Employer: ________

Employer Address: ________

City: ________ State: ______ Zip Code: ________ Telephone: (_____) _____-_______

Primary Care Physician No.: _____ Primary Care Physician Name: Anita Rambo

Insured Information

Primary Insured's Last Name: Inella First: Mona MI: U

Primary Insured's Address: 475 Hidden Lane

City: Houston State: TX Zip Code: 77030-2190

Primary Insured's Social Security No.: 216-55-2342 Insured's Telephone: (713) 555-0122

Primary Insured's Occupation: Retired Employer: ________

Employer Address: ________

City: ________ State: ______ Zip Code: ________ Telephone: (_____) _____-_______

Relationship of Patient to Insured: ☑ Self ☐ Spouse ☐ Dependent

Secondary Insured's Last Name: ________ First: ________ MI: ___

Secondary Insured's Address: ________

City: ________ State: ______ Zip Code: ________

Secondary Insured's Social Security No.: ________ Insured's Telephone: (_____) _____-_______

Secondary Insured's Occupation: ________ Employer: ________

Employer Address: ________

City: ________ State: ______ Zip Code: ________ Telephone: (_____) _____-_______

Relationship of Patient to Insured: ☐ Self ☐ Spouse ☐ Dependent

Primary Insurance

Primary Insurance: ☐ United ☐ MetHealth ☐ TexMut ☑ Medicare

Other Insurance Company Name: ________

Insurance Company Address: 42 Bellevue Avenue

City: Dallas State: TX Zip Code: 75201 Telephone: (214) 555-0189

Policy No.: 216552342 Group No.: 42A

Secondary Insurance

Secondary Insurance Company: ________

Insurance Company Address: ________

City: ________ State: ______ Zip Code: ________

Policy No.: ________ Group No.: ________

Out-Patient Services Order

16–6

Physician Information	**Patient Information**
Physician's No.: 9	
Physician's Name: Albino (Last) Ramon (First)	Patient's Name: Lopreti (Last) Albert (First)
Street Address: 111 Northern Lane	Date of Birth: 1/19/47 Sex ✓ M ___ F
City: Dallas State: TX Zip: 76346	Patient's Phone No.: (817) 555 - 0183

ICD DIAGNOSIS CODES: 788.41, 780.79

Diagnosis: Urinary frequency, Fatigue and malaise

CPT PANELS

_____ BASIC METABOLIC – Calcium, chloride, Glucose, Sodium, Carbon Dioxide (CO2), Creatinine, Potassium, urea nitrogen (BUN) –80048

_____ COMPREHENSIVE METABOLIC – Albumin, Alkaline, Phosphatase, ALT/SGPT; AST/SGOT; bilirubin, total; Calcium; Carbon Dioxide; Chloride; Creatinine; Glucose; Potassium; Protein, total; Sodium; Urea Nitrogen –80053

_____ CORONARY RISK PROFILE (LIPID PANEL) – Total Cholesterol, HDO cholesterol, LDL Cholesterol calculated), Triglycerides –80061

CHEMISTRY

_____	ALBUMIN	82040
_____	ALK PHOSPHATASE	84075
_____	ALK/SGPT	84460
_____	T4, TOTAL	84436
_____	TSH	84443
_____	T3, TOTAL	84480
_____	TRIGLYCERIDES	84478
_____	UREA NITROGEN (BUN)	84520

BLOOD

✓	HEMATOCRIT	85013
_____	PARTIAL BLOOD COUNT	85021
✓	CBC/DIFF	85025
_____	CBC	85027
_____	RETICULOCYTE COUNT	85044
_____	PRO TIME/INR	85610
_____	AST/SGOT	85651

IMMUNOLOGY

_____	CEA	82378
_____	HEPATITIS B SURG AB	86706
_____	HEPATITIS C AB	86803
_____	HEPATITIS A AB (IGM)	86709
_____	HEPATITIS B SURG AG	87340

URINALYSIS/STOOL

✓	OCCULT BLOOD, DIAGNOSTIC	82270
✓	URINALYSIS, ROUTINE	81003
_____	URINE CULTURE	87086

GASTRIC

_____	EGD WITH BIOPSY	43239
_____	COLONOSCOPY	45380

NUCLEAR MEDICINE

✓	KIDNEY FLOW AND FUNCTION	76707
_____	THYROID UPTAKE MULTIPLE	78006

CARDIOLOGY

_____	BRAIN	78607
_____	EKG	93003

SURGICAL PATHOLOGY

_____	SPECIAL STAINS	80353
_____	BONE MARROW SME	80973
_____	DECALCIFICATION	83113

BREAST CENTER

_____	MAMMOGRAM LATERAL	76090
_____	DIAGNOSTIC MAMMOGRAM	76091
_____	STEREORTACTIC BREAST BIOPSY	76095
_____	NEEDLE LOCALIZATION	76096

GYNECOLOGICAL

_____	PAP SMEAR	99000
_____	GYN PROBLEM FOCUS	99212

DIAGNOSTIC RADIOLOGY

_____	NASAL BONES	72069
_____	SINUSES	70160
_____	ELBOW	73080
_____	KNEE	73564
_____	TIBIA/FIBULA	73590

CHEST IMAGING

_____	CHEST – PA/LATERAL	71020
_____	RIBS UNILATERAL	71120

DIAGNOSTIC ULTRASOUND

_____	US BREAST	75545
_____	US PREGNANT UTERUS	76805
_____	US SCROTUM	76870

MRI SERVICES

_____	MRI HEAD	70551
_____	MRI CERVICAL SPINE	72141
_____	MRI HEAD/NECK	70541
_____	MRI PELVIS	72198

GASTROINTESTINAL/ABDOMEN/URINARY TRACT

_____	ABDOMEN SURVEY	74000
_____	UPPER GI	74240

MISCELLANEOUS

_____	LYME, TOTAL	86618
_____	INJECTION	90788

Patient Information

To all returning patients: Fill in only the blanks that have changed since your last visit.

Social Security No.: 232-55-3245 Date of Birth: 01/19/1947 Sex: ☑ M ❑ F

Patient's Last Name: Lopreti First: Albert MI: R

Patient's Address: 128 Flintlock Road

City: Ft. Worth State: TX Zip Code: 91822

Patient Home Telephone No.: (817) 555 - 0183 Patient Work Telephone: (817) 555 - 0162

Occupation: Salesperson Employer: The Sports Shoe

Employer Address: 8372 Glasco Lane

City: Houston State: TX Zip Code: 77030 Telephone: (817) 555 - 0162

Primary Care Physician No.: ____ Primary Care Physician Name: Ramon Albino

Insured Information

Primary Insured's Last Name: Lopreti First: Albert MI: R

Primary Insured's Address: 128 Flintlock Road

City: Ft. Worth State: TX Zip Code: 91822

Primary Insured's Social Security No.: 232-55-3245 Insured's Telephone: (817) 555 - 0183

Primary Insured's Occupation: Salesperson Employer: The Sports Shoe

Employer Address: 8372 Glasco Lane

City: Houston State: TX Zip Code: 77030 Telephone: (817) 555 - 0162

Relationship of Patient to Insured: ☑ Self ❑ Spouse ❑ Dependent

Secondary Insured's Last Name: Lopreti First: Sonja MI: B

Secondary Insured's Address: 128 Flintlock Road

City: Ft. Worth State: TX Zip Code: 91822

Secondary Insured's Social Security No.: 292-55-2354 Insured's Telephone: (817) 555 - 0183

Secondary Insured's Occupation: Fitness Instructor Employer: Century City Fitness

Employer Address: 736 Hotel Row

City: Ft. Worth State: TX Zip Code: 91822 Telephone: (817) 555 - 0123

Relationship of Patient to Insured: ❑ Self ☑ Spouse ❑ Dependent

Primary Insurance

Primary Insurance: ☑ United ❑ MetHealth ❑ TexMut ❑ Medicare

Other Insurance Company Name: ____

Insurance Company Address: 2329 Lexton Lane

City: Ft. Worth State: TX Zip Code: 91822 Telephone: (817) 555 - 0149

Policy No.: UMS34-342 Group No.: 783392-L

Secondary Insurance

Secondary Insurance Company: American Managed Care

Insurance Company Address: 1602 Plaza Center

City: Houston State: TX Zip Code: 77030

Policy No.: TXS4500030 Group No.: Fitness

Out-Patient Services Order

16–7

Physician Information

Physician's No.: 8

Physician's Name: Sanchez (Last) Carlos (First)

Street Address: 4802 Parkway Blvd.

Dallas (City) TX (State) 75246 (Zip)

Patient Information

Patient's Name: Longin (Last) Paul (First)

Date of Birth: 7/5/1989 Sex ✓ M ___ F

Patient's Phone No.: (817) 555-0124

ICD DIAGNOSIS CODES: 789.00, 784.0, 783.2

Diagnosis: Abdominal pain, Headache, Weight loss, abnormal

CPT PANELS

___ BASIC METABOLIC – Calcium, chloride, Glucose, Sodium, Carbon Dioxide (CO2), Creatinine, Potassium, urea nitrogen (BUN) –80048

✓ COMPREHENSIVE METABOLIC – Albumin, Alkaline, Phosphatase, ALT/SGPT; AST/SGOT; bilirubin, total; Calcium; Carbon Dioxide; Chloride; Creatinine; Glucose; Potassium; Protein, total; Sodium; Urea Nitrogen –80053

___ CORONARY RISK PROFILE (LIPID PANEL) – Total Cholesterol, HDO cholesterol, LDL Cholesterol calculated), Triglycerides –80061

CHEMISTRY

___	ALBUMIN	82040
___	ALK PHOSPHATASE	84075
___	ALK/SGPT	84460
___	T4, TOTAL	84436
___	TSH	84443
___	T3, TOTAL	84480
___	TRIGLYCERIDES	84478
___	UREA NITROGEN (BUN)	84520

BLOOD

✓	HEMATOCRIT	85013
___	PARTIAL BLOOD COUNT	85021
___	CBC/DIFF	85025
✓	CBC	85027
___	RETICULOCYTE COUNT	85044
___	PRO TIME/INR	85610
___	AST/SGOT	85651

IMMUNOLOGY

___	CEA	82378
___	HEPATITIS B SURG AB	86706
___	HEPATITIS C AB	86803
___	HEPATITIS A AB (IGM)	86709
___	HEPATITIS B SURG AG	87340

URINALYSIS/STOOL

___	OCCULT BLOOD, DIAGNOSTIC	82270
___	URINALYSIS, ROUTINE	81003
✓	URINE CULTURE	87086

GASTRIC

___	EGD WITH BIOPSY	43239
___	COLONOSCOPY	45380

NUCLEAR MEDICINE

___	KIDNEY FLOW AND FUNCTION	76707
___	THYROID UPTAKE MULTIPLE	78006

CARDIOLOGY

___	BRAIN	78607
___	EKG	93003

SURGICAL PATHOLOGY

___	SPECIAL STAINS	80353
___	BONE MARROW SME	80973
___	DECALCIFICATION	83113

BREAST CENTER

___	MAMMOGRAM LATERAL	76090
___	DIAGNOSTIC MAMMOGRAM	76091
___	STEREORTACTIC BREAST BIOPSY	76095
___	NEEDLE LOCALIZATION	76096

GYNECOLOGICAL

___	PAP SMEAR	99000
___	GYN PROBLEM FOCUS	99212

DIAGNOSTIC RADIOLOGY

___	NASAL BONES	72069
___	SINUSES	70160
___	ELBOW	73080
___	KNEE	73564
___	TIBIA/FIBULA	73590

CHEST IMAGING

___	CHEST – PA/LATERAL	71020
___	RIBS UNILATERAL	71120

DIAGNOSTIC ULTRASOUND

___	US BREAST	75545
___	US PREGNANT UTERUS	76805
___	US SCROTUM	76870

MRI SERVICES

___	MRI HEAD	70551
___	MRI CERVICAL SPINE	72141
___	MRI HEAD/NECK	70541
___	MRI PELVIS	72198

GASTROINTESTINAL/ABDOMEN/URINARY TRACT

✓	ABDOMEN SURVEY	74000
✓	UPPER GI	74240

MISCELLANEOUS

___	LYME, TOTAL	86618
___	INJECTION	90788

Patient Information

16–7

To all returning patients: Fill in only the blanks that have changed since your last visit.

Social Security No.: 872-55-4101 Date of Birth: 07/05/1989 Sex: ☑ M ☐ F

Patient's Last Name: Longin First: Paul MI: M

Patient's Address: 1111 Morton Avenue

City: Ft. Worth State: TX Zip Code: 91822

Patient Home Telephone No.: (817) 555-0124 Patient Work Telephone: (____) ____-______

Occupation: Student Employer: ______

Employer Address: ______

City: ______ State: ______ Zip Code: ______ Telephone: (____) ____-______

Primary Care Physician No.: ______ Primary Care Physician Name: Carlos Sanchez

Insured Information

Primary Insured's Last Name: Longin First: John MI: M

Primary Insured's Address: 1111 Morton Avenue

City: Ft. Worth State: TX Zip Code: 91822

Primary Insured's Social Security No.: 283-55-2276 Insured's Telephone: (817) 555-0124

Primary Insured's Occupation: Engineer Employer: Texas Engineering

Employer Address: 2206 Wellworth Drive

City: Ft. Worth State: TX Zip Code: 91822 Telephone: (817) 555-0177

Relationship of Patient to Insured: ☐ Self ☐ Spouse ☑ Dependent

Secondary Insured's Last Name: Longin First: Jennifer MI: L

Secondary Insured's Address: 1111 Morton Avenue

City: Ft. Worth State: TX Zip Code: 91822

Secondary Insured's Social Security No.: 345-55-5732 Insured's Telephone: (817) 555-0124

Secondary Insured's Occupation: Nurse Employer: Centerville Nursing Center

Employer Address: 2603 Centerville Road

City: Ft. Worth State: TX Zip Code: 91822 Telephone: (817) 555-0165

Relationship of Patient to Insured: ☐ Self ☐ Spouse ☑ Dependent

Primary Insurance

Primary Insurance: ☐ United ☐ MetHealth ☑ TexMut ☐ Medicare

Other Insurance Company Name: ______

Insurance Company Address: 602 Insurance Center Drive

City: Houston State: TX Zip Code: 77030 Telephone: (713) 555-0167

Policy No.: TM1346573 Group No.: PL213-T

Secondary Insurance

Secondary Insurance Company: United Medical Services

Insurance Company Address: 2329 Lexton Lane

City: Ft. Worth State: TX Zip Code: 91822

Policy No.: UMS21-875 Group No.: 542636-L

Out-Patient Services Order

16–8

Physician Information

Physician's No.: 9

Physician's Name: Albino (Last) Ramon (First)

Street Address: 111 Northern Lane

Dallas (City) TX (State) 76346 (Zip)

Patient Information

Patient's Name: Lopes (Last) Gustavo (First)

Date of Birth: 3/25/50 Sex ✓ M ____ F

Patient's Phone No.: (817) 555-0183

ICD DIAGNOSIS CODES: 204.9

Diagnosis: Goiter

CPT PANELS

_____ BASIC METABOLIC – Calcium, chloride, Glucose, Sodium, Carbon Dioxide (CO2), Creatinine, Potassium, urea nitrogen (BUN) –80048

_____ COMPREHENSIVE METABOLIC – Albumin, Alkaline, Phosphatase, ALT/SGPT; AST/SGOT; bilirubin, total; Calcium; Carbon Dioxide; Chloride; Creatinine; Glucose; Potassium; Protein, total; Sodium; Urea Nitrogen –80053

_____ CORONARY RISK PROFILE (LIPID PANEL) – Total Cholesterol, HDO cholesterol, LDL Cholesterol calculated), Triglycerides –80061

CHEMISTRY

_____ALBUMIN 82040
_____ALK PHOSPHATASE 84075
_____ALK/SGPT 84460
_____T4, TOTAL 84436
_____TSH 84443
_____T3, TOTAL 84480
_____TRIGLYCERIDES 84478
_____UREA NITROGEN (BUN) 84520

BLOOD

_____HEMATOCRIT 85013
_____PARTIAL BLOOD COUNT 85021
_____CBC/DIFF 85025
_____CBC 85027
_____RETICULOCYTE COUNT 85044
_____PRO TIME/INR 85610
_____AST/SGOT 85651

IMMUNOLOGY

_____CEA 82378
_____HEPATITIS B SURG AB 86706
_____HEPATITIS C AB 86803
_____HEPATITIS A AB (IGM) 86709
_____HEPATITIS B SURG AG 87340

URINALYSIS/STOOL

_____OCCULT BLOOD, DIAGNOSTIC 82270
_____URINALYSIS, ROUTINE 81003
_____URINE CULTURE 87086

GASTRIC

_____EGD WITH BIOPSY 43239
_____COLONOSCOPY 45380

NUCLEAR MEDICINE

_____KIDNEY FLOW AND FUNCTION 76707
__✓__THYROID UPTAKE MULTIPLE 78006

CARDIOLOGY

_____BRAIN 78607
_____EKG 93003

SURGICAL PATHOLOGY

_____SPECIAL STAINS 80353
_____BONE MARROW SME 80973
_____DECALCIFICATION 83113

BREAST CENTER

_____MAMMOGRAM LATERAL 76090
_____DIAGNOSTIC MAMMOGRAM 76091
_____STEREORTACTIC BREAST BIOPSY 76095
_____NEEDLE LOCALIZATION 76096

GYNECOLOGICAL

_____PAP SMEAR 99000
_____GYN PROBLEM FOCUS 99212

DIAGNOSTIC RADIOLOGY

_____NASAL BONES 72069
_____SINUSES 70160
_____ELBOW 73080
_____KNEE 73564
_____TIBIA/FIBULA 73590

CHEST IMAGING

_____CHEST – PA/LATERAL 71020
_____RIBS UNILATERAL 71120

DIAGNOSTIC ULTRASOUND

_____US BREAST 75545
_____US PREGNANT UTERUS 76805
_____US SCROTUM 76870

MRI SERVICES

_____MRI HEAD 70551
_____MRI CERVICAL SPINE 72141
_____MRI HEAD/NECK 70541
_____MRI PELVIS 72198

GASTROINTESTINAL/ABDOMEN/URINARY TRACT

_____ABDOMEN SURVEY 74000
_____UPPER GI 74240

MISCELLANEOUS

_____LYME, TOTAL 86618
_____INJECTION 90788

Patient Information

16–8

To all returning patients: Fill in only the blanks that have changed since your last visit.

Social Security No.: 234-55-2356 Date of Birth: 03/25/1950 Sex: ☑ M ❑ F

Patient's Last Name: Lopes First: Gustavo MI: N

Patient's Address: 6 Pheasant Lane

City: Corsicana State: TX Zip Code: 75151

Patient Home Telephone No.: (817) 555-0193 Patient Work Telephone: (817) 555-0123

Occupation: Plant Manager Employer: Mercury Fabricating

Employer Address: 33493 Industrial Lane

City: Corsicana State: TX Zip Code: 75151 Telephone: (817) 555-0123

Primary Care Physician No.: ____ Primary Care Physician Name: Ramon Albino

Insured Information

Primary Insured's Last Name: Lopes First: Gustavo MI: N

Primary Insured's Address: 6 Pheasant Lane

City: Corsicana State: TX Zip Code: 75151

Primary Insured's Social Security No.: 234-55-2356 Insured's Telephone: (817) 555-0193

Primary Insured's Occupation: Plant Manager Employer: Mercury Fabricating

Employer Address: 33493 Industrial Lane

City: Corsicana State: TX Zip Code: 75151 Telephone: (817) 555-0123

Relationship of Patient to Insured: ☑ Self ❑ Spouse ❑ Dependent

Secondary Insured's Last Name: ____ First: ____ MI: ____

Secondary Insured's Address: ____

City: ____ State: ____ Zip Code: ____

Secondary Insured's Social Security No.: ____ Insured's Telephone: (____) ____-____

Secondary Insured's Occupation: ____ Employer: ____

Employer Address: ____

City: ____ State: ____ Zip Code: ____ Telephone: (____) ____-____

Relationship of Patient to Insured: ❑ Self ❑ Spouse ❑ Dependent

Primary Insurance

Primary Insurance: ❑ United ☑ MetHealth ❑ TexMut ❑ Medicare

Other Insurance Company Name: ____

Insurance Company Address: 1702 Broadway

City: Kansas City State: KS Zip Code: 66101 Telephone: (913) 555-0125

Policy No.: GL837-KC Group No.: TX-3929-M

Secondary Insurance

Secondary Insurance Company: ____

Insurance Company Address: ____

City: ____ State: ____ Zip Code: ____

Policy No.: ____ Group No.: ____

Out-Patient Services Order

16–9

Physician Information

Physician's No.: 2

Physician's Name: Lincoln (Last) Steven (First)

Street Address: 2206 Bldg. B

Dallas (City) TX (State) 75204 (Zip)

Patient Information

Patient's Name: Miller (Last) Susan (First)

Date of Birth: 3/23/70 Sex ___ M ✓ F

Patient's Phone No.: (214) 555 - 0153

ICD DIAGNOSIS CODES: 788.2, 789.00, 783.2

Diagnosis: Cough, Abdominal pain, Weight loss, abnormal

CPT PANELS

_____ BASIC METABOLIC – Calcium, chloride, Glucose, Sodium, Carbon Dioxide (CO2), Creatinine, Potassium, urea nitrogen (BUN) –80048

✓ COMPREHENSIVE METABOLIC – Albumin, Alkaline, Phosphatase, ALT/SGPT; AST/SGOT; bilirubin, total; Calcium; Carbon Dioxide; Chloride; Creatinine; Glucose; Potassium; Protein, total; Sodium; Urea Nitrogen –80053

_____ CORONARY RISK PROFILE (LIPID PANEL) – Total Cholesterol, HDO cholesterol, LDL Cholesterol calculated), Triglycerides –80061

CHEMISTRY

_____	ALBUMIN	82040
_____	ALK PHOSPHATASE	84075
_____	ALK/SGPT	84460
_____	T4, TOTAL	84436
_____	TSH	84443
_____	T3, TOTAL	84480
_____	TRIGLYCERIDES	84478
_____	UREA NITROGEN (BUN)	84520

BLOOD

_____	HEMATOCRIT	85013
_____	PARTIAL BLOOD COUNT	85021
✓	CBC/DIFF	85025
_____	CBC	85027
_____	RETICULOCYTE COUNT	85044
_____	PRO TIME/INR	85610
_____	AST/SGOT	85651

IMMUNOLOGY

_____	CEA	82378
_____	HEPATITIS B SURG AB	86706
_____	HEPATITIS C AB	86803
_____	HEPATITIS A AB (IGM)	86709
_____	HEPATITIS B SURG AG	87340

URINALYSIS/STOOL

✓	OCCULT BLOOD, DIAGNOSTIC	82270
✓	URINALYSIS, ROUTINE	81003
_____	URINE CULTURE	87086

GASTRIC

_____	EGD WITH BIOPSY	43239
_____	COLONOSCOPY	45380

NUCLEAR MEDICINE

_____	KIDNEY FLOW AND FUNCTION	76707
_____	THYROID UPTAKE MULTIPLE	78006

CARDIOLOGY

_____	BRAIN	78607
_____	EKG	93003

SURGICAL PATHOLOGY

_____	SPECIAL STAINS	80353
_____	BONE MARROW SME	80973
_____	DECALCIFICATION	83113

BREAST CENTER

_____	MAMMOGRAM LATERAL	76090
_____	DIAGNOSTIC MAMMOGRAM	76091
_____	STEREORTACTIC BREAST BIOPSY	76095
_____	NEEDLE LOCALIZATION	76096

GYNECOLOGICAL

_____	PAP SMEAR	99000
_____	GYN PROBLEM FOCUS	99212

DIAGNOSTIC RADIOLOGY

_____	NASAL BONES	72069
_____	SINUSES	70160
_____	ELBOW	73080
_____	KNEE	73564
_____	TIBIA/FIBULA	73590

CHEST IMAGING

_____	CHEST – PA/LATERAL	71020
_____	RIBS UNILATERAL	71120

DIAGNOSTIC ULTRASOUND

_____	US BREAST	75545
_____	US PREGNANT UTERUS	76805
_____	US SCROTUM	76870

MRI SERVICES

_____	MRI HEAD	70551
_____	MRI CERVICAL SPINE	72141
_____	MRI HEAD/NECK	70541
_____	MRI PELVIS	72198

GASTROINTESTINAL/ABDOMEN/URINARY TRACT

✓	ABDOMEN SURVEY	74000
_____	UPPER GI	74240

MISCELLANEOUS

_____	LYME, TOTAL	86618
_____	INJECTION	90788

Patient Information

16–9

To all returning patients: Fill in only the blanks that have changed since your last visit.

Social Security No.: 234-55-3453 Date of Birth: 03/23/1970 Sex: ☐ M ☑ F

Patient's Last Name: Miller First: Susan MI: E

Patient's Address: 893 Canter Lane

City: Dallas State: TX Zip Code: 75238

Patient Home Telephone No.: (214) 555-0153 Patient Work Telephone: (214) 555-0156

Occupation: Consultant Employer: Langley Personnel

Employer Address: 3827 Oriole Boulevard

City: Dallas State: TX Zip Code: 75238-6103 Telephone: (214) 555-0156

Primary Care Physician No.: ____ Primary Care Physician Name: Steven Lincoln

Insured Information

Primary Insured's Last Name: Miller First: Susan MI: E

Primary Insured's Address: 893 Canter Lane

City: Dallas State: TX Zip Code: 75238

Primary Insured's Social Security No.: 234-55-3453 Insured's Telephone: (214) 555-0153

Primary Insured's Occupation: Consultant Employer: Langley Personnel

Employer Address: 3827 Oriole Boulevard

City: Dallas State: TX Zip Code: 75238-6103 Telephone: (214) 555-0156

Relationship of Patient to Insured: ☑ Self ☐ Spouse ☐ Dependent

Secondary Insured's Last Name: ____ First: ____ MI: ____

Secondary Insured's Address: ____

City: ____ State: ____ Zip Code: ____

Secondary Insured's Social Security No.: ____ Insured's Telephone: (____) ____-____

Secondary Insured's Occupation: ____ Employer: ____

Employer Address: ____

City: ____ State: ____ Zip Code: ____ Telephone: (____) ____-____

Relationship of Patient to Insured: ☐ Self ☐ Spouse ☐ Dependent

Primary Insurance

Primary Insurance: ☐ United ☐ MetHealth ☑ TexMut ☐ Medicare

Other Insurance Company Name: ____

Insurance Company Address: 602 Insurance Center Drive

City: Houston State: TX Zip Code: 77030 Telephone: (713) 555-0167

Policy No.: TM827392 Group No.: LML394M

Secondary Insurance

Secondary Insurance Company: ____

Insurance Company Address: ____

City: ____ State: ____ Zip Code: ____

Policy No.: ____ Group No.: ____

Out-Patient Services Order

16–10

Physician Information

Physician's No.: 6

Physician's Name: Ling (Last) Su (First)

Street Address: 6208 Medical Center

Dallas (City) TX (State) 75246 (Zip)

Patient Information

Patient's Name: Torres (Last) Jeff (First)

Date of Birth: 6/10/1994 Sex ✓ M ___ F

Patient's Phone No.: (817) 555-0153

ICD DIAGNOSIS CODES: 785.2, 786.59

Diagnosis: Cardiac murmur, Chest pain, unspecified

CPT PANELS

_____ BASIC METABOLIC – Calcium, chloride, Glucose, Sodium, Carbon Dioxide (CO2), Creatinine, Potassium, urea nitrogen (BUN) –80048

_____ COMPREHENSIVE METABOLIC – Albumin, Alkaline, Phosphatase, ALT/SGPT; AST/SGOT; bilirubin, total; Calcium; Carbon Dioxide; Chloride; Creatinine; Glucose; Potassium; Protein, total; Sodium; Urea Nitrogen –80053

✓ CORONARY RISK PROFILE (LIPID PANEL) – Total Cholesterol, HDO cholesterol, LDL Cholesterol calculated), Triglycerides –80061

CHEMISTRY

_____ALBUMIN 82040
_____ALK PHOSPHATASE 84075
_____ALK/SGPT 84460
_____T4, TOTAL 84436
_____TSH 84443
_____T3, TOTAL 84480
_____TRIGLYCERIDES 84478
_____UREA NITROGEN (BUN) 84520

BLOOD

_____HEMATOCRIT 85013
_____PARTIAL BLOOD COUNT 85021
_____CBC/DIFF 85025
_____CBC 85027
_____RETICULOCYTE COUNT 85044
_____PRO TIME/INR 85610
_____AST/SGOT 85651

IMMUNOLOGY

_____CEA 82378
_____HEPATITIS B SURG AB 86706
_____HEPATITIS C AB 86803
_____HEPATITIS A AB (IGM) 86709
_____HEPATITIS B SURG AG 87340

URINALYSIS/STOOL

_____OCCULT BLOOD, DIAGNOSTIC 82270
_____URINALYSIS, ROUTINE 81003
_____URINE CULTURE 87086

GASTRIC

_____EGD WITH BIOPSY 43239
_____COLONOSCOPY 45380

NUCLEAR MEDICINE

_____KIDNEY FLOW AND FUNCTION 76707
_____THYROID UPTAKE MULTIPLE 78006

CARDIOLOGY

_____BRAIN 78607
✓ EKG 93003

SURGICAL PATHOLOGY

_____SPECIAL STAINS 80353
_____BONE MARROW SME 80973
_____DECALCIFICATION 83113

BREAST CENTER

_____MAMMOGRAM LATERAL 76090
_____DIAGNOSTIC MAMMOGRAM 76091
_____STEREORTACTIC BREAST BIOPSY 76095
_____NEEDLE LOCALIZATION 76096

GYNECOLOGICAL

_____PAP SMEAR 99000
_____GYN PROBLEM FOCUS 99212

DIAGNOSTIC RADIOLOGY

_____NASAL BONES 72069
_____SINUSES 70160
_____ELBOW 73080
_____KNEE 73564
_____TIBIA/FIBULA 73590

CHEST IMAGING

_____CHEST – PA/LATERAL 71020
_____RIBS UNILATERAL 71120

DIAGNOSTIC ULTRASOUND

_____US BREAST 75545
_____US PREGNANT UTERUS 76805
_____US SCROTUM 76870

MRI SERVICES

_____MRI HEAD 70551
_____MRI CERVICAL SPINE 72141
_____MRI HEAD/NECK 70541
_____MRI PELVIS 72198

GASTROINTESTINAL/ABDOMEN/URINARY TRACT

_____ABDOMEN SURVEY 74000
_____UPPER GI 74240

MISCELLANEOUS

_____LYME, TOTAL 86618
_____INJECTION 90788

Out-Patient Services Order

17

Physician Information

Physician's No.: 8

Physician's Name: Sanchez (Last) Carlos (First)

Street Address: 4802 Parkway Blvd.

Dallas (City) TX (State) 75246 (Zip)

Patient Information

Patient's Name: Mitchell (Last) Laurie (First)

Date of Birth: 2/4/1956 Sex ___M ✓ F

Patient's Phone No.: (214) 555-0185

ICD DIAGNOSIS CODES: 569.0

Diagnosis: Rectal polyps

CPT PANELS

____ BASIC METABOLIC – Calcium, chloride, Glucose, Sodium, Carbon Dioxide (CO2), Creatinine, Potassium, urea nitrogen (BUN) –80048

____ COMPREHENSIVE METABOLIC – Albumin, Alkaline, Phosphatase, ALT/SGPT; AST/SGOT; bilirubin, total; Calcium; Carbon Dioxide; Chloride; Creatinine; Glucose; Potassium; Protein, total; Sodium; Urea Nitrogen –80053

____ CORONARY RISK PROFILE (LIPID PANEL) – Total Cholesterol, HDO cholesterol, LDL Cholesterol calculated), Triglycerides –80061

CHEMISTRY

____	ALBUMIN	82040
____	ALK PHOSPHATASE	84075
____	ALK/SGPT	84460
____	T4, TOTAL	84436
____	TSH	84443
____	T3, TOTAL	84480
____	TRIGLYCERIDES	84478
____	UREA NITROGEN (BUN)	84520

BLOOD

✓	HEMATOCRIT	85013
____	PARTIAL BLOOD COUNT	85021
____	CBC/DIFF	85025
____	CBC	85027
____	RETICULOCYTE COUNT	85044
____	PRO TIME/INR	85610
____	AST/SGOT	85651

IMMUNOLOGY

____	CEA	82378
____	HEPATITIS B SURG AB	86706
____	HEPATITIS C AB	86803
____	HEPATITIS A AB (IGM)	86709
____	HEPATITIS B SURG AG	87340

URINALYSIS/STOOL

✓	OCCULT BLOOD, DIAGNOSTIC	82270
____	URINALYSIS, ROUTINE	81003
____	URINE CULTURE	87086

GASTRIC

____	EGD WITH BIOPSY	43239
✓	COLONOSCOPY	45380

NUCLEAR MEDICINE

____	KIDNEY FLOW AND FUNCTION	76707
____	THYROID UPTAKE MULTIPLE	78006

CARDIOLOGY

____	BRAIN	78607
____	EKG	93003

SURGICAL PATHOLOGY

____	SPECIAL STAINS	80353
____	BONE MARROW SME	80973
____	DECALCIFICATION	83113

BREAST CENTER

____	MAMMOGRAM LATERAL	76090
____	DIAGNOSTIC MAMMOGRAM	76091
____	STEREORTACTIC BREAST BIOPSY	76095
____	NEEDLE LOCALIZATION	76096

GYNECOLOGICAL

____	PAP SMEAR	99000
____	GYN PROBLEM FOCUS	99212

DIAGNOSTIC RADIOLOGY

____	NASAL BONES	72069
____	SINUSES	70160
____	ELBOW	73080
____	KNEE	73564
____	TIBIA/FIBULA	73590

CHEST IMAGING

____	CHEST – PA/LATERAL	71020
____	RIBS UNILATERAL	71120

DIAGNOSTIC ULTRASOUND

____	US BREAST	75545
____	US PREGNANT UTERUS	76805
____	US SCROTUM	76870

MRI SERVICES

____	MRI HEAD	70551
____	MRI CERVICAL SPINE	72141
____	MRI HEAD/NECK	70541
____	MRI PELVIS	72198

GASTROINTESTINAL/ABDOMEN/URINARY TRACT

____	ABDOMEN SURVEY	74000
____	UPPER GI	74240

MISCELLANEOUS

____	LYME, TOTAL	86618
____	INJECTION	90788

Out-Patient Services Order

16–10

Physician Information

Physician's No.: 6

Physician's Name: Ling (Last) Su (First)

Street Address: 6208 Medical Center

Dallas (City) TX (State) 75246 (Zip)

Patient Information

Patient's Name: Torres (Last) Jeff (First)

Date of Birth: 6/10/1994 Sex ✓ M ___ F

Patient's Phone No.: (817) 555-0153

ICD DIAGNOSIS CODES: 785.2, 786.59

Diagnosis: Cardiac murmur, Chest pain, unspecified

CPT PANELS

_____ BASIC METABOLIC – Calcium, chloride, Glucose, Sodium, Carbon Dioxide (CO2), Creatinine, Potassium, urea nitrogen (BUN) –80048

_____ COMPREHENSIVE METABOLIC – Albumin, Alkaline, Phosphatase, ALT/SGPT; AST/SGOT; bilirubin, total; Calcium; Carbon Dioxide; Chloride; Creatinine; Glucose; Potassium; Protein, total; Sodium; Urea Nitrogen –80053

✓ CORONARY RISK PROFILE (LIPID PANEL) – Total Cholesterol, HDO cholesterol, LDL Cholesterol calculated), Triglycerides –80061

CHEMISTRY

_____ ALBUMIN 82040
_____ ALK PHOSPHATASE 84075
_____ ALK/SGPT 84460
_____ T4, TOTAL 84436
_____ TSH 84443
_____ T3, TOTAL 84480
_____ TRIGLYCERIDES 84478
_____ UREA NITROGEN (BUN) 84520

BLOOD

_____ HEMATOCRIT 85013
_____ PARTIAL BLOOD COUNT 85021
_____ CBC/DIFF 85025
_____ CBC 85027
_____ RETICULOCYTE COUNT 85044
_____ PRO TIME/INR 85610
_____ AST/SGOT 85651

IMMUNOLOGY

_____ CEA 82378
_____ HEPATITIS B SURG AB 86706
_____ HEPATITIS C AB 86803
_____ HEPATITIS A AB (IGM) 86709
_____ HEPATITIS B SURG AG 87340

URINALYSIS/STOOL

_____ OCCULT BLOOD, DIAGNOSTIC 82270
_____ URINALYSIS, ROUTINE 81003
_____ URINE CULTURE 87086

GASTRIC

_____ EGD WITH BIOPSY 43239
_____ COLONOSCOPY 45380

NUCLEAR MEDICINE

_____ KIDNEY FLOW AND FUNCTION 76707
_____ THYROID UPTAKE MULTIPLE 78006

CARDIOLOGY

_____ BRAIN 78607
✓ EKG 93003

SURGICAL PATHOLOGY

_____ SPECIAL STAINS 80353
_____ BONE MARROW SME 80973
_____ DECALCIFICATION 83113

BREAST CENTER

_____ MAMMOGRAM LATERAL 76090
_____ DIAGNOSTIC MAMMOGRAM 76091
_____ STEREORTACTIC BREAST BIOPSY 76095
_____ NEEDLE LOCALIZATION 76096

GYNECOLOGICAL

_____ PAP SMEAR 99000
_____ GYN PROBLEM FOCUS 99212

DIAGNOSTIC RADIOLOGY

_____ NASAL BONES 72069
_____ SINUSES 70160
_____ ELBOW 73080
_____ KNEE 73564
_____ TIBIA/FIBULA 73590

CHEST IMAGING

_____ CHEST – PA/LATERAL 71020
_____ RIBS UNILATERAL 71120

DIAGNOSTIC ULTRASOUND

_____ US BREAST 75545
_____ US PREGNANT UTERUS 76805
_____ US SCROTUM 76870

MRI SERVICES

_____ MRI HEAD 70551
_____ MRI CERVICAL SPINE 72141
_____ MRI HEAD/NECK 70541
_____ MRI PELVIS 72198

GASTROINTESTINAL/ABDOMEN/URINARY TRACT

_____ ABDOMEN SURVEY 74000
_____ UPPER GI 74240

MISCELLANEOUS

_____ LYME, TOTAL 86618
_____ INJECTION 90788

Patient Information

16–10

To all returning patients: Fill in only the blanks that have changed since your last visit.

Social Security No.: 354-55-2314 Date of Birth: 06/10/1994 Sex: ☑ M ❑ F

Patient's Last Name: Torres First: Jeff MI: R

Patient's Address: 2093 Springdale Road

City: Ft. Worth State: TX Zip Code: 91822

Patient Home Telephone No.: (817) 555-0153 Patient Work Telephone: (____) ____-______

Occupation: Student Employer: __________

Employer Address: __________

City: ________ State: ____ Zip Code: ______ Telephone: (____) ____-______

Primary Care Physician No.: ____ Primary Care Physician Name: Su Ling

Insured Information

Primary Insured's Last Name: Torres First: Emilio MI: P

Primary Insured's Address: 263 Horseshoe Lane

City: Nashville State: TN Zip Code: 37215

Primary Insured's Social Security No.: 982-55-1604 Insured's Telephone: (615) 555-0153

Primary Insured's Occupation: Talent Agent Employer: Music City Rhythms

Employer Address: 3827 Music Row

City: Nashville State: TN Zip Code: 37215 Telephone: (615) 555-9283

Relationship of Patient to Insured: ❑ Self ❑ Spouse ☑ Dependent

Secondary Insured's Last Name: Levittis First: Malana MI: B

Secondary Insured's Address: 2093 Springdale Road

City: Ft. Worth State: TX Zip Code: 91822

Secondary Insured's Social Security No.: 425-55-2203 Insured's Telephone: (817) 555-0153

Secondary Insured's Occupation: Real estate broker Employer: Corporate Leasing

Employer Address: 101-C Oakdale Drive

City: Ft. Worth State: TX Zip Code: 91822 Telephone: (817) 555-0176

Relationship of Patient to Insured: ❑ Self ❑ Spouse ☑ Dependent

Primary Insurance

Primary Insurance: ❑ United ❑ MetHealth ❑ TexMut ❑ Medicare

Other Insurance Company Name: National Insurers

Insurance Company Address: 2302 Patriot Drive

City: Ft. Lauderdale State: FL Zip Code: 33329 Telephone: (754) 555-0167

Policy No.: TNS3400082 Group No.: Talent

Secondary Insurance

Secondary Insurance Company: Merchant's Medical Insurance

Insurance Company Address: 1642 Parkway

City: Dallas State: TX Zip Code: 75201

Policy No.: 0156 Group No.: 2847B

Patient Information

To all returning patients: Fill in only the blanks that have changed since your last visit.

Social Security No.: 915-55-6174 Date of Birth: ________ Sex: ❑ M ❑ F

Patient's Last Name: Mitchell First: Laurie MI: R

Patient's Address: ________

City: ________ State: ________ Zip Code: ________

Patient Home Telephone No.: (____) ____-____ Patient Work Telephone: (817) 555-0177

Occupation: ________ Employer: Anderson

Employer Address: ________

City: Abeline State: TX Zip Code: 78796 Telephone: (817) 555-0177

Primary Care Physician No.: ____ Primary Care Physician Name: ________

Insured Information

Primary Insured's Last Name: ________ First: ________ MI: ____

Primary Insured's Address: ________

City: ________ State: ________ Zip Code: ________

Primary Insured's Social Security No.: ________ Insured's Telephone: (____) ____-____

Primary Insured's Occupation: ________ Employer: Anderson

Employer Address: ________

City: Abeline State: TX Zip Code: 78796 Telephone: (817) 555-0177

Relationship of Patient to Insured: ❑ Self ❑ Spouse ❑ Dependent

Secondary Insured's Last Name: ________ First: ________ MI: ____

Secondary Insured's Address: ________

City: ________ State: ________ Zip Code: ________

Secondary Insured's Social Security No.: ________ Insured's Telephone: (____) ____-____

Secondary Insured's Occupation: ________ Employer: ________

Employer Address: ________

City: ________ State: ____ Zip Code: ________ Telephone: (____) ____-____

Relationship of Patient to Insured: ❑ Self ❑ Spouse ❑ Dependent

Primary Insurance

Primary Insurance: ❑ United ❑ MetHealth ☑ TexMut ❑ Medicare

Other Insurance Company Name: ________

Insurance Company Address: ________

City: ________ State: ____ Zip Code: ________ Telephone: (____) ____-____

Policy No.: TM642391-M Group No.: URS320-C

Secondary Insurance

Secondary Insurance Company: ________

Insurance Company Address: ________

City: ________ State: ________ Zip Code: ________

Policy No.: ________ Group No.: ________

Out-Patient Services Order

17

Physician Information

Physician's No.: 8

Physician's Name: Sanchez (Last) Carlos (First)

Street Address: 4802 Parkway Blvd.

Dallas (City) TX (State) 75246 (Zip)

Patient Information

Patient's Name: Mitchell (Last) Laurie (First)

Date of Birth: 2/4/1956 Sex ___M ✓ F

Patient's Phone No.: (214) 555-0185

ICD DIAGNOSIS CODES: 569.0

Diagnosis: Rectal polyps

CPT PANELS

____ BASIC METABOLIC – Calcium, chloride, Glucose, Sodium, Carbon Dioxide (CO2), Creatinine, Potassium, urea nitrogen (BUN) –80048

____ COMPREHENSIVE METABOLIC – Albumin, Alkaline, Phosphatase, ALT/SGPT; AST/SGOT; bilirubin, total; Calcium; Carbon Dioxide; Chloride; Creatinine; Glucose; Potassium; Protein, total; Sodium; Urea Nitrogen –80053

____ CORONARY RISK PROFILE (LIPID PANEL) – Total Cholesterol, HDO cholesterol, LDL Cholesterol calculated), Triglycerides –80061

CHEMISTRY

____	ALBUMIN	82040
____	ALK PHOSPHATASE	84075
____	ALK/SGPT	84460
____	T4, TOTAL	84436
____	TSH	84443
____	T3, TOTAL	84480
____	TRIGLYCERIDES	84478
____	UREA NITROGEN (BUN)	84520

BLOOD

✓	HEMATOCRIT	85013
____	PARTIAL BLOOD COUNT	85021
____	CBC/DIFF	85025
____	CBC	85027
____	RETICULOCYTE COUNT	85044
____	PRO TIME/INR	85610
____	AST/SGOT	85651

IMMUNOLOGY

____	CEA	82378
____	HEPATITIS B SURG AB	86706
____	HEPATITIS C AB	86803
____	HEPATITIS A AB (IGM)	86709
____	HEPATITIS B SURG AG	87340

URINALYSIS/STOOL

✓	OCCULT BLOOD, DIAGNOSTIC	82270
____	URINALYSIS, ROUTINE	81003
____	URINE CULTURE	87086

GASTRIC

____	EGD WITH BIOPSY	43239
✓	COLONOSCOPY	45380

NUCLEAR MEDICINE

____	KIDNEY FLOW AND FUNCTION	76707
____	THYROID UPTAKE MULTIPLE	78006

CARDIOLOGY

____	BRAIN	78607
____	EKG	93003

SURGICAL PATHOLOGY

____	SPECIAL STAINS	80353
____	BONE MARROW SME	80973
____	DECALCIFICATION	83113

BREAST CENTER

____	MAMMOGRAM LATERAL	76090
____	DIAGNOSTIC MAMMOGRAM	76091
____	STEREORTACTIC BREAST BIOPSY	76095
____	NEEDLE LOCALIZATION	76096

GYNECOLOGICAL

____	PAP SMEAR	99000
____	GYN PROBLEM FOCUS	99212

DIAGNOSTIC RADIOLOGY

____	NASAL BONES	72069
____	SINUSES	70160
____	ELBOW	73080
____	KNEE	73564
____	TIBIA/FIBULA	73590

CHEST IMAGING

____	CHEST – PA/LATERAL	71020
____	RIBS UNILATERAL	71120

DIAGNOSTIC ULTRASOUND

____	US BREAST	75545
____	US PREGNANT UTERUS	76805
____	US SCROTUM	76870

MRI SERVICES

____	MRI HEAD	70551
____	MRI CERVICAL SPINE	72141
____	MRI HEAD/NECK	70541
____	MRI PELVIS	72198

GASTROINTESTINAL/ABDOMEN/URINARY TRACT

____	ABDOMEN SURVEY	74000
____	UPPER GI	74240

MISCELLANEOUS

____	LYME, TOTAL	86618
____	INJECTION	90788

Patient Information

To all returning patients: Fill in only the blanks that have changed since your last visit.

Social Security No.: 915-55-6120 Date of Birth: ______ Sex: ❑ M ❑ F

Patient's Last Name: Swenson First: Joshua MI: R

Patient's Address: 340 Oak Street

City: Ft. Worth State: TX Zip Code: 91822

Patient Home Telephone No.: (713) 555-0169 Patient Work Telephone: (____) ____-____

Occupation: ______ Employer: ______

Employer Address: ______

City: ______ State: ______ Zip Code: ______ Telephone: (____) ____-____

Primary Care Physician No.: ______ Primary Care Physician Name: ______

Insured Information

Primary Insured's Last Name: ______ First: ______ MI: ____

Primary Insured's Address: 340 Oak Street

City: Ft. Worth State: TX Zip Code: 91822

Primary Insured's Social Security No.: ______ Insured's Telephone: (713) 555-0169

Primary Insured's Occupation: ______ Employer: Brown & Sons

Employer Address: 233 West Johnson Street

City: Ft. Worth State: ______ Zip Code: 91822 Telephone: (713) 555-0187

Relationship of Patient to Insured: ❑ Self ❑ Spouse ❑ Dependent

Secondary Insured's Last Name: ______ First: ______ MI: ____

Secondary Insured's Address: ______

City: ______ State: ______ Zip Code: ______

Secondary Insured's Social Security No.: ______ Insured's Telephone: (____) ____-____

Secondary Insured's Occupation: ______ Employer: ______

Employer Address: ______

City: ______ State: ______ Zip Code: ______ Telephone: (____) ____-____

Relationship of Patient to Insured: ❑ Self ❑ Spouse ❑ Dependent

Primary Insurance

Primary Insurance: ❑ United ❑ MetHealth ❑ TexMut ❑ Medicare

Other Insurance Company Name: ______

Insurance Company Address: ______

City: ______ State: ______ Zip Code: ______ Telephone: (____) ____-____

Policy No.: TM897645-M Group No.: URS450

Secondary Insurance

Secondary Insurance Company: ______

Insurance Company Address: ______

City: ______ State: ______ Zip Code: ______

Policy No.: ______ Group No.: ______

Out-Patient Services Order

17

Physician Information

Physician's No.: 7

Physician's Name: Mair (Last) Ad-Med (First)

Street Address: 7109 Medical Center

Dallas (City) TX (State) 75246 (Zip)

Patient Information

Patient's Name: Swenson (Last) Joshua (First)

Date of Birth: 11/16/94 Sex ✓ M ___ F

Patient's Phone No.: (713) 555-0169

ICD DIAGNOSIS CODES: 466.0

Diagnosis: Bronchitis, acute

CPT PANELS

_____ BASIC METABOLIC – Calcium, chloride, Glucose, Sodium, Carbon Dioxide (CO2), Creatinine, Potassium, urea nitrogen (BUN) –80048

_____ COMPREHENSIVE METABOLIC – Albumin, Alkaline, Phosphatase, ALT/SGPT; AST/SGOT; bilirubin, total; Calcium; Carbon Dioxide; Chloride; Creatinine; Glucose; Potassium; Protein, total; Sodium; Urea Nitrogen –80053

_____ CORONARY RISK PROFILE (LIPID PANEL) – Total Cholesterol, HDO cholesterol, LDL Cholesterol calculated), Triglycerides –80061

CHEMISTRY

_____ ALBUMIN 82040
_____ ALK PHOSPHATASE 84075
_____ ALK/SGPT 84460
_____ T4, TOTAL 84436
_____ TSH 84443
_____ T3, TOTAL 84480
_____ TRIGLYCERIDES 84478
_____ UREA NITROGEN (BUN) 84520

BLOOD

✓ HEMATOCRIT 85013
_____ PARTIAL BLOOD COUNT 85021
_____ CBC/DIFF 85025
✓ CBC 85027
_____ RETICULOCYTE COUNT 85044
_____ PRO TIME/INR 85610
_____ AST/SGOT 85651

IMMUNOLOGY

_____ CEA 82378
_____ HEPATITIS B SURG AB 86706
_____ HEPATITIS C AB 86803
_____ HEPATITIS A AB (IGM) 86709
_____ HEPATITIS B SURG AG 87340

URINALYSIS/STOOL

_____ OCCULT BLOOD, DIAGNOSTIC 82270
✓ URINALYSIS, ROUTINE 81003
_____ URINE CULTURE 87086

GASTRIC

_____ EGD WITH BIOPSY 43239
_____ COLONOSCOPY 45380

NUCLEAR MEDICINE

_____ KIDNEY FLOW AND FUNCTION 76707
_____ THYROID UPTAKE MULTIPLE 78006

CARDIOLOGY

_____ BRAIN 78607
_____ EKG 93003

SURGICAL PATHOLOGY

_____ SPECIAL STAINS 80353
_____ BONE MARROW SME 80973
_____ DECALCIFICATION 83113

BREAST CENTER

_____ MAMMOGRAM LATERAL 76090
_____ DIAGNOSTIC MAMMOGRAM 76091
_____ STEREORTACTIC BREAST BIOPSY 76095
_____ NEEDLE LOCALIZATION 76096

GYNECOLOGICAL

_____ PAP SMEAR 99000
_____ GYN PROBLEM FOCUS 99212

DIAGNOSTIC RADIOLOGY

_____ NASAL BONES 72069
_____ SINUSES 70160
_____ ELBOW 73080
_____ KNEE 73564
_____ TIBIA/FIBULA 73590

CHEST IMAGING

✓ CHEST – PA/LATERAL 71020
_____ RIBS UNILATERAL 71120

DIAGNOSTIC ULTRASOUND

_____ US BREAST 75545
_____ US PREGNANT UTERUS 76805
_____ US SCROTUM 76870

MRI SERVICES

_____ MRI HEAD 70551
_____ MRI CERVICAL SPINE 72141
_____ MRI HEAD/NECK 70541
_____ MRI PELVIS 72198

GASTROINTESTINAL/ABDOMEN/URINARY TRACT

_____ ABDOMEN SURVEY 74000
_____ UPPER GI 74240

MISCELLANEOUS

_____ LYME, TOTAL 86618
_____ INJECTION 90788

Patient Information

To all returning patients: Fill in only the blanks that have changed since your last visit.

Social Security No.: 621-55-3021 Date of Birth: ______ Sex: ❑ M ❑ F

Patient's Last Name: Lehman First: Susannah MI: T

Patient's Address: 44 Prairie Dog Blvd.

City: ______ State: ______ Zip Code: ______

Patient Home Telephone No.: (972) 555 - 0113 Patient Work Telephone: (972) 555 - 0115

Occupation: ______ Employer: Martha's Studio

Employer Address: 67 Bishop's Lane

City: Mesquite State: TX Zip Code: 75185 Telephone: (972) 555 - 0115

Primary Care Physician No.: ______ Primary Care Physician Name: ______

Insured Information

Primary Insured's Last Name: ______ First: ______ MI: ______

Primary Insured's Address: 44 Prairie Dog Blvd.

City: ______ State: ______ Zip Code: ______

Primary Insured's Social Security No.: ______ Insured's Telephone: (972) 555 - 0113

Primary Insured's Occupation: ______ Employer: Martha's Studio

Employer Address: 67 Bishop's Lane

City: Mesquite State: TX Zip Code: 75185 Telephone: (972) 555 - 0115

Relationship of Patient to Insured: ❑ Self ❑ Spouse ❑ Dependent

Secondary Insured's Last Name: ______ First: ______ MI: ______

Secondary Insured's Address: 44 Prairie Dog Blvd.

City: ______ State: ______ Zip Code: ______

Secondary Insured's Social Security No.: ______ Insured's Telephone: (972) 555 - 0113

Secondary Insured's Occupation: ______ Employer: ______

Employer Address: ______

City: ______ State: ______ Zip Code: ______ Telephone: (____) ____ - ____

Relationship of Patient to Insured: ❑ Self ❑ Spouse ❑ Dependent

Primary Insurance

Primary Insurance: ☑ United ❑ MetHealth ❑ TexMut ❑ Medicare

Other Insurance Company Name: ______

Insurance Company Address: ______

City: ______ State: ______ Zip Code: ______ Telephone: (____) ____ - ____

Policy No.: AMICC332 Group No.: 2253

Secondary Insurance

Secondary Insurance Company: ______

Insurance Company Address: ______

City: ______ State: ______ Zip Code: ______

Policy No.: ______ Group No.: ______

Out-Patient Services Order

17

Physician Information

Physician's No.: 10

Physician's Name: Larusso (Last) Mary (First)

Street Address: 2302 Parkway Blvd.

City: Dallas State: TX Zip: 75336

Patient Information

Patient's Name: Lehman (Last) Susannah (First)

Date of Birth: 6/12/60 Sex ___M ✓ F

Patient's Phone No.: (972) 555 - 0113

ICD DIAGNOSIS CODES: 340

Diagnosis: Multiple sclerosis

CPT PANELS

____ BASIC METABOLIC – Calcium, chloride, Glucose, Sodium, Carbon Dioxide (CO2), Creatinine, Potassium, urea nitrogen (BUN) –80048

✓ COMPREHENSIVE METABOLIC – Albumin, Alkaline, Phosphatase, ALT/SGPT; AST/SGOT; bilirubin, total; Calcium; Carbon Dioxide; Chloride; Creatinine; Glucose; Potassium; Protein, total; Sodium; Urea Nitrogen –80053

____ CORONARY RISK PROFILE (LIPID PANEL) – Total Cholesterol, HDO cholesterol, LDL Cholesterol calculated), Triglycerides –80061

CHEMISTRY

____ ALBUMIN 82040
____ ALK PHOSPHATASE 84075
____ ALK/SGPT 84460
____ T4, TOTAL 84436
____ TSH 84443
____ T3, TOTAL 84480
____ TRIGLYCERIDES 84478
____ UREA NITROGEN (BUN) 84520

BLOOD

✓ HEMATOCRIT 85013
____ PARTIAL BLOOD COUNT 85021
✓ CBC/DIFF 85025
✓ CBC 85027
____ RETICULOCYTE COUNT 85044
____ PRO TIME/INR 85610
____ AST/SGOT 85651

IMMUNOLOGY

____ CEA 82378
____ HEPATITIS B SURG AB 86706
____ HEPATITIS C AB 86803
____ HEPATITIS A AB (IGM) 86709
____ HEPATITIS B SURG AG 87340

URINALYSIS/STOOL

____ OCCULT BLOOD, DIAGNOSTIC 82270
✓ URINALYSIS, ROUTINE 81003
____ URINE CULTURE 87086

GASTRIC

____ EGD WITH BIOPSY 43239
____ COLONOSCOPY 45380

NUCLEAR MEDICINE

____ KIDNEY FLOW AND FUNCTION 76707
____ THYROID UPTAKE MULTIPLE 78006

CARDIOLOGY

____ BRAIN 78607
____ EKG 93003

SURGICAL PATHOLOGY

____ SPECIAL STAINS 80353
____ BONE MARROW SME 80973
____ DECALCIFICATION 83113

BREAST CENTER

____ MAMMOGRAM LATERAL 76090
____ DIAGNOSTIC MAMMOGRAM 76091
____ STEREORTACTIC BREAST BIOPSY 76095
____ NEEDLE LOCALIZATION 76096

GYNECOLOGICAL

____ PAP SMEAR 99000
____ GYN PROBLEM FOCUS 99212

DIAGNOSTIC RADIOLOGY

____ NASAL BONES 72069
____ SINUSES 70160
____ ELBOW 73080
____ KNEE 73564
____ TIBIA/FIBULA 73590

CHEST IMAGING

____ CHEST – PA/LATERAL 71020
____ RIBS UNILATERAL 71120

DIAGNOSTIC ULTRASOUND

____ US BREAST 75545
____ US PREGNANT UTERUS 76805
____ US SCROTUM 76870

MRI SERVICES

✓ MRI HEAD 70551
✓ MRI CERVICAL SPINE 72141
____ MRI HEAD/NECK 70541
____ MRI PELVIS 72198

GASTROINTESTINAL/ABDOMEN/URINARY TRACT

____ ABDOMEN SURVEY 74000
____ UPPER GI 74240

MISCELLANEOUS

____ LYME, TOTAL 86618
____ INJECTION 90788

Patient Information

To all returning patients: Fill in only the blanks that have changed since your last visit.

Social Security No.: 612-55-9421 Date of Birth: ________ Sex: ❑ M ❑ F
Patient's Last Name: Tylo First: Charles MI: M
Patient's Address: ________
City: ________ State: ________ Zip Code: ________
Patient Home Telephone No.: (____) ____-____ Patient Work Telephone: (972) 555-0147
Occupation: ________ Employer: Fox Realtors
Employer Address: 554 N. 23 Street
City: ________ State: ________ Zip Code: ________ Telephone: (972) 555-0147
Primary Care Physician No.: ____ Primary Care Physician Name: ________

Insured Information

Primary Insured's Last Name: ________ First: ________ MI: ____
Primary Insured's Address: ________
City: ________ State: ________ Zip Code: ________
Primary Insured's Social Security No.: ________ Insured's Telephone: (____) ____-____
Primary Insured's Occupation: ________ Employer: Fox Realtors
Employer Address: 554 N. 23rd Street
City: ________ State: ________ Zip Code: ________ Telephone: (972) 555-0147
Relationship of Patient to Insured: ❑ Self ❑ Spouse ❑ Dependent

Secondary Insured's Last Name: ________ First: ________ MI: ____
Secondary Insured's Address: ________
City: ________ State: ________ Zip Code: ________
Secondary Insured's Social Security No.: ________ Insured's Telephone: (____) ____-____
Secondary Insured's Occupation: ________ Employer: ________
Employer Address: ________
City: ________ State: ________ Zip Code: ________ Telephone: (____) ____-____
Relationship of Patient to Insured: ❑ Self ❑ Spouse ❑ Dependent

Primary Insurance

Primary Insurance: ❑ United ☑ MetHealth ❑ TexMut ❑ Medicare
Other Insurance Company Name: ________
Insurance Company Address: ________
City: ________ State: ________ Zip Code: ________ Telephone: (____) ____-____
Policy No.: CT660P Group No.: TX439M

Secondary Insurance

Secondary Insurance Company: ________
Insurance Company Address: ________
City: ________ State: ________ Zip Code: ________
Policy No.: ________ Group No.: ________

Out-Patient Services Order

17

Physician Information

Physician's No.: 3

Physician's Name: Killey (Last) Robert (First)

Street Address: 23-R Rodes Dr

Dallas (City) TX (State) 75246 (Zip)

Patient Information

Patient's Name: Tylo (Last) Charles (First)

Date of Birth: 5/12/75 Sex ✓ M ___ F

Patient's Phone No.: (972) 555-0156

ICD DIAGNOSIS CODES: 789.00, 789.30

Diagnosis: Abdominal pain, Abdominal swelling

CPT PANELS

___ BASIC METABOLIC – Calcium, chloride, Glucose, Sodium, Carbon Dioxide (CO2), Creatinine, Potassium, urea nitrogen (BUN) –80048

✓ COMPREHENSIVE METABOLIC – Albumin, Alkaline, Phosphatase, ALT/SGPT; AST/SGOT; bilirubin, total; Calcium; Carbon Dioxide; Chloride; Creatinine; Glucose; Potassium; Protein, total; Sodium; Urea Nitrogen –80053

___ CORONARY RISK PROFILE (LIPID PANEL) – Total Cholesterol, HDO cholesterol, LDL Cholesterol calculated), Triglycerides –80061

CHEMISTRY

___ALBUMIN 82040
___ALK PHOSPHATASE 84075
___ALK/SGPT 84460
___T4, TOTAL 84436
___TSH 84443
___T3, TOTAL 84480
___TRIGLYCERIDES 84478
___UREA NITROGEN (BUN) 84520

BLOOD

___HEMATOCRIT 85013
___PARTIAL BLOOD COUNT 85021
___CBC/DIFF 85025
___CBC 85027
___RETICULOCYTE COUNT 85044
___PRO TIME/INR 85610
___AST/SGOT 85651

IMMUNOLOGY

___CEA 82378
___HEPATITIS B SURG AB 86706
___HEPATITIS C AB 86803
___HEPATITIS A AB (IGM) 86709
___HEPATITIS B SURG AG 87340

URINALYSIS/STOOL

___OCCULT BLOOD, DIAGNOSTIC 82270
___URINALYSIS, ROUTINE 81003
___URINE CULTURE 87086

GASTRIC

___EGD WITH BIOPSY 43239
___COLONOSCOPY 45380

NUCLEAR MEDICINE

___KIDNEY FLOW AND FUNCTION 76707
___THYROID UPTAKE MULTIPLE 78006

CARDIOLOGY

___BRAIN 78607
___EKG 93003

SURGICAL PATHOLOGY

___SPECIAL STAINS 80353
___BONE MARROW SME 80973
___DECALCIFICATION 83113

BREAST CENTER

___MAMMOGRAM LATERAL 76090
___DIAGNOSTIC MAMMOGRAM 76091
___STEREORTACTIC BREAST BIOPSY 76095
___NEEDLE LOCALIZATION 76096

GYNECOLOGICAL

___PAP SMEAR 99000
___GYN PROBLEM FOCUS 99212

DIAGNOSTIC RADIOLOGY

___NASAL BONES 72069
___SINUSES 70160
___ELBOW 73080
___KNEE 73564
___TIBIA/FIBULA 73590

CHEST IMAGING

___CHEST – PA/LATERAL 71020
___RIBS UNILATERAL 71120

DIAGNOSTIC ULTRASOUND

___US BREAST 75545
___US PREGNANT UTERUS 76805
___US SCROTUM 76870

MRI SERVICES

___MRI HEAD 70551
___MRI CERVICAL SPINE 72141
___MRI HEAD/NECK 70541
___MRI PELVIS 72198

GASTROINTESTINAL/ABDOMEN/URINARY TRACT

✓ ABDOMEN SURVEY 74000
✓ UPPER GI 74240

MISCELLANEOUS

___LYME, TOTAL 86618
___INJECTION 90788

Patient Information

To all returning patients: Fill in only the blanks that have changed since your last visit.

Social Security No.: 415-55-9101 Date of Birth: ________ Sex: ❑ M ❑ F
Patient's Last Name: Volpe First: Clyde MI: N
Patient's Address: 55 Lincoln Drive
City: Mesquite State: TX Zip Code: 75185
Patient Home Telephone No.: (469) 555-0192 Patient Work Telephone: (____) ____-____
Occupation: ________ Employer: ________
Employer Address: ________
City: ________ State: ____ Zip Code: ______ Telephone: (____) ____-____
Primary Care Physician No.: ____ Primary Care Physician Name: ________

Insured Information

Primary Insured's Last Name: ________ First: ________ MI: ____
Primary Insured's Address: 55 Lincoln Drive
City: Mesquite State: TX Zip Code: 75185
Primary Insured's Social Security No.: ________ Insured's Telephone: (469) 555-0192
Primary Insured's Occupation: ________ Employer: ________
Employer Address: ________
City: ________ State: ____ Zip Code: ______ Telephone: (____) ____-____
Relationship of Patient to Insured: ❑ Self ❑ Spouse ❑ Dependent

Secondary Insured's Last Name: ________ First: ________ MI: ____
Secondary Insured's Address: ________
City: ________ State: ____ Zip Code: ______
Secondary Insured's Social Security No.: ________ Insured's Telephone: (____) ____-____
Secondary Insured's Occupation: ________ Employer: ________
Employer Address: ________
City: ________ State: ____ Zip Code: ______ Telephone: (____) ____-____
Relationship of Patient to Insured: ❑ Self ❑ Spouse ❑ Dependent

Primary Insurance

Primary Insurance: ❑ United ❑ MetHealth ❑ TexMut ❑ Medicare
Other Insurance Company Name: ________
Insurance Company Address: ________
City: ________ State: ____ Zip Code: ______ Telephone: (____) ____-____
Policy No.: ________ Group No.: ________

Secondary Insurance

Secondary Insurance Company: ________
Insurance Company Address: ________
City: ________ State: ____ Zip Code: ______
Policy No.: ________ Group No.: ________

Out-Patient Services Order

17

Physician Information

Physician's No.: 2

Physician's Name: Lincoln (Last) Steven (First)

Street Address: 2206 Bldg. B

City: Dallas State: TX Zip: 75204

Patient Information

Patient's Name: Volpe (Last) Clyde (First)

Date of Birth: 6/06/1922 Sex ✓ M ____ F

Patient's Phone No.: (469) 555-0192

ICD DIAGNOSIS CODES: 427.31, V17.4

Diagnosis: Atrial fibrillation, Cardiovascular disease

CPT PANELS

____ BASIC METABOLIC – Calcium, chloride, Glucose, Sodium, Carbon Dioxide (CO2), Creatinine, Potassium, urea nitrogen (BUN) –80048

✓ COMPREHENSIVE METABOLIC – Albumin, Alkaline, Phosphatase, ALT/SGPT; AST/SGOT; bilirubin, total; Calcium; Carbon Dioxide; Chloride; Creatinine; Glucose; Potassium; Protein, total; Sodium; Urea Nitrogen –80053

✓ CORONARY RISK PROFILE (LIPID PANEL) – Total Cholesterol, HDO cholesterol, LDL Cholesterol calculated), Triglycerides –80061

CHEMISTRY

____	ALBUMIN	82040
____	ALK PHOSPHATASE	84075
____	ALK/SGPT	84460
____	T4, TOTAL	84436
____	TSH	84443
____	T3, TOTAL	84480
____	TRIGLYCERIDES	84478
____	UREA NITROGEN (BUN)	84520

BLOOD

✓	HEMATOCRIT	85013
____	PARTIAL BLOOD COUNT	85021
✓	CBC/DIFF	85025
____	CBC	85027
____	RETICULOCYTE COUNT	85044
____	PRO TIME/INR	85610
____	AST/SGOT	85651

IMMUNOLOGY

____	CEA	82378
____	HEPATITIS B SURG AB	86706
____	HEPATITIS C AB	86803
____	HEPATITIS A AB (IGM)	86709
____	HEPATITIS B SURG AG	87340

URINALYSIS/STOOL

____	OCCULT BLOOD, DIAGNOSTIC	82270
____	URINALYSIS, ROUTINE	81003
____	URINE CULTURE	87086

GASTRIC

____	EGD WITH BIOPSY	43239
____	COLONOSCOPY	45380

NUCLEAR MEDICINE

____	KIDNEY FLOW AND FUNCTION	76707
____	THYROID UPTAKE MULTIPLE	78006

CARDIOLOGY

____	BRAIN	78607
✓	EKG	93003

SURGICAL PATHOLOGY

____	SPECIAL STAINS	80353
____	BONE MARROW SME	80973
____	DECALCIFICATION	83113

BREAST CENTER

____	MAMMOGRAM LATERAL	76090
____	DIAGNOSTIC MAMMOGRAM	76091
____	STEREORTACTIC BREAST BIOPSY	76095
____	NEEDLE LOCALIZATION	76096

GYNECOLOGICAL

____	PAP SMEAR	99000
____	GYN PROBLEM FOCUS	99212

DIAGNOSTIC RADIOLOGY

____	NASAL BONES	72069
____	SINUSES	70160
____	ELBOW	73080
____	KNEE	73564
____	TIBIA/FIBULA	73590

CHEST IMAGING

____	CHEST – PA/LATERAL	71020
____	RIBS UNILATERAL	71120

DIAGNOSTIC ULTRASOUND

____	US BREAST	75545
____	US PREGNANT UTERUS	76805
____	US SCROTUM	76870

MRI SERVICES

____	MRI HEAD	70551
____	MRI CERVICAL SPINE	72141
____	MRI HEAD/NECK	70541
____	MRI PELVIS	72198

GASTROINTESTINAL/ABDOMEN/URINARY TRACT

____	ABDOMEN SURVEY	74000
____	UPPER GI	74240

MISCELLANEOUS

____	LYME, TOTAL	86618
____	INJECTION	90788

Patient Information

To all returning patients: Fill in only the blanks that have changed since your last visit.

Social Security No.: 876-55-4402 Date of Birth: ______ Sex: ☐ M ☐ F

Patient's Last Name: Harlan First: Tabitha MI: S

Patient's Address: ______

City: ______ State: ______ Zip Code: ______

Patient Home Telephone No.: (____) ____-____ Patient Work Telephone: (____) ____-____

Occupation: Store Manager Employer: Colonial Boutique

Employer Address: 380 W. Vermont Street

City: Dallas State: TX Zip Code: 75204 Telephone: (214) 555-0166

Primary Care Physician No.: ____ Primary Care Physician Name: ______

Insured Information

Primary Insured's Last Name: Harlan First: Tabitha MI: S.

Primary Insured's Address: ______

City: ______ State: ______ Zip Code: ______

Primary Insured's Social Security No.: 876-55-4402 Insured's Telephone: (____) ____-____

Primary Insured's Occupation: Store Manager Employer: Colonial Boutique

Employer Address: 380 W. Vermont

City: ______ State: ______ Zip Code: ______ Telephone: (214) 555-0166

Relationship of Patient to Insured: ☑ Self ☐ Spouse ☐ Dependent

Secondary Insured's Last Name: Harlan First: Ronnie MI: ____

Secondary Insured's Address: 22B University Lane

City: Dallas State: TX Zip Code: 75204

Secondary Insured's Social Security No.: 782-55-2203 Insured's Telephone: (214) 555-0198

Secondary Insured's Occupation: Sales Employer: Casa de Ville

Employer Address: 9287 Twin Oaks Drive

City: Dallas State: TX Zip Code: 75204 Telephone: (214) 555-0163

Relationship of Patient to Insured: ☐ Self ☑ Spouse ☐ Dependent

Primary Insurance

Primary Insurance: ☑ United ☐ MetHealth ☐ TexMut ☐ Medicare

Other Insurance Company Name: Merchant's Medical Insurance (Delete)

Insurance Company Address: 2329 Lexton Lane

City: Ft. Worth State: TX Zip Code: 91822 Telephone: (817) 555-0149

Policy No.: UMS87-523 Group No.: 454310-C

Secondary Insurance

Secondary Insurance Company: Texas Mutual Medical Insurance

Insurance Company Address: 602 Insurance Center Drive

City: Houston State: TX Zip Code: 77030

Policy No.: TM487322-M Group No.: URS761-C

Out-Patient Services Order

17

Physician Information

Physician's No.: 7

Physician's Name: Mair (Last) Ad-Med (First)

Street Address: 7109 Medical Center

Dallas (City) TX (State) 75246 (Zip)

Patient Information

Patient's Name: Harlan (Last) Tabitha (First)

Date of Birth: 2/1/51 Sex ___M ✓ F

Patient's Phone No.: (214) 555-0198

ICD DIAGNOSIS CODES: 610.0

Diagnosis: Breast cyst

CPT PANELS

_____ BASIC METABOLIC – Calcium, chloride, Glucose, Sodium, Carbon Dioxide (CO2), Creatinine, Potassium, urea nitrogen (BUN) –80048

_____ COMPREHENSIVE METABOLIC – Albumin, Alkaline, Phosphatase, ALT/SGPT; AST/SGOT; bilirubin, total; Calcium; Carbon Dioxide; Chloride; Creatinine; Glucose; Potassium; Protein, total; Sodium; Urea Nitrogen –80053

_____ CORONARY RISK PROFILE (LIPID PANEL) – Total Cholesterol, HDO cholesterol, LDL Cholesterol calculated), Triglycerides –80061

CHEMISTRY

_____	ALBUMIN	82040
_____	ALK PHOSPHATASE	84075
_____	ALK/SGPT	84460
_____	T4, TOTAL	84436
_____	TSH	84443
_____	T3, TOTAL	84480
_____	TRIGLYCERIDES	84478
_____	UREA NITROGEN (BUN)	84520

BLOOD

_____	HEMATOCRIT	85013
_____	PARTIAL BLOOD COUNT	85021
_____	CBC/DIFF	85025
_____	CBC	85027
_____	RETICULOCYTE COUNT	85044
_____	PRO TIME/INR	85610
_____	AST/SGOT	85651

IMMUNOLOGY

_____	CEA	82378
_____	HEPATITIS B SURG AB	86706
_____	HEPATITIS C AB	86803
_____	HEPATITIS A AB (IGM)	86709
_____	HEPATITIS B SURG AG	87340

URINALYSIS/STOOL

_____	OCCULT BLOOD, DIAGNOSTIC	82270
_____	URINALYSIS, ROUTINE	81003
_____	URINE CULTURE	87086

GASTRIC

_____	EGD WITH BIOPSY	43239
_____	COLONOSCOPY	45380

NUCLEAR MEDICINE

_____	KIDNEY FLOW AND FUNCTION	76707
_____	THYROID UPTAKE MULTIPLE	78006

CARDIOLOGY

_____	BRAIN	78607
_____	EKG	93003

SURGICAL PATHOLOGY

_____	SPECIAL STAINS	80353
_____	BONE MARROW SME	80973
_____	DECALCIFICATION	83113

BREAST CENTER

_____	MAMMOGRAM LATERAL	76090
_____	DIAGNOSTIC MAMMOGRAM	76091
_____	STEREORTACTIC BREAST BIOPSY	76095
✓	NEEDLE LOCALIZATION	76096

GYNECOLOGICAL

_____	PAP SMEAR	99000
_____	GYN PROBLEM FOCUS	99212

DIAGNOSTIC RADIOLOGY

_____	NASAL BONES	72069
_____	SINUSES	70160
_____	ELBOW	73080
_____	KNEE	73564
_____	TIBIA/FIBULA	73590

CHEST IMAGING

_____	CHEST – PA/LATERAL	71020
_____	RIBS UNILATERAL	71120

DIAGNOSTIC ULTRASOUND

_____	US BREAST	75545
_____	US PREGNANT UTERUS	76805
_____	US SCROTUM	76870

MRI SERVICES

_____	MRI HEAD	70551
_____	MRI CERVICAL SPINE	72141
_____	MRI HEAD/NECK	70541
_____	MRI PELVIS	72198

GASTROINTESTINAL/ABDOMEN/URINARY TRACT

_____	ABDOMEN SURVEY	74000
_____	UPPER GI	74240

MISCELLANEOUS

_____	LYME, TOTAL	86618
_____	INJECTION	90788

Patient Information

To all returning patients: Fill in only the blanks that have changed since your last visit.

Social Security No.: 212-55-0620 Date of Birth: ______ Sex: ❑ M ❑ F

Patient's Last Name: Lopez First: Alina MI: S

Patient's Address: 32 Maple Road

City: ______ State: ______ Zip Code: ______

Patient Home Telephone No.: (214) 555-0188 Patient Work Telephone: (____) ____-____

Occupation: ______ Employer: ______

Employer Address: ______

City: ______ State: ______ Zip Code: ______ Telephone: (____) ____-____

Primary Care Physician No.: ______ Primary Care Physician Name: ______

Insured Information

Primary Insured's Last Name: ______ First: ______ MI: ______

Primary Insured's Address: 32 Maple Road

City: ______ State: ______ Zip Code: ______

Primary Insured's Social Security No.: ______ Insured's Telephone: (214) 555-0188

Primary Insured's Occupation: Sales Rep. Employer: Waters Communications

Employer Address: 32 Waters Ave.

City: ______ State: ______ Zip Code: ______ Telephone: (214) 555-0137

Relationship of Patient to Insured: ❑ Self ❑ Spouse ❑ Dependent

Secondary Insured's Last Name: ______ First: ______ MI: ______

Secondary Insured's Address: ______

City: ______ State: ______ Zip Code: ______

Secondary Insured's Social Security No.: ______ Insured's Telephone: (____) ____-____

Secondary Insured's Occupation: ______ Employer: ______

Employer Address: ______

City: ______ State: ______ Zip Code: ______ Telephone: (____) ____-____

Relationship of Patient to Insured: ❑ Self ❑ Spouse ❑ Dependent

Primary Insurance

Primary Insurance: ☑ United ❑ MetHealth ❑ TexMut ❑ Medicare

Other Insurance Company Name: ______

Insurance Company Address: 2329 Lexton Lane

City: Ft. Worth State: TX Zip Code: 91822 Telephone: (817) 555-0149

Policy No.: UMS21-411 Group No.: 488910-C

Secondary Insurance

Secondary Insurance Company: ______

Insurance Company Address: ______

City: ______ State: ______ Zip Code: ______

Policy No.: ______ Group No.: ______

Out-Patient Services Order

17

Physician Information

Physician's No.: 4

Physician's Name: Appleby Suzanne
Last First

Street Address: 16-B Hospital Tower

Dallas TX 75336
City State Zip

Patient Information

Patient's Name: Lopez Alina
Last First

Date of Birth: 2/3/91 Sex ___ M ✓ F

Patient's Phone No.: (214) 555-0188

ICD DIAGNOSIS CODES: 466.0

Diagnosis: Bronchitis, acute

CPT PANELS

_____ BASIC METABOLIC – Calcium, chloride, Glucose, Sodium, Carbon Dioxide (CO2), Creatinine, Potassium, urea nitrogen (BUN) –80048

_____ COMPREHENSIVE METABOLIC – Albumin, Alkaline, Phosphatase, ALT/SGPT; AST/SGOT; bilirubin, total; Calcium; Carbon Dioxide; Chloride; Creatinine; Glucose; Potassium; Protein, total; Sodium; Urea Nitrogen –80053

_____ CORONARY RISK PROFILE (LIPID PANEL) – Total Cholesterol, HDO cholesterol, LDL Cholesterol calculated), Triglycerides –80061

CHEMISTRY

_____	ALBUMIN	82040
_____	ALK PHOSPHATASE	84075
_____	ALK/SGPT	84460
_____	T4, TOTAL	84436
_____	TSH	84443
_____	T3, TOTAL	84480
_____	TRIGLYCERIDES	84478
_____	UREA NITROGEN (BUN)	84520

BLOOD

✓	HEMATOCRIT	85013
_____	PARTIAL BLOOD COUNT	85021
_____	CBC/DIFF	85025
✓	CBC	85027
_____	RETICULOCYTE COUNT	85044
_____	PRO TIME/INR	85610
_____	AST/SGOT	85651

IMMUNOLOGY

_____	CEA	82378
_____	HEPATITIS B SURG AB	86706
_____	HEPATITIS C AB	86803
_____	HEPATITIS A AB (IGM)	86709
_____	HEPATITIS B SURG AG	87340

URINALYSIS/STOOL

_____	OCCULT BLOOD, DIAGNOSTIC	82270
_____	URINALYSIS, ROUTINE	81003
_____	URINE CULTURE	87086

GASTRIC

_____	EGD WITH BIOPSY	43239
_____	COLONOSCOPY	45380

NUCLEAR MEDICINE

_____	KIDNEY FLOW AND FUNCTION	76707
_____	THYROID UPTAKE MULTIPLE	78006

CARDIOLOGY

_____	BRAIN	78607
_____	EKG	93003

SURGICAL PATHOLOGY

_____	SPECIAL STAINS	80353
_____	BONE MARROW SME	80973
_____	DECALCIFICATION	83113

BREAST CENTER

_____	MAMMOGRAM LATERAL	76090
_____	DIAGNOSTIC MAMMOGRAM	76091
_____	STEREORTACTIC BREAST BIOPSY	76095
_____	NEEDLE LOCALIZATION	76096

GYNECOLOGICAL

_____	PAP SMEAR	99000
_____	GYN PROBLEM FOCUS	99212

DIAGNOSTIC RADIOLOGY

_____	NASAL BONES	72069
_____	SINUSES	70160
_____	ELBOW	73080
_____	KNEE	73564
_____	TIBIA/FIBULA	73590

CHEST IMAGING

✓	CHEST – PA/LATERAL	71020
_____	RIBS UNILATERAL	71120

DIAGNOSTIC ULTRASOUND

_____	US BREAST	75545
_____	US PREGNANT UTERUS	76805
_____	US SCROTUM	76870

MRI SERVICES

_____	MRI HEAD	70551
_____	MRI CERVICAL SPINE	72141
_____	MRI HEAD/NECK	70541
_____	MRI PELVIS	72198

GASTROINTESTINAL/ABDOMEN/URINARY TRACT

_____	ABDOMEN SURVEY	74000
_____	UPPER GI	74240

MISCELLANEOUS

_____	LYME, TOTAL	86618
_____	INJECTION	90788

Patient Information

To all returning patients: Fill in only the blanks that have changed since your last visit.

Social Security No.: 659-55-9642 Date of Birth: ____ Sex: ❑ M ❑ F

Patient's Last Name: McDonald First: Andrew MI: R

Patient's Address: ____

City: ____ State: ____ Zip Code: ____

Patient Home Telephone No.: (____) ____-____ Patient Work Telephone: (____) ____-____

Occupation: ____ Employer: ____

Employer Address: ____

City: ____ State: ____ Zip Code: ____ Telephone: (____) ____-____

Primary Care Physician No.: ____ Primary Care Physician Name: ____

Insured Information

Primary Insured's Last Name: ____ First: ____ MI: ____

Primary Insured's Address: ____

City: ____ State: ____ Zip Code: ____

Primary Insured's Social Security No.: ____ Insured's Telephone: (____) ____-____

Primary Insured's Occupation: ____ Employer: ____

Employer Address: ____

City: ____ State: ____ Zip Code: ____ Telephone: (____) ____-____

Relationship of Patient to Insured: ❑ Self ❑ Spouse ❑ Dependent

ivorced
move all
econdary
insured's
nformation

Secondary Insured's Last Name: McDonald First: Luanne MI: C

Secondary Insured's Address: 2165 Winfred Lane

City: Bedford State: TX Zip Code: 76021

Secondary Insured's Social Security No.: 354-55-8067 Insured's Telephone: (972) 555-0143

Secondary Insured's Occupation: Shipping Clerk Employer: URS Shipping

Employer Address: 2604 Transportation Drive

City: Dallas State: TX Zip Code: 75228 Telephone: (214) 555-0162

Relationship of Patient to Insured: ❑ Self ☑ Spouse ❑ Dependent

Primary Insurance

Primary Insurance: ❑ United ❑ MetHealth ❑ TexMut ❑ Medicare

Other Insurance Company Name: ____

Insurance Company Address: ____

City: ____ State: ____ Zip Code: ____ Telephone: (____) ____-____

Policy No.: ____ Group No.: ____

Secondary Insurance

Secondary Insurance Company: Texas Mutual Medical Insurance

Insurance Company Address: 602 Insurance Center Drive

City: Houston State: TX Zip Code: 77030

Policy No.: TM834967-M Group No.: URS620-C

Out-Patient Services Order

17

Physician Information

Physician's No.: 1

Physician's Name: Rambo Anita
Last First

Street Address: 6102 Medical Center

Dallas TX 75336
City State Zip

Patient Information

Patient's Name: McDonald Andrew
Last First

Date of Birth: 8/2/51 Sex ✓ M ___ F

Patient's Phone No.: (972) 555-0143

ICD DIAGNOSIS CODES: 486, 428

Diagnosis: Pneumonia, Congestive heart failure

CPT PANELS

_____ BASIC METABOLIC – Calcium, chloride, Glucose, Sodium, Carbon Dioxide (CO2), Creatinine, Potassium, urea nitrogen (BUN) –80048

_____ COMPREHENSIVE METABOLIC – Albumin, Alkaline, Phosphatase, ALT/SGPT; AST/SGOT; bilirubin, total; Calcium; Carbon Dioxide; Chloride; Creatinine; Glucose; Potassium; Protein, total; Sodium; Urea Nitrogen –80053

✓ CORONARY RISK PROFILE (LIPID PANEL) – Total Cholesterol, HDO cholesterol, LDL Cholesterol calculated), Triglycerides –80061

CHEMISTRY

_____ALBUMIN 82040
_____ALK PHOSPHATASE 84075
_____ALK/SGPT 84460
_____T4, TOTAL 84436
_____TSH 84443
_____T3, TOTAL 84480
_____TRIGLYCERIDES 84478
_____UREA NITROGEN (BUN) 84520

BLOOD

_____HEMATOCRIT 85013
_____PARTIAL BLOOD COUNT 85021
_____CBC/DIFF 85025
_____CBC 85027
_____RETICULOCYTE COUNT 85044
_____PRO TIME/INR 85610
_____AST/SGOT 85651

IMMUNOLOGY

_____CEA 82378
_____HEPATITIS B SURG AB 86706
_____HEPATITIS C AB 86803
_____HEPATITIS A AB (IGM) 86709
_____HEPATITIS B SURG AG 87340

URINALYSIS/STOOL

_____OCCULT BLOOD, DIAGNOSTIC 82270
_____URINALYSIS, ROUTINE 81003
_____URINE CULTURE 87086

GASTRIC

_____EGD WITH BIOPSY 43239
_____COLONOSCOPY 45380

NUCLEAR MEDICINE

_____KIDNEY FLOW AND FUNCTION 76707
_____THYROID UPTAKE MULTIPLE 78006

CARDIOLOGY

_____BRAIN 78607
✓ EKG 93003

SURGICAL PATHOLOGY

_____SPECIAL STAINS 80353
_____BONE MARROW SME 80973
_____DECALCIFICATION 83113

BREAST CENTER

_____MAMMOGRAM LATERAL 76090
_____DIAGNOSTIC MAMMOGRAM 76091
_____STEREORTACTIC BREAST BIOPSY 76095
_____NEEDLE LOCALIZATION 76096

GYNECOLOGICAL

_____PAP SMEAR 99000
_____GYN PROBLEM FOCUS 99212

DIAGNOSTIC RADIOLOGY

_____NASAL BONES 72069
_____SINUSES 70160
_____ELBOW 73080
_____KNEE 73564
_____TIBIA/FIBULA 73590

CHEST IMAGING

✓ CHEST – PA/LATERAL 71020
_____RIBS UNILATERAL 71120

DIAGNOSTIC ULTRASOUND

_____US BREAST 75545
_____US PREGNANT UTERUS 76805
_____US SCROTUM 76870

MRI SERVICES

_____MRI HEAD 70551
_____MRI CERVICAL SPINE 72141
_____MRI HEAD/NECK 70541
_____MRI PELVIS 72198

GASTROINTESTINAL/ABDOMEN/URINARY TRACT

_____ABDOMEN SURVEY 74000
_____UPPER GI 74240

MISCELLANEOUS

_____LYME, TOTAL 86618
_____INJECTION 90788

Patient Information

17

Melissa has remarried.

To all returning patients: Fill in only the blanks that have changed since your last visit.

Social Security No.: 212-55-6201 Date of Birth: ________ Sex: ❑ M ❑ F

Patient's Last Name: Connor First: Melissa MI: A

Patient's Address: 542 Cherry Street

City: ________ State: ________ Zip Code: ________

Patient Home Telephone No.: (817) 555 - 0199 Patient Work Telephone: (____) ____-____

Occupation: ________ Employer: ________

Employer Address: ________

City: ________ State: ________ Zip Code: ________ Telephone: (____) ____-____

Primary Care Physician No.: ____ Primary Care Physician Name: ________

Insured Information

Primary Insured's Last Name: Connor First: Melissa MI: A

Primary Insured's Address: 542 Cherry Street

City: ________ State: ________ Zip Code: ________

Primary Insured's Social Security No.: ________ Insured's Telephone: (817) 555 - 0199

Primary Insured's Occupation: ________ Employer: ________

Employer Address: ________

City: ________ State: ________ Zip Code: ________ Telephone: (____) ____-____

Relationship of Patient to Insured: ❑ Self ❑ Spouse ❑ Dependent

Secondary Insured's Last Name: Connor First: Michael MI: ____

Secondary Insured's Address: 542 Cherry Street

City: Ft. Worth State: TX Zip Code: 91822

Secondary Insured's Social Security No.: 321-55-0197 Insured's Telephone: (817) 555 - 0199

Secondary Insured's Occupation: Dental Hygienist Employer: Dr. Paula Traynor

Employer Address: 14S Dental Building

City: Ft. Worth State: TX Zip Code: 91822 Telephone: (817) 555 - 0101

Relationship of Patient to Insured: ❑ Self ☑ Spouse ❑ Dependent

Primary Insurance

Primary Insurance: ❑ United ❑ MetHealth ❑ TexMut ❑ Medicare

Other Insurance Company Name: ________

Insurance Company Address: ________

City: ________ State: ________ Zip Code: ________ Telephone: (____) ____-____

Policy No.: ________ Group No.: ________

Secondary Insurance

Secondary Insurance Company: ________

Insurance Company Address: ________

City: ________ State: ________ Zip Code: ________

Policy No.: UMS35-722 Group No.: 336810-C

Out-Patient Services Order

17

Physician Information

Physician's No.: 6

Physician's Name: Ling (Last) Su (First)

Street Address: 6208 Medical Center

Dallas (City) TX (State) 75246 (Zip)

Patient Information

Patient's Name: Connor (Last) Melissa (First)

Date of Birth: 5/4/49 Sex ___M ✓ F

Patient's Phone No.: (817) 555-0199

ICD DIAGNOSIS CODES: 820.8

Diagnosis: Fractures, elbow

CPT PANELS

_____ BASIC METABOLIC – Calcium, chloride, Glucose, Sodium, Carbon Dioxide (CO2), Creatinine, Potassium, urea nitrogen (BUN) –80048

_____ COMPREHENSIVE METABOLIC – Albumin, Alkaline, Phosphatase, ALT/SGPT; AST/SGOT; bilirubin, total; Calcium; Carbon Dioxide; Chloride; Creatinine; Glucose; Potassium; Protein, total; Sodium; Urea Nitrogen –80053

_____ CORONARY RISK PROFILE (LIPID PANEL) – Total Cholesterol, HDO cholesterol, LDL Cholesterol calculated), Triglycerides –80061

CHEMISTRY

_____	ALBUMIN	82040
_____	ALK PHOSPHATASE	84075
_____	ALK/SGPT	84460
_____	T4, TOTAL	84436
_____	TSH	84443
_____	T3, TOTAL	84480
_____	TRIGLYCERIDES	84478
_____	UREA NITROGEN (BUN)	84520

BLOOD

_____	HEMATOCRIT	85013
_____	PARTIAL BLOOD COUNT	85021
_____	CBC/DIFF	85025
_____	CBC	85027
_____	RETICULOCYTE COUNT	85044
_____	PRO TIME/INR	85610
_____	AST/SGOT	85651

IMMUNOLOGY

_____	CEA	82378
_____	HEPATITIS B SURG AB	86706
_____	HEPATITIS C AB	86803
_____	HEPATITIS A AB (IGM)	86709
_____	HEPATITIS B SURG AG	87340

URINALYSIS/STOOL

_____	OCCULT BLOOD, DIAGNOSTIC	82270
_____	URINALYSIS, ROUTINE	81003
_____	URINE CULTURE	87086

GASTRIC

_____	EGD WITH BIOPSY	43239
_____	COLONOSCOPY	45380

NUCLEAR MEDICINE

_____	KIDNEY FLOW AND FUNCTION	76707
_____	THYROID UPTAKE MULTIPLE	78006

CARDIOLOGY

_____	BRAIN	78607
_____	EKG	93003

SURGICAL PATHOLOGY

_____	SPECIAL STAINS	80353
_____	BONE MARROW SME	80973
_____	DECALCIFICATION	83113

BREAST CENTER

_____	MAMMOGRAM LATERAL	76090
_____	DIAGNOSTIC MAMMOGRAM	76091
_____	STEREORTACTIC BREAST BIOPSY	76095
_____	NEEDLE LOCALIZATION	76096

GYNECOLOGICAL

_____	PAP SMEAR	99000
_____	GYN PROBLEM FOCUS	99212

DIAGNOSTIC RADIOLOGY

_____	NASAL BONES	72069
_____	SINUSES	70160
✓	ELBOW	73080
_____	KNEE	73564
_____	TIBIA/FIBULA	73590

CHEST IMAGING

_____	CHEST – PA/LATERAL	71020
_____	RIBS UNILATERAL	71120

DIAGNOSTIC ULTRASOUND

_____	US BREAST	75545
_____	US PREGNANT UTERUS	76805
_____	US SCROTUM	76870

MRI SERVICES

_____	MRI HEAD	70551
_____	MRI CERVICAL SPINE	72141
_____	MRI HEAD/NECK	70541
_____	MRI PELVIS	72198

GASTROINTESTINAL/ABDOMEN/URINARY TRACT

_____	ABDOMEN SURVEY	74000
_____	UPPER GI	74240

MISCELLANEOUS

_____	LYME, TOTAL	86618
_____	INJECTION	90788

Patient Information

To all returning patients: Fill in only the blanks that have changed since your last visit.

Social Security No.: 313-55-2203 Date of Birth: ______ Sex: ❑ M ❑ F

Patient's Last Name: Daniels First: Louis MI: P

Patient's Address: ______

City: ______ State: ______ Zip Code: ______

Patient Home Telephone No.: (____) ____-______ Patient Work Telephone: (214) 555-0199

Occupation: ______ Employer: Smith & Bros. Landscaping

Employer Address: 864 Red Pepper Avenue

City: Dallas State: ______ Zip Code: 75201 Telephone: (214) 555-0199

Primary Care Physician No.: ______ Primary Care Physician Name: ______

Insured Information

Primary Insured's Last Name: ______ First: ______ MI: ______

Primary Insured's Address: ______

City: ______ State: ______ Zip Code: ______

Primary Insured's Social Security No.: ______ Insured's Telephone: (____) ____-______

Primary Insured's Occupation: ______ Employer: Smith & Bros. Landscaping

Employer Address: 864 Red Pepper Avenue

City: Dallas State: TX Zip Code: 75201 Telephone: (214) 555-0199

Relationship of Patient to Insured: ❑ Self ❑ Spouse ❑ Dependent

Secondary Insured's Last Name: ______ First: ______ MI: ______

Secondary Insured's Address: ______

City: ______ State: ______ Zip Code: ______

Secondary Insured's Social Security No.: ______ Insured's Telephone: (____) ____-______

Secondary Insured's Occupation: ______ Employer: ______

Employer Address: ______

City: ______ State: ______ Zip Code: ______ Telephone: (____) ____-______

Relationship of Patient to Insured: ❑ Self ❑ Spouse ❑ Dependent

Primary Insurance

Primary Insurance: ❑ United ❑ MetHealth ☑ TexMut ❑ Medicare

Other Insurance Company Name: ______

Insurance Company Address: ______

City: ______ State: ______ Zip Code: ______ Telephone: (____) ____-______

Policy No.: TM884521-M Group No.: URS476-C

Secondary Insurance

Secondary Insurance Company: ______

Insurance Company Address: ______

City: ______ State: ______ Zip Code: ______

Policy No.: ______ Group No.: ______

Out-Patient Services Order

17

Physician Information

Physician's No.: 8

Physician's Name: Sanchez (Last) Carlos (First)

Street Address: 4802 Parkway Blvd.

Dallas (City) TX (State) 75246 (Zip)

Patient Information

Patient's Name: Torres (Last) Serena (First)

Date of Birth: 5/14/77 Sex ___M ✓ F

Patient's Phone No.: (817) 555-0142

ICD DIAGNOSIS CODES: 796.2

Diagnosis: Elevated blood pressure

CPT PANELS

_____ BASIC METABOLIC – Calcium, chloride, Glucose, Sodium, Carbon Dioxide (CO2), Creatinine, Potassium, urea nitrogen (BUN) –80048

_____ COMPREHENSIVE METABOLIC – Albumin, Alkaline, Phosphatase, ALT/SGPT; AST/SGOT; bilirubin, total; Calcium; Carbon Dioxide; Chloride; Creatinine; Glucose; Potassium; Protein, total; Sodium; Urea Nitrogen –80053

_____ CORONARY RISK PROFILE (LIPID PANEL) – Total Cholesterol, HDO cholesterol, LDL Cholesterol calculated), Triglycerides –80061

CHEMISTRY

_____ALBUMIN 82040
_____ALK PHOSPHATASE 84075
_____ALK/SGPT 84460
_____T4, TOTAL 84436
_____TSH 84443
_____T3, TOTAL 84480
_____TRIGLYCERIDES 84478
_____UREA NITROGEN (BUN) 84520

BLOOD

✓ HEMATOCRIT 85013
_____PARTIAL BLOOD COUNT 85021
✓ CBC/DIFF 85025
✓ CBC 85027
_____RETICULOCYTE COUNT 85044
_____PRO TIME/INR 85610
_____AST/SGOT 85651

IMMUNOLOGY

_____CEA 82378
_____HEPATITIS B SURG AB 86706
_____HEPATITIS C AB 86803
_____HEPATITIS A AB (IGM) 86709
_____HEPATITIS B SURG AG 87340

URINALYSIS/STOOL

_____OCCULT BLOOD, DIAGNOSTIC 82270
_____URINALYSIS, ROUTINE 81003
_____URINE CULTURE 87086

GASTRIC

_____EGD WITH BIOPSY 43239
_____COLONOSCOPY 45380

NUCLEAR MEDICINE

_____KIDNEY FLOW AND FUNCTION 76707
_____THYROID UPTAKE MULTIPLE 78006

CARDIOLOGY

_____BRAIN 78607
✓ EKG 93003

SURGICAL PATHOLOGY

_____SPECIAL STAINS 80353
_____BONE MARROW SME 80973
_____DECALCIFICATION 83113

BREAST CENTER

_____MAMMOGRAM LATERAL 76090
_____DIAGNOSTIC MAMMOGRAM 76091
_____STEREORTACTIC BREAST BIOPSY 76095
_____NEEDLE LOCALIZATION 76096

GYNECOLOGICAL

_____PAP SMEAR 99000
_____GYN PROBLEM FOCUS 99212

DIAGNOSTIC RADIOLOGY

_____NASAL BONES 72069
_____SINUSES 70160
_____ELBOW 73080
_____KNEE 73564
_____TIBIA/FIBULA 73590

CHEST IMAGING

_____CHEST – PA/LATERAL 71020
_____RIBS UNILATERAL 71120

DIAGNOSTIC ULTRASOUND

_____US BREAST 75545
_____US PREGNANT UTERUS 76805
_____US SCROTUM 76870

MRI SERVICES

_____MRI HEAD 70551
_____MRI CERVICAL SPINE 72141
_____MRI HEAD/NECK 70541
_____MRI PELVIS 72198

GASTROINTESTINAL/ABDOMEN/URINARY TRACT

_____ABDOMEN SURVEY 74000
_____UPPER GI 74240

MISCELLANEOUS

_____LYME, TOTAL 86618
_____INJECTION 90788

Patient Information

To all returning patients: Fill in only the blanks that have changed since your last visit.

Social Security No.: 313-55-2203 Date of Birth: ____________ Sex: ❑ M ❑ F

Patient's Last Name: Daniels First: Louis MI: P

Patient's Address: ____________

City: ____________ State: ______ Zip Code: ______

Patient Home Telephone No.: (____) ____-______ Patient Work Telephone: (214) 555-0199

Occupation: ____________ Employer: Smith & Bros. Landscaping

Employer Address: 864 Red Pepper Avenue

City: Dallas State: ______ Zip Code: 75201 Telephone: (214) 555-0199

Primary Care Physician No.: ______ Primary Care Physician Name: ____________

Insured Information

Primary Insured's Last Name: ____________ First: ____________ MI: ____

Primary Insured's Address: ____________

City: ____________ State: ______ Zip Code: ______

Primary Insured's Social Security No.: ____________ Insured's Telephone: (____) ____-______

Primary Insured's Occupation: ____________ Employer: Smith & Bros. Landscaping

Employer Address: 864 Red Pepper Avenue

City: Dallas State: TX Zip Code: 75201 Telephone: (214) 555-0199

Relationship of Patient to Insured: ❑ Self ❑ Spouse ❑ Dependent

Secondary Insured's Last Name: ____________ First: ____________ MI: ____

Secondary Insured's Address: ____________

City: ____________ State: ______ Zip Code: ______

Secondary Insured's Social Security No.: ____________ Insured's Telephone: (____) ____-______

Secondary Insured's Occupation: ____________ Employer: ____________

Employer Address: ____________

City: ____________ State: ______ Zip Code: ______ Telephone: (____) ____-______

Relationship of Patient to Insured: ❑ Self ❑ Spouse ❑ Dependent

Primary Insurance

Primary Insurance: ❑ United ❑ MetHealth ☑ TexMut ❑ Medicare

Other Insurance Company Name: ____________

Insurance Company Address: ____________

City: ____________ State: ______ Zip Code: ______ Telephone: (____) ____-______

Policy No.: TM884521-M Group No.: URS476-C

Secondary Insurance

Secondary Insurance Company: ____________

Insurance Company Address: ____________

City: ____________ State: ______ Zip Code: ______

Policy No.: ____________ Group No.: ____________

Out-Patient Services Order

17

Physician Information

Physician's No.: 9

Physician's Name: Albino (Last) Ramon (First)

Street Address: 111 Northern Lane

Dallas (City) TX (State) 76346 (Zip)

Patient Information

Patient's Name: Daniels (Last) Louis (First)

Date of Birth: 1/1/59 Sex ✓ M ___ F

Patient's Phone No.: (214) 555-0119

ICD DIAGNOSIS CODES: v17.4

Diagnosis: Cardiovascular disease

CPT PANELS

____ BASIC METABOLIC – Calcium, chloride, Glucose, Sodium, Carbon Dioxide (CO2), Creatinine, Potassium, urea nitrogen (BUN) –80048

✓ COMPREHENSIVE METABOLIC – Albumin, Alkaline, Phosphatase, ALT/SGPT; AST/SGOT; bilirubin, total; Calcium; Carbon Dioxide; Chloride; Creatinine; Glucose; Potassium; Protein, total; Sodium; Urea Nitrogen –80053

✓ CORONARY RISK PROFILE (LIPID PANEL) – Total Cholesterol, HDO cholesterol, LDL Cholesterol calculated), Triglycerides –80061

CHEMISTRY

	Test	Code
____	ALBUMIN	82040
____	ALK PHOSPHATASE	84075
____	ALK/SGPT	84460
____	T4, TOTAL	84436
____	TSH	84443
____	T3, TOTAL	84480
____	TRIGLYCERIDES	84478
____	UREA NITROGEN (BUN)	84520

BLOOD

	Test	Code
____	HEMATOCRIT	85013
____	PARTIAL BLOOD COUNT	85021
____	CBC/DIFF	85025
____	CBC	85027
____	RETICULOCYTE COUNT	85044
____	PRO TIME/INR	85610
____	AST/SGOT	85651

IMMUNOLOGY

	Test	Code
____	CEA	82378
____	HEPATITIS B SURG AB	86706
____	HEPATITIS C AB	86803
____	HEPATITIS A AB (IGM)	86709
____	HEPATITIS B SURG AG	87340

URINALYSIS/STOOL

	Test	Code
____	OCCULT BLOOD, DIAGNOSTIC	82270
____	URINALYSIS, ROUTINE	81003
____	URINE CULTURE	87086

GASTRIC

	Test	Code
____	EGD WITH BIOPSY	43239
____	COLONOSCOPY	45380

NUCLEAR MEDICINE

	Test	Code
____	KIDNEY FLOW AND FUNCTION	76707
____	THYROID UPTAKE MULTIPLE	78006

CARDIOLOGY

	Test	Code
____	BRAIN	78607
✓	EKG	93003

SURGICAL PATHOLOGY

	Test	Code
____	SPECIAL STAINS	80353
____	BONE MARROW SME	80973
____	DECALCIFICATION	83113

BREAST CENTER

	Test	Code
____	MAMMOGRAM LATERAL	76090
____	DIAGNOSTIC MAMMOGRAM	76091
____	STEREORTACTIC BREAST BIOPSY	76095
____	NEEDLE LOCALIZATION	76096

GYNECOLOGICAL

	Test	Code
____	PAP SMEAR	99000
____	GYN PROBLEM FOCUS	99212

DIAGNOSTIC RADIOLOGY

	Test	Code
____	NASAL BONES	72069
____	SINUSES	70160
____	ELBOW	73080
____	KNEE	73564
____	TIBIA/FIBULA	73590

CHEST IMAGING

	Test	Code
____	CHEST – PA/LATERAL	71020
____	RIBS UNILATERAL	71120

DIAGNOSTIC ULTRASOUND

	Test	Code
____	US BREAST	75545
____	US PREGNANT UTERUS	76805
____	US SCROTUM	76870

MRI SERVICES

	Test	Code
____	MRI HEAD	70551
____	MRI CERVICAL SPINE	72141
____	MRI HEAD/NECK	70541
____	MRI PELVIS	72198

GASTROINTESTINAL/ABDOMEN/URINARY TRACT

	Test	Code
____	ABDOMEN SURVEY	74000
____	UPPER GI	74240

MISCELLANEOUS

	Test	Code
____	LYME, TOTAL	86618
____	INJECTION	90788

Patient Information

To all returning patients: Fill in only the blanks that have changed since your last visit.

Social Security No.: 624-55-0319 Date of Birth: ______ Sex: ❑ M ❑ F

Patient's Last Name: Torres First: Serena MI: I

Patient's Address: ______

City: ______ State: ______ Zip Code: ______

Patient Home Telephone No.: (____) ____-______ Patient Work Telephone: (____) ____-______

Occupation: ______ Employer: ______

Employer Address: ______

City: ______ State: ______ Zip Code: ______ Telephone: (____) ____-______

Primary Care Physician No.: ______ Primary Care Physician Name: ______

Insured Information

Primary Insured's Last Name: ______ First: ______ MI: ______

Primary Insured's Address: ______

City: ______ State: ______ Zip Code: ______

Primary Insured's Social Security No.: ______ Insured's Telephone: (____) ____-______

Primary Insured's Occupation: ______ Employer: ______

Employer Address: ______

City: ______ State: ______ Zip Code: ______ Telephone: (____) ____-______

Relationship of Patient to Insured: ❑ Self ❑ Spouse ❑ Dependent

Secondary Insured's Last Name: ______ First: ______ MI: ______

Secondary Insured's Address: ______

City: ______ State: ______ Zip Code: ______

Secondary Insured's Social Security No.: ______ Insured's Telephone: (____) ____-______

Secondary Insured's Occupation: ______ Employer: ______

Employer Address: ______

City: ______ State: ______ Zip Code: ______ Telephone: (____) ____-______

Relationship of Patient to Insured: ❑ Self ❑ Spouse ❑ Dependent

Primary Insurance

Primary Insurance: ☑ United ❑ MetHealth ❑ TexMut ❑ Medicare

Other Insurance Company Name: ______

Insurance Company Address: ______

City: ______ State: ______ Zip Code: ______ Telephone: (____) ____-______

Policy No.: UMS23-477 Group No.: 429510-C

Secondary Insurance

Secondary Insurance Company: ______

Insurance Company Address: ______

City: ______ State: ______ Zip Code: ______

Policy No.: ______ Group No.: ______

Out-Patient Services Order

17

Physician Information

Physician's No.: 8

Physician's Name: Sanchez (Last) Carlos (First)

Street Address: 4802 Parkway Blvd.

Dallas (City) TX (State) 75246 (Zip)

Patient Information

Patient's Name: Torres (Last) Serena (First)

Date of Birth: 5/14/77 Sex ___M ✓ F

Patient's Phone No.: (817) 555-0142

ICD DIAGNOSIS CODES: 796.2

Diagnosis: Elevated blood pressure

CPT PANELS

____ BASIC METABOLIC – Calcium, chloride, Glucose, Sodium, Carbon Dioxide (CO2), Creatinine, Potassium, urea nitrogen (BUN) –80048

____ COMPREHENSIVE METABOLIC – Albumin, Alkaline, Phosphatase, ALT/SGPT; AST/SGOT; bilirubin, total; Calcium; Carbon Dioxide; Chloride; Creatinine; Glucose; Potassium; Protein, total; Sodium; Urea Nitrogen –80053

____ CORONARY RISK PROFILE (LIPID PANEL) – Total Cholesterol, HDO cholesterol, LDL Cholesterol calculated), Triglycerides –80061

CHEMISTRY

____	ALBUMIN	82040
____	ALK PHOSPHATASE	84075
____	ALK/SGPT	84460
____	T4, TOTAL	84436
____	TSH	84443
____	T3, TOTAL	84480
____	TRIGLYCERIDES	84478
____	UREA NITROGEN (BUN)	84520

BLOOD

✓	HEMATOCRIT	85013
____	PARTIAL BLOOD COUNT	85021
✓	CBC/DIFF	85025
✓	CBC	85027
____	RETICULOCYTE COUNT	85044
____	PRO TIME/INR	85610
____	AST/SGOT	85651

IMMUNOLOGY

____	CEA	82378
____	HEPATITIS B SURG AB	86706
____	HEPATITIS C AB	86803
____	HEPATITIS A AB (IGM)	86709
____	HEPATITIS B SURG AG	87340

URINALYSIS/STOOL

____	OCCULT BLOOD, DIAGNOSTIC	82270
____	URINALYSIS, ROUTINE	81003
____	URINE CULTURE	87086

GASTRIC

____	EGD WITH BIOPSY	43239
____	COLONOSCOPY	45380

NUCLEAR MEDICINE

____	KIDNEY FLOW AND FUNCTION	76707
____	THYROID UPTAKE MULTIPLE	78006

CARDIOLOGY

____	BRAIN	78607
✓	EKG	93003

SURGICAL PATHOLOGY

____	SPECIAL STAINS	80353
____	BONE MARROW SME	80973
____	DECALCIFICATION	83113

BREAST CENTER

____	MAMMOGRAM LATERAL	76090
____	DIAGNOSTIC MAMMOGRAM	76091
____	STEREORTACTIC BREAST BIOPSY	76095
____	NEEDLE LOCALIZATION	76096

GYNECOLOGICAL

____	PAP SMEAR	99000
____	GYN PROBLEM FOCUS	99212

DIAGNOSTIC RADIOLOGY

____	NASAL BONES	72069
____	SINUSES	70160
____	ELBOW	73080
____	KNEE	73564
____	TIBIA/FIBULA	73590

CHEST IMAGING

____	CHEST – PA/LATERAL	71020
____	RIBS UNILATERAL	71120

DIAGNOSTIC ULTRASOUND

____	US BREAST	75545
____	US PREGNANT UTERUS	76805
____	US SCROTUM	76870

MRI SERVICES

____	MRI HEAD	70551
____	MRI CERVICAL SPINE	72141
____	MRI HEAD/NECK	70541
____	MRI PELVIS	72198

GASTROINTESTINAL/ABDOMEN/URINARY TRACT

____	ABDOMEN SURVEY	74000
____	UPPER GI	74240

MISCELLANEOUS

____	LYME, TOTAL	86618
____	INJECTION	90788

Patient Information

To all returning patients: Fill in only the blanks that have changed since your last visit.

17

Social Security No.: 345-55-2354 Date of Birth: ________ Sex: ❑ M ❑ F

Patient's Last Name: Swerdlow First: Frank MI: J

Patient's Address: ________

City: ________ State: ________ Zip Code: ________

Patient Home Telephone No.: (____) ____-____ Patient Work Telephone: (____) ____-____

Occupation: ________ Employer: ________

Employer Address: ________

City: ________ State: ____ Zip Code: ________ Telephone: (____) ____-____

Primary Care Physician No.: ____ Primary Care Physician Name: ________

Insured Information

Primary Insured's Last Name: ________ First: ________ MI: ____

Primary Insured's Address: ________

City: ________ State: ________ Zip Code: ________

Primary Insured's Social Security No.: ________ Insured's Telephone: (____) ____-____

Primary Insured's Occupation: ________ Employer: ________

Employer Address: ________

City: ________ State: ____ Zip Code: ________ Telephone: (____) ____-____

Relationship of Patient to Insured: ❑ Self ❑ Spouse ❑ Dependent

Secondary Insured's Last Name: Swerdlow First: Betty MI: ____

Secondary Insured's Address: 1105 Edgewood Road

City: Ft. Worth State: TX Zip Code: 91822

Secondary Insured's Social Security No.: 901-55-3426 Insured's Telephone: (713) 555-0126

Secondary Insured's Occupation: Public Relations VP Employer: Clark Publications

Employer Address: 742 West River Drive

City: Ft. Worth State: TX Zip Code: 91822 Telephone: (713) 555-0133

Relationship of Patient to Insured: ❑ Self ☑ Spouse ❑ Dependent

Primary Insurance

Primary Insurance: ❑ United ❑ MetHealth ❑ TexMut ❑ Medicare

Other Insurance Company Name: ________

Insurance Company Address: ________

City: ________ State: ____ Zip Code: ________ Telephone: (____) ____-____

Policy No.: ________ Group No.: ________

Secondary Insurance

Secondary Insurance Company: American Medical Insurance

Insurance Company Address: 1204 Boulevard Center

City: Ft. Worth State: TX Zip Code: 91822

Policy No.: AMICC477 Group No.: 9981

Out-Patient Services Order

17

Physician Information

Physician's No.: 9

Physician's Name: Albino (Last) Ramon (First)

Street Address: 111 Northern Lane

Dallas (City) TX (State) 76346 (Zip)

Patient Information

Patient's Name: Swerdlow (Last) Frank (First)

Date of Birth: 4/14/44 Sex ✓ M ___ F

Patient's Phone No.: (713) 555-0126

ICD DIAGNOSIS CODES: 573.3

Diagnosis: Hepatitis, unspecified

CPT PANELS

____ BASIC METABOLIC – Calcium, chloride, Glucose, Sodium, Carbon Dioxide (CO_2), Creatinine, Potassium, urea nitrogen (BUN) –80048

____ COMPREHENSIVE METABOLIC – Albumin, Alkaline, Phosphatase, ALT/SGPT; AST/SGOT; bilirubin, total; Calcium; Carbon Dioxide; Chloride; Creatinine; Glucose; Potassium; Protein, total; Sodium; Urea Nitrogen –80053

____ CORONARY RISK PROFILE (LIPID PANEL) – Total Cholesterol, HDO cholesterol, LDL Cholesterol calculated), Triglycerides –80061

CHEMISTRY

____	ALBUMIN	82040
____	ALK PHOSPHATASE	84075
____	ALK/SGPT	84460
____	T4, TOTAL	84436
____	TSH	84443
____	T3, TOTAL	84480
____	TRIGLYCERIDES	84478
____	UREA NITROGEN (BUN)	84520

BLOOD

✓	HEMATOCRIT	85013
____	PARTIAL BLOOD COUNT	85021
____	CBC/DIFF	85025
✓	CBC	85027
____	RETICULOCYTE COUNT	85044
____	PRO TIME/INR	85610
____	AST/SGOT	85651

IMMUNOLOGY

____	CEA	82378
____	HEPATITIS B SURG AB	86706
✓	HEPATITIS C AB	86803
____	HEPATITIS A AB (IGM)	86709
____	HEPATITIS B SURG AG	87340

URINALYSIS/STOOL

____	OCCULT BLOOD, DIAGNOSTIC	82270
____	URINALYSIS, ROUTINE	81003
____	URINE CULTURE	87086

GASTRIC

____	EGD WITH BIOPSY	43239
____	COLONOSCOPY	45380

NUCLEAR MEDICINE

____	KIDNEY FLOW AND FUNCTION	76707
____	THYROID UPTAKE MULTIPLE	78006

CARDIOLOGY

____	BRAIN	78607
____	EKG	93003

SURGICAL PATHOLOGY

____	SPECIAL STAINS	80353
____	BONE MARROW SME	80973
____	DECALCIFICATION	83113

BREAST CENTER

____	MAMMOGRAM LATERAL	76090
____	DIAGNOSTIC MAMMOGRAM	76091
____	STEREORTACTIC BREAST BIOPSY	76095
____	NEEDLE LOCALIZATION	76096

GYNECOLOGICAL

____	PAP SMEAR	99000
____	GYN PROBLEM FOCUS	99212

DIAGNOSTIC RADIOLOGY

____	NASAL BONES	72069
____	SINUSES	70160
____	ELBOW	73080
____	KNEE	73564
____	TIBIA/FIBULA	73590

CHEST IMAGING

____	CHEST – PA/LATERAL	71020
____	RIBS UNILATERAL	71120

DIAGNOSTIC ULTRASOUND

____	US BREAST	75545
____	US PREGNANT UTERUS	76805
____	US SCROTUM	76870

MRI SERVICES

____	MRI HEAD	70551
____	MRI CERVICAL SPINE	72141
____	MRI HEAD/NECK	70541
____	MRI PELVIS	72198

GASTROINTESTINAL/ABDOMEN/URINARY TRACT

____	ABDOMEN SURVEY	74000
____	UPPER GI	74240

MISCELLANEOUS

____	LYME, TOTAL	86618
____	INJECTION	90788

Car Insurance Application: Customer Information ❶

Date of Application (MM/DD/YYYY): 07 / 28 / 200x

Customer name: Hopkinson (Last) Sylvia (First) M (M.I.) Customer ID: ____________

Street: 675 E. Slocum St. Apt. Number ____________

City, State, Zip: Barrington RI 58966-4310

Phone (daytime): (401) 555 - 0134 Phone (evening): (401) 555 - 0154

Sex (M/F): F Date of Birth (MM/DD/YYYY): 11 / 18 / 1982

Social Security No.: 854 - 89 - 5481

State in which customer is licensed: RI License type: D

Date license was issued (MM//YYYY): 05 / 2001 License number: 764968412

Car Insurance Application: Customer Information ❶

Date of Application (MM/DD/YYYY): 07 / 28 / 200x

Customer name: Spefansky (Last) Dana (First) S (M.I.) Customer ID: ____________

Street: 7801 Milford Rd. Apt. Number ____________

City, State, Zip: St. Cloud MN 56395

Phone (daytime): (320) 555 - 0125 Phone (evening): (320) 555 - 0137

Sex (M/F): F Date of Birth (MM/DD/YYYY): 12 / 14 / 1953

Social Security No.: 485 - 22 - 9733

State in which customer is licensed: MN License type: C

Date license was issued (MM//YYYY): 05 / 2002 License number: 741395526

Car Insurance Application: Customer Information

1

Date of Application (MM/DD/YYYY): 07 / 28 / 200X

Customer name: Mebrat (Last) Christopher (First) L (M.I.) Customer ID: ________

Street: 458 N. 15th St. Apt. Number 6

City, State, Zip: Rochester New York 14606-1250

Phone (daytime): (585) 555 - 0166 Phone (evening): (585) 555 - 0182

Sex (M/F): M Date of Birth (MM/DD/YYYY): 02 / 03 / 1972

Social Security No.: 554 - 54 - 8063

State in which customer is licensed: NY License type: D

Date license was issued (MM//YYYY): 07 / 2000 License number: 842654217

Car Insurance Application: Customer Information

1

Date of Application (MM/DD/YYYY): 07 / 28 / 200x

Customer name: Fabrizio (Last) Henry (First) C (M.I.) Customer ID: ________

Street: 77 Chestnut St. Apt. Number ________

City, State, Zip: Greensboro NC 27407-4077

Phone (daytime): (____) 555 - 0132 Phone (evening): (____) 555 - 0163

Sex (M/F): M Date of Birth (MM/DD/YYYY): 03 / 25 / 1969

Social Security No.: 591 - 88 - 4230

State in which customer is licensed: NC License type: D

Date license was issued (MM//YYYY): 08 / 1999 License number: 487621445

Car Insurance Application: Customer Information

1

Date of Application (MM/DD/YYYY): 07 / 28 / 200x

Customer name: Dalal (Last) Mina (First) R (M.I.) Customer ID: ______

Street: 902 N 66th St Apt. Number 201A

City, State, Zip: Lansing Michigan 48924-2413

Phone (daytime): (517) 555 - 0154 Phone (evening): (517) 555 - 0121

Sex (M/F): F Date of Birth (MM/DD/YYYY): 07 / 18 / 1937

Social Security No.: 548 - 96 - 7432

State in which customer is licensed: TX License type: B

Date license was issued (MM//YYYY): 01 / 2001 License number: 869344102

Car Insurance Application: Customer Information

1

Date of Application (MM/DD/YYYY): 07 / 28 / 200X

Customer name: Alvarez (Last) Ramon (First) O (M.I.) Customer ID: ______

Street: 506 Coulter Dr. Apt. Number ______

City, State, Zip: Torrington Connecticut

Phone (daytime): (____) 555 - 0145 Phone (evening): (____) 555 - 0111

Sex (M/F): M Date of Birth (MM/DD/YYYY): 08 / 28 / 1981

Social Security No.: 964 - 87 - 5240

State in which customer is licensed: NY License type: D

Date license was issued (MM//YYYY): 02 / 1995 License number: 875921068

Car Insurance Application: Customer Information

1

Date of Application (MM/DD/YYYY): 07 / 28 / 200x

Customer name: Scribner (Last) Natalya (First) E (M.I.) Customer ID: ______

Street: 4865 Lawrence Dr. Apt. Number ______

City, State, Zip: Spokane WA 99212-1212

Phone (daytime): (509) 555 - 0125 Phone (evening): (509) 555 - 0172

Sex (M/F): F Date of Birth (MM/DD/YYYY): 09 / 01 / 1975

Social Security No.: 877 - 06 - 0348

State in which customer is licensed: WA License type: D

Date license was issued (MM//YYYY): 05 / 2001 License number: 579036400

Car Insurance Application: Customer Information

1

Date of Application (MM/DD/YYYY): 07 / 28 / 200x

Customer name: Lam (Last) Wanda (First) S (M.I.) Customer ID: ______

Street: 899 Blue Grass Rd. Apt. Number ______

City, State, Zip: Fresno CA 93710-1945

Phone (daytime): (____) 555 - 0142 Phone (evening): (____) 555 - 0169

Sex (M/F): F Date of Birth (MM/DD/YYYY): 03 / 18 / 1944

Social Security No.: 869 - 22 - 7301

State in which customer is licensed: CA License type: D

Date license was issued (MM//YYYY): 06 / 2002 License number: 491279143

Car Insurance Application: Customer Information

1

Date of Application (MM/DD/YYYY): 07 / 28 / 200x

Customer name: Rangnow (Last) Barbara (First) G (M.I.) Customer ID: ____

Street: 4957 Academy Rd. Apt. Number 1C

City, State, Zip: Charleston WV 26322

Phone (daytime): (304) 555 - 0156 Phone (evening): (304) 555 - 0194

Sex (M/F): F Date of Birth (MM/DD/YYYY): 01 / 21 / 1964

Social Security No.: 562 - 77 - 4288

State in which customer is licensed: WV License type: D

Date license was issued (MM//YYYY): 11 / 2000 License number: 459855962

Car Insurance Application: Customer Information

1

Date of Application (MM/DD/YYYY): 07 / 28 / 200x

Customer name: Klepchick (Last) Peter (First) L (M.I.) Customer ID: ____

Street: 485 Cowden St. Apt. Number ____

City, State, Zip: Manhattan KS 66505

Phone (daytime): (785) 555 - 0123 Phone (evening): (785) 555 - 0112

Sex (M/F): M Date of Birth (MM/DD/YYYY): 11 / 04 / 1945

Social Security No.: 973 - 44 - 8625

State in which customer is licensed: KS License type: D

Date license was issued (MM//YYYY): 02 / 2001 License number: 886330240

Car Insurance Application: Customer Information ❶

Date of Application (MM/DD/YYYY): 07 / 28 / 200x

Customer name: Breary (Last) Elliot (First) M (M.I.) Customer ID: ____________

Street: 7384 Alberta Dr. Apt. Number Apt 2A

City, State, Zip: Flagstaff Arizona 86018-1804

Phone (daytime): (928) 555 - 0146 Phone (evening): (928) 555 - 0139

Sex (M/F): M Date of Birth (MM/DD/YYYY): 03 / 19 / 1975

Social Security No.: 963 - 45 - 7815

State in which customer is licensed: AZ License type: D

Date license was issued (MM//YYYY): 11 / 2000 License number: 457195623

Car Insurance Application: Customer Information ❶

Date of Application (MM/DD/YYYY): 07 / 28 / 200X

Customer name: Heller-Klein (Last) Kimberly (First) G (M.I.) Customer ID: ____________

Street: 624 Rockwell Ave Apt. Number 4

City, State, Zip: Tacoma WA 98403-3004

Phone (daytime): (253) 555 - 0186 Phone (evening): (253) 555 - 0144

Sex (M/F): F Date of Birth (MM/DD/YYYY): 06 / 24 / 1981

Social Security No.: 541 - 68 - 8623

State in which customer is licensed: WA License type: C

Date license was issued (MM//YYYY): 03 / 2002 License number: 452198623

Crandle Insurance — Car Insurance Application: Customer Information (1)

Date of Application (MM/DD/YYYY): 07 / 28 / 200x

Customer name: Madigan (Last) Gayle (First) M (M.I.) Customer ID: ______

Street: 352 E Sedgely Rd. Apt. Number ______

City, State, Zip: Grand Rapids MI 49506

Phone (daytime): (____) 555 - 0188 Phone (evening): (____) 555 - 0111

Sex (M/F): F Date of Birth (MM/DD/YYYY): 07 / 01 / 1942

Social Security No.: 490 - 33 - 5421

State in which customer is licensed: MI License type: D

Date license was issued (MM//YYYY): 12 / 1998 License number: 526364217

Crandle Insurance — Car Insurance Application: Customer Information (1)

Date of Application (MM/DD/YYYY): 07 / 28 / 200x

Customer name: Shen (Last) Lindsay (First) A (M.I.) Customer ID: ______

Street: 571 Jasper St. Apt. Number ______

City, State, Zip: Wilmington DE 19890-1906

Phone (daytime): (302) 555 - 0190 Phone (evening): (302) 555 - 0127

Sex (M/F): F Date of Birth (MM/DD/YYYY): 9 / 30 / 1984

Social Security No.: 562 - 77 - 8842

State in which customer is licensed: DE License type: A

Date license was issued (MM//YYYY): 03 / 2001 License number: 642541726

Car Insurance Application: Customer Information

1

Date of Application (MM/DD/YYYY): 07 / 28 / 200X

Customer name: Madison (Last) Leila (First) T (M.I.) Customer ID: ______

Street: 7408 Henry Ave. Apt. Number ______

City, State, Zip: Columbus OH 43220

Phone (daytime): (614) 555 - 0195 Phone (evening): (614) 555 - 0136

Sex (M/F): F Date of Birth (MM/DD/YYYY): 03 / 03 / 1955

Social Security No.: 642 - 26 - 5216

State in which customer is licensed: IN License type: D

Date license was issued (MM//YYYY): 04 / 2001 License number: 475963226

Crandle Insurance

Car Insurance Application: Customer Information

1

Date of Application (MM/DD/YYYY): 07 / 28 / 200x

Customer name: Faulkner (Last) Shawn (First) B (M.I.) Customer ID: ______

Street: 781 N Parrish St. Apt. Number Apt 3

City, State, Zip: Manchester NH 03109-0320

Phone (daytime): (____) 555 - 0194 Phone (evening): (____) 555 - 0125

Sex (M/F): M Date of Birth (MM/DD/YYYY): 10 / 23 / 1979

Social Security No.: 632 - 45 - 7412

State in which customer is licensed: NH License type: D

Date license was issued (MM//YYYY): 12 / 2000 License number: 452684745

Car Insurance Application: Vehicle Information

2

Customer name: Hopkinson Sylvia M Customer ID: 695234
Last First M.I.

Vehicle make: Honda Model: Civic Year: 1996

VIN: 1HYDL2873USO7654 Mileage: 75,468

Date of purchase (MM//YYYY): 04 / 1998 Usage code: 2 Miles per day: 38

Coverage code: 6 Liability limit: 25ØK

Car Insurance Application: Vehicle Information

2

Customer name: Spefansky Dana S Customer ID: 761285
Last First M.I.

Vehicle make: Chevrolet Model: Cavalier Year: 1990

VIN: 1JULI3826OSO8765 Mileage: 114,812

Date of purchase (MM//YYYY): 05 / 2000 Usage code: 5 Miles per day: 26

Coverage code: 4 Liability limit: 1ØØK

Crandle Insurance — Car Insurance Application: Vehicle Information **2**

Customer name: Mebrat (Last) Christopher (First) L (M.I.) Customer ID: 642377

Vehicle make: Mercury Model: Sable Year: 1996

VIN: 1UYIU8270JIO2987 Mileage: 80,467

Date of purchase (MM//YYYY): 08 / 1995 Usage code: 3 Miles per day: 48

Coverage code: 3 Liability limit: 250K

Crandle Insurance — Car Insurance Application: Vehicle Information **2**

Customer name: Fabrizio (Last) Henry (First) C (M.I.) Customer ID: 803141

Vehicle make: Dodge Model: Durango Year: 1999

VIN: 1IJGY1768URO8379 Mileage: 33,980

Date of purchase (MM//YYYY): 10 / 1998 Usage code: 2 Miles per day: 58

Coverage code: 5 Liability limit: 50K

Car Insurance Application: Vehicle Information

2

Customer name: Dalal (Last) Mina (First) R (M.I.) Customer ID: 420399

Vehicle make: Saturn Model: LW Year: 1995

VIN: 1IUJI789ØIUJ7365 Mileage: 68,425

Date of purchase (MM//YYYY): 04 / 1999 Usage code: 3 Miles per day: 68

Coverage code: 4 Liability limit: 5ØK

Car Insurance Application: Vehicle Information

2

Customer name: Alvarez (Last) Ramon (First) O (M.I.) Customer ID: 770526

Vehicle make: Acura Model: Integra Year: 2002

VIN: 1UIHU288OUIO8276 Mileage: 23,098

Date of purchase (MM//YYYY): 07 / 2001 Usage code: 4 Miles per day: 72

Coverage code: 3 Liability limit: 5ØØK

Crandle Insurance Car Insurance Application: Vehicle Information ❷

Customer name: Scribner (Last) Natalya (First) E (M.I.) Customer ID: 596403

Vehicle make: Subaru Model: Legacy Year: 1999

VIN: 1UHIJ1768UIO6725 Mileage: 52,384

Date of purchase (MM//YYYY): 01 / 1999 Usage code: 3 Miles per day: 56

Coverage code: 4 Liability limit: 150K

Crandle Insurance Car Insurance Application: Vehicle Information ❷

Customer name: Lam (Last) Wanda (First) S (M.I.) Customer ID: 692114

Vehicle make: Pontiac Model: Grand Am Year: 1997

VIN: 1UIYJ1789HUO2873 Mileage: 78,632

Date of purchase (MM//YYYY): 02 / 1997 Usage code: 3 Miles per day: 48

Coverage code: 4 Liability limit: 100K

Crandle Insurance — Car Insurance Application: Vehicle Information

2

Customer name: Rangnow (Last) Barbara (First) G (M.I.) Customer ID: 497251

Vehicle make: Ford Model: Escort Year: 1996

VIN: 1HGWU1765WUO8276 Mileage: 84,330

Date of purchase (MM//YYYY): 12 / 1999 Usage code: 4 Miles per day: 56

Coverage code: 3 Liability limit: 1ØØK

Crandle Insurance — Car Insurance Application: Vehicle Information

2

Customer name: Klepchick (Last) Peter (First) L (M.I.) Customer ID: 631402

Vehicle make: Buick Model: Riviera Year: 1999

VIN: 1HYUI2817UIO9854 Mileage: 42,381

Date of purchase (MM//YYYY): 09 / 1998 Usage code: 4 Miles per day: 42

Coverage code: 5 Liability limit: 15ØK

Crandle Insurance — Car Insurance Application: Vehicle Information

2

Customer name: Breary (Last) Elliot (First) M (M.I.) Customer ID: 751264

Vehicle make: Honda Model: Civic Year: 1999

VIN: 1UHIJ2762UAO8765 Mileage: 68,990

Date of purchase (MM//YYYY): 03 / 1999 Usage code: 3 Miles per day: 54

Coverage code: 6 Liability limit: 2ØØK

Crandle Insurance — Car Insurance Application: Vehicle Information

2

Customer name: Heller-Klein (Last) Kimberly (First) G (M.I.) Customer ID: 724659

Vehicle make: Hyundai Model: Excel Year: 2003

VIN: 1GUYY287UIO2876 Mileage: 24,705

Date of purchase (MM//YYYY): 12 / 2002 Usage code: 2 Miles per day: 48

Coverage code: 1 Liability limit: 25ØK

Crandle Insurance — Car Insurance Application: Vehicle Information 2

Customer name: Madigan (Last) Gayle (First) M (M.I.) Customer ID: 987426

Vehicle make: Ford Model: Tempo Year: 1995

VIN: 1UEIW879ØIYO6342 Mileage: 92,790

Date of purchase (MM//YYYY): 08 / 2000 Usage code: 3 Miles per day: 37

Coverage code: 7 Liability limit: 1ØØK

Crandle Insurance — Car Insurance Application: Vehicle Information 2

Customer name: Shen (Last) Lindsay (First) A (M.I.) Customer ID: 541203

Vehicle make: Saturn Model: SW Year: 1996

VIN: 1HGDI376OIUO9876 Mileage: 78,956

Date of purchase (MM//YYYY): 04 / 1998 Usage code: 5 Miles per day: 63

Coverage code: 2 Liability limit: 2ØØK

Crandle Insurance — Car Insurance Application: Vehicle Information ❷

Customer name: Madison (Last) Leila (First) T (M.I.) Customer ID: 547126

Vehicle make: Volvo Model: 760 Year: 1991

VIN: 1HHDI1736IEO3928 Mileage: 157,639

Date of purchase (MM//YYYY): 06 / 1995 Usage code: 4 Miles per day: 42

Coverage code: 6 Liability limit: 15ØK

Crandle Insurance — Car Insurance Application: Vehicle Information ❷

Customer name: Faulkner (Last) Shawn (First) B (M.I.) Customer ID: 623526

Vehicle make: Buick Model: LeSabre Year: 2002

VIN: 1ETGS7364IOO3Ø28 Mileage: 16,895

Date of purchase (MM//YYYY): 02 / 2004 Usage code: 5 Miles per day: 27

Coverage code: 2 Liability limit: 2ØØK

Customer Information Update Form

3

Date of Application (MM/DD/YYYY): 01 / 14 / 200x

Customer name: Fabrizio (Last) Henry (First) C (M.I.) Customer ID: 803141

Street: 77 Chestnut St. Apt. Number: ______

City, State, Zip: Greensboro NC 27407-4077

Phone (daytime): (336) 555-0132 Phone (evening): (336) 555-0163

Sex (M/F): M Date of Birth (MM/DD/YYYY): 03 / 25 / 1969

Social Security No.: 591-88-4230

State in which customer is licensed: NC License type: D

Date license was issued (MM//YYYY): 08 / 1999 License number: 487621445

Vehicle Information

Customer name: Fabrizio (Last) Henry (First) C (M.I.) Customer ID: ______

Vehicle make: Jeep Model: Wrangler Year: 2000

VIN: 1IJKK1657UIO6754 Mileage: 42,817

Date of purchase (MM//YYYY): 10 / 2002 Usage code: 2 Miles per day: 100

Coverage code: 3 Liability limit: 1ØØK

Customer Information Update Form

3

Date of Application (MM/DD/YYYY): 01 / 14 / 200x

Customer name: Scribner (Last) Natalya (First) E (M.I.) Customer ID: 596403

Street: 289 Forest Rd. Apt. Number: ______

City, State, Zip: Spokane WA 99206

Phone (daytime): (509) 555-0125 Phone (evening): (509) 555-0103

Sex (M/F): F Date of Birth (MM/DD/YYYY): 09 / 01 / 1975

Social Security No.: 877-06-0348

State in which customer is licensed: WA License type: D

Date license was issued (MM//YYYY): 05 / 2001 License number: 579036400

Vehicle Information

Customer name: Scribner (Last) Natalya (First) E (M.I.) Customer ID: ______

Vehicle make: Subaru Model: Legacy Year: 1999

VIN: 1UHIJ1768UIO6725 Mileage: 52,384

Date of purchase (MM//YYYY): 01 / 1999 Usage code: 3 Miles per day: 42

Coverage code: 3 Liability limit: 15ØK

Crandle Insurance — Customer Information Update Form

3

Date of Application (MM/DD/YYYY): 01 / 14 / 200X

Customer name: Lam (Last) Wanda (First) S (M.I.) Customer ID: 692114

Street: 899 Blue Grass Rd. Apt. Number:

City, State, Zip: Fresno CA 93710-1945

Phone (daytime): (559) 555 - 0142 Phone (evening): (559) 555 - 0169

Sex (M/F): F Date of Birth (MM/DD/YYYY): 03 / 18 / 1944

Social Security No.: 869 - 22 - 7301

State in which customer is licensed: CA License type: D

Date license was issued (MM//YYYY): 06 / 2002 License number: 491279143

Vehicle Information

Customer name: Lam (Last) Wanda (First) S (M.I.) Customer ID:

Vehicle make: Acura Model: Legend Year: 2003

VIN: 1IOYU7987HUI2763 Mileage: 13,985

Date of purchase (MM//YYYY): 07 / 2004 Usage code: 3 Miles per day: 48

Coverage code: 4 Liability limit: 100K

Crandle Insurance — Customer Information Update Form

3

Date of Application (MM/DD/YYYY): 01 / 14 / 200x

Customer name: Rangnow (Last) Barbara (First) G (M.I.) Customer ID: 497251

Street: 4957 Academy Rd. Apt. Number: Apt 1C

City, State, Zip: Charleston WV 26322

Phone (daytime): (304) 555 - 0165 Phone (evening): (304) 555 - 0194

Sex (M/F): F Date of Birth (MM/DD/YYYY): 01 / 21 / 1964

Social Security No.: 562 - 77 - 4288

State in which customer is licensed: WV License type: D

Date license was issued (MM//YYYY): 11 / 2000 License number: 459855962

Vehicle Information

Customer name: Rangnow (Last) Barbara (First) G (M.I.) Customer ID:

Vehicle make: Ford Model: Escort Year: 1996

VIN: 1HGWU1765WUO8276 Mileage: 84,330

Date of purchase (MM//YYYY): 12 / 1999 Usage code: 4 Miles per day: 34

Coverage code: 5 Liability limit: 150K

Customer Information Update Form

3

Date of Application (MM/DD/YYYY): 01 / 14 / 200x

Customer name: Klepchick (Last) Peter (First) L (M.I.) Customer ID: 631402

Street: 521 Water St. Apt. Number: Apt 3

City, State, Zip: Manhattan KS 66507

Phone (daytime): (785) 555-0123 Phone (evening): (785) 555-0186

Sex (M/F): M Date of Birth (MM/DD/YYYY): 11 / 04 / 1945

Social Security No.: 973-44-8625

State in which customer is licensed: KS License type: D

Date license was issued (MM//YYYY): 02 / 2001 License number: 886330240

Vehicle Information

Customer name: Klepchick (Last) Peter (First) L (M.I.) Customer ID:

Vehicle make: Buick Model: Riviera Year: 1999

VIN: 1HYUI2817UIO9854 Mileage: 42,381

Date of purchase (MM//YYYY): 09 / 1998 Usage code: 3 Miles per day: 36

Coverage code: 5 Liability limit: 150K

Customer Information Update Form

3

Date of Application (MM/DD/YYYY): 01 / 14 / 200X

Customer name: Shen (Last) Lindsay (First) A (M.I.) Customer ID: 541203

Street: 865 Moorehouse Ln. Apt. Number:

City, State, Zip: Westover Hills DE 19805

Phone (daytime): (302) 555-0190 Phone (evening): (302) 555-0149

Sex (M/F): F Date of Birth (MM/DD/YYYY): 09 / 30 / 1984

Social Security No.: 562-77-8842

State in which customer is licensed: DE License type: A

Date license was issued (MM//YYYY): 03 / 2001 License number: 642541726

Vehicle Information

Customer name: Shen (Last) Lindsay (First) A (M.I.) Customer ID:

Vehicle make: Saturn Model: SW Year: 1996

VIN: 1HGDI376OIUO9876 Mileage: 78,956

Date of purchase (MM//YYYY): 04 / 1998 Usage code: 5 Miles per day: 38

Coverage code: 2 Liability limit: 200K

Crandle Insurance — Customer Information Update Form

3

Date of Application (MM/DD/YYYY): 01 / 14 / 200x

Customer name: Faulkner (Last) Shawn (First) B (M.I.) Customer ID: 623526

Street: 781 N Parrish St. Apt. Number: Apt 3

City, State, Zip: Manchester NH 03109-0320

Phone (daytime): (603) 555-0194 Phone (evening): (603) 555-0125

Sex (M/F): M Date of Birth (MM/DD/YYYY): 10 / 23 / 1979

Social Security No.: 632-45-7412

State in which customer is licensed: NH License type: D

Date license was issued (MM//YYYY): 12 / 2000 License number: 452684745

Vehicle Information

Customer name: Faulkner (Last) Shawn (First) B (M.I.) Customer ID: ______

Vehicle make: Honda Model: CRX Year: 2003

VIN: IGHRF1876UIJ7365 Mileage: 12,623

Date of purchase (MM//YYYY): 09 / 2002 Usage code: 5 Miles per day: 27

Coverage code: 2 Liability limit: 2ØØK

Crandle Insurance — Customer Information Update Form

3

Date of Application (MM/DD/YYYY): 01 / 14 / 200x

Customer name: Breary (Last) Elliot (First) M (M.I.) Customer ID: 751264

Street: 2645 Altman Ave. Apt. Number: 1203-B

City, State, Zip: Flagstaff AZ 86024

Phone (daytime): (928) 555-0146 Phone (evening): (928) 555-0178

Sex (M/F): M Date of Birth (MM/DD/YYYY): 03 / 19 / 1975

Social Security No.: 963-45-7815

State in which customer is licensed: AZ License type: D

Date license was issued (MM//YYYY): 11 / 2000 License number: 457195623

Vehicle Information

Customer name: Breary (Last) Elliot (First) M (M.I.) Customer ID: ______

Vehicle make: Honda Model: Civic Year: 1999

VIN: 1UHIJ2762UAO8765 Mileage: 68,990

Date of purchase (MM//YYYY): 03 / 1999 Usage code: 2 Miles per day: 44

Coverage code: 6 Liability limit: 2ØØK

Crandle Insurance

Customer Information Update Form

3

Date of Application (MM/DD/YYYY): 01 / 14 / 200X

Customer name: Dalal (Last) Mina (First) R (M.I.) Customer ID: 420399

Street: 902 N 66th St Apt. Number: Apt 201A

City, State, Zip: Lansing MI 48924-2413

Phone (daytime): (517) 555 - 0154 Phone (evening): (517) 555 - 0121

Sex (M/F): F Date of Birth (MM/DD/YYYY): 07 / 18 / 1937

Social Security No.: 548 - 96 - 7432

State in which customer is licensed: TX License type: B

Date license was issued (MM//YYYY): 01 / 2001 License number: 869344102

Vehicle Information

Customer name: Dalal (Last) Mina (First) R (M.I.) Customer ID: ______

Vehicle make: Isuzu Model: Impulse Year: 2002

VIN: IHRYF1652UIY7654 Mileage: 18,807

Date of purchase (MM//YYYY): 06 / 2005 Usage code: 3 Miles per day: 68

Coverage code: 6 Liability limit: 150K

8

Purchase Order

Vendor number: 87513

Vendor name and address:
Malcom and Malcom
9485 Collins Road
Dryden, MI

Ship to:
Attn: Tom Jansen
Funwear, Inc.
8990 Hamilton Boulevard
Deer Creek, IA 67093

Bill to:
Accounts Payable
Funwear, Inc.
PO Box 6895
Deer Creek, IA 67093

Ship via: UPS 3-day

UPC Number	Qty	Description	Unit Price	Subtotal
95426	150	Men's cotton polo shirt	11.00	1,650.00
82415	300	Men's cotton crew-neck sweater	20.00	6,000.00
62187	250	Men's oxford dress shirt	14.00	3,500.00
24625	800	Ribbed cotton socks	3.00	2,400.00

Payment terms: Net 30

Total:

8

Purchase Order

Vendor number: 52694

Vendor name and address:
Fleece Mania
867 Winter Street
Lincoln, IL

Ship to:
Attn: Tom Jansen
Funwear, Inc.
8990 Hamilton Boulevard
Deer Creek, IA 67093

Bill to:
Accounts Payable
Funwear, Inc.
PO Box 6895
Deer Creek, IA 67093

Ship via: UPS ground

UPC Number	Qty	Description	Unit Price	Subtotal
26703	225	Child's fleece jacket	12.00	2,700.00
61456	300	Women's fleece vest	16.00	4,800.00
41128	400	Women's fleece pullover	19.00	7,600.00
76220	250	Adult's fleece hat	6.00	1,500.00
46929	250	Fleece scarf	4.00	1,000.00

Payment terms: Net 30

Total:

Purchase Order

8

Vendor number: 20224

Vendor name and address:
Bathwares, Inc.
994 Whistler Drive
Grand Rapids, MI 49506

Ship to:
Attn: Tom Jansen
Funwear, Inc.
8990 Hamilton Boulevard
Deer Creek, IA 67093

Bill to:
Accounts Payable
Funwear, Inc.
PO Box 6895
Deer Creek, IA 67093

Ship via: USPS 2-day

UPC Number	Qty	Description	Unit Price	Subtotal
36241	400	Terrycloth bath towel	7.00	2,800.00
64855	400	Terrycloth hand towel	4.00	1,600.00
86334	500	Terrycloth face cloth	2.50	1,250.00
55712	150	Cotton bathroom rug	8.00	1,200.00

Payment terms: Net 15

Total:

Purchase Order

8

Vendor number: 33875

Vendor name and address:
Sanderford Shoes
6348 Whitehorse Parkway
Sedalia, MO 65302

Ship to:
Attn: Tom Jansen
Funwear, Inc.
8990 Hamilton Boulevard
Deer Creek, IA 67093

Bill to:
Accounts Payable
Funwear, Inc.
PO Box 6895
Deer Creek, IA 67093

Ship via: USPS ground

UPC Number	Qty	Description	Unit Price	Subtotal
65934	200	Women's sling-back leather sandal	22.00	4,400.00
49532	150	Women's beach sandal	12.00	1,800.00
55976	225	Girl's canvas sneaker	9.00	2,025.00
20547	200	Boy's canvas sneaker	9.00	1,800.00

Payment terms: Net 30

Total:

8

Purchase Order

Vendor number: 39658

Vendor name and address:

Sweet Dreams
4421 Madington Drive
Yellow Springs, OH 45387

Ship to:

Attn: Tom Jansen
Funwear, Inc.
8990 Hamilton Boulevard
Deer Creek, IA 67093

Bill to:

Accounts Payable
Funwear, Inc.
PO Box 6895
Deer Creek, IA 67093

Ship via: RPS 3-day

UPC Number	Qty	Description	Unit Price	Subtotal
86330	125	Women's flannel pajamas	14.00	1,750.00
31490	150	Men's flannel pajamas	15.50	2,325.00
16229	200	Women's terrycloth bathrobe	21.00	4,200.00
69335	100	Child's pajama cover	13.00	1,300.00

Payment terms: Prepaid

Total:

8

Purchase Order

Vendor number: 62389

Vendor name and address:

Office Casual
904 Lakeshore Drive
St. Paul, MN 55182

Ship to:

Attn: Tom Jansen
Funwear, Inc.
8990 Hamilton Boulevard
Deer Creek, IA 67093

Bill to:

Accounts Payable
Funwear, Inc.
PO Box 6895
Deer Creek, IA 67093

Ship via: UPS 3-day

UPC Number	Qty	Description	Unit Price	Subtotal
69335	150	Khaki a-line skirt	22.00	3,300.00
34087	175	Pullover knit dress	21.00	3,675.00
71962	250	Short-sleeved cotton knit sweater	24.00	6,000.00
39668	225	Linen blazer	32.00	7,200.00
39660	225	Linen skirt	28.00	6,300.00

Payment terms: Net 30

Total:

Purchase Order

8

Vendor number: 36971

Vendor name and address:
Cotton Kingdom
302 Mammoth Road
Pocatello, ID 83201

Ship to:
Attn: Tom Jansen
Funwear, Inc.
8990 Hamilton Boulevard
Deer Creek, IA 67093

Bill to:
Accounts Payable
Funwear, Inc.
PO Box 6895
Deer Creek, IA 67093

Ship via: USPS 3-day

UPC Number	Qty	Description	Unit Price	Subtotal
96874	300	Women's roll-neck sweater	23.00	6,900.00
36225	250	Women's cable knit cardigan	24.00	6,000.00

Payment terms: Prepaid

Total:

Purchase Order

8

Vendor number: 35298

Vendor name and address:
Hanson's Swimwear
788 Cadmium Drive
Macon, GA 31212

Ship to:
Attn: Tom Jansen
Funwear, Inc.
8990 Hamilton Boulevard
Deer Creek, IA 67093

Bill to:
Accounts Payable
Funwear, Inc.
PO Box 6895
Deer Creek, IA 67093

Ship via: USPS ground

UPC Number	Qty	Description	Unit Price	Subtotal
02485	450	Men's nylon swim trunks	15.00	6,750.00
59861	350	Boys' nylon swim trunks	10.00	3,500.00
36974	300	Women's streamlined tank swimsuit	18.00	5,400.00
95782	350	Girls' tank swimsuit	12.00	4,200.00

Payment terms: Net 30

Total:

8

Purchase Order

Vendor number: 36791

Vendor name and address:

Atlanta Mills
203 Peachtree Boulevard
Atlanta, GA 30033

Ship to:

Attn: Tom Jansen
Funwear, Inc.
8990 Hamilton Boulevard
Deer Creek, IA 67093

Bill to:

Accounts Payable
Funwear, Inc.
PO Box 6895
Deer Creek, IA 67093

Ship via: USPS 3-day

UPC Number	Qty	Description	Unit Price	Subtotal
83735	200	Boy's cardigan	42.00	8,400.00
28265	150	Men's jacket	89.00	13,350.00

Payment terms: Prepaid

Total:

8

Purchase Order

Vendor number: 35264

Vendor name and address:

Ladies Emporium
7823 Landon Lane
Nashville, TN 37217

Ship to:

Attn: Tom Jansen
Funwear, Inc.
8990 Hamilton Boulevard
Deer Creek, IA 67093

Bill to:

Accounts Payable
Funwear, Inc.
PO Box 6895
Deer Creek, IA 67093

Ship via: USPS ground

UPC Number	Qty	Description	Unit Price	Subtotal
93837	250	Ladies' nightgown	25.00	6,250.00
38372	200	Women's t-shirt	10.00	2,000.00
378462	300	Girls' chemise	18.00	5,400.00
09283	250	Ladies hose	12.00	3,000.00

Payment terms: Net 30

Total:

Guest's Web Site Feedback

Name: Rosemary Thornton

Zip code: 99705

Date: Current date

Phone number: 907-555-0175

Email address: rthornton@rol.net

Comments: I just want to acknowledge the wonderful service I received from the manager on duty the night I arrived at your hotel. I had been delayed at the airport and had not had a chance to call to inform the hotel management that I would miss the arrival deadline. According to hotel policy, I should have lost my reservation, but the manager on duty, Mary Robbins, was extremely kind and went out of her way to have an extra room cleaned so that I would have a place to stay. She made my check-in easy, and I was made to feel very welcome and I greatly appreciate the extra effort that was made to accommodate me.

Guest's Web Site Feedback

Name: Thanh Nguyen

Zip code: 11207

Date: Current date

Phone number: 716-555-0343

Email address: argus248@yourmail.com

Comments: I had a bad experience overall during my last stay at Western Suites. The equipment in the business center was down, and I had to go to an outside copy store to run copies that I needed. There was a lot of noise very late at night coming from several rooms at the end of my hall. I called the front desk to notify the clerk, but he did not take a great interest in my problem and seemed impatient with my call. Eventually it quieted down, but other guests and I should not have been kept awake for as long as we were. Thank you.

Guest's Web Site Feedback

Name: Adele Celeste

Zip code: 55111-8564

Date: Current date

Phone number: 651-555-0185

Email address: aceleste@msn.com

Comments: I stay at Western Suites twice a month when I come for business meetings. I often have trouble opening the fitness center door and sometimes the equipment is broken. I always work out in the mornings, and this is becoming very frustrating. This is affecting my overall impression of Western Suites.

Guest's Web Site Feedback

12

Name: Aaron Manning

Zip code: 20906

Date: Current date

Phone number: 301-555-0190

Email address: amann326@waterworks.com

Comments: I would appreciate it if the hotel were more child-friendly. I understand that you cater mostly to business travelers, but many of your customers are families on personal trips and many of those families have children with them. When I took my ten-year-old and my eight-year-old to the pool, they were treated very harshly by the lifeguard and I was asked to "keep them under control." They were not out of control at all, just behaving like normal children. Also, there were no children's portions for room service. Please keep in mind that many of your customers have children and expect their children to be welcomed. Thank you.

Guest's Web Site Feedback

Name: Nancy Ling

Zip code: 73104-3865

Date: Current date

Phone number: 405-555-0144

Email address: ling_nancy@earthnet.com

Comments: I really appreciate the extra details that make guests feel welcome. The coffee pot in the room, the front-desk staff that greets me by name, the general friendliness—I always enjoy coming back to Western Suites. Overall, it's a great experience.

Guest's Web Site Feedback

Name: Isabel Cervantes

Zip code: 11230

Date: Current date

Phone number: 718-555-0130

Email address: cervantes23@aol.com

Comments: The room service was wonderful! A terrific selection, and everything was fresh, delicious, and elegantly presented in my beautiful big room.

Guest's Web Site Feedback

Name: Florence Silveri

Zip code: 45231

Date: Current date

Phone number: 513-555-0166

Email address: fsilveri@morris.com

Comments: I would like to have had better lighting in the room. I spend a lot of time working when I am on the road, and Western Suites has good desks and other facilities, but the lights are pretty dim. A bright standing lamp would be an excellent addition to the room.

Guest's Web Site Feedback

Name: Samuel Zimmerman

Zip code: 02145-9863

Date: Current date

Phone number: 617-555-0191

Email address: zimmerman@chem.sfu.edu

Comments: I really appreciate the airport shuttle service that you've set up as a part of the check-out procedures It makes everything so much easier and the shuttles are always right there when I arrive at the airport. It improves my overall opinion of Western Suites.